POSTCARDS FROM THE ROAD

POSTCARDS FROM THE ROAD

ROBERT FRANK'S 'THE AMERICANS'

JONATHAN DAY

intellect Bristol, UK / Chicago, USA

First published in the UK in 2014 by
Intellect, The Mill, Parnall Road, Fishponds, Bristol, BS16 3JG, UK

First published in the USA in 2014 by
Intellect, The University of Chicago Press, 1427 E. 60th Street, Chicago,
IL 60637, USA

A catalogue record for this book is available from the
British Library.

Cover designer: Holly Rose and Stephanie Sarlos
Production managers: Tim Elameer and Tom Newman
Copy-editor: Lisa Cordaro
Typesetting: Stephanie Sarlos

ISBN 978-1-78320-186-0
ePDF ISBN 978-1-78320-281-2
ePUB ISBN 978-1-78320-282-9

Printed & bound by Gwasg Gomer Cyf / Gomer Press Ltd, UK

my ship it leaves tomorrow shallow oh shallow brown
and it fills my heart with sorrow shallow oh shallow brown
miss Beverley is feeding oysters shallow oh shallow brown
to the twinkle-eyed filthy travellers road dirty and full of grace
in Mobile the cranes are rusting shallow oh shallow brown
on a chrome and eggshell morning as the seafoam green gulf curls quietly
the shrimp boats their nets unfurling on dragonfly wings they're sailing
while Jesus' red heart is burning for the mud brown levees that could not hold
in the Clover Grill a half man is toasting meat against the darkness
so I run to the Christ's blood mountains and the high white church of kindness
a triangle sun is setting for Daniella's baby, dying quietly
the most beautiful girl child is sitting on a miner's tomb, she does not understand
in the wide plains of Nebraska I sleep among the unquiet dead
on their warm beasts dressed in buckskin or the snow white covered wagons forever lost
so I cling to Stella Maris and the Virgin of Guadeloupe
desperately hoping I'll make it home again

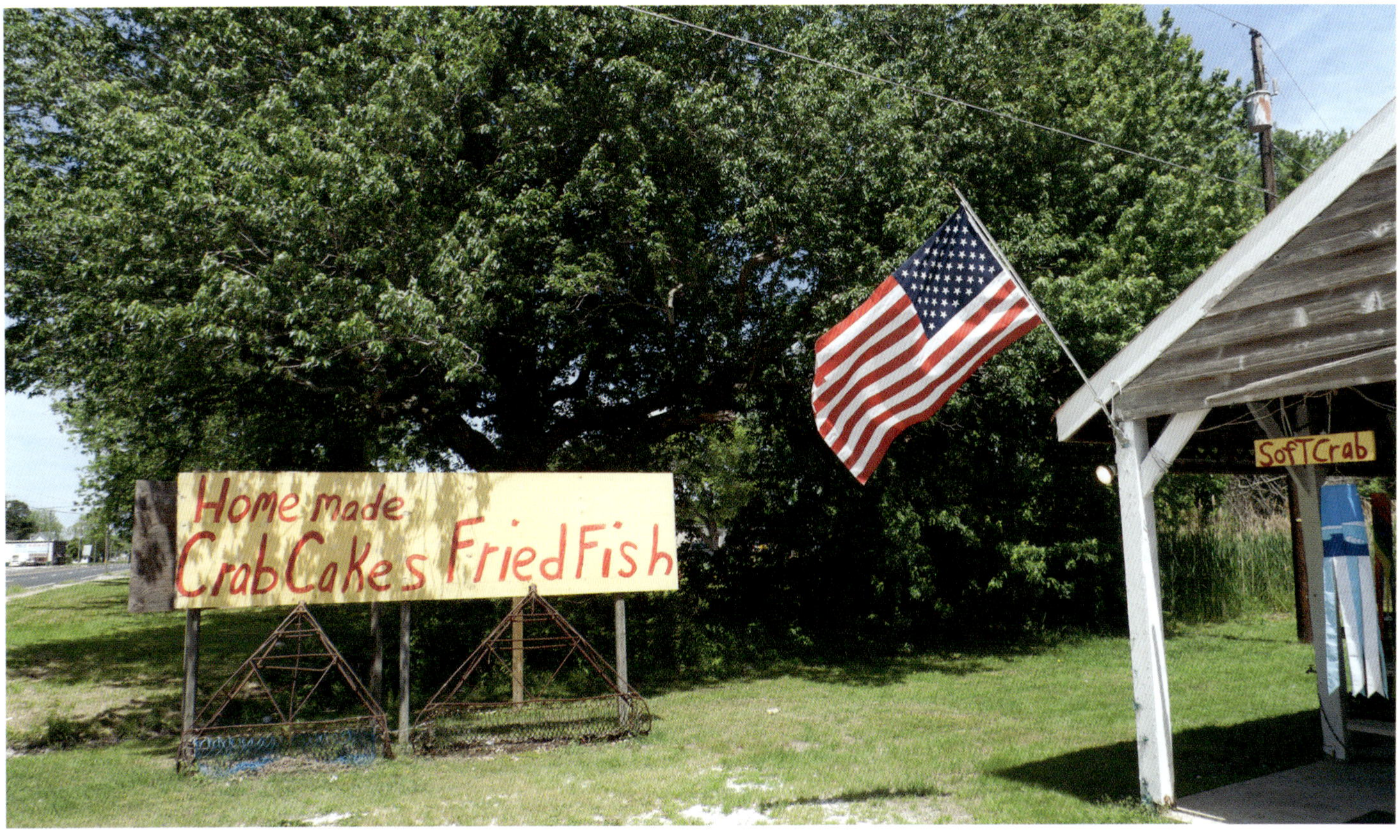
Home made
CrabCakes FriedFish
SofTCrab

INTRODUCTION

I have for a long time been fascinated by the photographs in Robert Frank's book *The Americans*. They shine a searchlight back onto a time that is lost to us now, staring mutely out of the pages. The book was published in the year I was born: it helps explain my world. No surprise, then, that I should set out to search for the remnants of the America he pictured, to see how 50 years have changed it—what has gone and what remains.

Jack Kerouac, too, has been so important. His *On the Road* was a life-affirming text for me as someone already travelling, already on my own road, when I encountered his. Through him I noticed others of the 'Beats', and their world view seemed to chime with mine, sharing an interest in Zen and an appreciation of music and painting. I wanted to see what lasting effect their freewheeling rhetoric and often radical lives had on America. Was there any real trace of them left in its warp and weft? Or are they consigned to the footnotes of history—like the quirky *San Fran Beat Museum*, an occasional TV documentary and the less-than-spectacular reception of the recent *On the Road* cinema release?

This isn't my first book about *The Americans*. My first one was wordy, with even some bestseller appearances in a few countries around the world. I like it, but I wanted to do something—not more exactly, but different. I'm a maker as well as a writer, and thereby hangs a tale. Many of my visually creative friends view text with extreme caution. Acres of the printed word leave them skittish and uncertain. A good number of them take it further, reacting with something like fear to the sight of a pictureless book. It's not that they are philistine or uninformed: they will discuss and weigh an argument for hours and with precision. It is something about those serried pages, waiting in line for consideration, that has them running for the door. So I wanted to make a book that tunnelled beneath them, like mediaeval pioneers undermining a wall, mollified the danger and threat, opened its arms and drew them, warm and cuddly, in.

This is it. Pictures and words, even handed—not illustrations serving text, or captions serving images—hand in hand the two, instead, in hierarchical equality. The structure follows Frank's: radical, non-linear, enter where you like and make your own journey through this little snow globe America. Treat it like a pensieve, the alchemists' future reflecting mirror. Look in and see if you can find yourself there, smiling back. For this to make sense, you'll never have to read more than two or three pages at a time.

The Americans is a complicated book. The photographs are often part of interconnected sequences examining the nature of human love, for example, or the imagery of the cross. At the same time, many of them contribute to non-consecutive thematic considerations—the car, for instance, or the Stars and Stripes. These devices work architecturally, knitting the book together like the interwoven trunks of a yew tree or the convoluted fibres in jade. Extracting and presenting these threads is a difficult business, and I think maybe the book you're holding does it most transparently. All the ideas are here gathered together, hanging on the meat hooks of the pictures.

These photographs were taken in America, over a period of years and perhaps 20,000 miles of road. They react to Frank's originals, sometimes taken in the same place, but mostly not. He was searching for moments, things which caught his eye, ways of talking about the world. I knew I wasn't going to find them in the same places—although I did, actually, once or twice. I thought about his messages, glass bottled and arcane, and how time has changed things—looked for the impressions he and the Beats made, or at their absence, the negative American space where they used to stand.

Each picture has a commentary, a story of its making, a postcard from the road. Also a section about Robert's photograph—the one that inspired me, to which I react. His pictures are not here, which I think is as it should be. They are available cheaply in the excellent Steidl facsimile, or online, for free. The order of presentation is the same as in *The Americans*, so if you know it well the progression should be plain.

PREFACE: *VESUVIO*

The Vesuvio Café, San Francisco, is old, like the district. In the Gold Rush when China-town was threatened by the authorities, the shop owners shot at the council until they desisted. The ghost of that defiance lingers here still, seeping up through drain covers and pooling in gutters. Stained glass windows canonise bottles of Sierra Nevada, an amber shining amidst Titian blue skies, colouring the howling night, brightening the darkness in Kerouac Alley outside. The air in here is stained with bleach, vomit and alcohol, all melding together like washed out watercolour paint. A mirror in the bathroom is scratched with the names of pilgrims. I drink in the gallery, between a photograph of '50s women and a Gold Rush era nude. One is a record of real women, who maybe Kerouac and Cassady wooed on these very stools. Certainly they are gift-wrap layered like their lovers: powder, eyeliner, 'Victory' red lipstick, corsets, nylons and New Look chiffon. The painting is a naked promise, soft as marshmallow, smooth as rose petals, the ancient pigment pert and willing. It is cracked now, as the oils (like skin) have dried, revealing the lie; nonetheless charming, nonetheless comforting for me. I feel I am at sea in a wide, wild ocean, far from home, far from land. Content though, carried on these stormy gusts. It's a relief, a need I've spent a lifetime knowing, hungering deeply within for something, still unsatisfied yet. Something I know is out there, something I know Kerouac found, even if he couldn't hold it long, even if (in the end) it let him down.

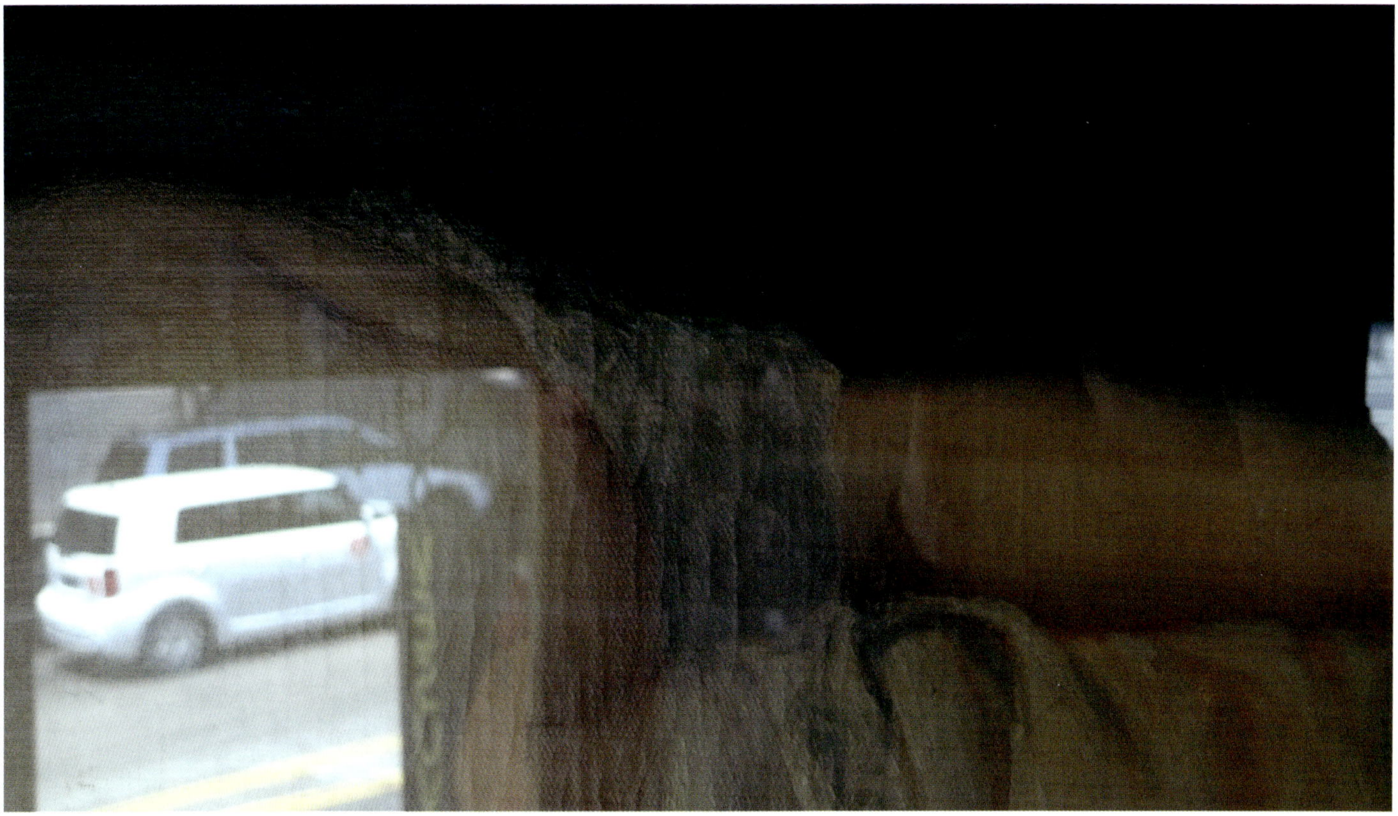

HOW LONG DOES IT TAKE TO FALL IN LOVE? A minute, an hour, a day? The bright, strange Carolina night is high and brilliant, as I knew it would be on those long miles down from the mountains. Fireflies are dancing with the stars—only the scent of Mimosa stops them flying away for ever. Sound of wind and waves outside my door, sunrise over the water, intense light filling the air and turning it the quietest kind of golden. Tiny seabirds are dancerly scurrying along the bite marks of the breakers.

Breakfast from a shack selling quesadillas and an old man passionately hawking fruit. South, afterwards, to Hatteras and the North Carolina ferry (toll free) squatting on the ocean like a water boatman bug. The ferry captain still weaves between shoals, as the pirates did sailing to the haunt of Blackbeard. Sitting on the porch of Ocracoke Coffee, heavy with the scent of Carolina Jasmine and Mimosa, I'm shaded by Lonesome pines as a warm breeze rustles the leaves, brilliant green against the light. It's everything I'd almost forgotten about summer. Sunlight on the dusty streets hangs in the air between low wooden buildings hiding in the bushes. The kids selling me coffee were celebrating their English teacher's appearance on the TV show *Jeopardy*. Hope he did well.

Out along the brilliant beach, scattered with more of the darting waders, legs a-blur as they trot up and down the sand, choreographed by waves and tide. Phalaropes, turnstones and dunlin: they seem happy with their lives. Dead creatures lie on the strand line: their dance is done and their broken remains feed again the land from which their fiery incredible beings were born. Somewhere among the sands and pools I saw an osprey casually fly over with a fish in its talons. Just as if this was everyday and not at all spectacular—which I guess for an osprey it is. The evening sucked the colour from the russet bill of a cormorant and the brilliant crimson of a blackbird's red wing. Sunrise and sunset over the Atlantic, from this debatable land, lost out there somewhere in the waves.

PARADE—HOBOKEN, NEW JERSEY

The American flag is its country's most recognizable symbol. It is a pictogram of nationhood, of unity, of the American way. In songs and dreams, it flies from a high White House or is raised by passionate marine hands on Iwo Jima. Frank, not surprisingly, chose to structure *The Americans* around this strongest of ciphers. His initial book maquette was arranged in four sections, each divided by a blank page and introduced by a flag (Greenough 2009: 133). The dividing pages were removed in the final editions, aiding the book's continuity. Flags nonetheless remain highly significant within the work, and are crucial to its intent.

Parade—Hoboken, New Jersey is the book's opening photograph. Two women stand in separate windows in a wall. On the left, a woman in a spotted dress stares grimly out. Next to her is another in a clean, buttoned coat, her face hidden by the flag's flap. The caption tells us why the flag is tied to the window: there is a parade.

Alfred Eisenstaedt provides a telling contrast in his iconic parade-picture, *V-J Day in Times Square* (1945, *Life* archives, Getty Museum). This photograph is principally a celebration of spontaneous human joy, but it is also a celebration of Americans and America. The dark-uniformed sailor kisses a young nurse, whose glorious transient beauty is defined in an exposed stocking top. Frank's women, by contrast, are faceless and grimacing. Eisenstaedt's revellers celebrate a 'Brave New World', a world at peace, a world which had just capitulated through conflict to the Anglo-American way. Whatever reason Frank's heroine had for tying a flag to her window appears, from her expression, to have little to do with goodwill to all men. Frank reveals, as his frontispiece, a misanthropic stare at the heart of the parade. This photograph, in turn, is the heart of *The Americans*. Frank invites his readers to look at the American flag waving in its everyday reality, away from the hype and the lionizing. His photograph questions and modifies the received wisdom created by so many images of smiling flag-wavers. He said in his statement in the 1958 *US Camera Annual*, "It is important to see what is invisible to others—perhaps the look of hope or the look of sadness" (Frank, in Maloney 1958: 115). He is looking to photograph that which is occluded, those moments that might be caught in the corner of an eye and dismissed. The critic and galleryist Jane Livingston recognized that Frank captured "things found around the edges, things half invisible

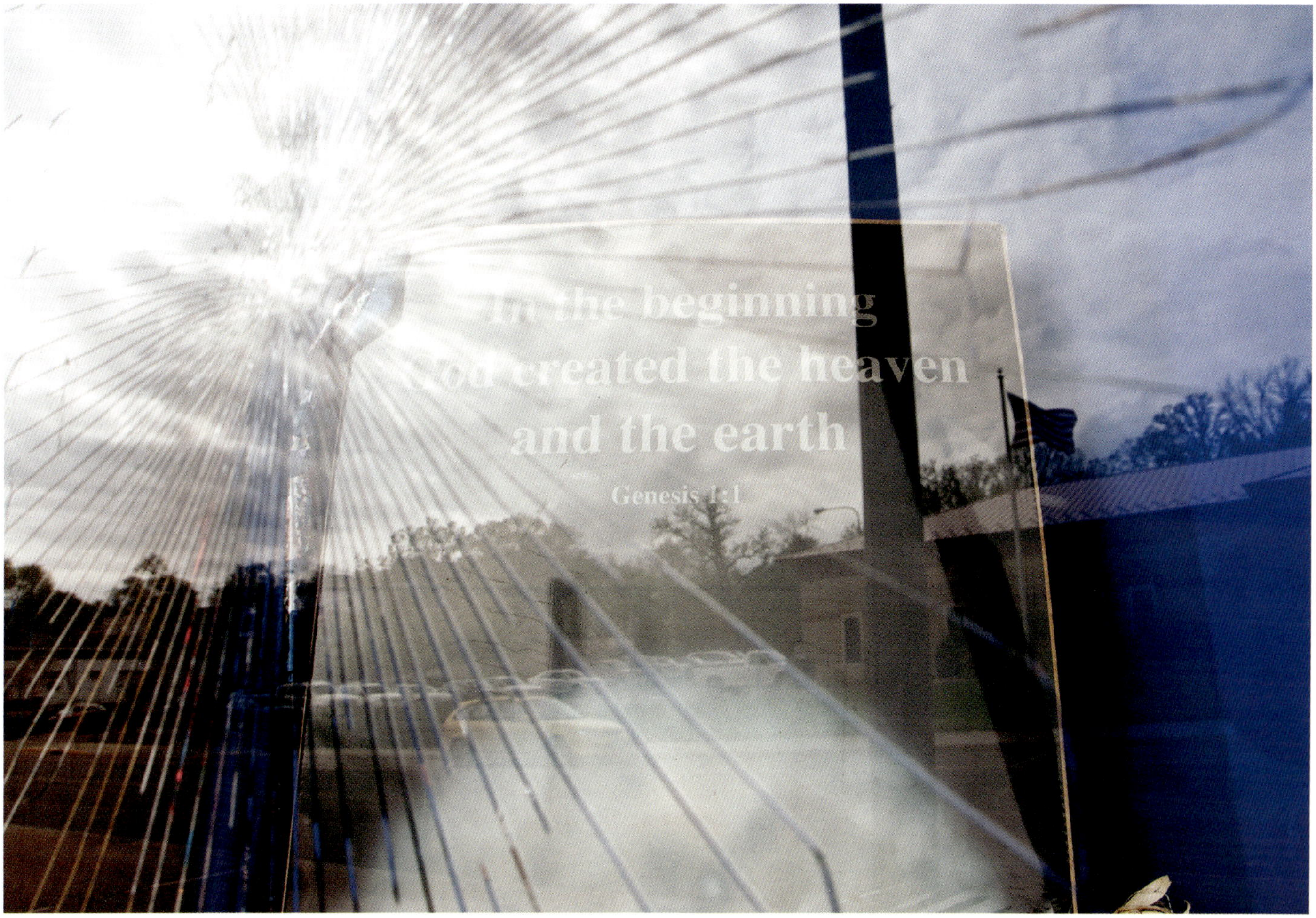
the beginning
created the heaven
and the earth
Genesis 1:1

to most of us most of the time" (1992: 343).

This askance-seeing, deliberately avoiding the orthodoxies of enculturation, is not the only challenge of *Parade—Hoboken*. A brick wall occupies the centre of the picture. It is blandly regular, jerry-built, functional, without beauty. Its dominance of the photograph challenges viewers' expectations. Images that include human beings very often make them the principal subject. Here they are marginalised, cramped into the corners of the composition. They appear no more important in the image's visual hierarchy than the wall that divides them. These women are fitted into this block not because it suits them or is a desirable residence, but because there is nowhere else they can go. The photograph's tenement claustrophobia is heightened by the cropped flag and window frames and by the almost unbearably close picture plane. Frank has achieved a foreshortening through his head-on view: all of the objects in the photograph are at about the same distance from the camera. This unrelenting flatness invades our personal space; it is too close for comfort. The photograph's viewpoint is at the level of the women's rooms, implying another window across the street. The horizon of their vision is, then, defined by another brick wall.

This photograph is about alienation. The women are divided by their wall from each other within the house, and divided from the parade below. The house separates them, and even more surely, keeps them from us. The claustrophobic picture plane is an effective stylistic analogue to their tenement reality. There is no association here between the flag and beautiful, youthful exuberance—no admirable sentiments, no smiling face or stocking tops. There is ugliness, banality and a tantalizing glimpse of Frank's dense and challenging intention.

Frank talked of his work in terms of 'love' (in Maloney 1958: 115) and 'vision' (1954, in Tucker and Brookman 1986: 20), so there must be more to *Parade—Hoboken* if he is not to be proved a liar. These women are not demons, they are everyday. They have to live in this forbidding place, but something in their thrown-up, four-square lives must surely embody their hope, if they are to survive. Karl Marx, talking about the religious inclination in humanity, wrote: "Religion is the sigh of the oppressed creature, the heart of a heartless world, and the soul of soulless conditions." (Marx 1977 [1843]: 127). However fatuous or compromised, the Stars and Stripes is the nearest thing the women have to a symbol for their wild hope, a conduit for their doubting and uncertain faith. In the backstreet reality of the American Dream, real women still take a moment out of their lives to stand beside it and watch a parade.

The ugliness of *Parade—Hoboken* was too much for many of Frank's readers. Writing in *Popular Photography* in 1960, Bruce Downs commented:

> Frank is sensitive, but apparently he is without love. There is no pity in his images. They are images of hate and hopelessness, of desolation and preoccupation with death. They are images of America by a man who hates the country of his adoption [...] It is a world shrouded in immense grey tragic boredom. (Downs, in Tucker and Brookman 1986: 36)

John Durniak wrote in the same publication, "If this is America (the United States) we should burn it down and start again" (in Tucker and Brookman 1986: 36). James Zanutto, paraphrasing Kerouac, called it a "sad poem for sick people" (in Tucker and Brookman 1986: 37). Even with the benefit of hindsight, there is something in these criticisms that carries a disturbing kernel of truth. How do we square the undoubted ugliness and desperate disempowerment of Frank's Hoboken women? Perhaps Marx again says it best:

> To call on them [humanity] to give up their illusions about their condition is to call on them to give up a condition that requires illusions. The criticism of religion is, therefore, in embryo, the criticism of that vale of tears of which religion is the halo. (Marx 1977 [1843]: 127)

As long as people suffer, they will need dreams. Surely *Parade—Hoboken* is Frank's 'criticism coming out of love'. He is facing and describing this 'grey tragic boredom' in the hope of contributing towards bringing it to an end. Frank said in an interview: "I think at that time I was compassionate. I had a feeling of compassion for the people on the street" (Frank, in Wheeler 1977: 22).

At the same time as allowing the idly flapping flag to simultaneously embody and challenge hope, Frank presses it further into a manifesto for his book. A woman's face, the thing that most characterizes human beings as individuals, is here obscured by the flag. *The Americans* is an examination of the nature of a people, a look through a flag at the faces hidden behind it, and the extent to which these faces are stained by its red, white and blue.

SAN FRANCISCO—CITY OF DREAMS FOR ME, AS A CHILD IN AFRICA. Walking the whites-only streets of Johannesburg, I longed for the flowers in your hair. Nine years old, I was eye level with the hemlines of mini dresses. I still recall the perfectly tanned thighs and paisley clad bottoms of two girls walking in Berea. I knew their liberation was thanks to you and, though having no clear understanding yet of the deep joy those swinging hips would bring, was grateful.

Now a chill potato patch fog grips the morning, chill and damp. The Golden Gate is a hollow maw, growling deepest grey. Last night a jazz trumpeter played as the homeless howled a night-long litany outside my boutique hotel window. Take a trolley bus to North Point and Chinatown, I'm in the dark thick dream of it now. Found a strange and jarring place—the Beat Museum, made of tin-tack typewriters and ratty couches facing dead faces, talking from the grave. Old and obscure paperbacks around, and an over-zealous assistant, his hard sell inadequately obscured by excessive obsequiousness. Fun though, in a way, to browse the fake and barely believable ephemera. Something of a sense of how these streets might have been before they were (in)famous. Funnily, amongst the tat, a book called *Jesus was a Beatnik*. And there it is, the soul-question and definition-heart of Frank. Robert said he was "pursuing, sometimes catching the essence of the black and white, the knowledge of where God is" (Frank 1991: after plate 63), and Jack Kerouac called him out with a line or two:

> I wanted to take off. Somewhere along the line I knew there'd be girls, visions, everything. Somewhere along the line the pearl would be handed to me. (Kerouac 1972[1957]: 11)

Understanding, I guess, is what they were seeking, something standing strong against the blizzard of bewilderment. Dharma bums, saddhus of the American streets. That makes them Saints then, certainly—but not ones any church I know would canonise.

This *Political Rally* picture, what's it all about? Like the rest of *The Americans*, a signpost, a word to the wise. It's a yin–yang balance thing, a negative space, a searching by subtraction. It shows us clearly where God is not and Robert tells us you'd better be sure of that and make no mistake, if you really want to take this trip and find out where He/She/It (the challenging taxonomy of God…) is. For this is honesty, this is reality, this is no bullshit. Let's get that clear right at the beginning.

CITY FATHERS—HOBOKEN, NEW JERSEY

City Fathers—Hoboken, New Jersey is *The Americans*' second image, which signals its significance. The contact sheet (Greenough 2009: 379) shows several takes of the same scene: a group of politicians on a dais. We might call this 'speculative photography', Frank reaching for something, sensing that there is something important there, some potential, hoping that it might reveal itself to the lens, without really knowing exactly what it is, or even exactly what he is hoping for.

The shot before the one eventually chosen (frame 27 on the contact) is rather busy. The eye wanders aimlessly; there is no clear compositional focus. The most attractive visual element is a large tricolour rosette. The photograph ringed in red crayon (frame 28) which was selected, moves the previously dominant rosette down, placing it a fifth of the way up from the base of the photograph, along a golden section line. The heads of the row of politicians are no longer cut off, creating space in the image. They occupy the centre band, focusing our attention on them. The upward rake of their heads leads the eye towards the enigmatic expression of the man at the extreme right, making him the subject of the photograph. Frank has cropped the image for every edition of *The Americans*, always removing the head of a politician to the right (Greenough 2009: 461) in order to heighten this focus and amplify the aspects of his 'personal vision' that the photograph embodies.

So what has Frank's personal vision fixed on in this picture, what is the story that he is so keen to tell? The politicians' top-hatted pomp is juxtaposed with their stolid, bored expressions. There is a supporting character in the image, playing a subsidiary role. He is second from right and characterizes the corrupt, power-hungry mandarin, dismissive of the event, not even dressed for the occasion. He could be Joseph Kennedy, Randolph Hearst or any one of Hollywood's depictions of the

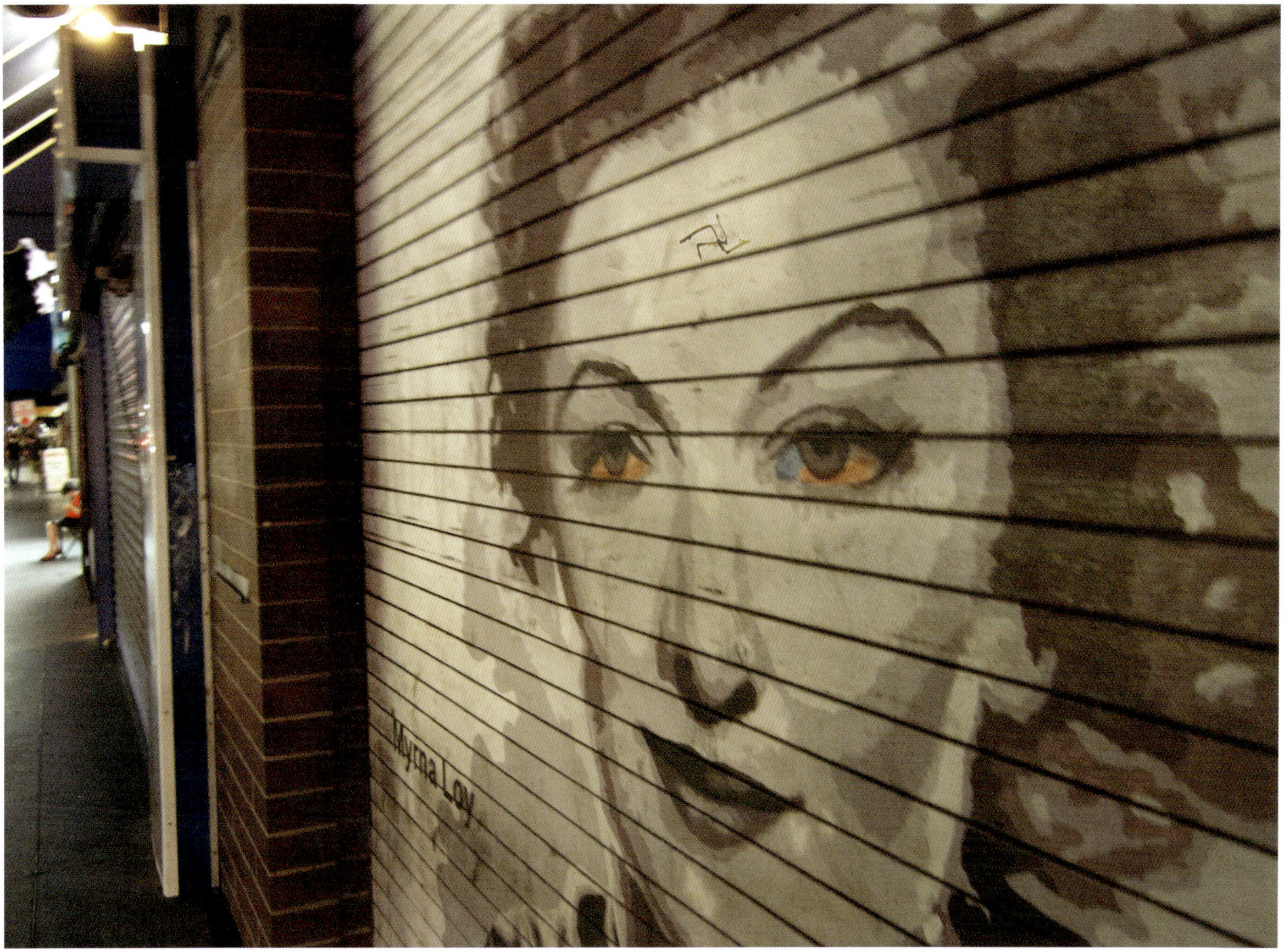
Myrna Loy

dark world of American politics. Richard Nixon was vice-president at this time, a man who could suitably be invoked here. The man at extreme right, though, is the focus of the image. His expression is incongruous and unexpected. Is he praying? Blowing a kiss? If so, to whom? The overwhelming impression is of arrogance, confident defiance and self-satisfaction: it is a distinctly 'kiss my ass' gesture. Jack Kerouac, in his introduction to *The Americans*, recognized that the picture's importance lay in the capturing of this particular moment. He described it as:

> Hoboken in the winter, platform full of politicians all ordinary looking till suddenly at the far end to the right you see one of them pursing his lips in prayer politico (yawning probably) not a soul cares. (Kerouac, in Frank 1959: 2)

The expression of the politician was the necessary element, supported by a composition that draws the eye towards the enigma. *City Fathers* captures something of the particular kind of 'decisive moment' that Frank was seeking, a moment which was manipulated and included in order to communicate Frank's vision.

City Fathers—Hoboken, New Jersey is a successful single image. Its communication is extended significantly, however, when it is considered alongside the image that precedes it. Philip Brookman (Coke and Du Pont 1986: 124) says that *City Fathers* was taken during a parade, linking it intimately with *Parade—Hoboken, New Jersey*, which comes before. This link is important, picking up as it does one of the book's abiding themes: the juxtaposition of unknown and insignificant poor Americans with their more eminent and well-heeled compatriots. Frank described this as "the faces of the leaders and the faces of the followers" in his Guggenheim application (Frank, in Greenough 2009: 362). These images also demonstrate another of Frank's interests: looking and being watched. He said: "The first four or five pictures are of people looking, spectators. And then you see what they're looking at" (Frank, in Alexander 1997: 38).

WALKING THE HOLLYWOOD HILLS, from a small gate opening out of a dead-end apartmented street, neatly tree lined. By the tube piped door a drive owner has placed a table filled with water, bottled and granola, barred. Into and up the dry canyon, friable earth crumbly and large grained, full of small sharp stones—a thousand hanging on a thread waiting for the next rain to free them and rip up the road. Spiky bushes, armed against heat and desiccating desert air. Higher up we looked down on dark raptors, riding the city's updraught, all of the brilliant coloured fumes of Los Angeles rising eternally past them, up into the air. We crested the ridge, somewhere near Mulholland Drive, overlooking sizable houses, held back for the super rich. They were nothing too special, expensive because of where they sit in the social rules of this little world. Arching higher and higher, these hills, in a happy analogue for Hollywood hierarchy. Prickly pears were everywhere around an ochre dusted path. In a moment I saw, disappearing, three Hispanics, an adult and two kids. In decent clothes, for sure, and carrying plastic bags enormously obese with empty plastic bottles. Bounty hunters chasing down the levy. On the ovoid, jungle-green leaf of a cactus someone had cut "Obama, Yes!".

Always the (vain) hope we have of a saviour, here is another more newly named. Someone who can bring everyone together, the rich in their compounds, the bottle hunters in their bins. Who was the saviour in Robert's famous picture? For whom did the staid, suited man climb a building and fling open his arms?

POLITICAL RALLY—CHICAGO

Frank's first two images make a powerful pair, examining rich and poor, politically influential and insignificant, leaders and followers. The use of pairs, diptychs, is a central practice in documentary photography, allowing the exploration of interrelationships, most frequently 'ironic juxtapositions'—a key approach in street photography. *The Americans* does this certainly, but not in a rigid or mechanistic manner: its linear structure is much more sophisticated. A favourite practice later in the book is a three-way linking, with each photograph having a visual or thematic link that a second picture will pick up. This middle image then passes something forward to a third photograph, in a kind of pictorial leap-frog or relay. Frank also very often presents extended series of linked images. Finally, there are occasional pictures which act as *caesura*, pauses in which the flow is momentarily halted by photographs which do not seem to discernibly relate in any particular way to their adjacent pictures.

We have seen that *Parade—Hoboken, New Jersey* and *City Fathers—Hoboken, New Jersey* are a thematically linked pair, but they are also part of an extended series of related adjacent images. The series here is characterized by the representation of gesture. The flag-obscured lady on the right hand side of *Parade* holds her hand to her mouth in a gesture that looks like uncertainty. The hatted politician in *City Fathers* makes a gesture of opposition, sharing none of her ambivalence and pursing his lips in a supremely confident and defiant gesture. *Political Rally—Chicago* is also a study of gesture: in this case a kind of ecstasy, however misplaced or bizarre. Following him, a pensive black man looks quietly on in *Funeral—St. Helena, South Carolina.* He too is holding his hand to his mouth, a gesture echoed by the man in a lighter suit behind him and the man to his left. The gravity of their remembrance of a life lived and over is held in their contemplative gestures. They are followed by a photograph of a small group with a tall man at centre wearing a hat. He again holds his hand to his chin. He is smoking a cigar, which leads us into the next image, also of a cigar smoker, as Frank dispenses with gesture as his linking thread.

So, then, the book's complexity is apparent. The opening image can be read firstly as itself, secondly as part of a thematically linked pair and thirdly as part of a short series of visually related adjacent images. It doesn't, of course, end there. Frank decided early on to divide his book into four parts, beginning each part with a photograph of the American flag (Frank, in Alexander 1997: 38) thus making it part of his extended, complex and sophisticated consideration of the iconography of the Stars and Stripes. *Political Rally—Chicago*, similarly, extends beyond even this series: it is directly paired with another image of the same name, later in *The Americans*. Both of these feature in the discussion of leaders and followers.

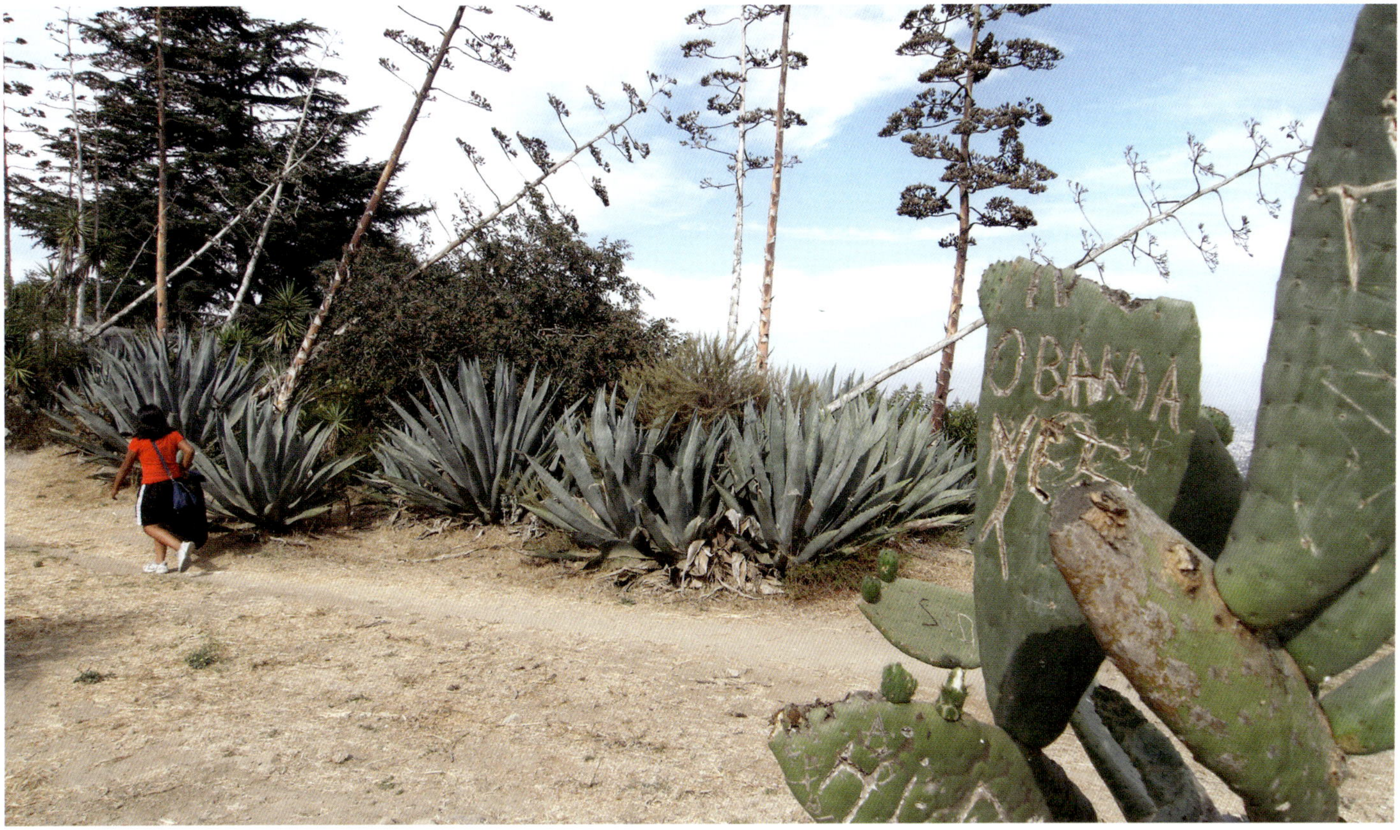
OBAMA

"EL REY DEL POP HA MUERTO". Sitting in a Mexican bar in Silverlake, Los Angeles, my bass-player friend was schmoozing the locals—jazz players and bare-midrifted hangers on. The walls were dripping graffiti, like a Santa Cruz surfer's pectoral. In a corner of the dingy, ply-boarded room, set like an icon in a Tzarist church, a screen announced the involuntary manslaughter of the Man in the Mirror. Here, in his home town. We joined the flood of bodies in Brownian motion, sucked coriolis clockwise onto Hollywood Boulevard, in search of the Star. A heap of tributes, looking like landfill, unceremoniously swept away every few minutes by garbage men. People laughing, pushing, crying.

Is it fear of forgetting that drives us? Is it memory that's cybernetically enhanced, as glowing blue electronic retinas record the moment—or are we afraid to look into the eyes of the dead?

FUNERAL—ST. HELENA, SOUTH CAROLINA

Funeral—St. Helena, South Carolina figures suited and hatted mourners standing in a circle among their cars, watching the proceedings. Two of the men, intent perhaps on the address, lean on a black car, their faces mournful. There is no perception of incongruity apparent—the car is accepted in this profound and intimate moment.

Central to the impact and success of *The Americans* is Frank's recognition and presentation of significant symbols which act to define America's emerging civilization. These include filling stations, diners, jukeboxes and, perhaps most eloquently of all, the automobile. Frank measures out a life in Chevrolets and Cadillacs. He images cars that are present at conception, that serve as nannies and childhood friends; cars that facilitate romance, are the seat of great endeavours and the objects of worship; cars that perpetrate murder and become the conduits and memorials of the dead. The notion of a life lived 'on the road' is not unique to Frank, reflecting, rather, an allegory of life's journey and the pursuit of paradise on earth widely expressed and examined in near-contemporary culture. Jack Kerouac's novel *On the Road* (1972[1957]), along with F. Scott Fitzgerald's *The Great Gatsby* (1994[1925]), films such as *Of Mice and Men* (Milestone 1939) and *The Grapes of Wrath* (Ford 1940), alongside *Rebel Without a Cause* (Ray 1955) and *The Wild One* (Benedek 1954) and experimental and innovative music from John Coltrane, Charlie Parker and Woody Guthrie, all enfold Frank's series of pictures.

The road and car are highly significant in American culture. Frank himself chose a 1950 second-hand Ford Business Coupe and the road as the conduit for his Guggenheim Foundation funded study. It is not surprising that the highway should feature so prominently in *The Americans*. Kerouac's novel was finished in the same year as the publication in France of the first version of Frank's book. The car and the road for him were a place of pilgrimage:

> I could see Denver looming ahead of me like the promised land, way out there beneath the stars, across the prairie of Iowa and the plains of Nebraska. (Kerouac 1972[1957]: 11)

The notion of quest, seeking some kind of latter-day grail, is common to both artists. Frank described his goal for this journey as: "pursuing, sometimes catching [...] the knowledge of where God is" (Frank 1991: after plate 63).

The still-new American interstate network and the wide, wild vastness of America were an appropriate place to look. Travelling these roads also has a spiritual association: they are an analogue for the journey we all undertake. Kerouac's 'pearl' or Frank's 'knowledge of where God is' are the promise at the end of the road, literally the suggestion of enlightenment, if only the end may be reached. The road to it is undeniably luminous, the travelling will be along its brightness, riding between darkness to the left and right. F. Scott Fitzgerald, writing thirty years earlier, saw the highway in similar terms:

> Out of the corner of his eye Gatsby saw that the blocks of the sidewalks really formed a ladder and mounted to a secret place above the trees. He could climb to it, if he climbed alone, and once there he could suck on the pap of life, gulp down the incomparable milk of wonder. (Fitzgerald 1994[1925]: 118)

Gatsby, like Frank and Kerouac, dreams of paradise at the end of the road. Frank though, as we have already noted, will brook no sentimentality or 'magic realism'. He wants to see it all, in the full and raw light of everyday. So here, chins cupped in contemplative fingers, men who are still travelling their lives' roads look on as one of their number is interred: journey done, all brightness seen, all wonder consumed and, now, forgotten.

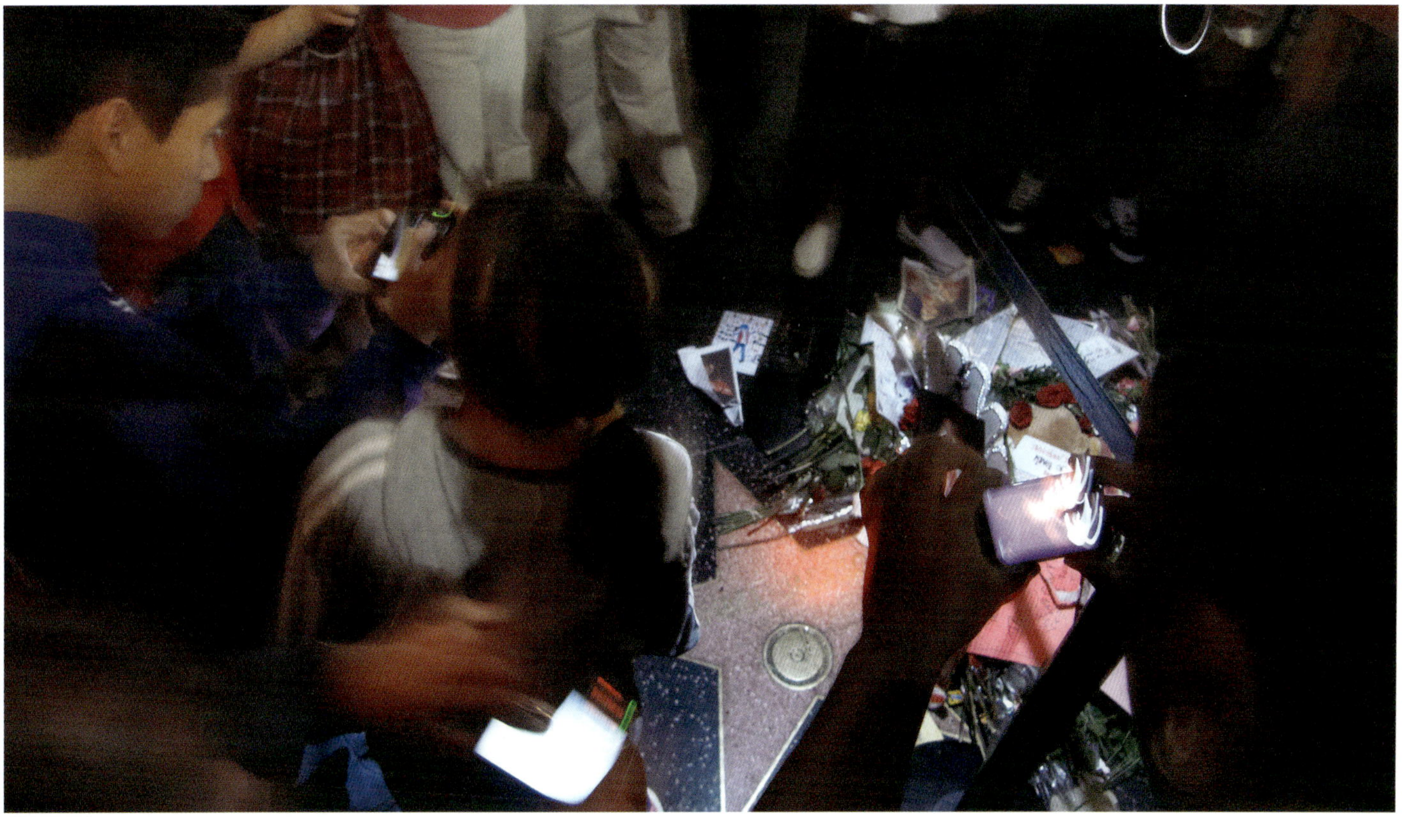

INTO THE RESERVATION OF THE OGLALA SIOUX WHERE THE ROAD IS DIRT—a US Highway number, but no funding, so it's almost impassable. Miles of muddy sliding past litter-wreathed trailer houses in various states of decay. Every now and then, one looked more tidy and cared for. Made it through to Pine Ridge, eventually, for gas and lunch. Most of the young people are dressed slouchily in baseball gear and sweats—the older men look like cowboys. They're talking to each other in English. The counter clerk has an imperious air, really seems impressively invulnerable. I really don't know how to be—here, today—I am another passing white man and this is an unrecognisable place. So many years I've read and dreamed about this place, seen old photographs and wondered how it would be. So impressed by the look and the descriptions of the way of life of these people's ancestors—on horseback, in Tipis, self sufficient, celebratory. The town reminds me of my inner city childhood, looks like a hundred other deprived housing projects I've seen, in Tipton, Glasgow, East Berlin. My sense of the vision's loss is acute, like a sudden tragedy that one struggles to process. I'm not sure for a moment if their whole beautiful past is an invention of my imagination, and thrash around inwardly, looking for acknowledgement from someone else. They quietly continue conversations and munch on burgers and fries. Something in me is deeply at risk—I sense the danger.

Heading out to Wounded Knee, the buildings are graffitied. On a scrubby Great Plains sand-hill I saw a church ahead, and the little monument. I've seen this place in documentaries and photographs. Harrowing pictures of frozen bodies of old men, women and children cut down by artillery and carbines. The epic documentary *The West* shows it in almost black and white, the monument solemn and dignified in ice—hauntingly beautiful and terribly sad. Descriptions of the little boys, in schoolboy grey, playing one day, all dead the next. The reality made me catch my breath. It's small—the names for the dead, quite shockingly, are numbered. The patch of ground where they are buried is unmowed and full of dandelion seed heads. Tributes, tatty, cheaply made and kitsch are fading and weatherbeaten behind a rough, poorly erected chain link fence. Newer graves are there, too, the broken earth covering still visible through the grass.

Milling around were many Lakota, all of them hawking something or other. One fresh-faced kid was collecting for his drum circle. A tall, heavily scarred 21 year old talked of his emerging career as a rapper called 'Mandate'. His career until now had been fighting and carnivals. His still healing eyebrow-cut joined his scars in testament to a street fighting life. Trying to sell me beadwork was a young woman called Natasha, saying the money was for her baby. An old, tired beggars' story of which I was inwardly sceptical. She pointed to a little girl, sleeping a way off in the porch of the church in her young father's arms. Her bead work was really beautiful. Dodging through the dollar chasing, I felt a connection to these kids. They are friendly and soon get past the hustling. We talked of fusion music, and I wondered whether the rapper and the drummer might get together. I told them how inspired I'd been by their people's art and old way of living—a strong contrast to now, litter strewn and unkempt. There was such a gleam of hope in the drummer's clever eyes and such a strength in Natasha's mother love for the tiny girl wrapped against the rain. The story of peoples is one thing—beneath it all there's always you and I. An older Lakota man tells me a story, me hoping to hear someone speaking like Black Elk. No thunder in his words though and I left feeling bereaved, chastened and awakened. The world seemed cold and bleaker at my leaving, inconsolable they and I—at the grey reality held in bullets that killed their bodies, and ended their Dance for the Ghosts. All their generations of loved ones, lost for ever. It's a cold hard thing the destruction of dreaming. Harsh, harrowing, an ice shiver driven into bone. It is also liberating. I could barely sense it yet, on that low cloud day, the quietly growing realisation that the strange, ancient and utterly inhuman Universe has a wonder of its own, beyond the skerries of our dreams.

RODEO—DETROIT

Rodeo—Detroit is an image of a tall, white man in an oversize western hat. He is contemplative, like the mourners in the last photograph, and again holds his hand to his chin. His expression is serious, certainly, but lacks the sombre tones of the preceding image. His contemplation is of something off to the photograph's right, presumably the rodeo of the caption. He is smoking a cigar, which leads us into the next image, also of a cigar smoker, as Frank dispenses with gesture as his linking

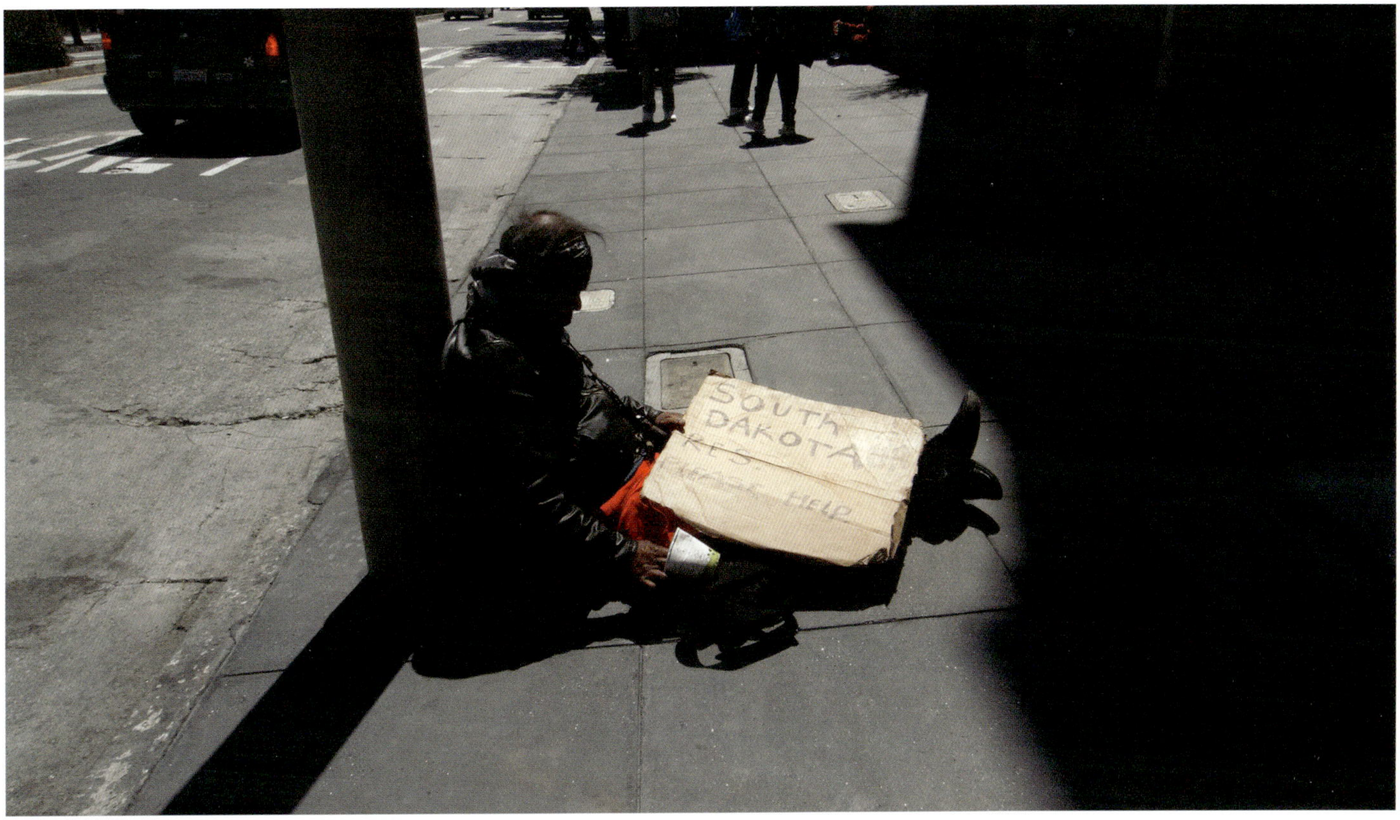
SOUTH
DAKOTA
HELP

thread. One of Frank's favourite structural devices in *The Americans* is a three-way connection, with an image looking back to its predecessor through some shared visual or thematic aspect, while also looking forward with another, different shared link. In this case the backwards look is the chin-in-hand, and the forwards one the cigar.

PULLING INTO THE COMPLEXITIES OF NASHVILLE IN THE EVENING LIGHT, how my heart sank at the chaotic, industrial defeat. Last night I was in the wild, on mile-high Balsam Mountain, reeking of resin in the cold air, no lights anywhere in the Smoky Mountain vastness save the stars and I, with raven, bear and fox as bedfellows.

The Nashville suburbs did not disappoint—exactly as tawdry as they'd at first appeared. I'd arrived late, so tried a local bar—a place for less than a happy hour, gagging on stale cigarette smoke and trying to like the house band. The next day in Downtown was different though: Broadway after a grubby and unloved Days Inn was another story. A South Carolinian, handsome, not lovely, sang Patsy Cline enough to bring down the stars. Tootsies Orchid Lounge—a thousand old photographs dimmed by the holiest of grime. Her gorgeous voice always was interrupted by coach parties of tourists, in for one drink, too loud laughing (so we all would notice) at their genial tour guides' over-practised jokes and out again in the middle of the most exquisite heartbreak.

Among the Bud waving, straw cowboy-hatted ladies and their pressed shirted companions, relishing the scheduled fun, I saw a man in a Viet Nam Veteran hat. I think I saw something in his eyes—was it really there? All those deaths he could not process, the lost friends and enemies he still needed to remember? Ghosts he could never forget. No sure and stogie wielding soldier he, striding like Frank's, through Savannah. This man wears his colours on the inside: you can see them blowing ragged in his eyes.

SAVANNAH, GEORGIA

Savannah, Georgia is a photograph of a cigar smoker, again accompanied by a lady friend, echoing the previous image, *Rodeo*. This smoker is a soldier, a link that will carry us into the following image. The soldier eyes the photographer with suspicion. This is a response that is frequently seen in *The Americans*, reflecting something of the spirit of the times, but also reminding us of the relative novelty for most people in the '50s, of being photographed. It serves also to remind us frequently of the eye behind the camera, of the man whose vision this is. The kind of suspicion pictured here reached its apogee when Frank was arrested by Lieutenant Brown of the Little Rock Police due to

> the man's appearance, the fact that he was a foreigner and had in his possession cameras [...] we are continually being advised to watch out for any persons illegally in the country in the employ of some unfriendly foreign power and the possibility of Communist affiliations. (Frank, in Tucker and Brookman 1986: 24)

America in the '50s was waging a crusade against communism, partially as a response to the explosion of the first Russian nuclear bomb in 1949. Senator Joe McCarthy's Committee for Anti-American Activities practiced its inquisition-like witch hunts and celebrated their associated *auto da fé*. Political unconformity was effectively outlawed. Xenophobia and racism were rife, deeply woven into the texture of the nation. By a significant coincidence, the very same Little Rock in which Frank was arrested would explode into violence three years later, as white elitists attempted to prevent the racial integration of its Central High School. This would require the army's intervention. Frank felt this: "Seeing those faces, those people, the kind of hidden violence in the country at that time, the McCarthy period I felt it very strongly" (Frank, in Janis and MacNeil 1977: 54).

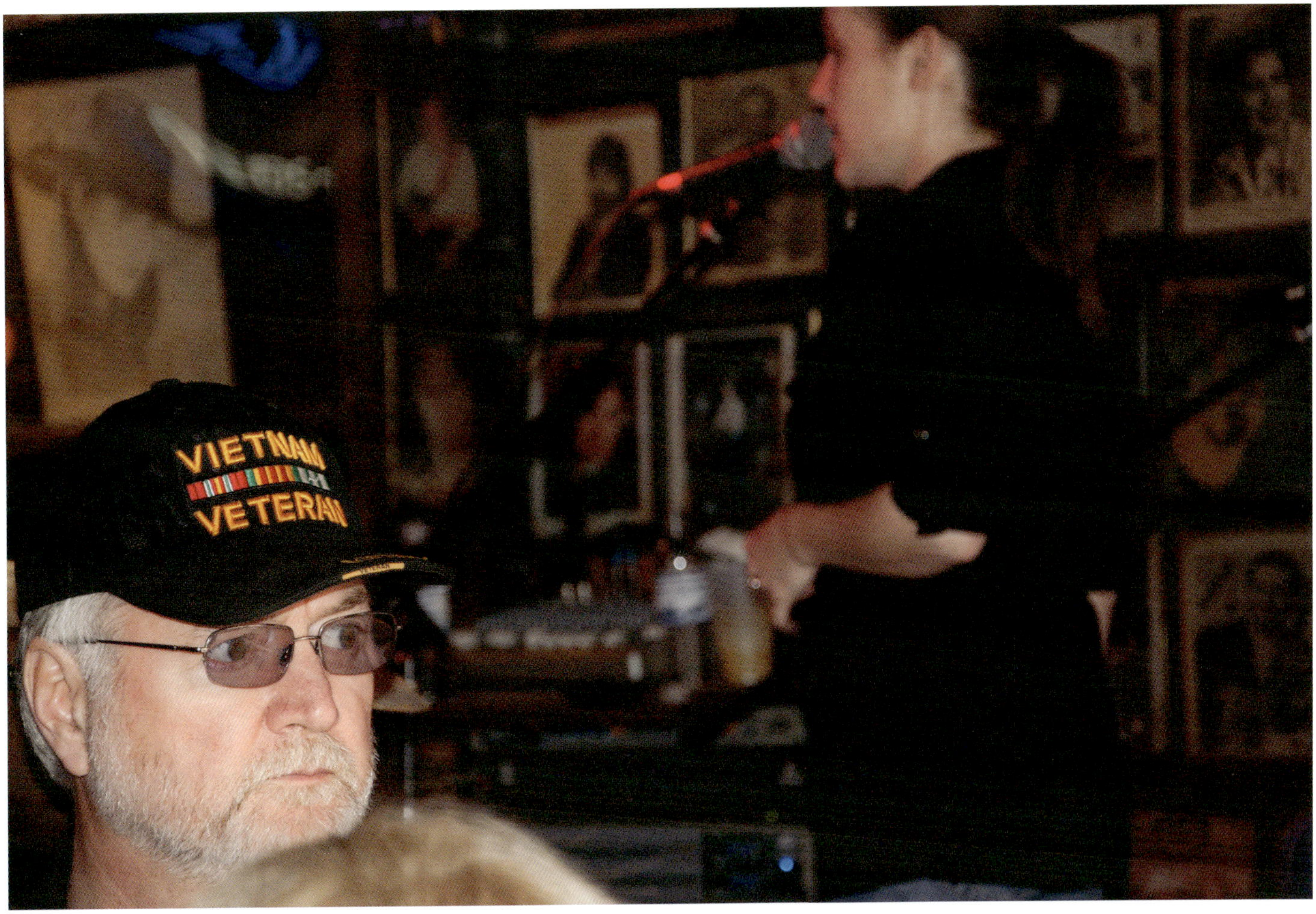
VIETNAM
VETERAN

RIDING THE FREE FERRY IN THE MARINE CORP TRAINING COASTLANDS OF CAROLINA, I looked down from the gantry onto a well kept camper. The gun laws of America—controversy on controversy, a fat rat-a-tat journalist jousting the Omega Man over the children's deaths in Columbine—and now years later more children in Newport, Connecticut. A teacher there, hearing gunfire, *knew what was happening* and heroically herded her charges into cupboards and closets, knowing she was about to die. When the crazed man came she lied convincingly enough to fool him. She succeeded—and died. She can't value our tributes or know her dead face is famous, or that she deservedly now represents everything about humanity that is great and good. I hold in my heart a torch high for her, like the children in *Harry Potter* for Dumbledore. No, I do not trivialise. She is the reality which the movie imaginatively admires. But what of the other, the killer of children? My god, I can barely stand to think inside the morass of his mind.

And yet Americans are free, in a different way than Europeans ever can be. Britain is mostly free of gun crime, but the people are controlled by forces who are armed in a way they cannot be. So this 'freedom' helps keep British people subjects and never citizens, more likely to be killed by a Policeman than a terrorist. A friend in Minnesota could barely stand to leave his children unprotected, dropping them at school the day after the shooting. For my English children I have no such fears.

Which of us is more nearly free?

NAVY RECRUITING STATION, POST OFFICE—BUTTE, MONTANA

Navy Recruiting Station, Post Office—Butte, Montana is another *Americans* photograph featuring the flag. Usually Frank reserves the flag for section-heading images: he uses four other flag pictures, each indicating the start of a section. In *Navy Recruiting Station,* the flag is one among many motifs. It hangs vertically in an office lit by daylight. Set against a dark framing door, the Star Spangled Banner supplies the entry point into this photograph. It points down at the recruiting officer's indolently crossed feet. These rest on his desk, in strong contrast with the active soldier of the last image. Beneath them is a sign saying 'Join the Navy, ask me about it.' The ironic juxtaposition of the conventional dream of the dynamic glory of the US Navy with the tawdry, typically small-town, somnolent office is supported by the flag, but does not rely on it.

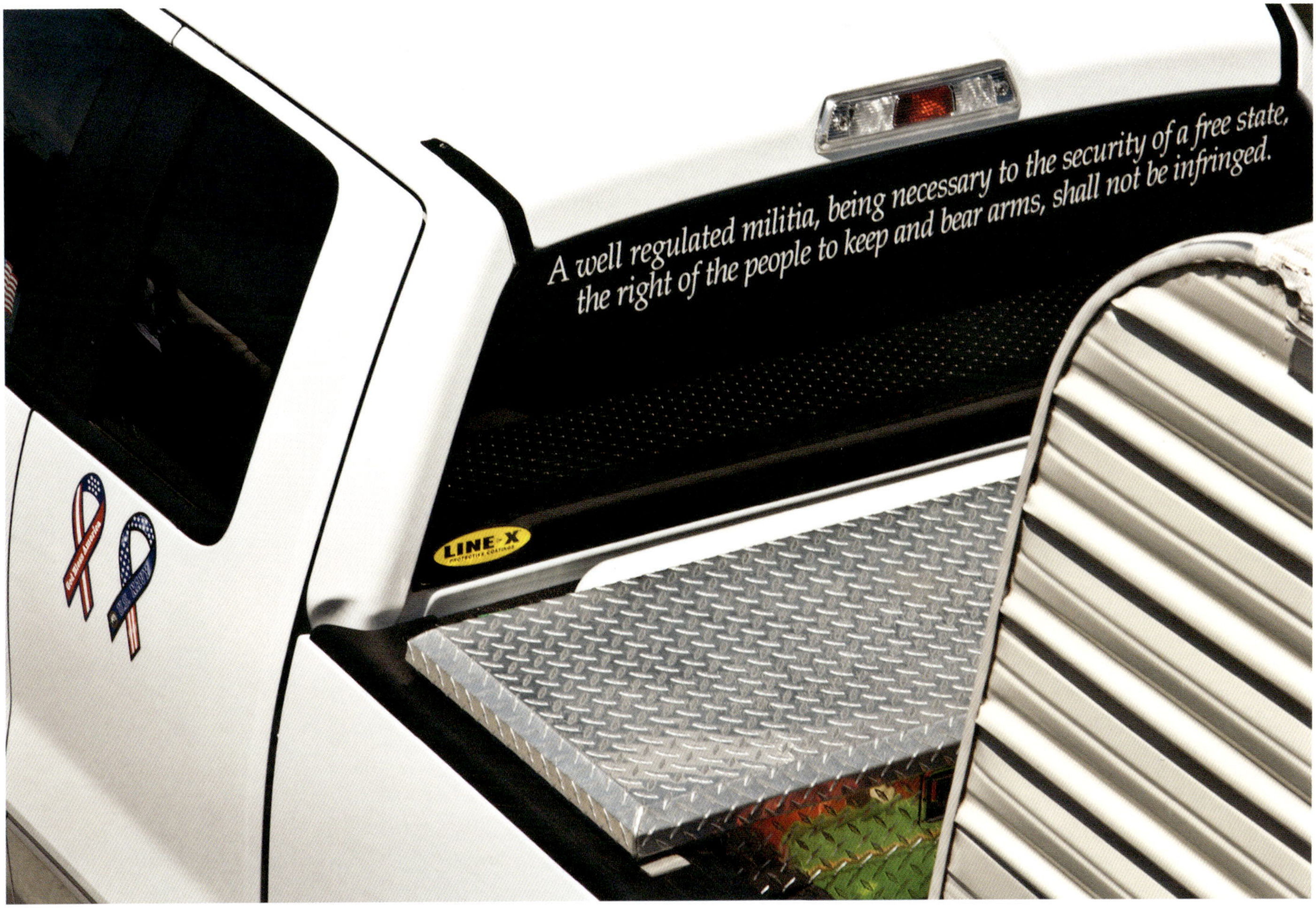
A well regulated militia, being necessary to the security of a free state,
the right of the people to keep and bear arms, shall not be infringed.
LINE-X

I REMEMBER A FROZEN WORLD. My first time in Minnesota, minus 40 degrees, riding a white highway in a howling wind. Telegraph wires draped like tinsel, heavy with six pointed crystals. The ice-sun hung in the coldest of skies, around it smudges of rainbow, dogging its heels. In the Lower Sioux Casino a full blood Dakota woman was serving tables. She co-owns the land, but works for the out-of-reservation money that squats here, concrete and gaudy against the cold. She gently exhorted me to stay warm, the quiet voice of her generations, still buried waist deep in this ground, offered up to the incomer, wide eyed and inexperienced.

It is not she tonight who waits at my table—maybe her sister, or a cousin? Her ancient eyes are attentive on us, waiting for requirements, serving with a smile. But the irony bites me, sitting at the 'Prairie Waters' table with these worthies, and genuine, tourist facilitating, developmental planners. All white we are, mostly Nordic descended. This table is our reservation, for we own the Waters, and will decide the administration and give ourselves awards. All the great Northern flowings—Mississippi and Minnie Sota, Lac qui Parle and Boundary Waters are ours by right of conquest. And this tiny place is theirs still, sundogged and bald eagled, bullrushed and deeply frozen. Like the conspirators in the Club Car on Robert's Congressional Special express, all here talk tryst and bargain. I, a wanderer walking between worlds, will take the words of the Dakota woman and make sure I stay warm.

EN ROUTE FROM NEW YORK TO WASHINGTON, CLUB CAR

The stasis and complacency of the recruiting office is contrasted with energy and engagement in *En route from New York to Washington, Club Car.* The train's dining car is lit with fluorescent light. Half of the photograph is occupied by the backs of two tweed-jacketed men. They are hunched conspiratorially, blocking us out. The camera is at chair level, looking up, a viewpoint that heightens the sense of exclusion. Between the jackets is a bald man's head. He listens to the left-hand jacket, fully occupied in the discussion, ignoring the camera utterly. Though not physically active, their body language evidences their engagement. There is a strong visual echo with the last image: the illuminated stars above the service counter of this train car recall the stars on the flag of the last image. There is also a conceptual link. Although not acknowledged in the title, this train is the 'Congressional Special', an express carrying, at premium cost, businessmen between New York and Washington. The contrast between the idle American Navy recruiting officer and these earnest, engaged American power-brokers is effective.

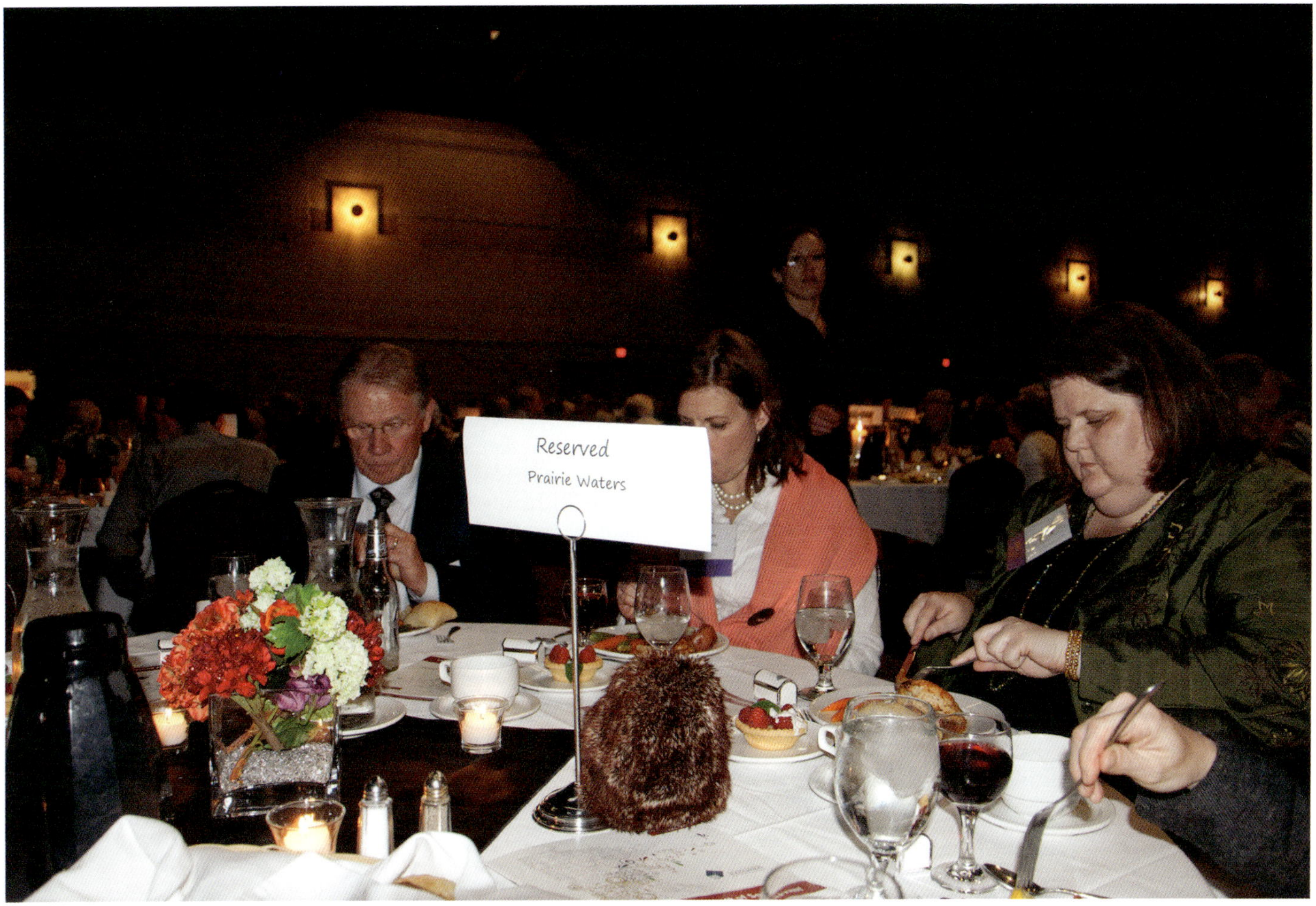
Reserved
Prairie Waters

IT'S AN ALMOST TOKEN GESTURE, THE LA SUBWAY—perfunctory and vestigial, with just a couple of lines. It has underground stations, escalators and ticket machines—all the stuff you'd expect—paternosters, airflow towers and advertising. At each platform's end the dark hollow maws are appropriately full of dread and promise, symbolic wormholes drilling the city's roots. The issue is its scope: there just isn't enough of it to be taken seriously. The Chicago 'L' or the New York Subway, now those are places with definite cultures, deeply cinematic—think *Underworld* or *Spiderman*. But LA? Somehow it doesn't cut it.

Travelling to see a musician friend, marooned out in the Valley, I entered the hissing doors with a gaggle of others, San Fernando bound. A girl there, somehow, caught my attention. I've wondered if it was that she seemed so young to be in clothes so skimpy on this workaday train. But I don't think so—there were others also minimally dressed. It was something else, ineffable almost, like a shifting veil or a change in atmosphere that can bring far-off vistas close. She carried some condition, seeping somehow out of her pores. I took the photo on instinct, and forgot about the moment. Later I came across it again and for the first time I noticed, like a sigil, her Playboy tattoo. The Valley is the Hollywood of porn, the biggest manufacturer of sex films in the world. So young, trying so hard to be sexy—I don't know if my math is good; I'll leave the decision to you.

MOVIE PREMIERE—HOLLYWOOD

Sarah Greenough, in the excellent 2009 Frank retrospective exhibition catalogue *Looking In*, argues interestingly for a linguistic link between Frank's previous photograph, *Club Car*, and this image. *Movie Premiere—Hollywood* pictures a glamorously turned out young woman, and it is suggested that she might be described as a 'starlet', relating this photograph back to the stars in the train club car in the last image. I find this a little doubtful, as there are much stronger visual and conceptual links. The stark contrast between her fresh-faced vitality and the crabbed age of the power-brokers in the previous image balances their interdependence: she is part of the carefully constructed stucco and greasepaint facade that covers and disguises the ruthless capitalism of the Hollywood film industry: one of the industries that the men in the previous image underpin and control. The inclusion of 'Hollywood' in the title is significant, it being both a place and a cipher for a particular and powerful aspect of the American Dream. These images together strongly embody the notion of leaders and followers, which Frank described as a guiding principle for his work.

This glamorous girl instigates a series of photographs focusing on youth. Her aspirations and material well-being, evidenced by her situation and her fur stole, are contrasted in the next image with more humble, dowdily dressed young people. The isolation of the Hollywood *ingénue* contrasts with these crowded-together kids, Frank picturing eight people crammed into a small space. The girl at the premiere stands in front of a large art deco-styled stucco decoration. This is strongly echoed by the smaller, mass-produced, faux-gilt decoration on the *Candy store—New York City* jukebox.

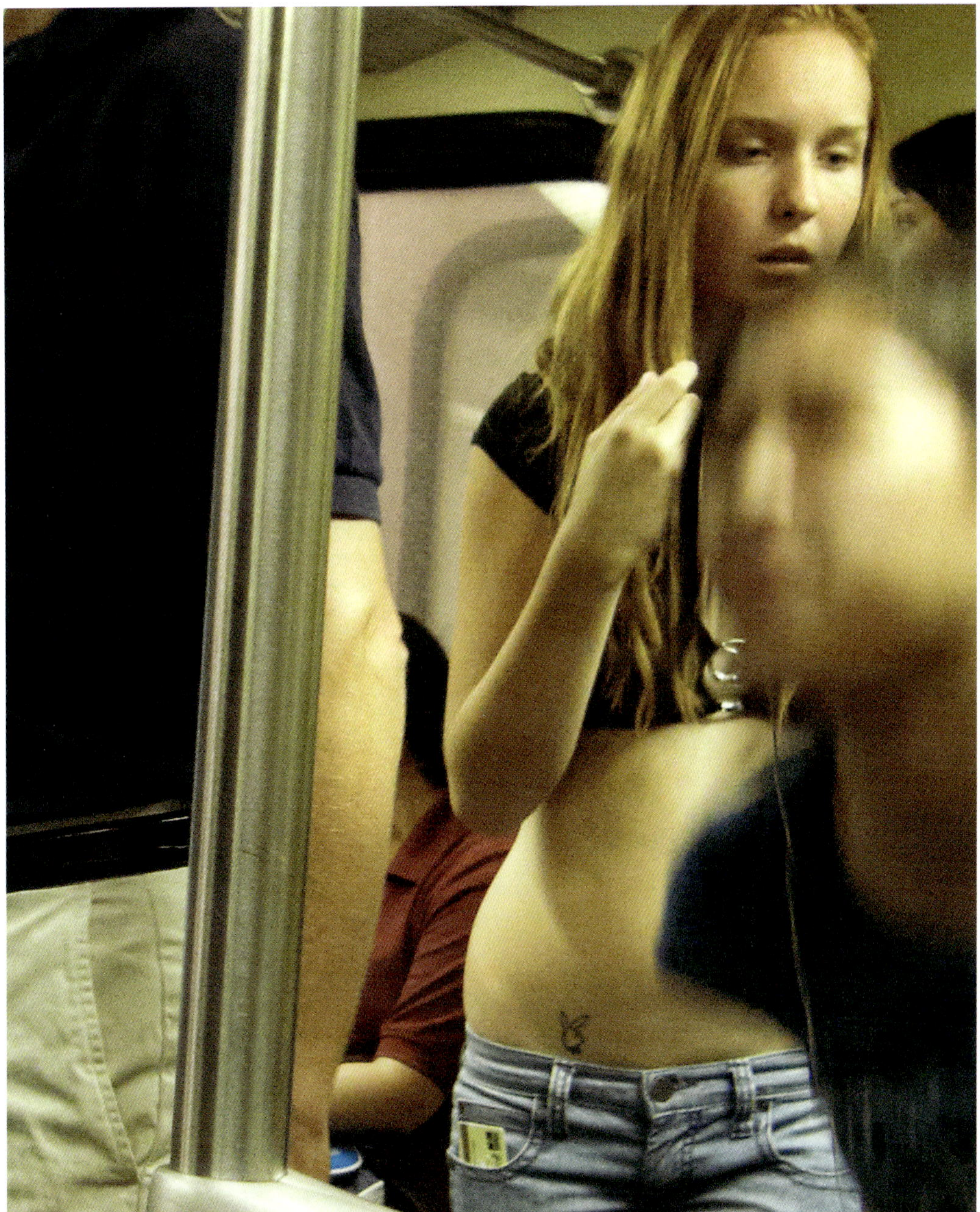

IN SANTA FE A JAZZ FUSION TRIO HAD ITS INSTRUMENTS AND AMPLIFIERS strewn across the pavement, in some kind of crazy order. These musical wanderers, fleeing DC and the double dip, were now caught in the flotsam sticks of a terracotta town, their station wagon beached and bleeding. Odysseus amongst the sirens, lost on the wine dark sea of America.

And I heard the sirens, across that bright morning park. Dark leaved trees, waxed against the mountain desert air, were waiting for the weather's onslaught like infantrymen, armed for drought and desiccation. It never comes, here in this manicured and cared for place. It's a wealthy town—tourists honey-potting draw in others who wait on their largesse. Four or five feral tramps, I saw there, teenage, maybe twenties. A red-dressed singer, her leg bandaged, stormy eyes—and grimy boys, deeply crazy, deeply cool, their crusted dirt as ancient as days. All stylish after the sub fashion of American travellers: trumpeting their difference to the staid and weary straights. Dogs on string lay bored and yawning, the bandstand planks were warm in the sun. An occasional rat appeared from the depths of their garments to take a proffered morsel between songs. Such music came from two battered ukuleles, skanking out satisfactory and sufficient progressions, a kid at the back clacking at a tiny washboard with thimbles. Well practised, their harmonies melded beautifully, so powerful their belief in music. Having rejected so much, this they have retained: music as a friend, music a philosophy. A bright and airy romp through Ralph Stanley's *Oh Death* brought apocalypse into the park on the pink wings of Zephyr. A whole series of the sweetest murder ballads and anarchist anthems had the chinoed and sport-shirted watchers humming along to tales of their destruction. Finally, one of their songs broke down mid verse. It happens—not really a problem—but the bandaged girl, whose powerful alto seemed to anchor them all, sensed their censure. She jabbed at their instruments, outraged that they were following her—why should they look to her, and why stop when she stopped? She was furious, the others cowed and irritated, sensing a storm they didn't want to wrestle with. They shrugged her off and let her rage. I can't help thinking I saw a nerve ending, a raw conduit into experiences on other days in other places, expectations that inhabit her voice and this song. She left and they mumbled their rebukes—just about audible was their practised level. The remnants performed another song of happy tune and murderous lyrics, before sloping off to the underbridges and railway culverts where they live.

CANDY STORE—NEW YORK CITY

Candy Store—New York City pictures a jukebox surrounded by young people. It's a gloriously ornate example, the Mother of Plastic. Around it are a range of expressions on adolescent faces: uncertainty, aggression, the looks of hope and sadness of which Frank was so fond.

The Wurlitzer is an adjunct to their adolescence, an essential aspect of the rites of passage of youth in 1950s America. The jukebox with its shining metal and obscure swirls and fins is not isolated, but absorbed without question into the world of these teenagers. It performs for them, creating a little concert, another world that they experience behind their eyes. Emphasising this, the youth at the bottom right solos on an imaginary trumpet, absorbed by his inner vision. The box is a projection of the strange and wonderful inner America, usually only glimpsed in two-dimensional movies or on billboards. It is solid and tangible, the box relished and cherished for what it embodies, more significant than the tawdry candy bar in which it sits. It is, in the imaginations of these youths, more real. Frank's photograph records the movement of an invisible power, which hangs unseen yet apparent at the centre of this picture. Ulrich Keller sees these images as depictions of poverty. He argues that:

> What makes his [Frank's]calculation of the wealth and deficit of culture so poignant is the recognition that ultimately its material lavishness translated into human poverty, the poverty of technologically colonized minds. (Keller 1986: 23)

The question of colonisation is certainly powerful in these images. Frank has chosen situations that highlight the strangeness of these machines, and their ready acceptance by humanity. For Frank, though, 'material lavishness' does not necessarily equate with poverty. In *Candy Store*, the technology actualizes the dreams, emphasised by the shining pomp in which these cogs and motors are contained, the escape heightened by the ugliness of the environment. The young air trumpeter is blowing "The sigh" as Marx describes it "of the oppressed creature [...] who has not yet won through to himself" (Marx 1977[1843]: 127).

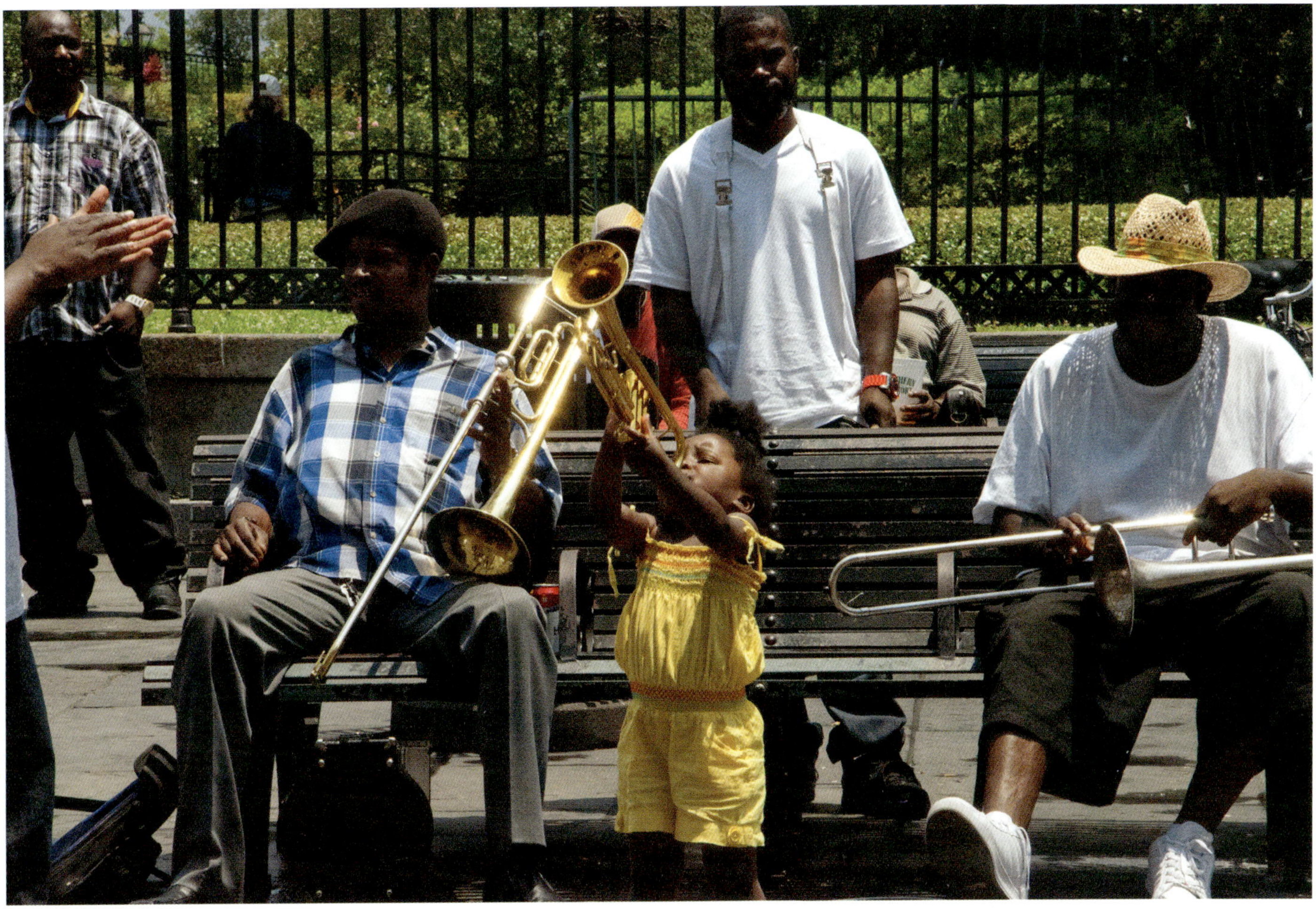

THE HOBOS OWN THE NIGHT. Several times on my first night I was cautioned to be careful. But this is the city of Kerouac, I will not skulk like a heeled tourist, self censored back inside, before the howling hour. So I fake myself as one of them, draw from inside a crazy staring-eyed self, who walks too fast, too straight, with too much intensity. Not so hard to do... no one says anything to me now. Trolley bus to North Point and Chinatown, in the dark thick dream of it. Feel so foolish to have misread Kerouac: he didn't obfuscate, he in-full-detail described these drunks and crazies. But I didn't see them, as the vision-smoke rose from the pages—saw instead radical hipsters, self contained and composed, their four sheets to the wind only trumpeting their rejection of bourgeois society, inebriation a conscious finger flick at all things straight. In my mind from those Kerouac pages I saw someone like Camus, raincoated, shouting "The only way to deal with an unfree world is to become so absolutely free that your very existence is an act of rebellion." The reality is grim and sad, not any kind of freedom I recognize or could aspire to. And it's all there in the books! I just didn't see it.

MOTORAMA—LOS ANGELES

Frank continues his life-in-cars with *Motorama—Los Angeles.* Three children are pictured sitting inside a large black sedan. One is behind the wheel, while two others occupy the rear seat. They are smartly dressed and the image speaks of affluence. There is no sense of question in these children's faces: they seem to entirely accept the place of this lump of technology in their childhood world. Their interior is brightly lit, surrounded by a world in darkness. There is the suggestion of protection. Steve Fitch in *Diesels and Dinosaurs* remembers this sense:

> Certain objects would acquire a symbolic—even ritualistic—stature in my still unfashioned psyche. The Buick itself became an icon of sorts: to me it was a landed fish, a large benevolent animal. Sitting in it was like riding in the belly of a whale. The world outside the car was dangerous and obscure. Everything was bent and mysterious. I felt akin to an explorer on another planet. (Fitch 1976: 42)

The concentration of light and the photograph's crisp shadows suggest the use of flash. Frank thus highlights the comfort and ease of the children in the car against the uncertain darkness outside. They, like Fitch, ride the belly of a whale.

Frank has other pictures of children in cars, most notably *Bute, Montana* contrasting its homespun occupants with the wealthy ones of this photograph, and *Belle Isle—Detroit* featuring a black family grinning at the fun of their day out. These are part of Frank's examination of a 'life in cars'.

The car is, for his Americans, an unquestioned adjunct to existence, accepted at its core, as necessary as air.

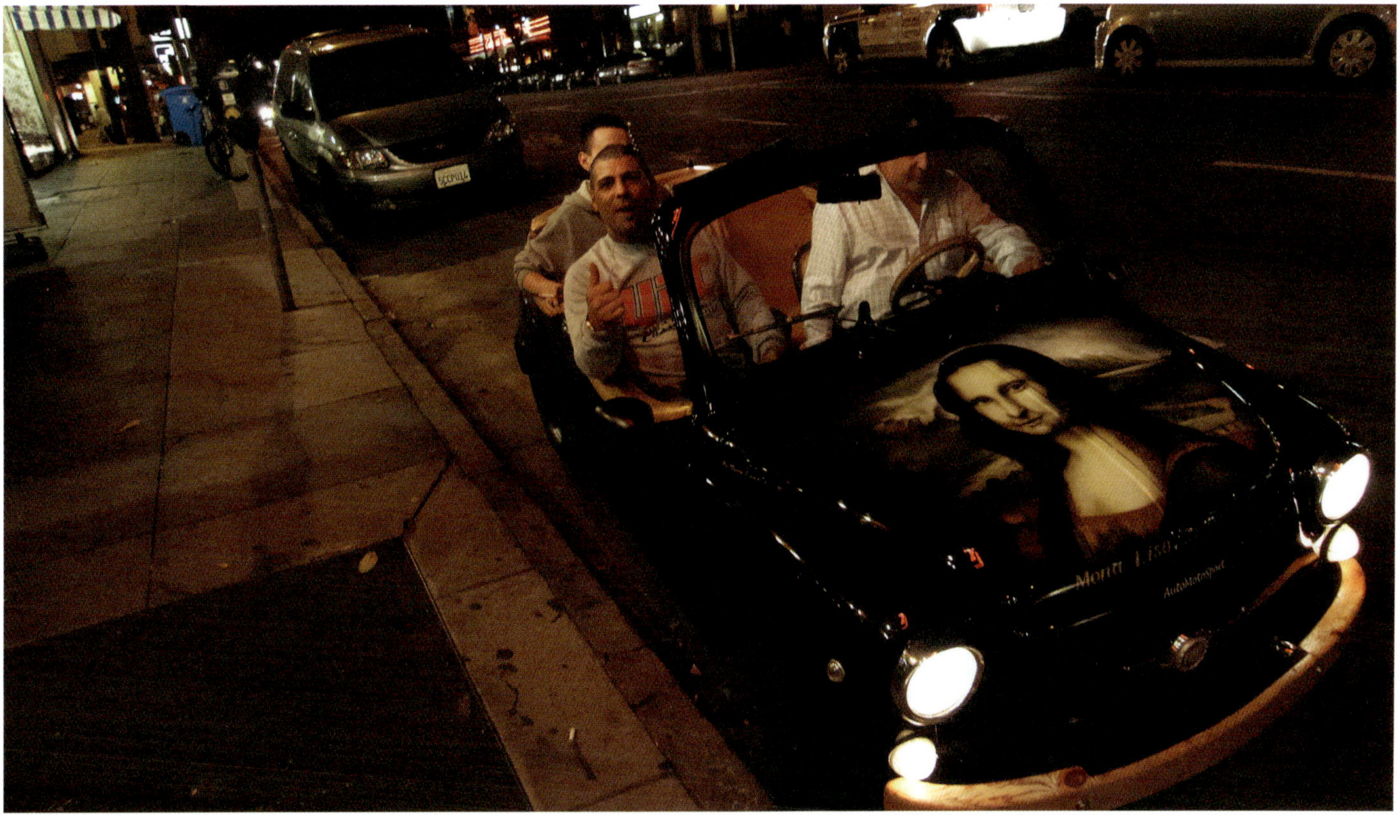

JACK KEROUAC ALLEY—A SMUTTY, DOG EARED PASSAGE through the backs of buildings. On the shit smirched pavement is a spiral of shiny letters, dedicating this non-place to the writer's memory. No bronze cast bust, no little statue, fenced around and grassily overgrown. Kerouac's monument is to be walked on, expectorated over, decorated with chewing gum. Flanked by the City Lights Bookstore and the Vesuvio Café—somehow they hold Kerouac between them in their arms, and I start to see something more than merely insult in the designation of his 'alley'. He is at home here hanging rather dissolute in this grubby netherworld, between intellectual endeavour and alcoholic dissolution. Writer Robert Lifton thought Jack craved an "authentic self", and looked for it somewhere between beautiful words and the vomit, booze and bleachy reek of the up-all-night bright and blousy Vesuvio. The existential Hipster, Lifton intoned, craved "experiential transcendence", a state in which the present moment is lived "with such intensity that time and death are, in effect, eliminated". Danger and drugs held a promise of such experience:

> The Beat and Hipster looked at vivid possibilities in the lives of new cultural heroes, individuals outside society either through personal rebellion or by social and racial circumstance: the jazz musician, hobo, black [this was the '50s...], criminal, insane person or dope addict. To be alienated, outside of social conventions and expectations, was to be set free, free to take to the road or to become part of the urban nether-world. (Lifton 1970: 53)

So here we have them, 50 years apart, Beat inspirations on a New York pavement and Beats on Hollywood Boulevard.

NEW YORK CITY

Youth is at the centre again in *New York City*—this time three young men, probably teenagers. They look black and Hispanic. Their sinuous poses, the faux dramatic manner in which one of them looks through his splayed fingers, and the partially plucked eyebrows of the boy to the left suggest a degree of gender play. The time-faded sign behind them, perhaps a playbill, says 'Don't Miss Mister Instin ...', I assume it is 'Instinct'. They are engaged fully with the camera, communicating through their eye contact with it, with Frank and thus ultimately with us. This engagement contrasts strongly with the distant and disinterested boys in *Motorama* and the seemingly oblivious youths in *Candy Store* and at the premiere.

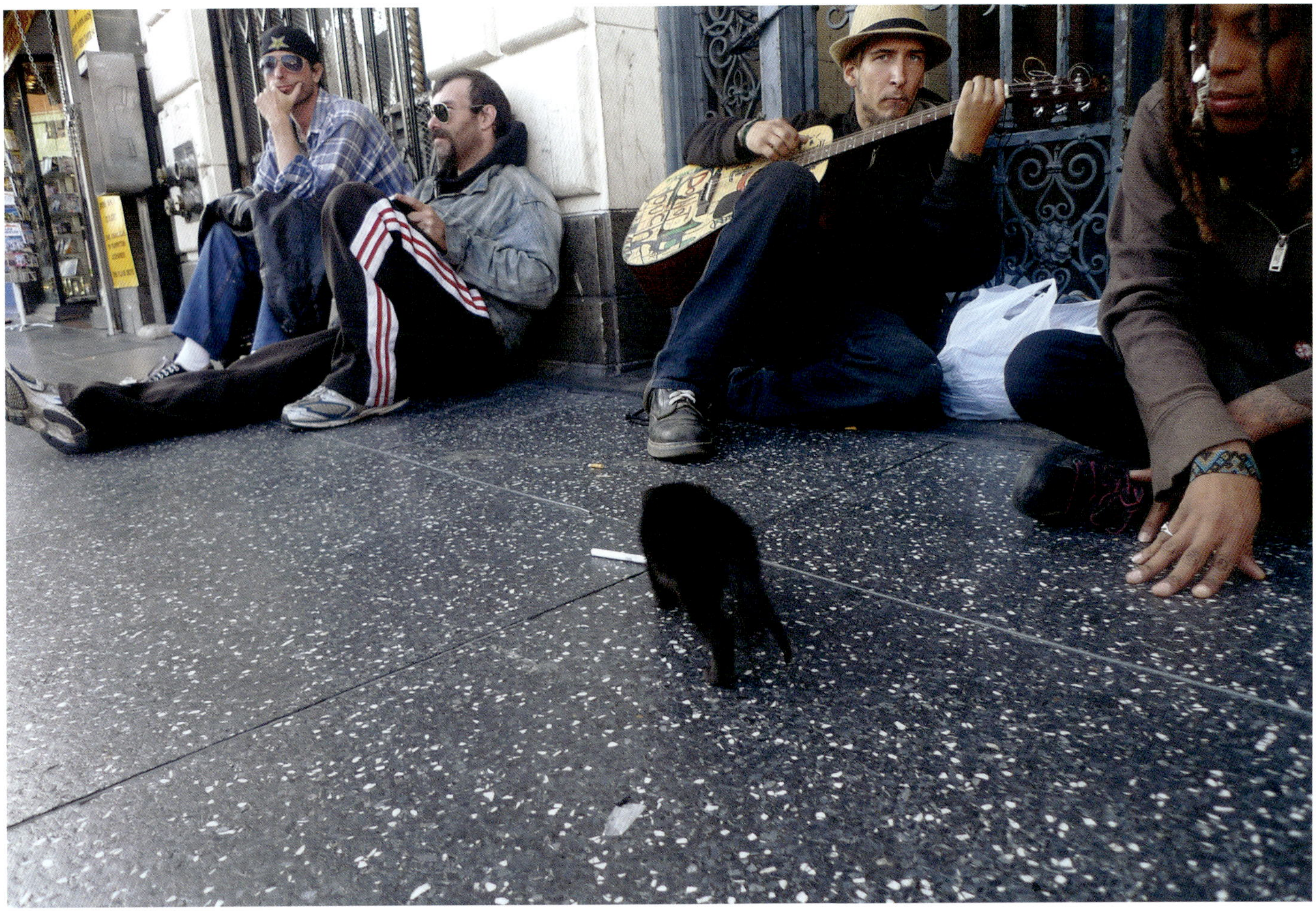

LOOK AT FRANK'S PICTURE. I couldn't help wondering what happened to the child…

I was up with the sun at Bull Hole, after a long sleep cradled by crickets and held in the strong quiet arms of the forest and the ocean islands. A crane flew between me and the sky, trailing three white birds like bridesmaids to a bride. Crimson Cardinals—better than their name—were bashful and intent, searching the grass for a leggy breakfast. I sat in the reeking car-rush as I closed on Charleston, trying to be present, ready for the incarnated moment. Sly as an antelope, cunning as coyotes, these moments are—as bashful as songbirds, and caring not a jot if they escape unnoticed.

Frank's photo had drawn me here, following, 50 years on, the ruts of his tyres. It deeply moved me when I first saw his picture of the blissful child, safe and secure in those strong black arms. Frank's camera so close I still smell the baby smell, every time I see it. Maybe in part because I too had a Nanny as a child—Bernice was her name, she was black and she lived in Soweto. "Slegs Blankes" it said on our playpark entrance, 'whites only'. She was allowed in too, only for the sake of her white children.

Robert's photograph mocks and eviscerates America's 'white on white' and 'black with black' censorship. It pre-dates the first scripted US TV interracial kiss by more than a decade. This colour coding, though, is still alive and well. Disney may finally have found a black heroine for *The Princess and The Frog*, but it's no surprise that her Prince turns out a swarthy foreigner of undisclosed—but certainly not white American or European—descent. 'Whites Only' is just a memory now in South Africa…

In Charleston, I couldn't help wondering what happened to the child.

CHARLESTON, SOUTH CAROLINA

One of the things Frank undertakes in *The Americans* is a virulent and swathing attack on *The Family of Man* exhibition (1955), curated by his friend Edward Steichen and staged initially at the Museum of Modern Art in New York. Frank assisted Steichen with research for the exhibition but had become disillusioned with it, saying:

> Steichen liked me a lot and he was very good to me. I just didn't agree with his sentimentality about photographs any more. I had used up the single, beautiful image. I was aware that I was living in a different world—that the world wasn't as good as that—that it was a myth that the sky was blue and that all photographs were beautiful. (Frank, in Johnson 1989: 37)

Frank wasn't simply, though, an *enfant terrible*, ripping up his former mentor's take on humanity and culture. He wrote:

> I have often been accused of deliberately twisting subject matter to my point of view [...] Opinion often consists of a kind of criticism. But criticism can come out of love. (Frank, in Maloney 1958: 115)

His critique, he claims, was from a perspective of love—a love that, unlike Steichen's, acknowledged the importance of honesty. *The Americans*' photographs often closely respond to particular images from *The Family of Man*: Frank sought the sometimes prosaic, sometimes challenging reality behind the exhibition's toothy smile.

The Family of Man included more than twenty images of a mother and child. All of these were racially matched. Two images especially represent the USA, one by Irving Penn from *Vogue* (collection of *Vogue*) and the other by Nell Dorr (Museum of Modern Art, New York). The first is an image of sophistication, the second of warm homeliness. Frank's photograph *Charleston, South Carolina* shows a smiling black nanny and her tiny white charge. They are clearly happy together. This figuration of motherhood, psychological rather than biological, echoes images of the Madonna and Child and recalls depictions of black Sarah, the Gypsy saint who was, apocryphally, the wet nurse of Christ. The implications are obvious: this is a relationship that transcends race. Jack Kerouac wrote his introduction to Frank's book at around the same time as the interracial violence in Little Rock, Arkansas was happening. He said of this picture:

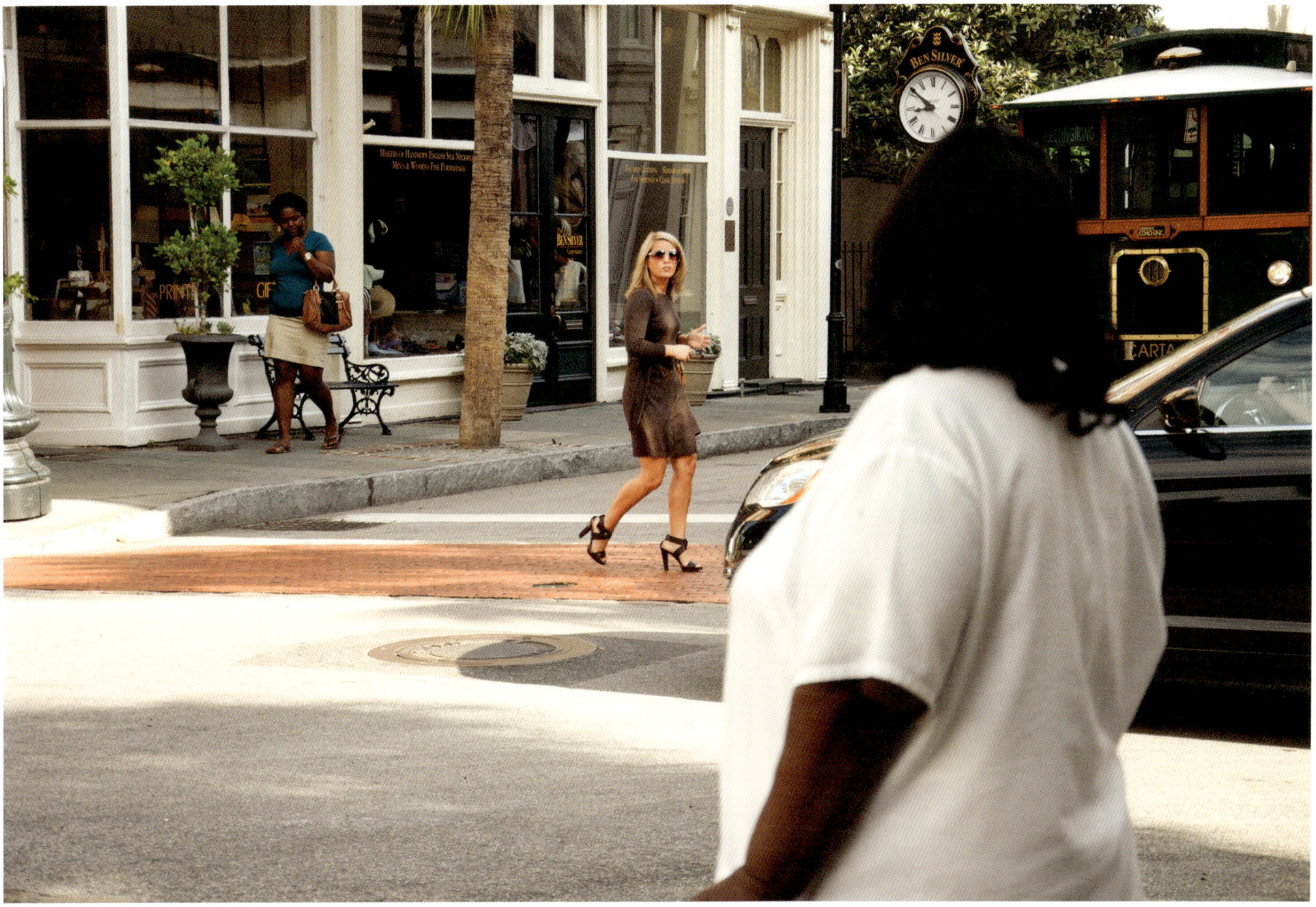
BEN SILVER
PRINTS

> —the sweet little white baby in the black nurse's arms both of them bemused in heaven, a picture that should have been hanged in Little Rock showing love under the sky and in the womb of our universe the Mother. (Kerouac, in Frank 1959: 6)

The woman in Irving Penn's picture looks as though she might be the employer of just such a nanny. This black woman is *in loco maternis*, more real to this child than her remote natural mother. Nell Dorr's picture of a blissful, nightgowned, breast-feeding mother is white on white on white. The bond between the white baby and a black breast is eschewed by Steichen, but eloquently addressed by Frank.

This image also begins a sequence of pictures concerned with what we might call the 'Ages of Man'. These run from babyhood through to senility, most often figuring parents and children, and contrasting youth with age.

THE CLOVER GRILL, NEW ORLEANS, UNCHANGED SINCE THE 70s, a perfect past age place. The manager is a man who flits and shimmies, acid tongued. In a flash of his eyes he tells the pain of his ill-fitting form, his passion to survive and prosper, his demand to be taken as he is and a quiet invitation to be his friend. Head cocked to one side, he sends me a challenge: "With me, or against me? Your choice baby" and dances off across the room. I try for the former. His friends he calls 'Ho'—I never make it that far, remain 'baby' the whole time. It's enough.

Later I play my Triangulin. It's a beautiful sound, hand made for me by a white-haired woodcarver, far away and long ago across the sea. One of the audience calls my playing 'soothing'. Outside is the coruscation of Bourbon Street—a caterwaul of sex and style, deep blue voudou on tubas and growl, uncomfortably close to invocation—aching country singers in intaglio, slashed vest Southern Lord-I-was-born-a-rambling men. A girl in the dark doorway of a 'Hustler' club shakes her thonged and unappealing ass at the world. I take 'soothing' with a smile.

RANCH MARKET—HOLLYWOOD

Frank's *Ranch Market—Hollywood* does two things within the book. It contrasts youth with age (embodied in a demoniacally grinning Santa, leering down on to a girl counter assistant), as did the last image, and it begins an extended examination—and critique of—the American diner. Jovial Americans consuming quantities of food were frequently represented and celebrated in the visual ephemera of the 1950s. The most significant source of these images for Frank was the Standard Oil of New Jersey Picture File, for reasons we will explore later on, but images of the diner were easily found. This is not surprising. By advertising its ability to feed its population (occasionally to the point of obesity), America contrasted itself starkly with the shortages and rationing being experienced throughout Europe. Eating is one of our most basic needs, and the American diner was represented as a microcosm of the land of plenty, peopled by well-fed, fecund women and well-fed, hard-working men coexisting in a happy and harmonious society. Smiling waitresses happily serve customers who are happy to be served. Photographer Sol Libsohn made images for a Standard Oil feature called 'Trucking Story' (1945). This story is important for us, and we'll encounter it again later. Libsohn's *Group of truckers in Eagle Grill, Akron, Ohio; May 1945* (Standard Oil Archive, University of Louisville) pictures a driver called Charles Henry and his associates drinking beer and coffee beneath a neon eagle. They sit in front of a door marked 'men'. A buxom young waitress serves them the latest in what appears to be a long line of drinks. She is smiling winningly at them, perhaps sharing a joke. The message is clear: this is the place for the men who serve the Eagle. Happiness and fulfilment, materially and socially, follow as a natural consequence of working for the nation. There is even an intimation of sexual promise. It may be limited to flirting, but for these crabbed drivers that pleasure may not be an inconsiderable one. The young waitress certainly accepts them and appears to enjoy her role and their company. Uncle Sam and his aquiline familiar are looking after their own.

Jack Kerouac, too, was not blind to the diner's charms. He celebrated the almost ritual intake of copious amounts of comestibles, in the party atmosphere of the eating-place. He wrote:

> We stopped along the road for a bite to eat. The cowboy went off to have a spare tire patched and Eddie and I sat down in a kind of homemade diner. I heard a great laugh, the greatest laugh in the world, and here came this rawhide old timer Nebraska farmer with a bunch of other boys into the diner; you could hear his raspy cries clear across the plains, across the whole grey world of them that day. Everybody else laughed with him. He didn't have a care in the world. (Kerouac, 1972[1957]: 19)

This is, of course, not surprising or anomalous. So many of the photographs that image the American diner echo Kerouac's experience. There is no doubt that many of these suggestions of a land of plenty and a happy society in which everyone, especially the stranger, is welcomed were reasonably accurate and ingenuous.

In *The Americans*, however, Frank's reactions to the figurations of the diner in the images of Standard Oil and others is typically considered and sophisticated. *Ranch Market—Hollywood* is an assault on American gastric bonhomie. In the pho-

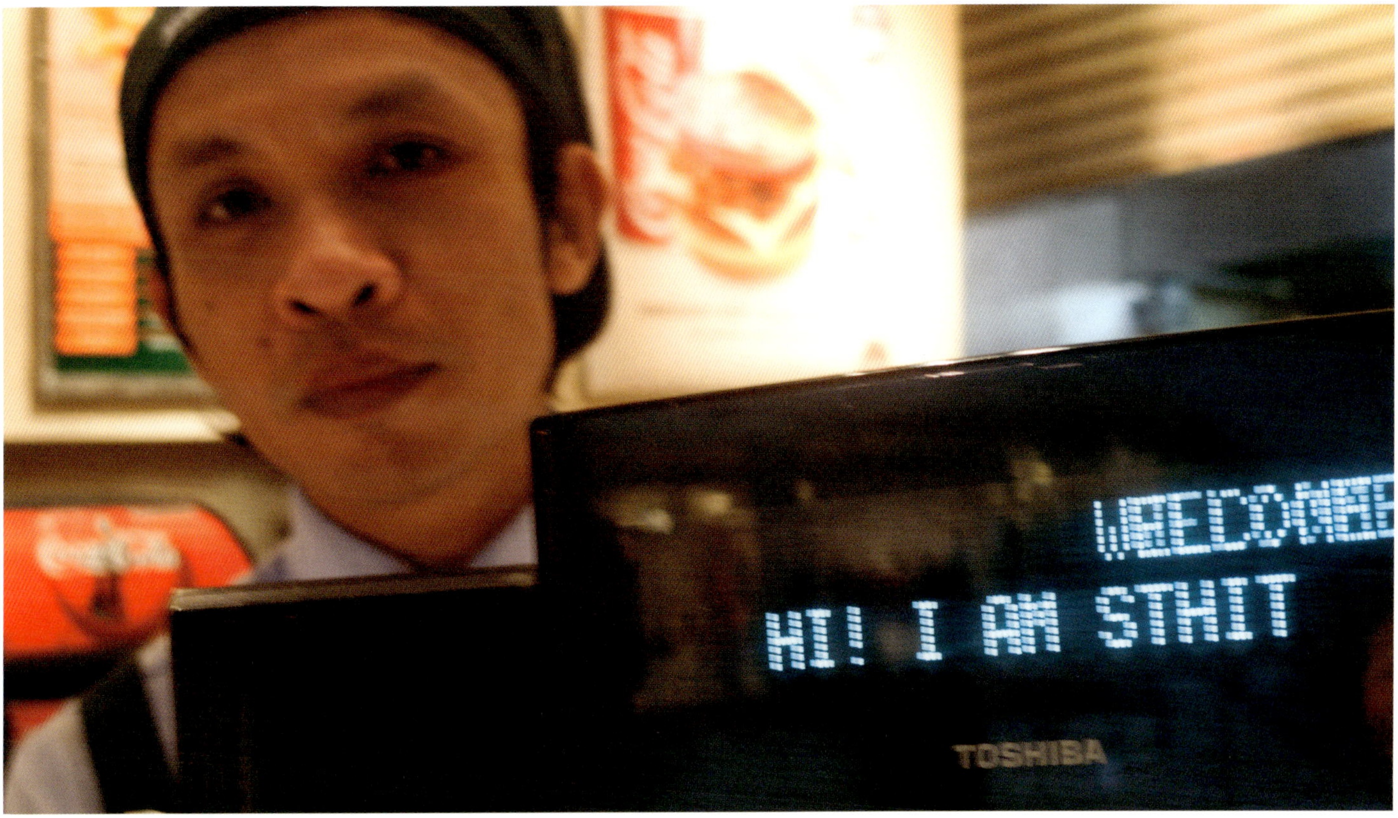
HI! I AM STHIT
TOSHIBA

tograph, a counter assistant glowers, staring out of shot, ignoring Frank and his camera. Her eyes are coldly half-closed, her lipsticked mouth pursed. Above her hang several signs. They proclaim the lack of filler in the market's burgers and their range of products and prices. The central sign is a maniacal Santa Claus with an alcoholic's red cheeks, proclaiming 'Merry Christmas' in a Gothic script. The lines of the ceiling and shelving converge slightly towards the left. This subtle view, neither fully sidelong nor fully frontal, revealing only the head of the waitress, is unfamiliar and uncomfortable. Is she irritated by a customer perhaps, or bored by the tedium of countless burgers and shakes? She has no Christmas spirit, merely standing behind her counter, defying the drudgery, defying the customers. She certainly has no smile for the Men of the Eagle. There is no suggestion of flirtatious willingness, no happy cafe society welcoming every passing driver. The demented Santa and this dour waitress stand against Libsohn's eagle and *ingénue* in Frank's unflattering revelation. It is not the whole truth, but it is an important part of it, part that needs acknowledgement. Frank here figures that part of the inconvenient truth which Standard Oil and others chose to ignore.

WE CAN GET REALLY LOST, tiny concatenations of cells, salts and fluids that we are, dragged screaming into consciousness and the cold light of day. Woody Allen, I remember, berates the direction of our lives—wishing we would instead grow from decrepitude to infancy, so that we become ever fresher through our living, finishing eventually with years when we are cherished and protected, cosseted and cooed over. Death, he posits, would follow months in a warm wet world, soothed by the heartbeats of our mothers. Instead we must face the immensity and wonder, trading intelligence for wisdom, the patina of time wasting ever more of our strength. Here on a sidewalk, in a country without access for his like to healthcare, a confused man is clinging to his copious suitcase, hiding behind its blue and crimson bulk as if it were a warm remembered place he wants to return to. Not so obviously evil as the enemy boiling Uzbek king, America is nonetheless a place that eats its children, Saturnalian on the Boulevard of Broken Dreams.

BUTTE, MONTANA

The market assistant of the last image leads us into another photograph contrasting youth with age, and another image of children in a car. It harks back clearly to *Motorama* and forms part of Frank's extensive and detailed critique of the nature and role of the car in American civilization. This small, light-coloured automobile contrasts with the bourgeois vehicle of the earlier image. The woman, probably a mother, and the two children in *Butte, Montana* are obviously intimate, and this too contrasts with the colder formality of the earlier image. The image of Butte is workaday, the car's rear full of food, the fruits, one assumes, of an earlier shopping expedition. The portly mother, poured into the front seat, is dressed in a plaid shirt and patterned apron, and watches together with her daughter, something out of shot to the left. Neither the car nor their clothing are down-at-heel, yet there is a homely, workaday feel about them which contrasts markedly with the earlier *Motorama*. Frank is revealing different American children from very different places, stuck in the back of cars. Their cars, like their clothes and their towns, signal their wealth and their perception of social status: cars are a significant opportunity for conspicuous consumption.

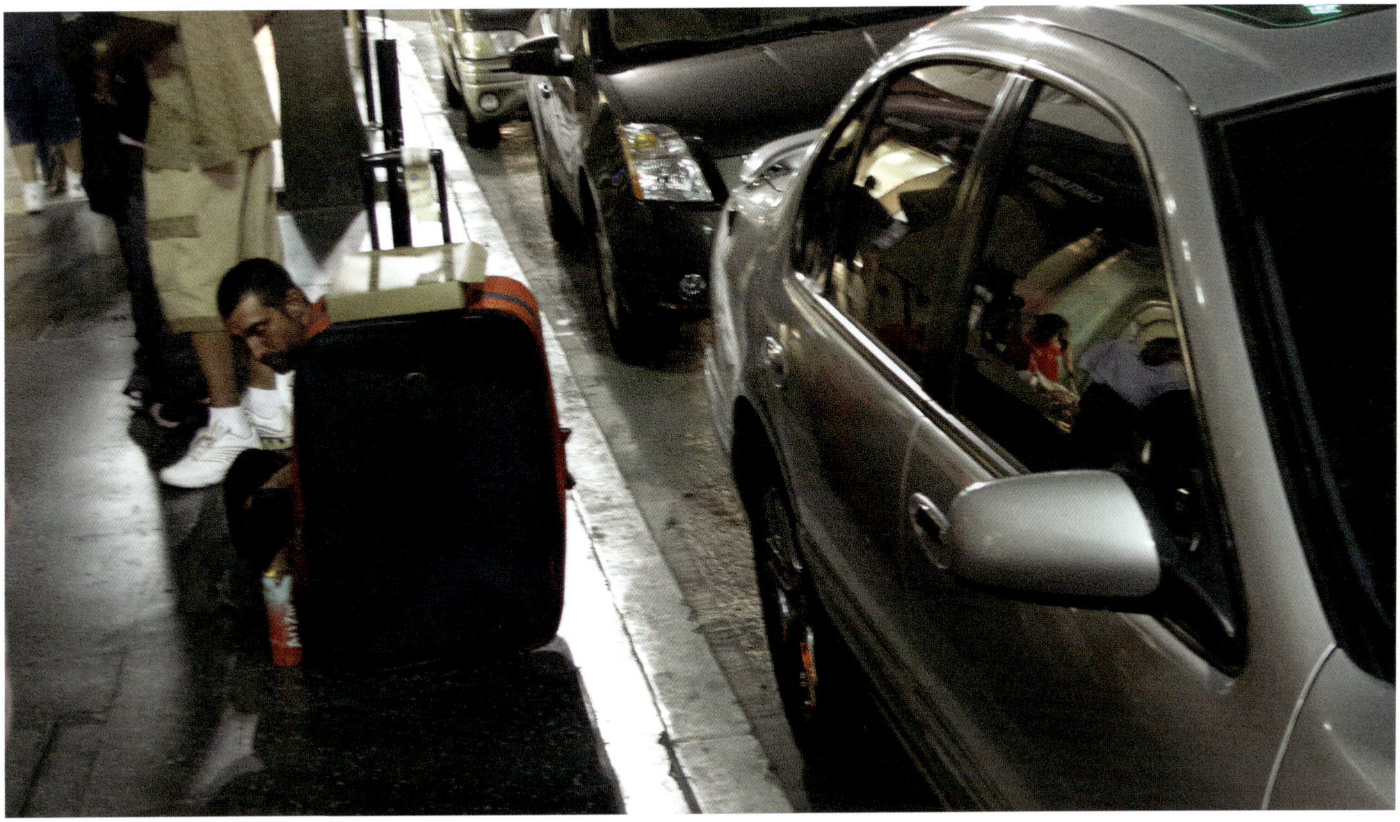

IN A STILL WORKING WATERMILL THAT ALSO SOLD GIFTS, I found with some surprise a Coonskin cap. Macabre but artful, the Racoon had been removed and its tanned skin carefully folded into quite an effective and comfortable hat. I'd seen so many of these as a child, but only in the electron dance of the cathode ray tube. My grandfather was a fan of Westerns, so those lost days and far places had filled my English Midlands childhood's imagination. Davy Crockett, king of the wild frontier, wore one. It was with a shock of cognition that I picked up this strange thing. In amongst all the faux fur and tat, this was a real road back to that earlier time, both in the history of this place and the history of me. It was a really profound moment, unexpected and powerful. If felt like I could hold the hand of the little boy I had been—and the little boy that I was could hold the hand of the man I now am. Both of me were able to smile at each other in this moment, something that is not always the case. This unlooked for and unbidden fulfilment of a profound and deeply held childhood dream was all the more powerful since the dream was near forgotten, thickly covered with the detritus of time. Forgotten but not gone. Here I was in the Cherokee mountains, at last wearing a Davy Crockett hat. The ghost of my grandfather lingered at the edge of the circle, while my own son's face so-lovingly smiled on, holding up his dreams in both hands for me to honour. Touching back and forward in time, the sacred flame of joy passed from an old man to a man to a boy. We pass the stories through the flames to renew them.

YOM KIPPUR—EAST RIVER, NEW YORK CITY

Frank's *Yom Kippur* photograph speaks now of many things. The overwhelming influence of Jewish people on the power structures and financial operations of America is no surprise—they either ran from Europe or were exterminated, and the United States was an obvious destination. So, fifty years on, in the light of the behaviour of the state of Israel and its wars and rumours of war this has undeniably become a political photograph. It's an ethnic photograph, too, these particular Jewish people belonging to a sect whose origins lie in the far-east and past of Europe. America is a concatenation of race, colour and creed, "Send us your unwanted" they said and they made a nation that holds more than a little of the future of our species in its hands. The US was full of new people in the '50s, including Robert Frank, one of these European Jews. It is full of new people now, from Cuba, Mexico, Eastern Europe, Asia. Despite the photograph's powerful significances, what strikes me most in this picture is the warm and comfortable familiarity between the man and the boy. Leaning on each other, without a need for face on face. So I and my grandfather and my son.

Although these last several images were part of a thematically linked sequence looking at youth and age, there is an even closer link between the previous photograph *Butte, Montana* and this one. The little family in the car is followed by this photograph of a group of Jewish men and a boy, beside a river. The image is divided along its vertical median line, with the grey-suited 'father', the boy dressed in lightly coloured clothes and the grey river on the right, contrasting with the mostly black left-hand side, occupied by the dark outfits of the Orthodox Jewish men. The boy in this photograph, like the little girl of the last image, is watching something out of frame, this time to the right, the two together thus creating a diptych of sorts. He is in bodily contact with the suited man's back, which might suggest he is a relative. In contrast with the last image, however, in which adult and child look together at the same thing, this adult and child are facing in separate directions, each engaged in his own separate thoughts.

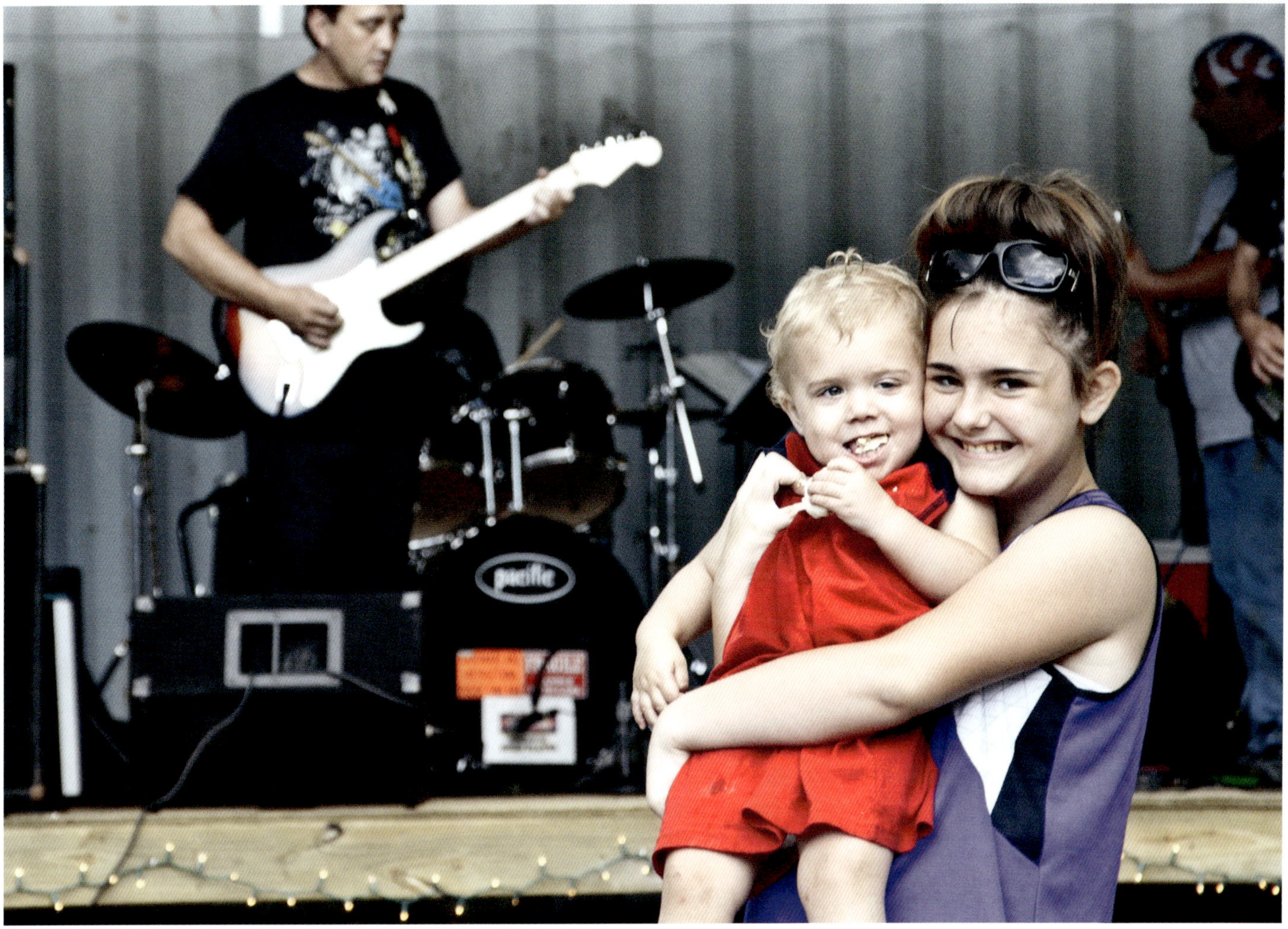
pacific

I WAS GIVEN A GRETSCH GUITAR. Deeply orange coloured, a cowboy stylee thing, stuck with bits of aluminium and chrome, a tractor driver's implement. Bringing together timber from the fields, the colour of the warm sun and bits of old valve radios, it fitted like a glove. I was given it to play in a cleaned out Fire House on a festival day, engines pulled close in the back, free root beer on tap.

Funny place Minnesota. Progressive, Democratic in its mission to Washington, far to the South. Something close to Yankee in its Viking Lutheran heritage, stoic for sure, ascetic somewhat—only way to survive the long deep-frozen winters. So wide and open, but lacking hills, at least in the parts I know best: it doesn't suffer from seeing too far. So much water flows from here, eating away at the deep black soil—this is a place that water flows from, not to, and the specks of deep black soil in the snow-melt carry Minnesota out to St Louis and New Orleans. The quiet harshness of winter and the wildflowered spring are the water's gifts to the gumbo cultures. The trade though is one way: none of their spice and complexity is carried north, reciprocally, on the wind. Appleton belongs here, a small town, hermetically sealed, watching a distant world from the hearthstones of kith and kin. A necessary tradition in a place where no one will certainly survive the 40 below, without family and friends coming to the call of need. A two edged sword—it cuts both ways, here where nothing is private, every detail of every life known, mulled over and judged in the balance. So, then, eating the staple beef and bread 'Commercial', a friend and I in a café speak in hushed voices to the consternation of ears three tables away. And my honesty is limited here, too, for the sakes of those that remain.

FOURTH OF JULY—JAY, NEW YORK

We've spoken frequently of Jack Kerouac, Frank's friend and the writer of his introduction. They met on a hot city street:

> I met Jack Kerouac on a hot summer night at a party in New York City. We sat down on the sidewalk, I showed Jack the photographs for *The Americans*. He said 'Sure I can write something about these pictures'. (Frank 1989: before the chapter headed 'United States')

Kerouac was an inspired choice. He had attended college, but as a football scholar. He was an intellectual, certainly: his erudition is evident, with wide and detailed knowledge of American literature and of Buddhist writing. He was also a hipster and a bum, comfortable riding on the back of trucks and flat cars and dating waitresses. He had lived for many years in this way, a condition he had celebrated in his novels *On the Road* (1972[1957]) and *The Dharma Bums* (2000[1958]). In the books he elevated the status of the vagabond and hobo to that of holy quester, equating the American tramp with the saddhus of India and the wandering monks of East Asia. There is another key aspect to Kerouac. He shrugged off any association between the notion of 'artist' or 'writer' and the elitism that was (and to a large degree still is) at the heart of European culture. He was not 'slumming it' as an artist, not wallowing in underclass life socially while associating with the rich and famous in galleries. He was fully part of the world of his characters, not an aloof observer but an equal-status participant. Kerouac's writing rolls with the rhythms of American street speech and is steeped in jazz, the racially integrated music of the American city. It is not pulp fiction by any means, but it is accessible and relevant to a wide demographic.

Kerouac's work often evidences a desire for 'direct' experience. He sought to live and see in a way unaltered by the goggles and filters that are forced on to us by our socialisation. Desire for directness is central to many of the Buddhist writings so beloved of Kerouac, particularly those in the Zen tradition (Various 2009). This desire for directness also plays its part in Kerouac's approach to communication, absorbing his experiences and then expressionistically recalling and recording them, describing and understanding what has passed, according to his vision.

Kerouac's approach is a clear analogue, in text, to Frank's photography. They are both striving to see beyond the externally imposed 'dream' of America, those aspects which in Buddhism are called *Samsara*: the world of illusions. Frank's photograph *Fourth of July—Jay, New York* wonderfully evidences this. It reveals a ghostly, dream-like American landscape seen through the banner, while at the same time depicting the ba-

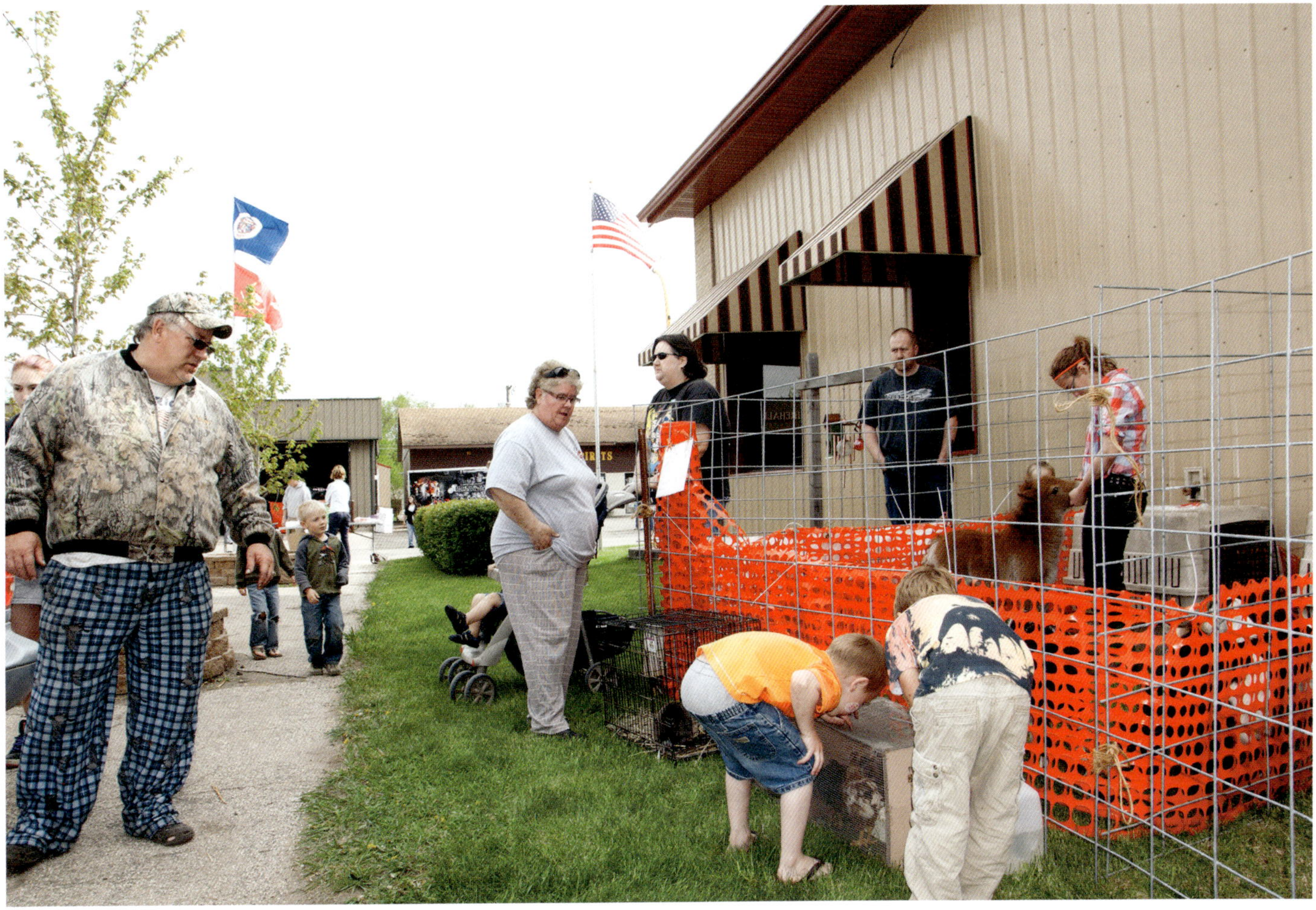

nality of this American day, seen around and beneath the tattered and repaired flag.

Fourth of July—Jay, New York is *The Americans'* second 'section-introducing' flag photograph. The huge Stars and Stripes hangs above a lawn. Frank has already indicated, through *Parade—Hoboken*, that he will describe the people who are covered and subsumed by the flag. Here he is further inviting us to look at the actual people, everyday individuals rather than archetypes or stereotypes, who stand beneath and at the edges of the Star Spangled Banner. The composition looks casual, rather snapshot. A bored young boy walks out of the bottom left corner of the photograph, his legs and arm cropped. Opposite him, in the bottom right corner, a man in shirtsleeves is also cropped. He chats to another, these two men and the boy clearly echoing the preceding image. Behind the flag, people amble around. Two girls in white party dresses, balloons in hand, run towards it. Theirs is the only focused activity in the photograph. This is the Fourth of July—Independence Day—a day on which America celebrates itself. It remembers the break with European hypocrisy, class divisions and tyranny, and represents the dream of a new way, a new and better life. The flag is the symbol of all this, yet here it hangs—torn, mended and mostly ignored. Its reality as a piece of faded, damaged cloth is clearly displayed. The symbol is thus subverted by its own materiality. The flag's patchwork questions America's shiny chrome dream. The flawless future of this flawless state is revealed as a much-used and repaired conception, more rustic than utopian, brought out by a stolid populus as they celebrate their unremarkable holiday. The dream represented by the flag cannot be too pressing or imminent, since no one in the photograph pays it any attention. They are concerned, instead, with their families, their neighbours and themselves. Everyday America is again emphatically revealed. This interest in the vernacular and commonplace reflects the growing focus on the lives and actions of ordinary working people, as an understandable reaction to the bankruptcy of European culture, with its aristocratic and grossly unfair class-based power structure, its colonialism and constant warmongering. It was also evidenced, wonderfully, by the painter Jasper Johns in his *Flag* of 1954 (Museum of Modern Art, New York). Johns' work used the archaic technique of encaustic, along with paint. Melted wax was used to build a textured surface. Beneath the wax, Johns placed cut out newspaper fragments, echoing the earlier Cubist collages of Picasso and others. Just as the copy on the newspaper fragments was sometimes part of the Cubists' intent, so it is important in Johns' piece. His clippings come from the small advertisements and anecdotal stories on the back pages of small-town American journals. He creates the icon of American identity from the humble happenings and concerns of its everyday unexceptional people. This is clearly a concern and a predilection powerfully shared by Frank.

We've seen that much of the landscape in *Fourth of July—Jay, New York* is seen through the flag. As with *Parade—Hoboken*, Frank photographs the flag as a filter through which its country is perceived. The trees and grass of its reality, like its people, are seen through the constructs of its red, white and blue. America sees itself, and is seen, through its dream. These preconceptions are almost impossible to ignore. Frank wanted to examine the reality within and behind the flag, within and behind America's public face, and invites us to join him in the exploration.

CRESCENT CITY, NEW ORLEANS, KATRINA TOWN. I caught the Trolley on a scraggy verge, steel rails dancing a tarantella with the traffic. Two small girls, their hair plaited to control the twisting curls, in mauve school shirts, untucked and grubby after a day's exertions, kicked their heels in the dust and waited alongside me. They seemed so small to be alone here, in the middle of a highway, in a city lost in water between Mississippi and Pontchartrain. Across the road an antebellum mansion was adorned with flags and bunting, the fabric lifting slightly as the hot, late afternoon air wriggled lazily, like an eel in muddy water. A gang of crisply suited young white men waited in line, facing the road. Valets for the day, away from college or store clerking or who-knows-what, hidden deep within the hot rank heart of the Big Easy. I was waiting for my Street Car Named Desire (am waiting still) though eventually a trolley bus did come. Drab in the waning sun, the apple of the schoolgirl's eye, it was unremarkable in every way. Nothing to photograph, nothing to see, save a reflection of my own Quixotic self—unnoticed, barely relevant to any of their passionate pursuits, their eyes blood blinded by the intensity of their everyday. And so I slipped along and slipped away, through the French Quarter and the *Monde Creole* to Grand Island asleep by the lapping sea. My only souvenir you see before you: the bus turning its camera, mockingly, on me.

TROLLEY—NEW ORLEANS

In *The Americans*, Robert Frank was taking a journey to the edge. He had been for some years a successful and celebrated photographer in New York, working for Alexey Brodovitch at *Harper's Bazaar* magazine, showing at well-known galleries and even assisting with the *Family of Man* exhibition at the Museum of Modern Art, New York. He had also featured in a variety of publications. Frank's work for *The Americans* was funded by the Guggenheim Foundation, and his receipt of this vaunted scholarship placed him among America's most noted photographers (Day 2011: 34). All of this was not enough for him. He complained that

> Mass production of uninspired photography without thought becomes anonymous merchandise. The air becomes infected with the smell of photography. (Frank, in Maloney 1958: 115)

Frank was looking for more. Along with many others Frank was feeling the changes, the opportunities and challenges for both this new nation and the wider world. In 1950s America, 'old world' European 'high' society was being deeply interrogated. It was dogged by war and inequality, was morally bankrupt, class ridden and apparently intent on self-destruction. It seemed to many that salvation might be found in the lives, culture and ideas of working people. Frank was deeply interested in exploring the visually ephemeral and vernacular in his search for "where God is" (Frank 1991: after plate 63). Frank found and celebrated the alternative galleries of the streets: billboards, hoardings and popular magazines. He seems to me to have had a particular interest in the photographic output of the Standard Oil Company's Picture File (Day 2011: 113), a group headed by Roy Stryker, who had famously directed the Farm Security Administration's photo section. The group documented the work of the Oil Company from exploration through extraction, refining and retailing. Their images were made freely available to magazines, newspapers, galleries, schools and universities.

The Civil Affairs Division of the US Army, for example, used the images to illustrate "the American Way of Life to People Overseas" (Stryker 1947). They featured in *Life*, *Look* and the *Saturday Evening Post*, among other magazines and newspapers. In 1949 alone, 667 Standard Oil file pictures were carried by the press. Another popular means of dissemination was panel-mounted display sequences. The Picture File produced 264 differently themed arrangements of photographs. In 1949 around 10,000 of these were needed to satisfy demand (Keller 1986: 47). Many galleries also featured Standard Oil's images. Harvard University and the Franklin Institute in Philadelphia both hosted an exhibition called *The Architecture of Oil*. The Museum of Modern Art in New York featured the work of four Standard Oil photographers in its *In and Out of Focus: A Survey of Today's Photography* exhibition (Museum of Modern Art exhibition number 373, 6 April—11 July, 1948). Steichen's *Family of Man* show included an image from the file, which showed children dancing in a circle outside a school in Peru, sited beneath an oil derrick. This again reveals the extent to which these images were known.

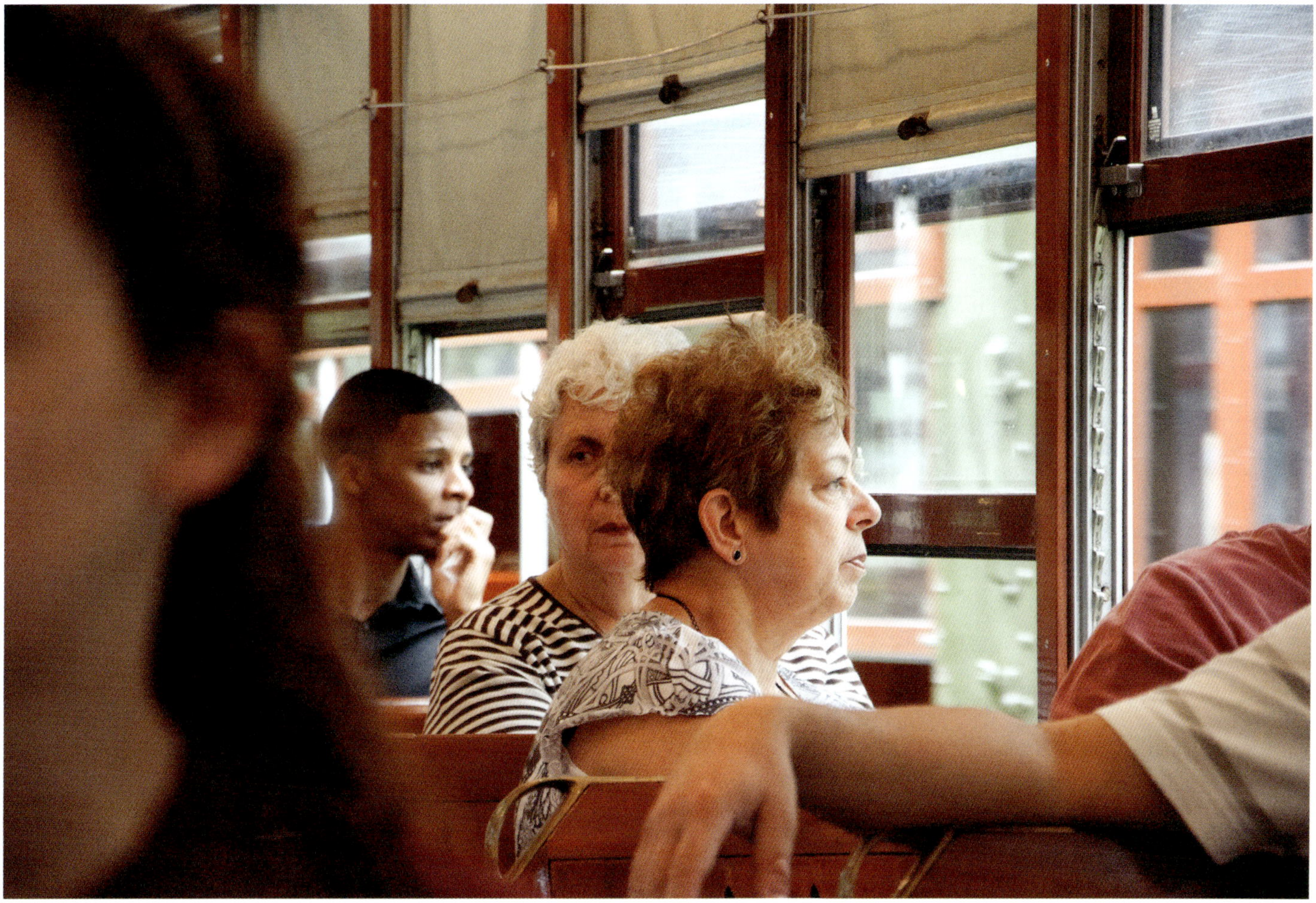

These Standard Oil pictures widely infiltrated the visual culture of America and Frank would certainly have had many opportunities to see them. The irony and strangeness of this 'shadow gallery', commercial images forming the content of a very different kind of exhibition, was not lost on Frank. The Standard Oil Picture File ripped the museum open and spread it willy-nilly across streets, markets, billboards and educational institutions. Images, in some cases by the same photographers who featured in the *Family of Man*, were reproduced en masse, printed and distributed free to anyone who asked for them.

Frank's photographs interrogate and criticise these Standard Oil originals at the same time as he pays them homage. In *The Americans* Frank refers as easily and frequently to these images as he does to Renaissance painting or Reformation engraving (Day 2011: 81, 114, 170–172, 185). He successfully challenges the conventional gallery and questions and subverts its hierarchical understanding of images. He opens the windows to the noise of the streets and lets the wind start to dissipate the 'infected' smell of photography. He combines the energy of the working world with his own sensibility, creating images which play with commercial originals but have an entirely different intent. He absorbs, comments on, juxtaposes and satirises works from across the range of cultural output. The exhibit and the advertisement coexist in *The Americans*, Frank thus subverting Marxist notions (Aronowitz 1990) of class predicated culture. He takes the images of humanity as his source material.

Trolley—New Orleans is one of Frank's pictures which echo Standard Oil's imagery. In 1947, photographer Esther Bubley made a series of works illustrating a cross-country bus journey. This appeared two years later, in volume 31 of *The Lamp*, Standard Oil's free-to-anyone corporate magazine, under the title 'Via Bus'. It also appeared in *Photo Memo,* a smaller, specialised magazine advertising the Picture File's latest photographs, under the alternative title 'By Bus'. Bubley photographed *Greyhound Bus Terminal, N.Y.C. Loaded bus ready to depart* (Standard Oil Archive, University of Louisville) in July of that year. Three side windows of a Greyhound fill the top half of the image. These are illuminated, the interior warm and busy against the darker tone of the bus's side. The affluent white passengers are furred and hatted: some smile, some are glum. Crisp, white-covered seats leave no doubt that every effort has been made to ensure their comfort. A legend painted along the coach reads 'Coast to Coast'. These travellers are, after all, the descendants of the pioneers; they also journey the wide land.

Frank's image is entirely other. Five windows similarly occupy the top half of the photograph, but the passengers thus framed are very different to Bubley's. White faces occupy the windows to the left. The first is evanescent behind the glass. The second passenger stares with unveiled suspicion and distaste at the photographer and, through him, by implication at the viewer. Black hair and a dark coat frame her disdain, an expression as evil as the witch in MGM's hugely popular 1939 version of *The Wizard of Oz*. Behind her, a white boy and his sister have a caged look, the boy clinging to the bar-like window frame. His hair, suit and bowtie define him as middle class and middle management in embryo. This boy stands in stark contrast to the dearly loved dream of adventurous and anarchic American boyhood described in *Tom Sawyer* and *Huckleberry Finn* (Twain, 1876 and 1884). This is boyhood at its most suppressed, exactly "the look of sadness" (Frank, in Maloney 1958: 115) that Frank sought. The matronly perpetrator of this bondage broods protectively in the shadows.

To the right, towards the back of the bus, sit two black people. They have no option but to sit here: the photograph was taken before the US Congress ruled that segregated buses were unconstitutional, on 20th December, 1956. The black man is powerfully built. He echoes the white boy's position, yet his open-shirted body language speaks an appeal. He appears to be in supplication. The white boy looks trapped, but at the same time holds himself with a confidence entirely lacking in the muscular adult behind. Not all of these colour-classified and restricted passengers seem uneasy with their demarcation. The black lady at extreme right seems to be staring unconcernedly out of shot. Frank's image is uncomfortable. It examines racism in America without overtly representing it. The photograph's tension exists in the unequal appearance and body language of its subjects. Its message is heightened enormously by its position, following *Fourth of July—Jay, New York*, a photograph of white families comfortably celebrating Independence Day beneath the red, white and blue supposed signifier of the equality of all men. Perhaps most significantly of all, the tension lies in the hindsight-equipped eye of the viewer. We are all, I suspect, looking for the unassuming Rosa Parks, quietly and unwittingly starting a revolution by refusing to give up her seat.

Frank, then, has taken Bubley's representative American image and rewritten it. His observation of the faces in *Trolley—New Orleans* reveals the reality of an America far more complex and divided than Standard Oil would dare depict.

FRANK SAID OF HIS JOURNEY

> 1955. I cross the States. For a year. 500 rolls of film. I go into post offices, Woolworths, 10 cent shops, bus stations. I sleep in cheap hotels. Around 7 in the morning I go to a nearby bar. I work all the time. I don't speak much. I try not to be seen. (Frank 1991: after plate 63)

A lonely pursuit. Many of the image-makers I know befriend their subjects. Some call it 'embedding'. Become friends, so that they relax and expose themselves in a way they otherwise wouldn't. Some will say that image maker and subject collaborate, conspire, connive together—and in my experience the subjects of these interrogations, whose friendship was sought because of what they represent or how they look, in a contrived and perhaps unnatural way, rarely complain about the outcomes. They are more often delighted by the observations and analyses brought to bear upon them.

Well, it was not so with Frank, and it is not so with me. I sometimes seek through a simple and single gesture (usually a questioning smile) someone's consent to capture a portrait. But, as often, I do not. Perhaps it is the poet in me, as against the sociologist? Maybe it is something more. A melancholy temperament, finding profundity more easily in silence than noise, seeing clarity in distance rather than the furnace fires of relationship and the almost undeniable human instinct towards empathy and shared belief. 'Stockholm syndrome' of the photographic kind.

Frank so often captures loneliness in his images. Perhaps because it is there, or perhaps because it reflects, more than is comfortable, the loneliness of the photographer. There is another possibility though: perhaps it allows him to see through the comfortable and upholstered eightfold arms of hearth, home, family, empathy and connection to the spaces of the infinite beyond.

CANAL STREET—NEW ORLEANS

Trolley—New Orleans is perhaps above all about loneliness—a loneliness imposed by distant but pressing legislators, whose icy and invisible fingers shape our daily lives, so often to our detriment. Also the loneliness of a more obscure separation, perhaps chosen, perhaps imposed. *Canal Street—New Orleans* continues this idea of loneliness. It figures an older man at centre, solitary in a thronging crowd. He is still-seeming within a mass of humanity, most of whom seem intent on navigating the *melée* without acknowledging or engaging with anyone else. The exceptions are familiar. Frank's 'man and boy' motif is repeated again at left, with the man smiling down on the child as if they are sharing some kind of joke. The observant face of a second child at extreme right similarly echoes the expression on the face of a dour and intent older woman. The selection and inclusion of this photograph, with its islands of warmth within a colder, harsher street scene, is not surprising since Frank was a parent, travelling for some of his journey with his family. These almost hidden moments of warmth give the lie to so much of the criticism of *The Americans* at the time of its release. There is a great deal of love and affection within its images; the problem is one of attention and application. Viewers used to the gushing and obvious representations of the *Family of Man* were not, I suspect, used to looking at photographs as one would look at a painting. Nor were they, in many cases and as Szarkowski observed, prepared to acknowledge that such everyday scenes could contain such profundity:

> The pictures took us by ambush then. We knew the America that they described, of course, but we knew it as one knows the background hum of a record player, not as a fact to recognize and confront. Nor had we understood that this stratum of our experience was a proper concern of artists. (Szarkowski, in Frank 1968: back cover)

The families notwithstanding, the isolation of the central figure is intense, emphasised by the whirl of inclusion all around.

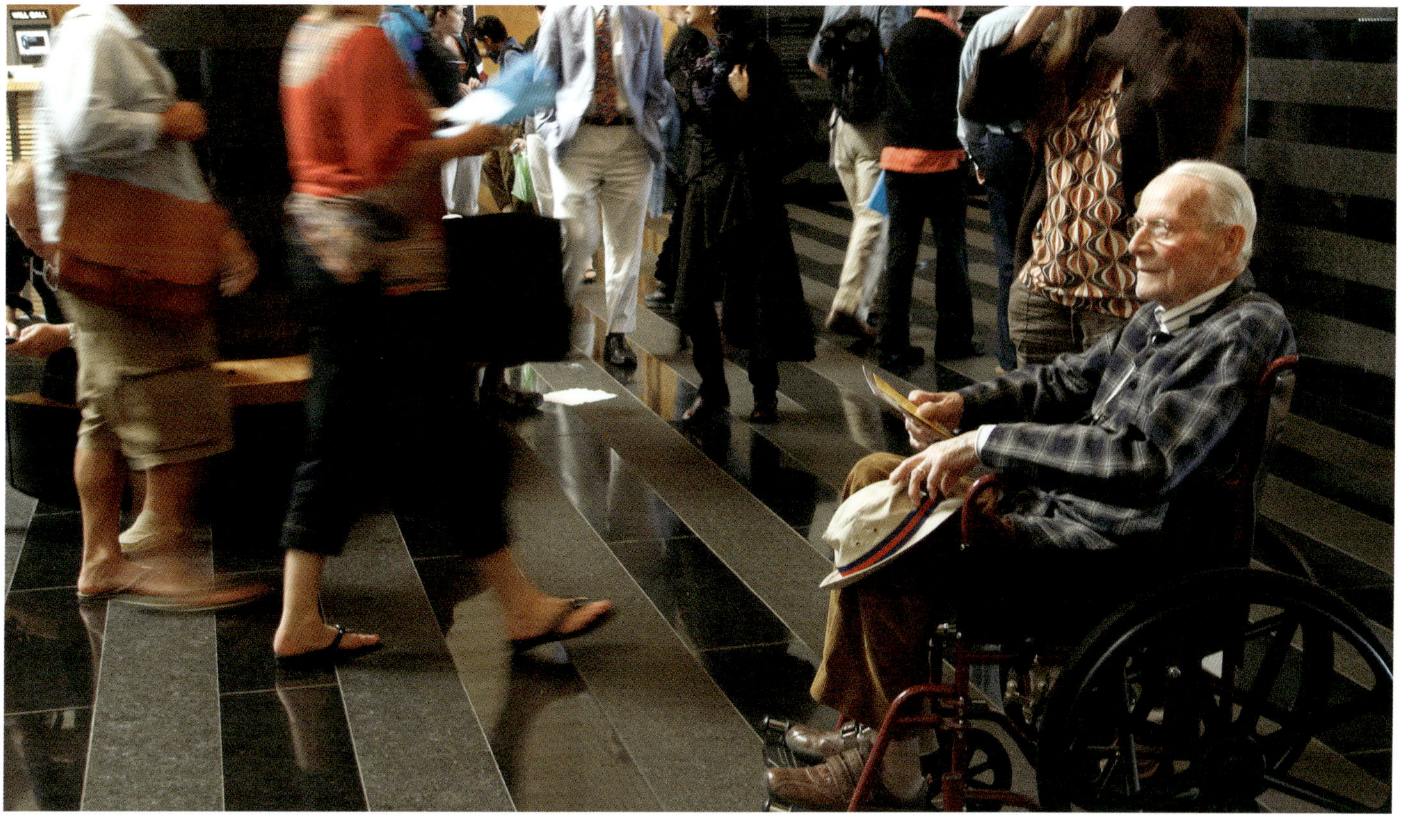

EVENTUALLY, IN AMARILLO, I FOUND THE WRONG EYED JESUS—hanging a hundred feet high and fifty feet wide. Just after I joined old Route 66 a truck stop passed by on the right, called the "Jesus is Lord, Not a Swear Word Truck Stop". Every usual truck stop thing inside, all stickered with the name of Christ. Next to the rough and reesty trucker's toilets was a tiny chapel. Two rescue trucks outside offered a variety of salvations. Sitting in a quiet, shaded corner were an old man and a little fluffy Chihuahua cross, like a lost and very far from home Disney fox cub. His name was Al Pickard ("like the Starship captain" he said), and hers Blondie. After a brain operation, he found the noise of living with others unbearable and set out along 66: his ratty camper was stickered with all the States he and the road so far had crossed. Something had broken in his engine, he thinks maybe the alternator bracket, but the mechanics can't fix it. So he's been living at the truck stop for three months. He says he has a family somewhere—I wonder if they know where he is? It's clear the counter clerks are looking out for him. So rare to find a Good Samaritan. Someone better than me, for sure, he is safer in their arms. I am surplus, save for conversation and news of another world—these things are about all I'm good for, in any case. The clerk is homely, lank haired and a little overweight, her flabby stomach bulging under a grubby sweatshirt over jeans. She is young, but brown teeth tell of a dodgy diet and poverty too great for dental care. Shy, uncertain, she feeds him McDonald's in the failing light, a dinner dropped off for her by a friend. Driving the East coast, the radio sang about "a girl in Amarillo", and the sunset in Santa Fe. She is that girl, for me, her beauty of another order. She is the Angel that Flies from Montgomery, here on the oily tarmac of a truckstop forecourt. She looks at me shyly and says she wishes it would rain. I think she sees the storms hanging quiet behind my eyes. In her care, ancient Al is content, clean and well fed. Part of me feels concern for him, part of me feels envy for the life they have together. I wonder if he's still there, and I wonder who will minister to me when I am old and lost.

ROOMING HOUSE—BUNKER HILL, LOS ANGELES

Solitude, age and loneliness continue in this Frank image. The children who surrounded the solitary man in the last photograph are gone now, and a single man is standing alone in the time-darkened, faded porch of *Rooming House—Bunker Hill, Los Angeles*. His face is hidden by the obliquely rising stair, and only his dark-suited body and walking stick are revealed. The architecture is a close analogy for his declined physical condition, both of them having had their glory days and both of them somewhat along the road to ruin. As Shakespeare wonderfully described it in *Othello*, they are "declined into the vale of years" (2007: 97).

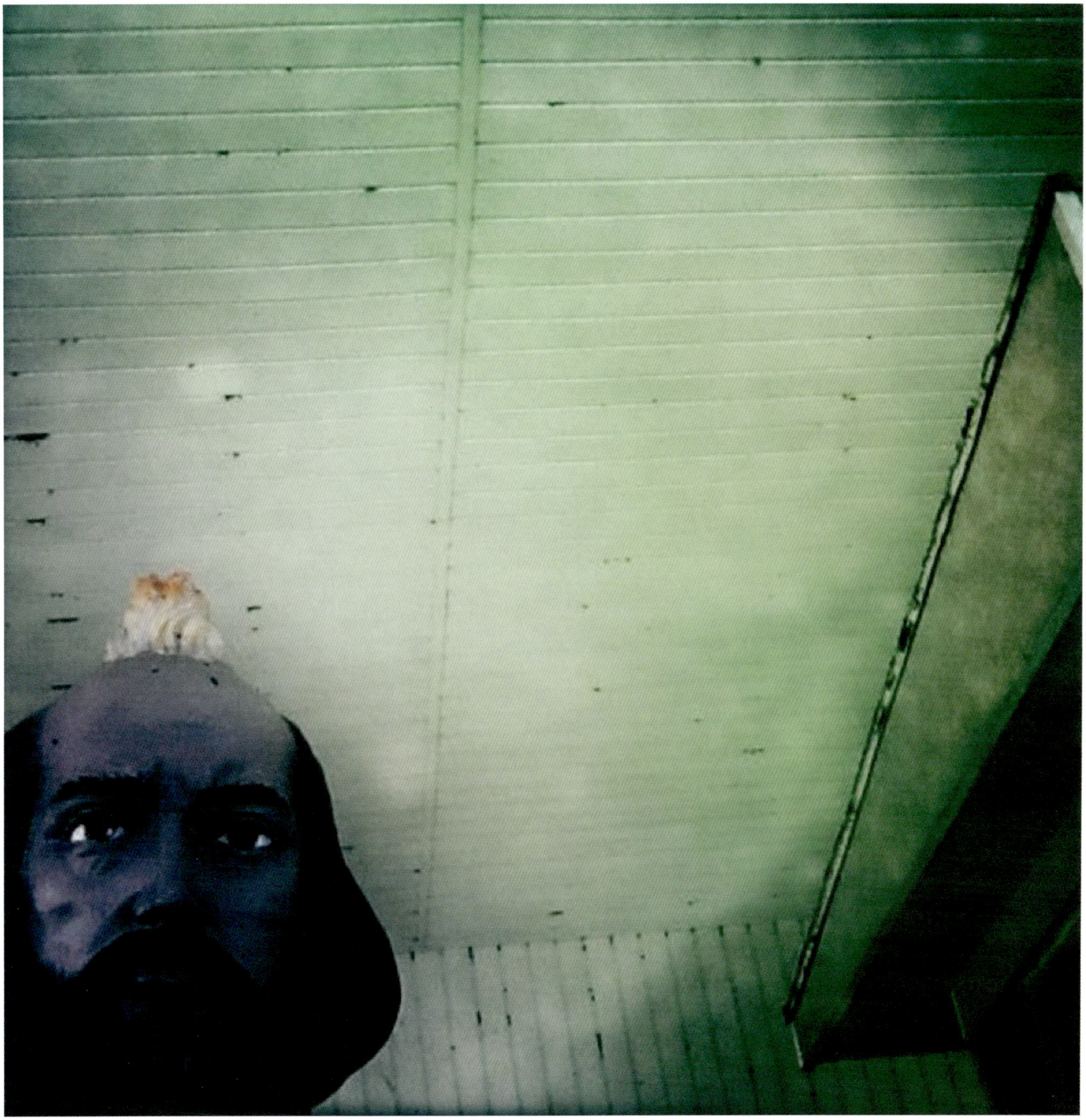

YESTERDAY AFTERNOON I REACHED MCCLELLANVILLE. A massive moment for me, this place marked on the map with one of those giant cinematic pins, half the size of a continent, where X marks the spot. All those long East-coast miles I had been expecting treasure. It's such a picture, the one Frank took here fifty years ago. Trailing clouds of photographic glory, an hommage not just to Walker Evans, as it so obviously is, but to the whole American tradition that he was remaking as he drove. All the time on my circumnavigation I was looking forward to the wonders to be found in absolutely the heart of America—Everyman's Everytown. I didn't find them.

It was great to be there, a real sense of resolution, of sucking the marrow of my days, but there was nothing to photograph—which I guess was always the point. The barbershops were gone. McClellanville is deeply surrounded by forest, off the side of Highway 17. An old relaxation place for Scottish plantation owners, sick of the heat and insects out on the delta, or really sick with insect-borne disease. It's easy and open between the buildings—a tidal creek there serves as a harbour.

By luck I met a professor, who also had come here because of Frank's photo—married a student and moved down. He's old now and, I detect, frustrated at the world's recent and growing indifference. Hard to be left alone by time, caught in the strandline jetsam, watching bright and newer creatures still busy as your life declines. He showed me the sites where the barbershops once stood: "The town is not the same," he continued, "old America is passing", even way out here. McClellanville oozed a quiet contentment that, like the inevitability he was fighting, could easily turn to tedium.

YALE COMMENCEMENT—
NEW HAVEN GREEN, NEW HAVEN, CONNECTICUT

The apparent dissolution and resignation of the old man in *Rooming House—Bunker Hill, Los Angeles* is contrasted with the still-engaged expression of the older man in *Yale Commencement—New Haven Green, New Haven, Connecticut*, continuing the theme of the ages of man. As he watches the stream of younger men walk by, he may appear a little cynical, an expression of world-weary indulgence towards these enthusiastic young things on his face, but his posture, his attire and the newspaper he holds attest to his continued involvement with the world of action. He is separate, but not lost to the world of the others in his photograph.

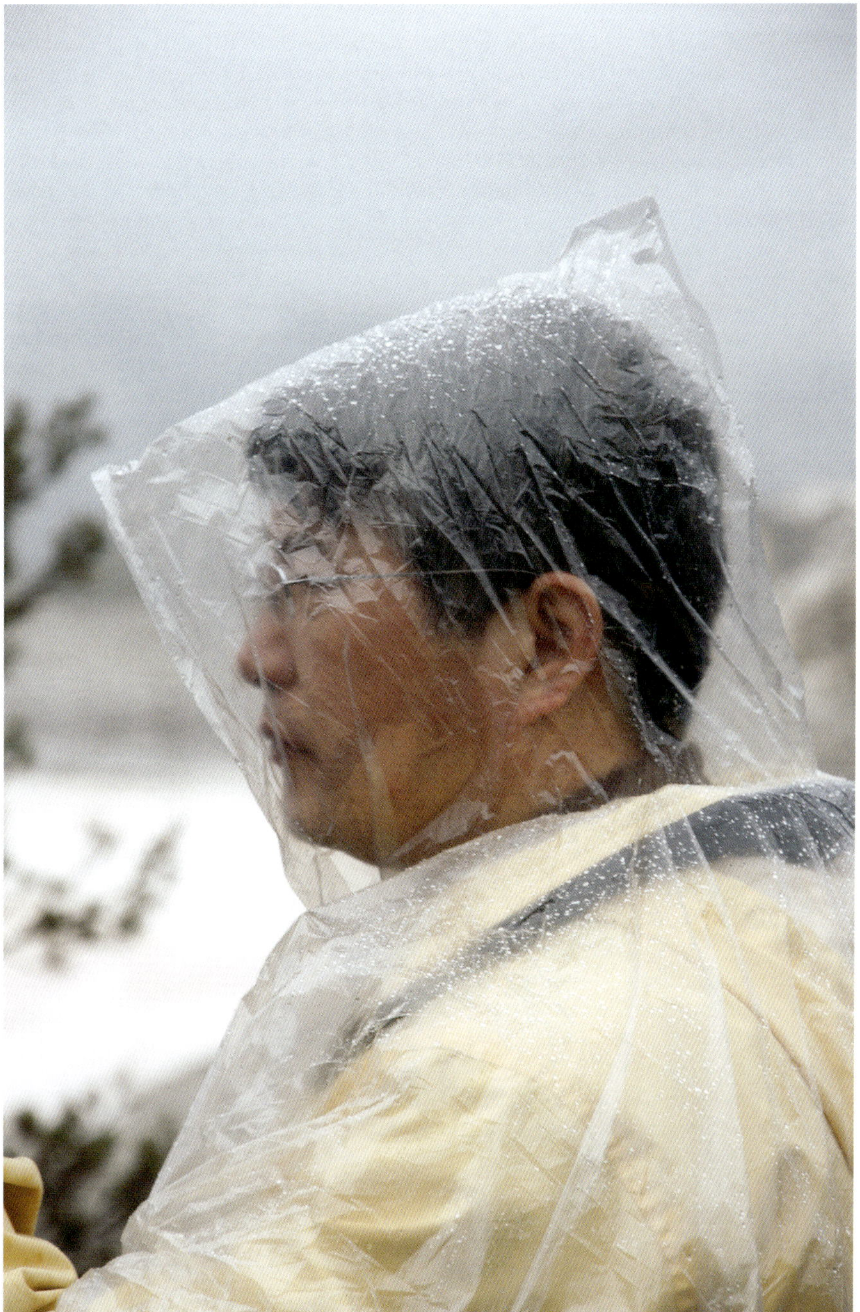

AN EASY NAVIGATION OUT OF TOWN AND ON DOWN 17 TOWARDS BEAUFORT. The first of many enormous thunderstorms hit me, precursors of Hurricane Beryl—rain so thick I could barely see out of my window. As I turned down a cloverleaf, heading for the sea, the deluge was followed in short order by steaming roads and vegetation, making this incredibly humid place wetter still. Beaufort (pronounced Byu-fud) was a small, quiet town—charming, clap boarded and truly pretty. A soft wind from the inlet cooled the heat a little, but not much. Over a white painted wooden viaduct heading across the water was an island. I was instantly intrigued. I wandered around the town and, with help from tourist guides at the Library, found the district where Frank's café was most likely located. There are no traces now and no one there to ask. I speculatively and perfunctorily photographed a couple of semi-derelict buildings where the small child may have lain on the floor, in front of the monolithic jukebox, 50 years before. I discovered most interestingly, and most distressingly, given my schedule, that the island across the water was St Helena. How had I never wondered in my looking at Frank's book, where exactly this place was, its photographs filled with black people? On this island, between the melons and sea marsh, Martin Luther King began his speech, "I have a dream". I began to notice the proud blackness in Beaufort too. On the main street amongst the tourist trash was the Gullah Gallery filled with paintings of famous black faces and a charmingly self-possessed curator, smiling and friendly. There are grand houses certainly, adorned with Daughters of the Confederacy memorial plaques, but alongside these, without any conflict I was aware of, were portraits aplenty of Robert Smalls, a slave who commandeered the ship on which he was wheelman, piloted it out to the Union blockade and became a Civil War hero. His mother was a lowcountry Gullah woman, his father almost certainly her white slave owner. Smalls was sent to Charleston aged 12 to find work, sending the money he earned back to his owner-father. He progressed through street lamplighter to dock worker to wheelsman, marrying along the way and having children of his own. His theft of the ship was wonderfully planned and executed, he impersonating the captain, using all the correctly coded signals and picking up his and his crew's families en route. But I wonder about his father—was he loving and kind to his half black child, setting him almost-free in Charleston? Or was he callous and profiteering, trying to make money from his denied offspring, living pompous and hypocritical? Like the sculpture outside the library in Beauford, South Carolina—its intention and its reality jarringly out of phase. Hard to see, sometimes, what is there before our eyes. Was Robert Smalls' father cuddling his bastard child, or doing something unspeakable and unforgiveable to that little human being? In Robert Frank's photograph the Gullah baby is cosy-feeling in the cabin café, despite the black sarcophagus of song. A friend said of my picture: "Someone thought this was a good idea…?". Hypocrisy, like the road to hell, is paved with good intentions.

CAFÉ—BEAUFORT, SOUTH CAROLINA

Frank's image pictures a baby next to a jukebox, standing incongruously in a timber *Café—Beaufort, South Carolina.* The jukebox appears almost to have landed there, like one of the spaceships that descended onto a startled earth in so many 1950s science fiction films. Frank recognizes the jukebox as a significant icon of '50s America, as we have seen. The relationship between the jukebox and the black baby is fascinating; it functions perhaps as a 'robot nanny', echoing science fiction again. The form of the machine resembles the much-celebrated robot 'butler' in Fred Wilcox's 1956 blockbuster film *Forbidden Planet.*

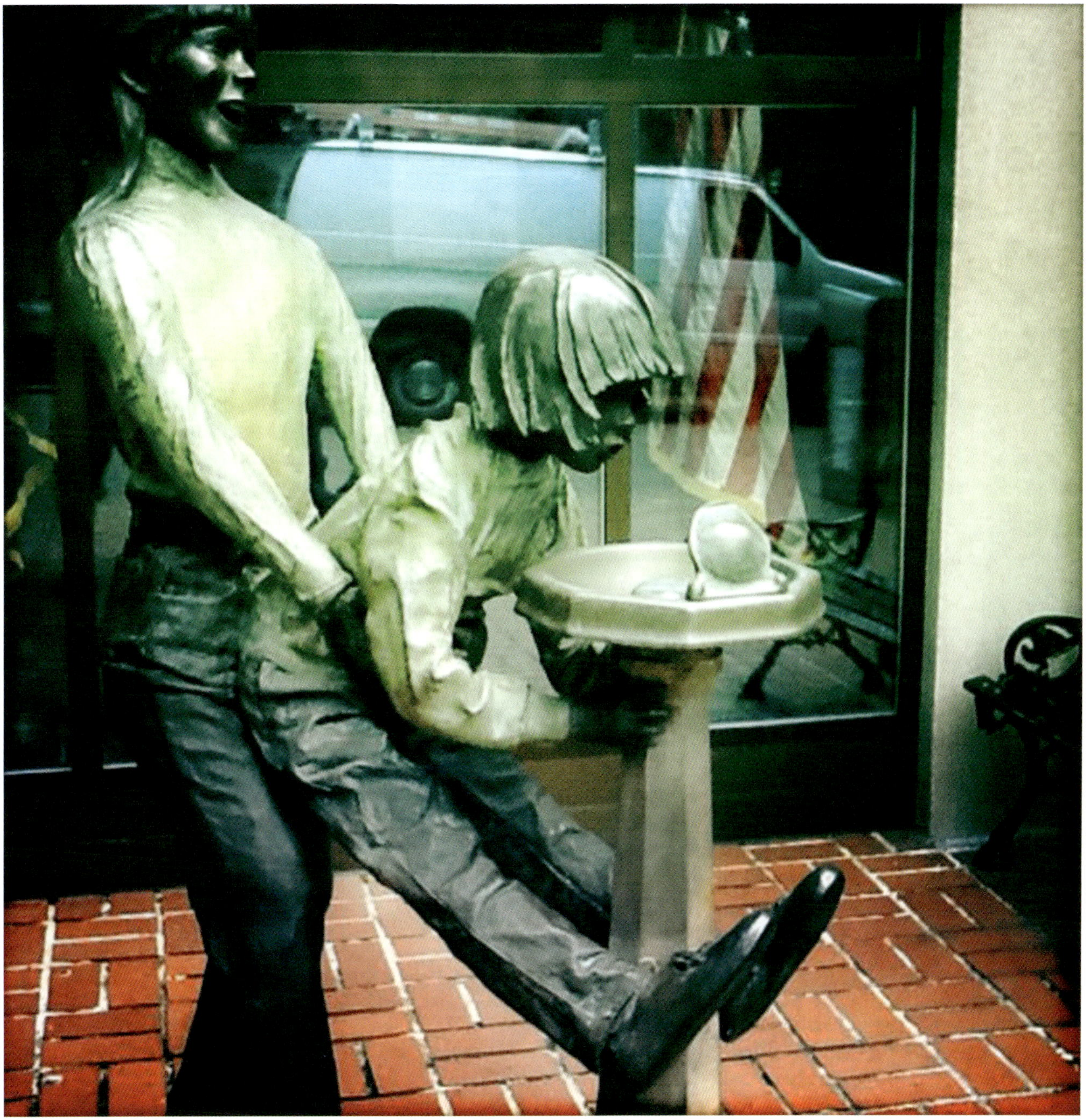

THE DARKLING OF THE DAY BROUGHT THE NEED OF A PLACE TO NEST. I favour the high and wild, so seek out mountains when I can, or forests. Somewhere I can breathe, somewhere I can see. Leaving Santa Fe this day I was uncertain. So many intriguing names on the map, each promising a different kind of doorway into a variety of lights. In hindsight, though, always only one way remains, our lives the traces of a thousand choices left unmade. I had to choose the way I would take my feet—and which possibilities I would ignore for ever. I turned, laggardly and uncertain, towards Taos. Names further on had confirmed it for me: Trinidad and Walsenburg, of which Woody Guthrie had written and I, copying him, had sung, and Cimarron, full of mountain wildness, stallions drumming on the roof of the world. I hadn't looked particularly carefully, and had no idea that I would follow the gorge of the Rio Grande until I did it. So, thereby, the most fateful moment of my trip was made inevitable, an encounter with life and death, powerful and with the smack of eternity. The water sparkled in sunlight, collapsing cliffs looming overhead. Deep in the gorge, I stopped for ice-cream and soda at the Sweet Take Out. A lovely old lady smiled from its service hatch, content with herself, with us and with the world. Her sign said "I'm retired so stop asking me to do stuff". Descendants of the indigenous had here turned themselves to tourism, living in this water-rich place for millennia, hunting in the desert to fill the bellies of their children and feed the home fires. Now, instead of hunting game, it's the tourist dollar they seek to spear. An intriguing creative collection was signposted 'Outsider Art'—Mad Max meets Pocahontas, sadly closed for business against the coming dark. I drove out over the lip of the canyon, saw it cut a knife gash across the high land. Distant mountains bookended the gently sloping sage-green plain—like a picture from a storybook, exactly like the Time Life Library Geography volume I had bought with my pocket money as a child. The Piedmont and peri-montane. Closing the circle of this, my little life. So beautiful a place, I thought I'd come back and watch the coming solar show from here, expecting to be alone.

After a high cold camp came a beautiful mountain morning (I didn't think too much about the 'Beware Rabies' signs nailed to the trees…) and a helter-skelter drive down to Taos Pueblo. I was unceremoniously waved away: it was closed. Turned out not to be an act of pique by the dwellers who still claim these ancient muddy condominiums—they were dancing a secret ritual for the Moon-Eats-Sun, ensuring she would regurgitate him, after their momentous congress was done.

I was wrong about the solitude—and I was glad. A happy party crowd of school kids and school Ma'ams, accountants, professors, local renegades temporarily returned and flat land dwellers up from the heat of the South. A kid, obsessive and clearly deeply loved, fetched an enormous telescope out of his father's car. Properly equipped with filters for the burning light, we saw the sun the size of a plate, and an orderly queue formed full of smiles and cell phone music. Unthinking I captured him, like St Anne in da Vinci's cartoon, pointing skyward, portentous, with a smile. A very pregnant blonde girl smiled and talked with me about travelling and her coming child. Up from Albuquerque, she and her Latvian man. I sang two lines of Dumshe Nachte, an old Baltic song I'd once learned. She was so excited at the coming birth, might even be during the eclipse. He was philosophical, thinking they had been lost in their lives before the child, who gave them purpose, a reason to be. The moon slid across the sun like a seductress assassin, with a knife hidden in her knickers. It darkened and the birds grew quiet, the shadow covering the mountain lands. A brilliant ring of fire remained and I captured it against all hope, perfectly through the telescope. Once he was fully dead, his fiery blood spilled for all to see, she, supercilious, self satisfied, replete, let him go slowly, like a dog freed finally by a bitch. The light did not return: it was sunset now. As the moon moved away a crescent sun hung in the sky. Over the ochre and sage brush plains, throat slit by the Rio Grande, the coral red star hung in a turquoise sky. It sank until only the crescent point remained—a triangle of sun setting, while the Tiwa kicked the dust and danced.

Amazing, I know. I can imagine a crone saying soothfully to me as a lad, "You'll live to see the setting sun triangular", and I would have thought her mad. But here it was and here am I to say how ever much we know, there can always come things entirely unexpected. And so they did. A while later, when I was home again, the Latvian father mailed me for copies of my photographs, which I'd promised. I asked after the three of them. Only two he replied: the baby had died. Oh that little life that brought his mother such joy, she said, in his tiny, hours-long life.

And that baby boy told his wisdom into our lives, too, on that distant road-side day. More attenuated we may be, our lives stretched out further, but only a little longer lived than he. He was born to indescribable beauty, life moulding, enrich-

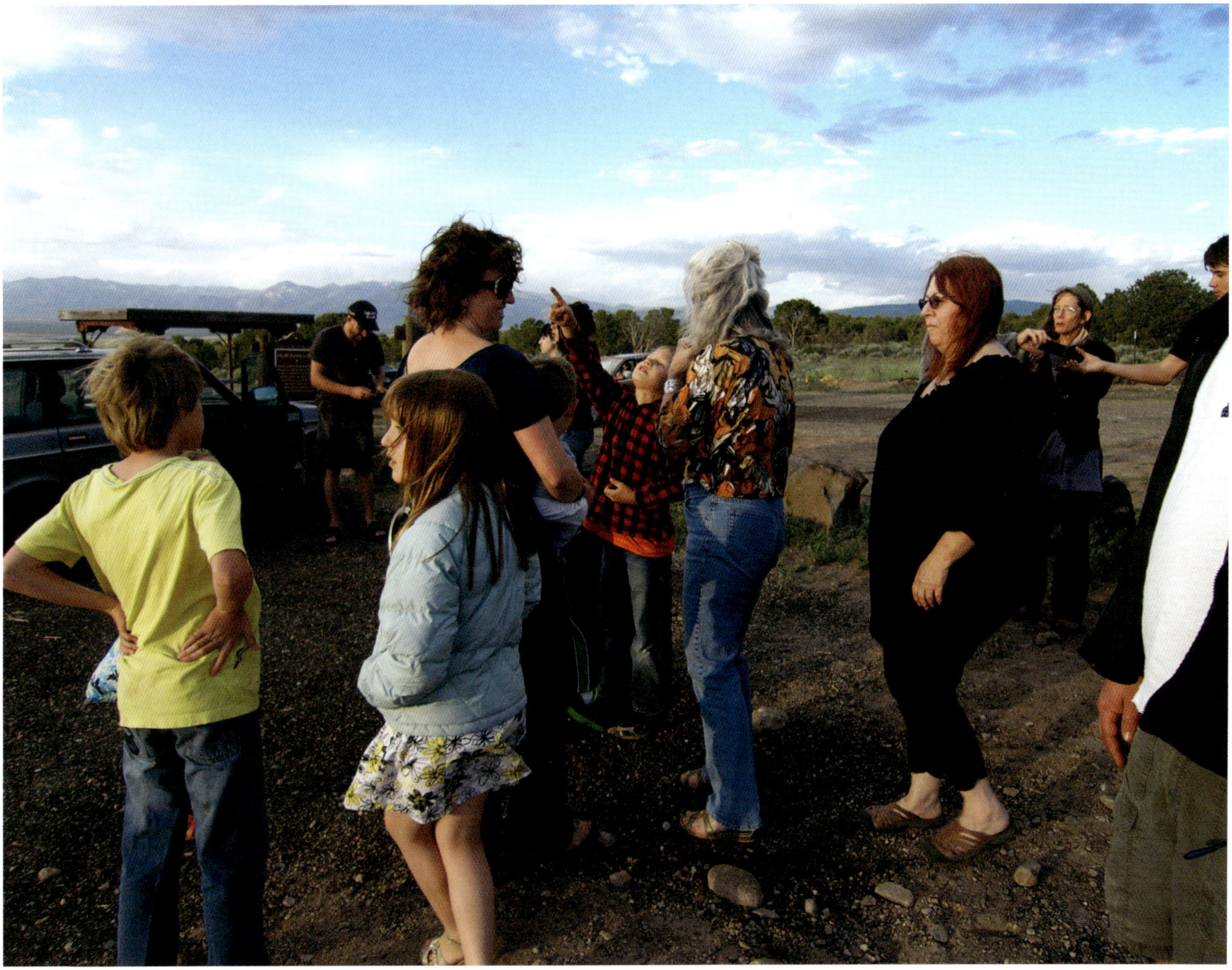

ing, affirming. And in the midst of our laughing and musical celebrations he stood hand-in-hand with death, this smallest and most beautiful, his potential untold. Trying to see the brilliance and its dark brother—holding them in balance is our challenge, I guess. Juggling the divine-seeming and the awful, and seeing still in the blue black halflight—beauty.

GEORGETOWN, SOUTH CAROLINA

The black baby is alone in *Café—Beaufort*, and contrasts with Frank's photograph, *Georgetown, South Carolina*, which features two women and a child in a classic pyramidal composition. The composition echoes a number of pyramidally composed Renaissance works depicting the Madonna and Christ. Leonardo da Vinci's *The Virgin and Child with St Anne and St John the Baptist* (National Gallery, London, 1499–1500) is an intriguing comparison. Instead of St Anne's enigmatic finger pointing towards heaven, the woman in Frank's rendering points upwards with a cigarette. The implication is obvious: there is nothing less significant or important about these women and children in contemporary America. They too are Madonnas and Saint Annes, and the anonymous toddler with them is every bit as significant for the contemporary American world as the Christ child or the Baptist. These unknown women are the 'everymen' in whose arcane ways the hope of the redundant world resides. The bankrupt culture of Europe, caught in a spiral of ever more devastating wars, and of which da Vinci and his contemporaries became pillars, must recognize and celebrate this moment of tenderness in Georgetown, or perish. This toddler in matronly company follows the lonely baby in the café in Beaufort: isolation is contrasted with community, and exposure with security.

WE'VE SEEN ALREADY IN *CAFÉ—BEAUFORT, SOUTH CAROLINA* that a black baby lies on a cushion close beside an ornate, black plastic and shining-metal jukebox. The box is huge in relation to the child, looming over it. Its monolithic presence is ambivalent. As with the car in *Motorama—Los Angeles*, also discussed earlier, there is no certainty as to whether this technology is protective or threatening. It is unquestionably alien. The box is self-contained, mobile, its mechanism obscure. It is from another place, another's mind, yet completely accepted. Frank's composition reveals a mother who is entirely comfortable leaving her unattended child in its care. In a corner of the low-tech, light filled room, the Rockola is so different from the bare-boards café and the flesh and blood baby as to almost require reverence. It is like the mouthpiece of a distant world, the gift of some obscure deity to the faithful. It is the high-tech inheritor of the megaphones built into the masks of ancient Greek actors, the amplifying acoustics of a Gothic cathedral or the shaman observed in Africa talking to the gods through a disconnected telephone. The jukebox's songs carry the dogma of the New World, the new way. The venue is a café, not a church, a prophecy, perhaps, of the primacy to come of McDonald's over Methodism, the golden arches replacing the Gothic arches as the people's meeting place of choice.

Bar—Las Vegas, Nevada examines another interior, lit brilliantly through its windows. There is nothing here that is homemade or homespun, however. Damaged linoleum covers the large, empty floor, with only a suggestion of furniture in the shadows at extreme left breaking the desolation. Against the right-hand wall, a jukebox, looking more like a lathe than anything religious, is the object of the rapt attention of the only person in the image. He is a dark man, light reflecting off his Brylcreemed hair, his casual flowered shirt signalling his leisure. He stands in obvious communion with the box: it is his companion, his associate. If he presses a button it will provide its comforting, well-known stock answers to the questions implicit in the language of his stance.

BAR—LAS VEGAS, NEVADA

The articulation between the last image, *Georgetown* and *Bar—Las Vegas, Nevada*, is wonderfully complex. There is certainly a *caesura*. Frank's book has a definite musicality to its structure and this notion of the musical pause is useful here. It is a momentary cessation, a break in the flow for reflection, consideration and to collect oneself ahead of the following activity—but certainly not a stop or a break. *Bar—Las Vegas* includes no children or older people. This is the first time in many images that these have not been represented. Its lone character is a mature male. Moreover, the photograph initiates a sequence of images that signally juxtapose poverty and affluence. It marks a change, then, but Frank does not let the movement cease—instead, he employs what curator John Szarkowski called "a little kind of syncopated carelessness, a kind of foot dragging rhythm" (Livingston 1992: 308). Across this thematic break, he creates a pictorial triptych. The central image of the three is *Georgetown*, the two women and the child, as we have already noted, forming a triangular composition that can be related to Renaissance religious paintings. This was preceded by a photograph of a lone black child, to the right of the centre of the image with a jukebox off to the left. The third image reflects this, with *Bar—Las Vegas, Nevada* having an Hispanic man occupying the central ground with a jukebox off to the right. In its provision of a few minutes of enculturating wisdom, each song being a message from the elevated world of pop stars and folk singers for the price of a nickel or a dime, the jukebox has an almost religious profundity and influence. It replaces, perhaps, the angelic messengers of God. It is appropriate, then, that these mechanical seraphs should feature as bracketing photographs for a composition characteristic of depictions of the holy family.

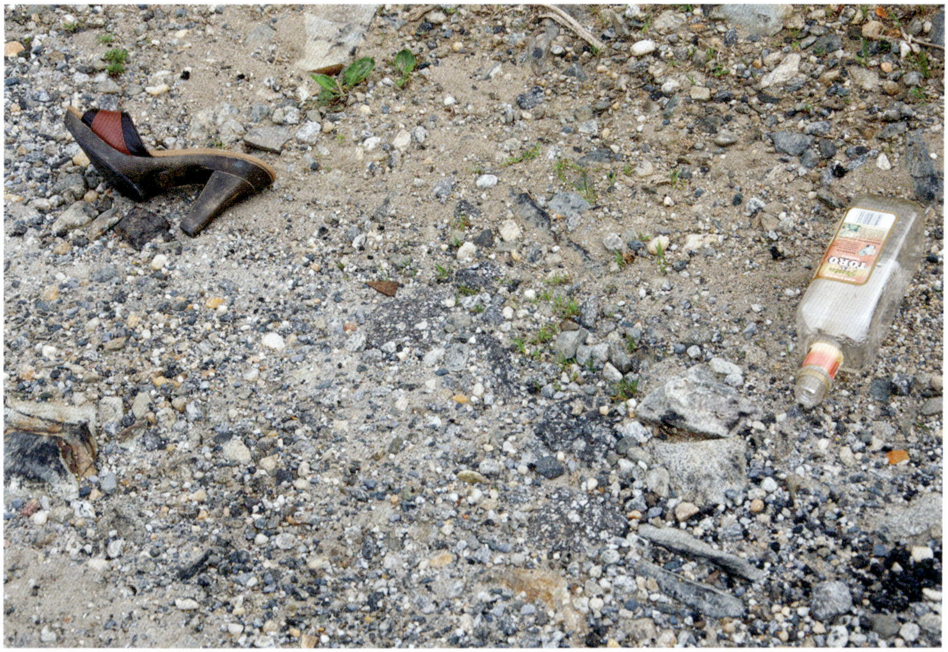

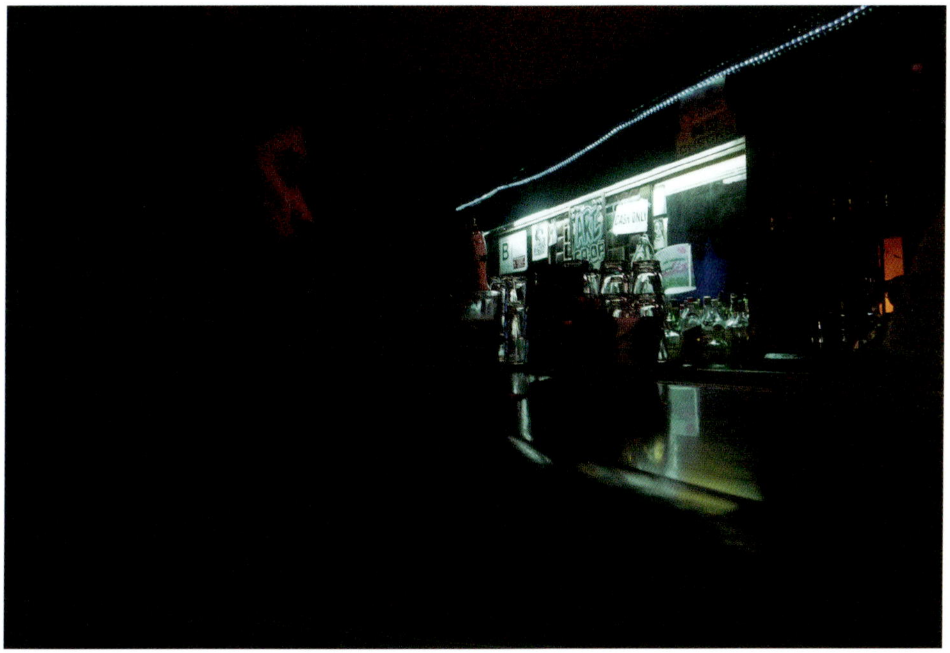
CASH ONLY

FINALLY THE BLUE RIDGE PARKWAY. 75 YEARS OLD, but only finished quite recently. Strange. A four hundred mile road with a forty five miles-per-hour limit and no commercial traffic. It weaves along the mountain's crest, on stilted viaducts and through tunnels when necessary, but always at the vertical limit, never for a moment doubting its purpose. Wreathed in mist most of the time, and frozenly inaccessible for much of the year, how is this not a wonderfully American idea? I rode it in cruise control, feeling like a kid manically turning the wheel of a toy car at an enormous theme park. As the evening shadows lengthened, I happened on a wilderness campsite—by a river in deep forest, just beyond Grandfather Mountain, which seemed to be snoring in its rocking chair and smoking a pipe. The camp seemed to me a very good idea.

It was half-filled with the most enormous Winnebagos, transformer toys for older people, lounges and kitchens popping out of the grey steel at the press of a switch. Wider than any English street, they are made to fit roads in a country that has space. Friendly and outrageously equipped, some of the inhabitants had not been home for years. These mountain fastness campsites are inexpensive and perfectly designed, allowing the nomadically inclined the freedom they require. Such a life is impossible in England, campsites are too infrequent and expensive and the owners of land too resolute and violent—I think of the famous Beanfield where the Henge lovers' lives were beaten and destroyed. Mostly these American campers are affluent: this is a recreated landscape, bought wholesale by Washington from farmers who'd exhausted the land. But there are poor people out there too—rubber tramps, like me, who find a way to make it down the highway, between dawn and the dimming of day.

HOTEL LOBBY—MIAMI BEACH

Hard on the heels of the single lackadaisical man in the *Bar* comes an image of a solid and affluent couple in a *Hotel Lobby—Miami Beach*. The woman is wrapped in mink, and sports large earrings. Her pose communicates casual confidence, while her companion is quietly threatening in his dour self-belief. The overall impression is of assuredness and comfort, in stark contrast to the uncertainty and visual poverty of the previous photograph.

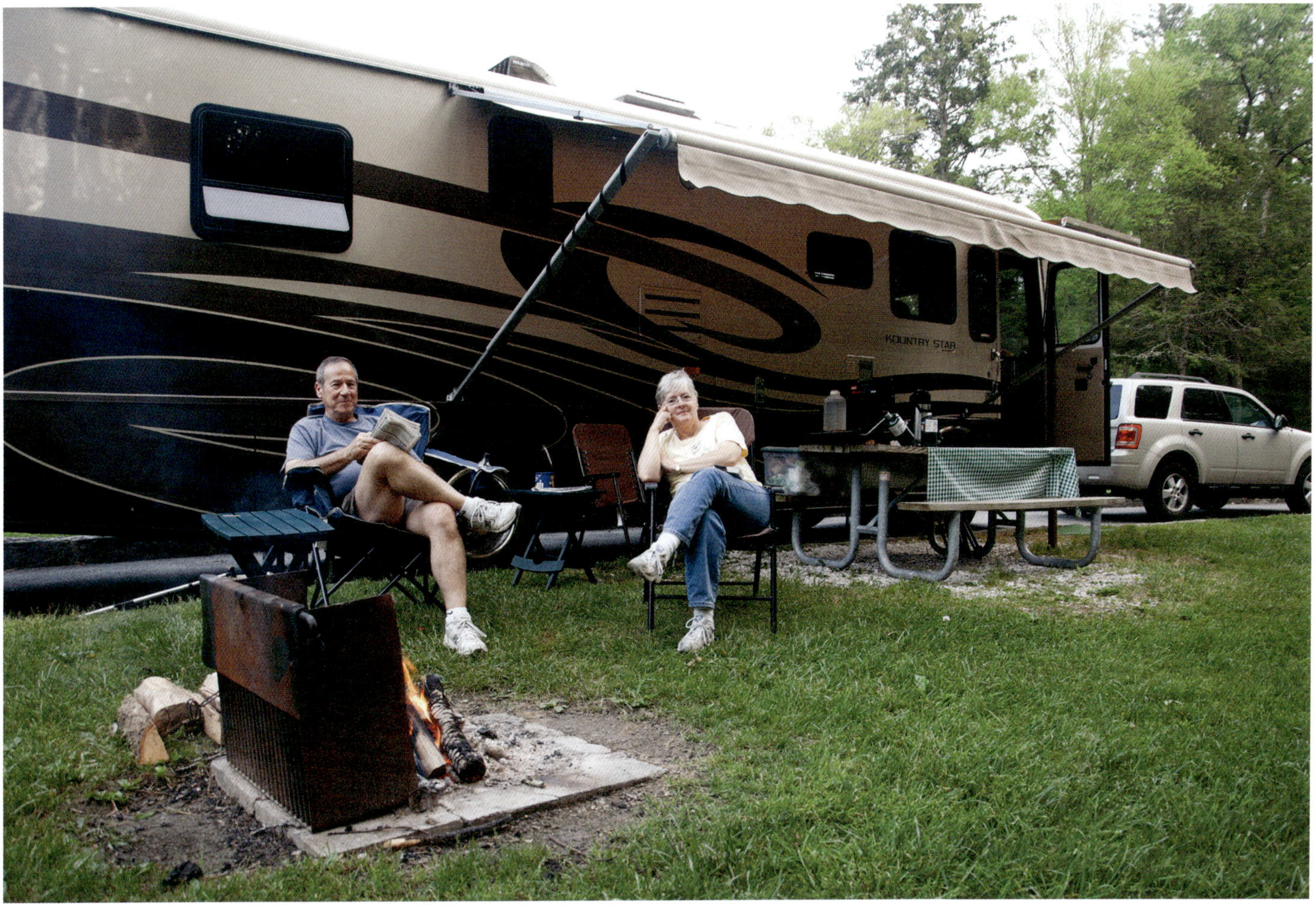
KOUNTRY STAR

I'D BEEN AT BELLE FOURCHE, THE GEOGRAPHICAL CENTRE OF AMERICA. It was flooded. The flags of every state were wallowing sodden and sulky, like flatfish caught on mud, in the damp, grey evening light. The streets were worm sided, brown and slick—the welcome flags were blowing backwards, caught by a contrary wind. I guess the reverse of 'Welcome' is 'Go Away'. I was tempted by the 212, the Beartooth Highway running west into the far mountains—but I turned instead onto the Interstate, on instinct I guess. The deluge was the wedding-dress bustle and train of the black storm dancers who had twirled for me yesterday. Their tarantella was beautiful as I watched it, but I heard they got carried away, and killed 90 people in Missouri. The day was grey as death. Out along the road, the misty rain eventually lifted, letting through a thin band of light, burning red and orange as the sun fell into High Plains. In the last of the cold light I came upon Gillette—an impossibly huge hole dug deep into Wyoming, the earth as black as night. These are the true marks of man on the land, forget the tiny Rushmore Presidents or Crazy Horse carved into Black Hills granite, here we see ourselves revealed. The mine is still small against the high country's vastness, but truly vast on the scale of me. Trains as long as English lanes drag the coal away—to fuel America. On a cat's cradle of conveyor belts it's hauled across the road to waiting furnaces, trading its ancient life for lights in the night. Long shallow pools show the strip mines by the road, reflecting the coldest, coldest silver I think I've ever seen—an evening entirely without warmth, bone cold, dog tired. The streets of the interchange, though, were bustling with cars and trucks, motel after motel for commercial travellers and migrant workers. "Where there's muck there's money" they say, and perhaps the busyness says that is so here.

A frozen factory town—I can barely imagine how harsh the lives of those who live here are. I remember, still, my own industrial childhood, in a town filled with iron works and fetid green pooled maufacturies. Strangely, I am attracted to places like this, although I hope I will not have to live in one again.

VIEW FROM HOTEL WINDOW—BUTTE, MONTANA

After figuring affluence and poverty as evidenced by people, Frank presents us with a pair of pictures that demonstrate affluence and poverty in the landscape. *View from Hotel Window—Butte, Montana* images sooty roofs receding between grey, rain-slicked roads, the whole outlook framed by grubby hotel voiles. This work holds, in silver nitrate, the sooty heart of industrial America. This is, interestingly, the first image in *The Americans* without any people.

Frank's view is taken from a high window. The dirty net curtains create a misty impression, echoing the smoke escaping from the engine house and the smog of this coal-fired, wintry city. Frank has photographed Butte in shadow on a dull day, the flat light exposing this miserable aspect of the functional, jerry-built town. The grey day is an analogue to the factories, flat industrial roofs and derelict land. Frank's high vantage point reveals the coal heaps, winding gear and slag tips.

Frank's image relates interestingly to one taken by John Collier for the Standard Oil Picture File called *Crested Butte, Coal Mining Town* (1948, Standard Oil archive, University of Louisville). Collier's image looks along a sunlit high street at a small collection of buildings. Behind them, verdant hills rise into a wispy-clouded sky. A silhouetted bell tower points the viewer heavenwards to the glory of summer. There is no evidence whatsoever of mining, despite the title. The road is a dirt track and the buildings are made of planks and corrugated steel, but there are no winding houses or slag tips in sight.

Frank, in his response to images from Standard Oil's Picture File (Day 2011: 113), seeks to see beyond the polemic to the actuality of the world before him. He examines the smile of Uncle Sam, pictured on the faces and landscape of America, and finds "what is invisible to others—the look of hope or the look of sadness" (Frank, in Maloney 1958: 115). As Frank had planned in his Guggenheim application, he found and recorded

> the things that are there, anywhere and everywhere—easily found, not easily selected and interpreted. (Frank 1954, in Greenough 2009: 362)

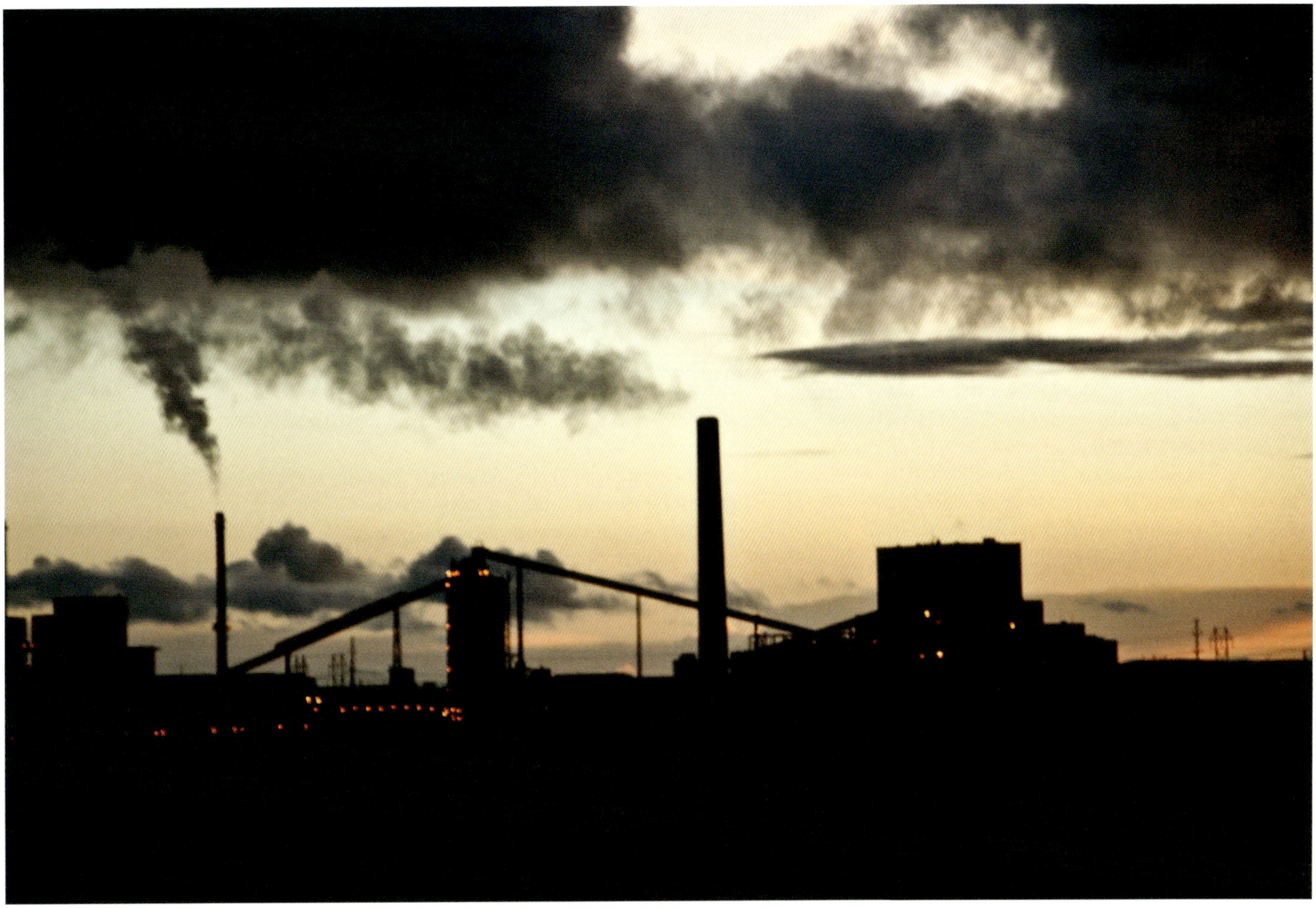

MAGAZINES AND BILLBOARDS ARE NOT A THING OF THE PAST. Print is buoyant, despite all the no-longer-new media. But the 50-years-on city scape is different, especially in Europe and America. The almost unimaginable profits extracted from a hungry for development world by the Eurocentric nations in the 20th century paved the Western cities and erected their monuments to modernism and the American way. Where did the money go? Because it is certainly gone. No more towers of white dressed stone, or aluminium griffons, staring the future in the eye. Pre-fabrications for the West now, as the money goes into the builders' pay—look to China or Malaysia or Dubai for architectural extravagance, where the workers are shipped in on tiny wages, and even that is sent off home. Hoardings now are lit from within, shimmering things, even if the messages remain as mundane. How do we fit, naked, human, within this technological world? So much of it beyond our understanding, alienating, estranging. Are these modular buildings and moving signs, though, any more alien than Frank's 50 years ago Metropolitan Life Building and serried ranks of magazines? For me they are—colder, less caring, less humane. I am warm, red and naked, against the cold silver silence of their possible tomorrow.

METROPOLITAN LIFE INSURANCE BUILDING—NEW YORK CITY

After the cold and dirty landscape of Butte,Montana—stuck by mines, sullied with slag heaps, a place as ratty and unwelcome as the strayest of dogs—we turn the page to another landscape, this time recording the *Metropolitan Life Insurance Building—New York City.* Instead of grimy curtains and streets on an overcast day, we see a multitude of windows set into the curves of a dove-grey building, many of them reflecting the brilliance of this very different day. In the foreground are a streetlight and a news-stand, the latter featuring a copy of *Bazaar*, the magazine that was formerly Frank's employer. Other titles are there too: *See*, *Paris Life, Art, Man's, Western, Seventeen* and *Companion.* The serried ranks of magazines visually echo the rising tiers of windows in the building behind. This is a tongue-in-cheek autobiographical photograph, its message contained in its title; this is the metropolitan life of New York, which was for so many years Frank's home. We noted earlier Frank's acknowledged dislike and eventual rejection of his work as a magazine photographer. He disliked the idea of 'hack' photojournalism, intent on the pursuit of notoriety and the security of money:

> I also wanted to follow my own intuition and do it my way, and not make concessions—not make a *Life* story. That was another thing I hated. (Frank, in Janis and MacNeil 1977: 56)

His implication in this photograph's amusing juxtaposition of ranks of magazines with ranks of windows in the four-square building is obvious: work for a magazine if you want the security of metropolitan success and acknowledgement. That life, though, can only ever be a half-truth—affluence in downtown New York rides on the back of poverty in Butte, Montana, but you could spend a lifetime never noticing that. The yin–yang interdependency of these landscapes, most interestingly, is not simply material but aesthetic, the sooty functionality of Butte highlighting the city's confident solidity. Be careful, though, as knowing the truth also carries a cost. It's a journey from which there can be no return.

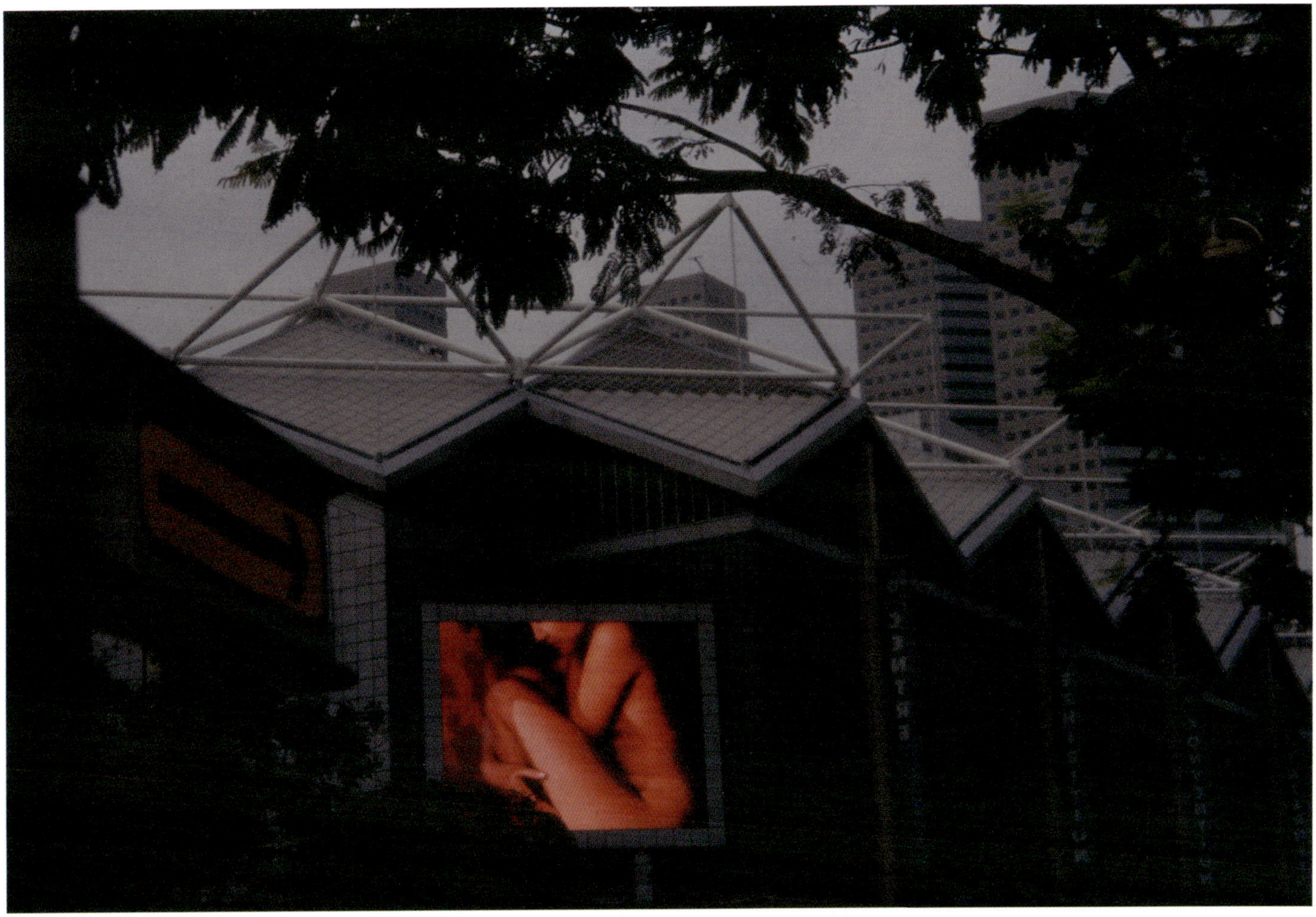

SALT LAKE CITY. After the cold, damp greyness of a Jackson Hole Rocky Mountain night and the glorious cloud-cut cerulean of the snow-floored, storm-blown-itself-out following morning, the place cascaded as the freshest, brightest, white-buildings-piling-down-a-mountainside town. The sense of pioneers is palpable, as the opal farms tumble down towards the Great Salt Lake. How it must have been to travel all this way on a horse drawn cart. I can really see why Brigham Young thought this must be a divinely appointed place. There are a lot of Mormons here, evidenced by billboards cursing 'Creationism' and extolling the joys of marriage (same sex? Perhaps not), pre-marital abstinence and opposing abortion. Along the eastern lakeshore the land rises slowly towards the mountains in a slow, fertile arc. At the apex, as the steep mountain terrain takes over, are a string of white, cathedral-like churches, shimmering pearl like in the afternoon light. A soft wind off the water against the bright sun on the day I drove through was ecstatic. A fantasy place, a new-feeling creation, much like the old that inspired it but displaced somehow, almost faux perhaps. The Mormon Cathedral high above the road, like Tolkien's white tower of Ecthelion, was snapping its banners in the breeze. It has such self confidence, such a solid self belief, like a bit of imagined England; picket fences, lawns and lanes somehow translated to a landscape almost lunar-strange. The Great Salt Lake is like a sea, and the shore a beach. The salty, ozone fresh wind blows onto and freshens the town. Westward, the sea abruptly ends in salt marsh fading quickly into dirt and sand and desert—in short it's an illusion, mountain surrounded, inland, of a remembered European strand, as the strip of towns is somehow an illusion, cross bred in memory from idealised mythical cities, somewhere between England and the sky. What intrigues me most of all is the extent to which these imaginings have been successfully made real: there are real social differences here, although I was too fleet footed through the place to attempt an analysis of what they are.

Appropriately, ironically, on the high stilt highway's side, an advertising hoarding boasts the date of the end of the world. May 21st, foretold by a prophet of the air (97.1 FM, 'The Bible Guarantees It'). Cry mightily unto God it exhorted me. As I drove by on the 26th, the world had the appearance of remaining. "Only the Earth endures" said the wisdom of America's former tenants. I heard later that the radio prophet declared a delay to Armageddon—when this postponement also passed, it became some kind of 'spiritual ending', followed finally by resignation—from the station. But his moment lives for ever now, emblazoned across these God fearing hills, his memory in pixels and chrome dots per inch, world without end, Amen.

JEHOVAH'S WITNESS—LOS ANGELES

Moving on now from the juxtaposition of poverty and affluence that had occupied him through the last several images, Frank chooses to reinforce his critique of magazines in case we might have missed the point. The next image features another magazine, this time emblazoned 'Awake!' It is in the hands of a *Jehovah's Witness—Los Angeles*, who is standing alone in front of the dove-grey stones of just such a building as was depicted in the last photograph. Away from the massed throng of photojournalistic output, of whatever shade, that filled the previous image's newsstand, we see this less commercial, cheaper publication, carrying this uncertain older man's faith. The image ascribes little nobility to the Witness, its tilted perspective rendering him somewhat foreshortened. He seems apologetic, even threatened, perhaps. Nonetheless, his cheap and tawdry looking publication is an aspect of his sincerity: he certainly isn't doing it for the money.

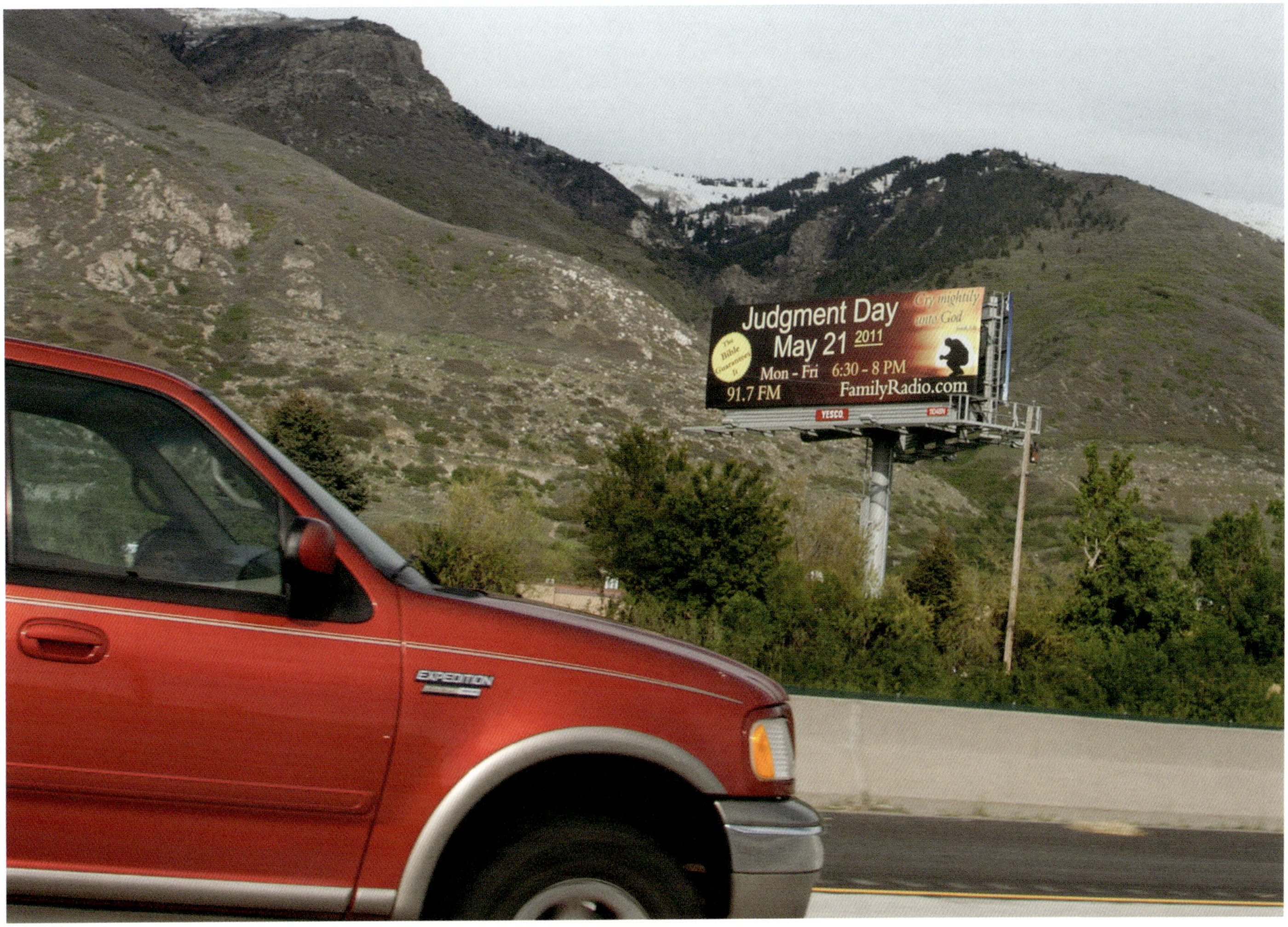
Judgment Day
May 21 2011
The Bible Guarantees It
Mon - Fri 6:30 - 8 PM
91.7 FM
FamilyRadio.com
Cry mightily unto God
YESCO
EXPEDITION

THE TEXAS PANHANDLE WAS PUNCTUATED with collapsing small towns, empty and eyeless single story buildings, hunkered low down, against the wind—seems people just moved out one day, a while ago in many cases, and these are houses returning to the earth. I especially remember a little filling station, not something preserved or cared for—this is not yet Route 66—just something old. The stench of giant cattle staging stations filled the last of the daylight, thousands of animals bound for burgers and steaks, to be eaten in gaudily advertised road houses everywhere across this state. Not at all appetising. In the distance I saw an otherworld display, something that maybe Christo or Walter de Maria might have dreamed of. Across miles and miles of high semi-desert a thousand red lights flashed on in concert, like a Christmas tree fallen sideways and enormous. As I drew closer, I saw in the darkness industrial scale windmills, each half-illuminated by its own cherry top. In a typically decaying town, I stopped at a single decked-out building, in good repair and well kept. It was filled with expensive nick nacks and a wide range of pecan-based confectionery. The owner was corpulent and over friendly in an unconvincing way: it was her sales ploy, and her hard business head was too visible beneath, not least in the way she spoke to her Spanish American assistants—peremptory, insistent, challenging. A hard bitten woman surviving in a hard bitten land.

BAR—GALLUP, NEW MEXICO

Bar—Gallup, New Mexico is another of Frank's explorations of exclusion and isolation in an apparently sociable place. We saw something similar in *En route from New York to Washington, Club Car* and will see it again in *Restaurant—U.S. 1 leaving Columbia, South Carolina.* These critiques of the American diner stand in stark contrast to the popular images of the day, most notably from the Standard Oil Picture File.

The brilliant coldness of fluorescent light bathes the photograph. The camera seems to be at knee height and the unusual angle of the composition suggests a photograph shot off without using the viewfinder, taken surreptitiously. The only person entirely in view is a cowboy-hatted man. He stands, relaxed yet confrontational, facing a group of figures whose black bulk occupies the right-hand third of the photograph. The picture is redolent of cinematic images of gunfights and Old West saloons, places of threat and fear rather than of welcome and bonhomie. This dark, foreboding place brings to mind Frank's experience "another time, in the South":

> a fellow turned up wearing a big hat. Same question. I say 'I'm looking, I'm travelling around'. He takes a big watch out of his pocket and says to me 'I'm the sheriff, you have one hour to leave town'. We think that only happens in films. (Frank 1991: 63)

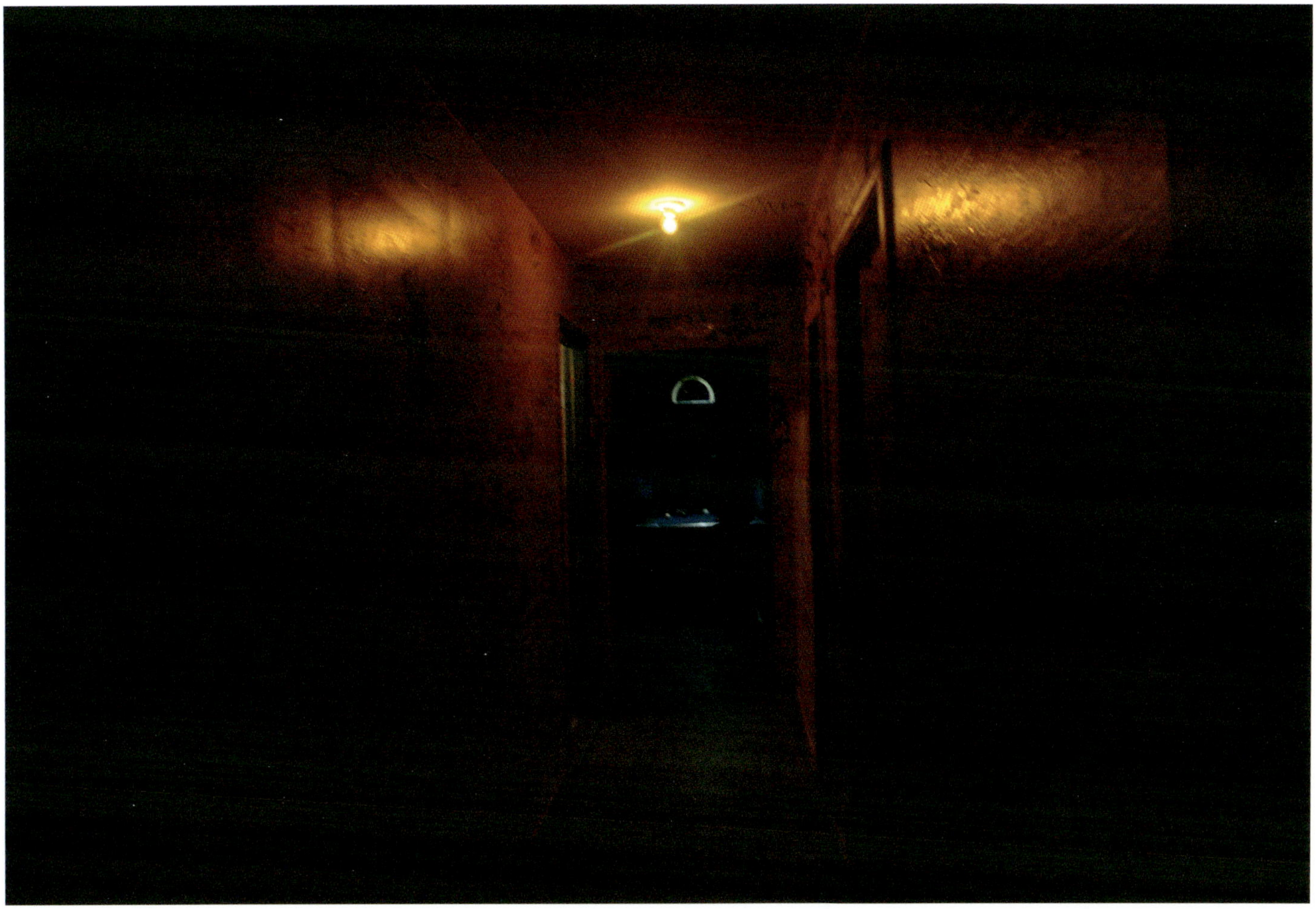

INTO THE WIDE FIELDS, WONDERING WHAT I'D FIND. The low Northern cloud blanket cleared as I rolled South, the country turning pasture green, no longer broken brown by the plough. Rolling low green knolls, azure pools sparkling in the sunlight... birds whose shapes and sizes are familiar, but their colours! A blackbirdish one, darting orange headed and white winged, a Scarlet Tangier, brilliant body against black wings. A Baltimore Oriole, sulphur yellow head and tail, barred with black. And my constant companions, the dainty and absorbed Red Winged Blackbirds. I think I've made it to Kansas at last—just looking for the yellow brick road.

I've eschewed the interstate for the two lane. Driving at 70 through the wide, wide land I seem always to be slowing down and down until I'm cruising in a five knot boat though an endless, kind green ocean.

The heat and the vast sky brew a storm between them, and huge curtains of charcoal waltz around the plains. Sometimes their sodden skirts pass within yards, at others they darken half the distant horizon. Lunch in Mill Town, in Bob's diner. Filled with local girls, some taking a lunch break away from their farms, some working half-heartedly with the food. One girl, gorgeously prettied by her smile, shouts 'Hey fence guy...' from the t-shirt on her back.

U.S. 30 BETWEEN OGALLALA AND NORTH PLATTE, NEBRASKA

What is remarkable about *U.S. 30 between Ogallala and North Platte, Nebraska* is how entirely unremarkable it is. It is one of a subset of four pictures all imaging the great American interior, the huge expanse of largely featureless country which is the hollow heart of the country. Mostly now these are called 'Flyover States'. The photograph depicts four houses, a telegraph pole and a letterbox on a prairie, seen from the road.

The American Dream requires the notion of travel. If its end is a chimera that cannot be reached, then it must always facilitate and invite further exploration, if the dream is not to die. Along the sides of the everyday, pragmatic road, on hoardings and store signs are dreamed the painted promises of glamour, beauty and excitement, somewhere outside in America. Frank in *The Americans* to an extent embraces this mythology, as we will see most noticeably in *U.S. 285*, later in our journey. His friend Jack Kerouac, after all, wrote *On the Road*, which remains the measure by which all other road texts, photographs and movies are judged. Frank's espousal of this automotive version of the dream is not entirely uncritical. In this image he shows us the uneventful everyday of these isolated plains dwellers. At other times he looks askance at the American Dream and, for a moment, beneath its glittering mantle, glimpses a cloven hoof.

European travellers before Frank had mostly marvelled at the American highway. Some saw the road as the defining aspect of American culture. Only a year before Walker Evans' *American Photographs* was published, the Russian writers Ilf and Petrov commented:

> America is located on a large Automobile Highway. When we shut our eyes and try to resurrect in memory the country, we see before us not Washington, not New York, not San Francisco, not hills, not factories, not canyons but the crossing of two roads and a gasoline station against the background of telegraph wires and advertising billboards. Roads are one of the most remarkable phenomena in American life. (Ilf and Petrov 1937: 76)

Wolfgang Koeppen, in his *American Journey*, so closely echoes Frank's account of the car that his work could serve as a summary of its role in *The Americans*:

> This garden wrested from the wilderness seemed to be inhabited less by humans than by automobiles. Motor vehicles dominated the landscape, stood in flocks before each house, camped in forest clearings, promenaded along the rivers, had their own drive in restaurants and theatre in the open field, their own hotels and huge immensely melancholy cemeteries. It was the automobiles that seemed to be lords of this continent. (Koeppen 1959: 45–46)

While the road may serve as a signifier of journey, associated with concepts of time, space and longing, Frank is intent on interrogating Koeppen's 'lords of this continent'. He examines the Americans' automobile existence and watches their rites of passage, with the car as conduit. We will encounter far more pithy and overtly critical images than this one, but it can serve as a beginning.

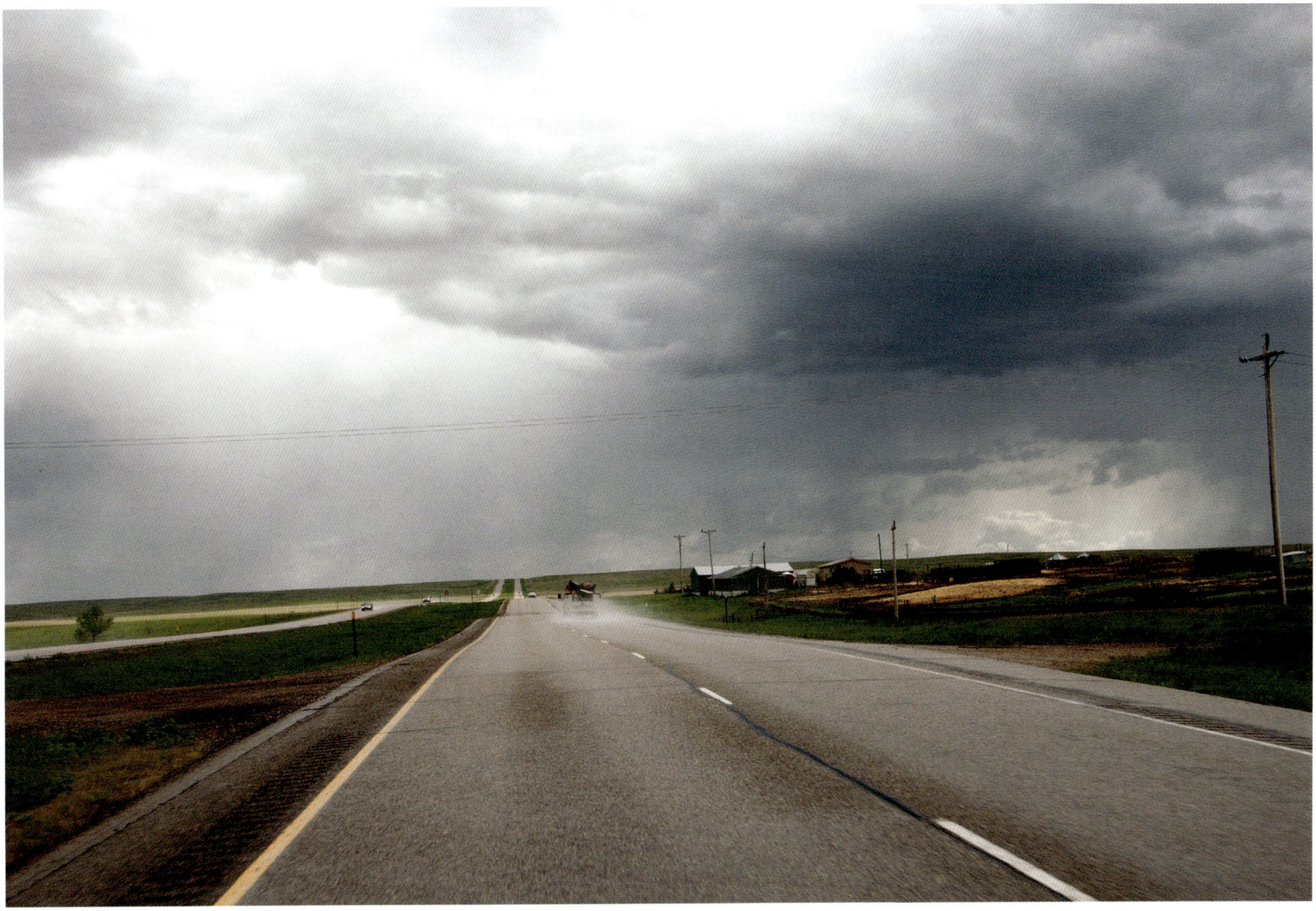

LEAVE ON A PENCIL GREY RAINY MORNING, out through the prairie reserves and the sodden peat black fields, past Ortonville with its carefully preserved four square western frontages. On a field exactly like the hundred others, a bald eagle is worrying the roadkill corpse of a coyote. In the grey light its stark, startling monochrome is diluted in the rain, everything sucked clean of colour. On then to Watertown—more of the same—foursquare old West, two lines of store frontages facing each other as if to shove away the yawning vastness which engulfs them. Walking down those short streets, the only dominantly human space in the wild, wide spiralling of prairie. Less well preserved than Orton, it's wreathed already by the wind, an intuition of the wild to come, blowing through its streets—still with half an eye, though, on the 'civilised' East, hunkering down against the prairie storms. Talking with a storekeeper, half Dakota, he exhorts me to respect the graves, and wonders why on earth I would come from England to here. In parting he calls me 'brother' and I thank him for that. The casino is on Indian land, their small flag flying behind the neon, flapping without illumination in the rain.

CASINO—ELKO, NEVADA

This short series of images were all taken in the great heartland. If America were a body, then most of it would be skin cells, millions clustered around the coasts. You can wade inland from the sea through ranks of houses sometimes two or three states deep, sometimes a single ribbon development of luxury retirement homes miles from anywhere, appropriately like death. But if you want any wilderness around the edges, better look to the National Parks and Forestry Service and their vestigial 'Heritage Coasts', preserved for those who need an end in sight, whether mountain or foreshore, river bank or forest wall. People thin out the nearer to the centre you drive. There are mountain range anomalies for sure, the Rockies, Sangre de Cristo or Big Horns/Black Hills, with their attendant civilizations built on minerals or skiing or holiday homes. The wide, flat, hollow heart is empty, pretty much: high plains for the drifter and miner and the Native born. Elko is a small town on the US 80 running from Salt Lake to Reno. It's cradled in the midst of a hundred mountain ranges, each rearing out of the sagebrush desert, only to fall into the rear view and be gone. It was refreshing being there, a high place after the heat of the salt plains, and a wind scoured night in Wendover, where the howling air rattled my cabin and shook the windows. Shook them so loudly that had I been a believing man, I would have sworn I heard a spirit voice, most likely one from *Scooby Doo* or Disney's *Atlantis 2*. The Elko Casino was unremarkable, but the shop ladies in a Cowboy outfitters were pleasant. An enormous flag blew over everything and its snap in the mountain wind answered that perennial question—why do cowboys sing?

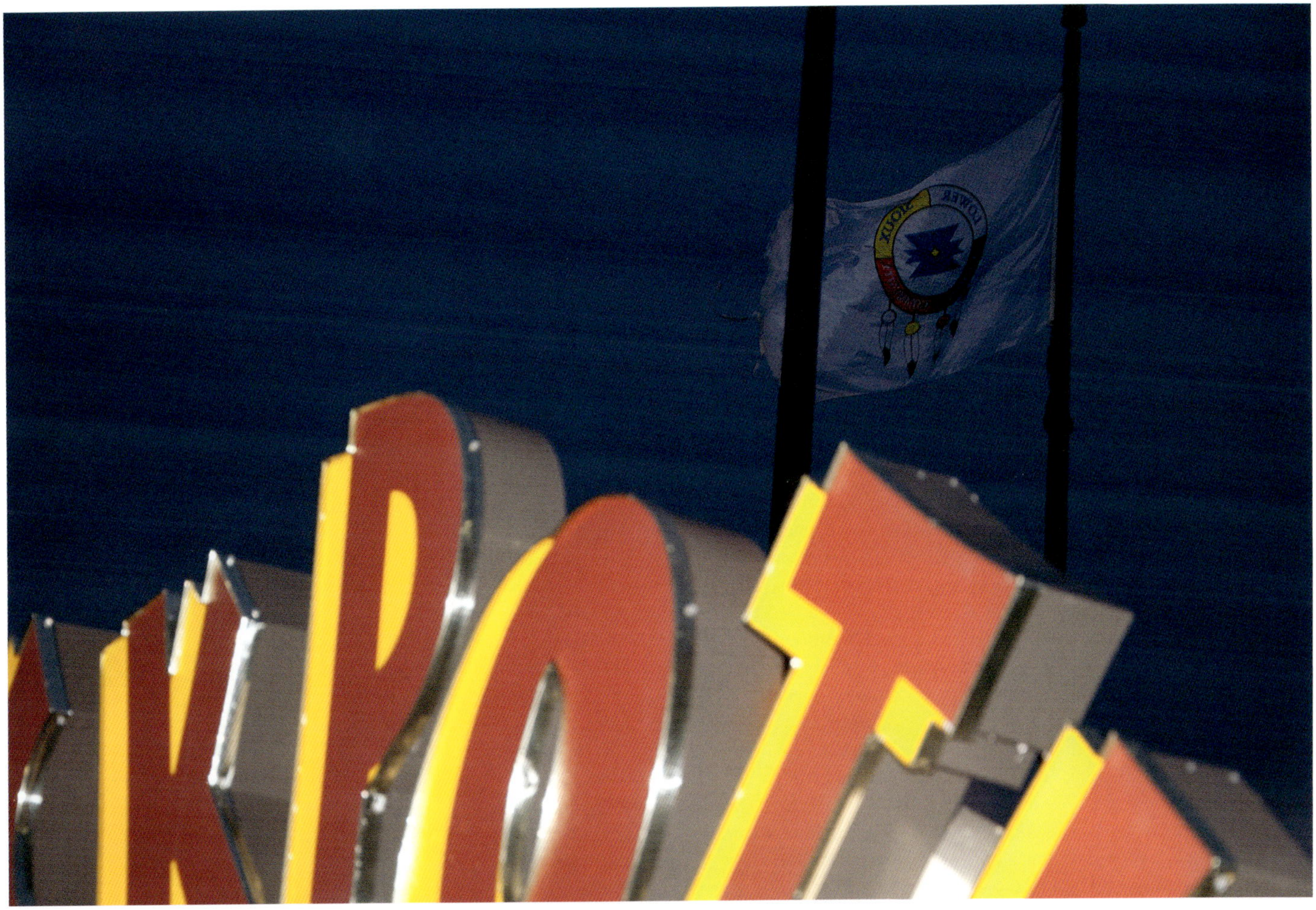

OVER THE HIGH SNOW FILLED PASS AND OUT FROM THE CENTRAL ROCKIES RIDGES, into the wave after wave of mountains that flank it—the temperature is rising courtesy of the sun and falling altitude. Little towns and miles of rangeland, remarkable rock outcrops striating the land. Out of the hills, eventually, and into Idaho Falls, a nondescript town, neither squalid nor notably swish. Fastfood, pharmacies, thrift stores, agricultural machinery. Along the freeway towards Blackfoot I drove over a lava field, geometric columns collapsed chaotically all around. Rarely have I seen the contrast between a roadway and the land so remarkable.

Blackfoot, Idaho is a town Frank visited. One of the hundred or so places I've mulled over and dreamed about. And, in that way, it has romance for me. I felt it for real in the lonesome whistle-blow of an enormous locomotive, matching me step by step on rails running along the street, but in little else. Frank when he was here had hitchhikers gunning his car in the semi-darkness. No hitchhikers for me, this bright and refreshingly warm afternoon. Two servers in a thrift shop drew me in and stood in the hitchers' places. They called it a one horse town, a hole in the wall, seemed happily unimpressed. There is a heavy emphasis on potatoes here—Potato Capital of America, apparently. Frank was following his own dark purposes, and left the unavoidable Potato Museum entirely unpictured. In that refusal to play the tourist, he found instead a photograph which pictures a universal: the beating blood passion of early maturity, the desperate rush and ambition for something, even if we don't know exactly what it is. Dowdy, homely, potato loving Blackfoot: for me for so long you were a place of dreams.

U.S. 91, LEAVING BLACKFOOT, IDAHO

U.S. 91, leaving Blackfoot, Idaho pictures two intent young men, wide-eyed and fresh-faced. They stare through the car's windshield at the road ahead. Their expressions suggest intensity of purpose, a full engagement with the issues and concerns of their lives. They are racing to meet their tomorrow in some small town, some diner or at some crossroads. The exterior world is burned out, brilliant white against the shady intimacy of the interior. This again describes the vehicle as a version of home, an extension of the dark warmth of womb or bed, the red comfort of the inside of our eyes. Unusually for *The Americans*, we know the story of this image. Kerouac, in his introduction, wrote:

> Robert picks up two hitch hikers and lets them drive the car, at night, and people look at their two faces looking grimly onward into the night ('Visionary Indian angels who were visionary Indian angels' says Allen Ginsberg) and people say 'Ooo how mean they look' but all they want to do is arrow on down that road and get back to the sack—Robert here tells us so... (Kerouac, in Frank 1959: 6)

The image does not seem to have been taken at night, but the intent hitchhikers are familiar. This mode of travelling was popular with Beat Generation artists, and has remained controversial, retaining an image of recklessness and danger. These intent young Americans seem to echo Kerouac's 'whoopee' as they gun Frank's car into the night, drawing always nearer to the promise of comfort, warmth, food. This idea of the road-as-intoxication was also a theme for Kerouac:

> How that truck disposed of the Nebraska nub—the nub that sticks out over Colorado! And soon I realized I was actually at last over Colorado. I yelled for joy. We passed the bottle. The great blazing stars came out, the far receding sand hills got dim. I felt like an arrow that could shoot out all the way. (Kerouac 1972[1957]: 27)

Frank is considering the energy of young men, their drive, ambition and focus. They are at the wheel in a world dominated by the car, passionately hurtling toward their destiny, minds and bodies engaged in the activity. There is a slight undertone of apprehension in their faces, a barely visible uncertainty. This shadow is entirely appropriate to Frank's purpose. His purposeful, physical-prime driver follows his chosen path with vigour, yet is hounded by the spectre of self-doubt, haunted by the knowledge that his course may be ill-advised and may result, ultimately, in irremediable failure.

U.S. 91, leaving Blackfoot, Idaho, begins a sequence of five images concerned with the iconography of the car. These introduce an extended consideration of new and representative icons of American civilization, which lasts for the next fifteen images.

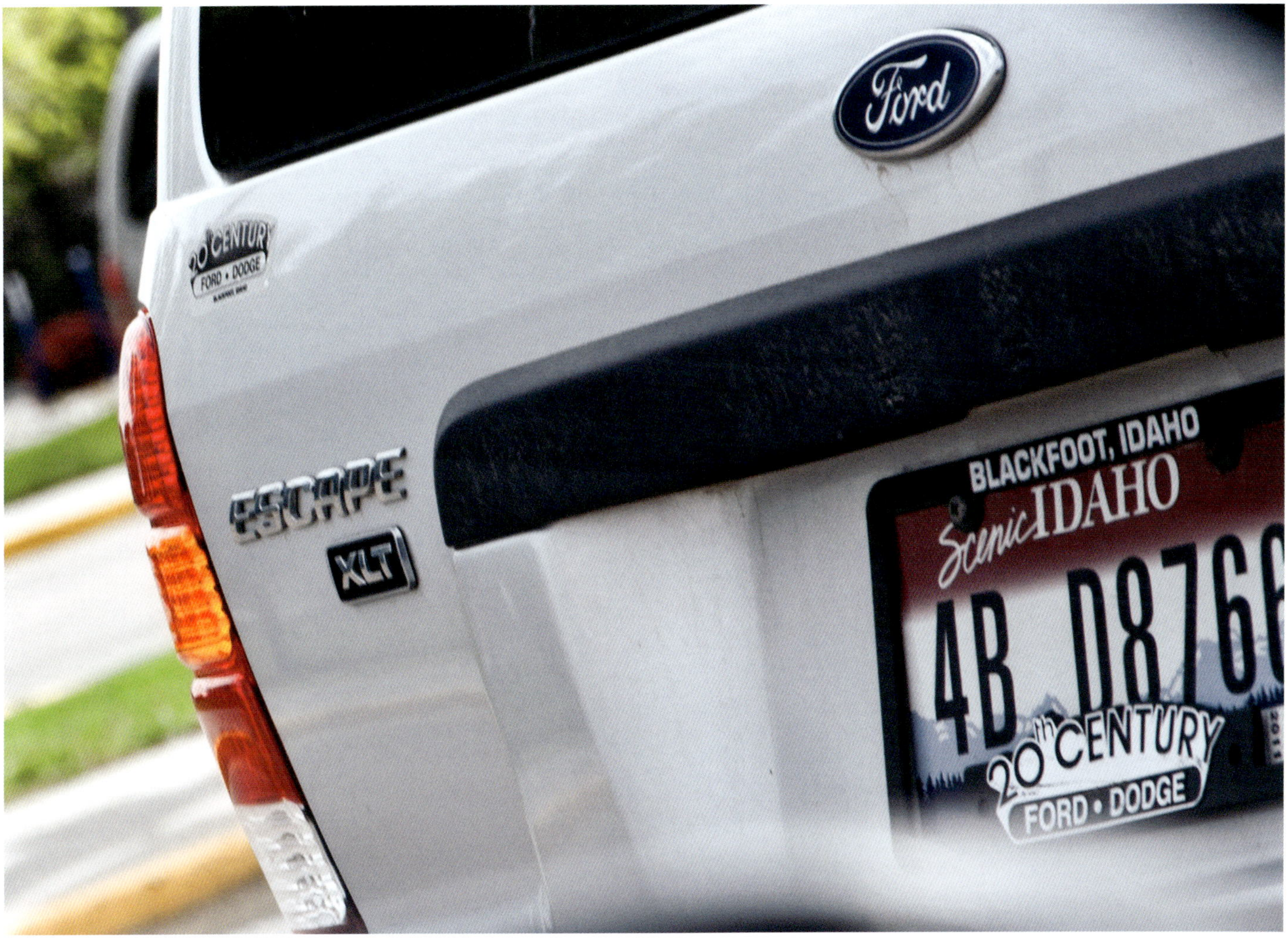
Ford
20th CENTURY
FORD • DODGE
ESCAPE
XLT
BLACKFOOT, IDAHO
Scenic IDAHO
4B D876
20th CENTURY
FORD • DODGE

ASTONISHINGLY QUIET, WITH ONLY ONE LIGHT VISIBLE in the whole wide world, was mile-high Balsam Mountain. Camped up in the gloaming, I lay down to sleep with the last of the light. Woke to the car rocking in the pitch black, thinking a bear was gnawing at my tyres. Couldn't see anything, thought maybe it was the wind. So much has been written about the restorative powers of wilderness: those who believe in it, like Eric Shipton who called it "a sophisticated escape from artificiality" (Dickinson, 1975, 20), through those who don't, like Coleridge, famously standing outside his Lakeland door, hoping in vain that the Fells might lift his depression. I feel renewed here, full of wonder, some deep and hidden place in me stoked to capacity with the will and means to survive. The smell of Balsam is so strongly hued. It's an olfactory reminder of youthful expeditions to the 'wilds' of my local forest, and hung heavy in the Cypress trees which ringed my Grandfather's garden. When he, my true parent, passed, I grieved through that fresh and amber scent. Now another place and time drives that aroma deeper in my heart, another cascade of memories every time it's in the air.

At 6.30 am a National Park's Ranger called Bill knocked on my car—to tell me there was a killer loose. A man shot some people down, yesterday in Cherokee—driving a black Pontiac, armed to the teeth. Rangers had been everywhere, looking. All night in the Great Smokies—just me, a killer and the darkness. All those cinematic moments that I'd laughingly dismissed, *Deliverance* (set just south of here in Georgia) or *The Road*. Could have been a convenient vehicle swap for him...

In the deep peace of Balsam Mountain there were lessons to learn. I cannot stop the frantic Human dance, but I won't fear what has not happened. And don't listen to the radio news—a wonderful wilderness night might have been spoiled, listening for the growl of a Pontiac.

Life is beautiful, but not safe: at least I am able to fight.

ST. PETERSBURG, FLORIDA

St. Petersburg, Florida contrasts the last image's energy with withered old people sitting back-to-back on benches. This is Main Street, Small Town, USA. Above their wizened faces and array of crisp but dubiously tasteful outfits, a long-finned duotone sedan cruises by, blurred by its speed. Is this the vehicle of the intent young men? These ancient Americans lack any of the conviction or urgency of their juniors; their lives have been pretty much lived and their actions have led to this appearance of peaceful passivity. They do not sit in cars; their desire for speed, perhaps, a thing of the past. They are oblivious to the passage of the young, at such a different place in their lives. Kerouac was again inspired to comment in his introduction:

> St. Petersburg Florida the retired old codgers on a bench in the busy mainstreet [...] As American a picture—the faces don't editorialize or criticize or say anything but "This is the way we are in real life and if you don't like it I don't know anything about it 'cause I'm living my own life my way and may God bless us all, mebbe" ... "if we deserve it"... (Kerouac, in Frank 1959: 6)

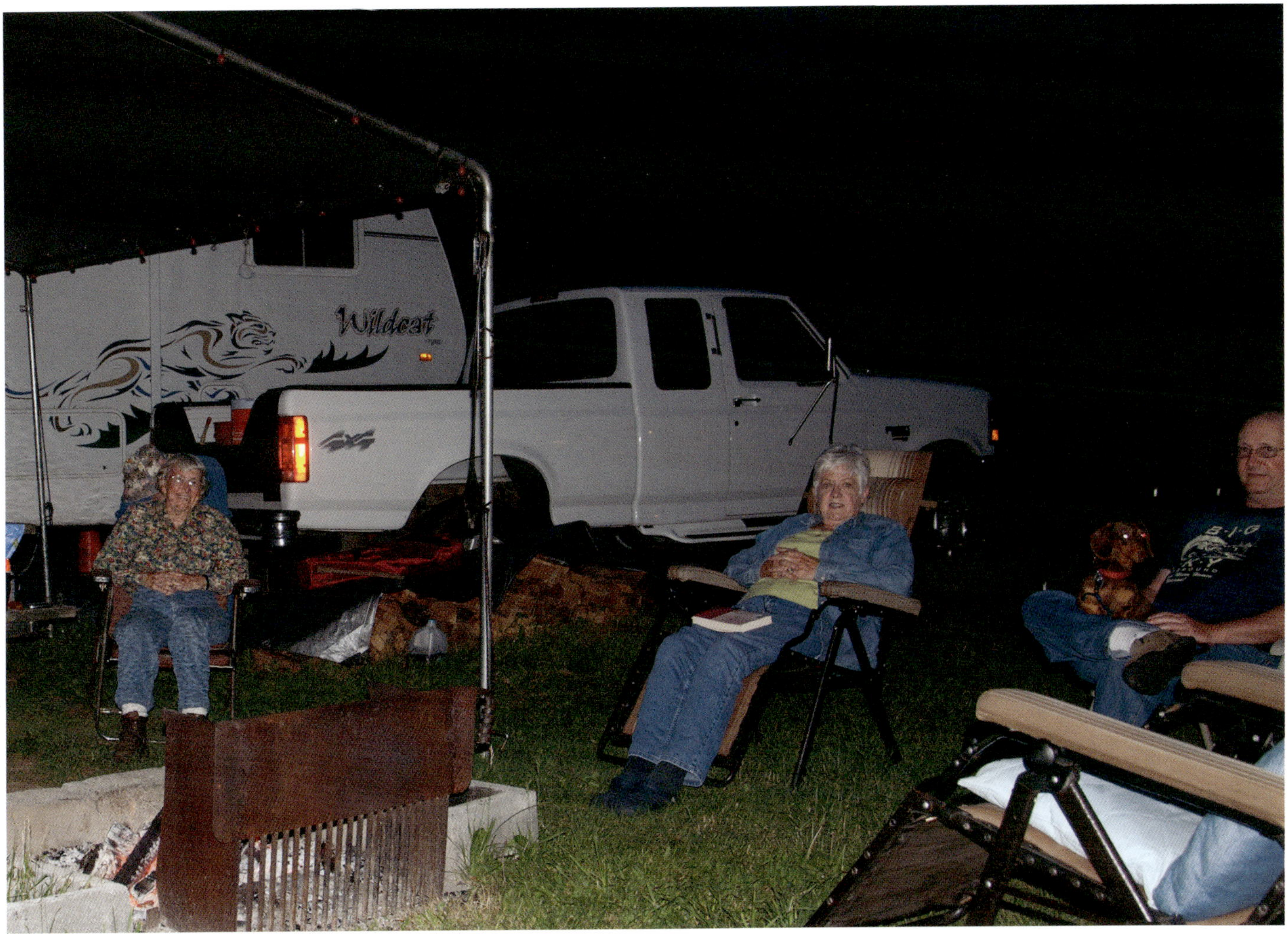
Wildcat

SO JACK'S BOOK, *ON THE ROAD*. Took fifty years to make it to the screen. With Marylou played by Snow White, a former vampire lover. Seems appropriate. *On the Road* and *The Road*, one word of difference and in that word a world and a civilization die. Like Kerouac and Frank, I've driven the filigree and shadows laid like lace across the land. On deep piled roads through salt marsh and estuary. On tarmac laid beyond belief across Idaho's laval plains, where even walking would be a near impossible challenge on the fallen over basalt columns, like a petrified squeeze from a Playdough factory. Along the summits of the Blue Ridge Mountains, high over Shenandoah I've waltzed with stone and mist. Around the world's greatest caldera, primed and smoking, ready to blow, with buffalo, wolf and bear, I've driven through yellow smoke and stone. The Roosevelt and Beartooth Highways, black roadways hidden between ramparts of snow.

Cormac McCarthy's *The Road* is a requiem. A look back in anger at what we lost from where we will soon be. A post-apocalyptic world, more pressing for its lack of narrative excess and refusal to detail the disaster's cause. It rings like Prophecy—no twopenny divination, but in the biblical sense, the declaration of truth. America's lace tracery of roads is rendered a shroud: in a world without fuel, the near sighted survivors are kings.

It's passing now, the world Kerouac visioned, for all our vestigial desire to see it flicker on the screen. Either preserved in aspic, like Tucumcari, or returning to the earth like the Trona Auto Repa., or the Shanty Barber Shop Pop-Inn. Cars are still pouring from the factories, and the greenhouse is stoked by the gas from their rears, but this world is passing, losing its currency. I am delighted, therefore, that you are with me here. And thankful, privileged more deeply than I can tell you, that I was able to see the world that had been laid out for me as a child, before the story of my times is lost in the grass.

COVERED CAR—LONG BEACH, CALIFORNIA

Frank has showed us the prosaic and everyday road through Nebraska, and some of the people who travel on it, and sit beside it, in the last two images. These are, though, a preparation, an *aperitif*, or the tentative first exclamations in the coruscation of a jazz solo.

Covered Car—Long Beach, California is quite possibly the most powerful and most accessible image in this whole collection. It is the apogee of Frank's consideration of the car as a holy object. If we have any remaining doubts about the religious allusions in his book, then *Covered Car* lays them to rest. At the same time, it examines the importance of the automobile for the mature American, living their lives somewhere between the "Visionary Indian angels" and the "old codgers" (Kerouac, in Frank 1959: 6).

A car stands in front of an unimpressive house. It is single-storey, blank concrete with tiny windows and a couple of ventilators in the wall. It could easily be a factory or garage, if not for the number '20' fixed to the door and, further to the right, fastened onto the fence. A small lantern above the number also suggests that this is a habitation. In front of the house two thick palm trees stand, like the columns of a Greek temple. Their leaves meet overhead against the sky, suggesting a portico. Between these trees is a parked car covered with a shining white cloth, either silk or a modern synthetic. The shape of headlights, aerial, roof and tail fins are just discernible beneath the cloth. The car is altar-like, waiting for prayer or sacrifice. It is cosseted in a way that the house is not. If the owner of the car is the owner of the house, as is assumed, then it is obvious which of these objects is their passion. The road and its potentialities represent more than the sedentary, humble house and deserve, therefore, more care, more reverence. All the clamouring voices warning about the mesmerising fallacy of the road/dream have fallen silent before this flowering of full-blown adulation, the car and the road representing, perhaps, the American Dream's most convincing materialisation.

Is it too fanciful, all this reading of religion into a picture of a car? Frank often sought nothing so resolutely as to photograph the indescribable; he was looking, in his words, for "the essence of the black and white, of where God is" (Frank 1991: after plate 63). Can we know with any certainty that he meant the framing palm trees to be portico-like, supplying a temple precinct for the automobile 'altar', complete with altar cloth? The image that follows, *Car accident—U.S. 66, between Winslow and Flagstaff, Arizona*, removes any doubt. Here, beneath a blanket or tarpaulin, on a cold day in the semi-desert, lie the victims of a car crash. It is a dour and sombre image, revealing for us the victims sacrificed on the altar of the car. This is the price paid for mass transit and the much-beloved American desire for the freedom to chase the dream. These two images echo each other compositionally as well, with the long, low shape of the covered car echoed by the covered bodies.

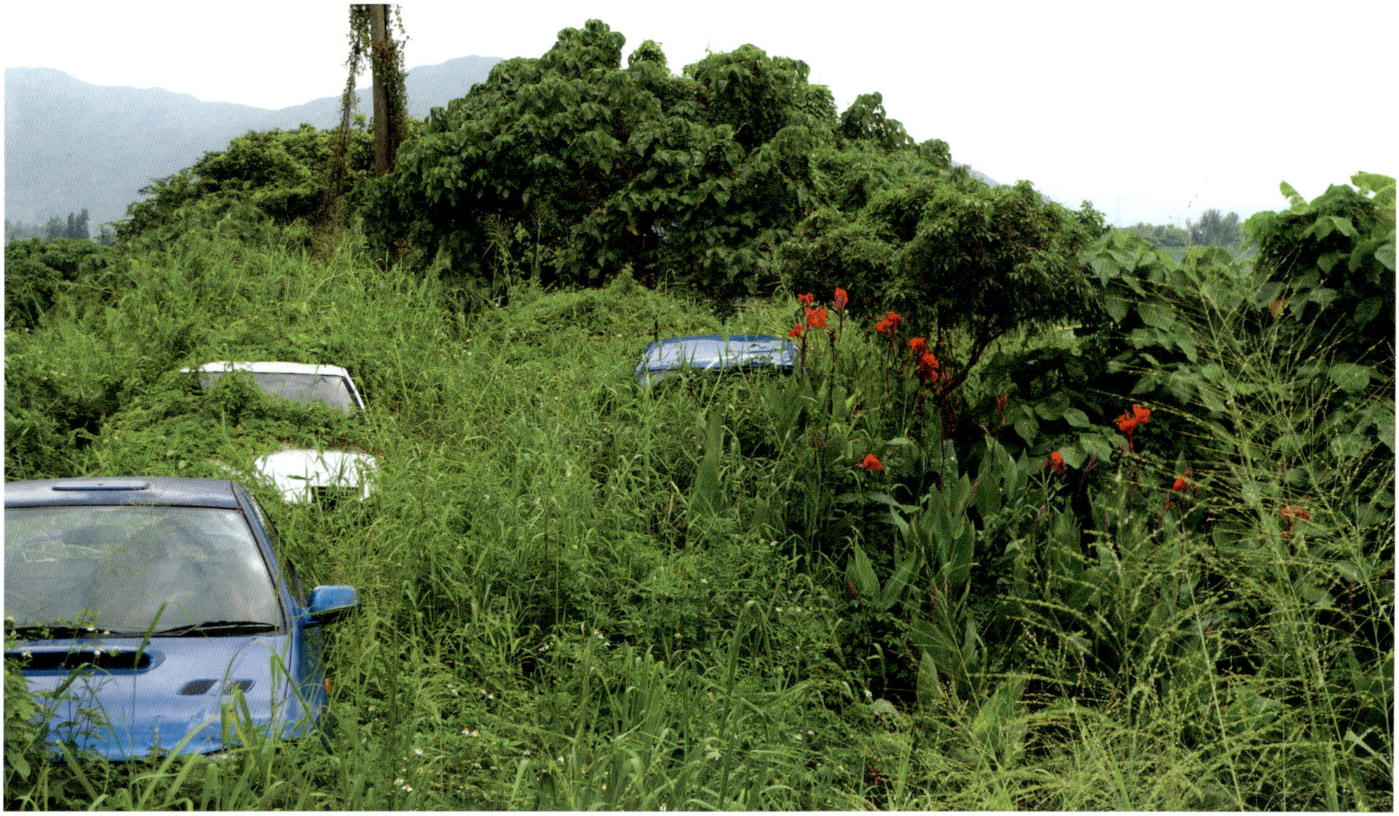

IN THE LAST RAGGED LIGHT OF A STORM-JUST-PASSED SUNSET, I ran into Gillette, perhaps the coldest place I've known. Even the bitter light was fading: it lit strip mine pools that were the touch of icy steel on bone. I should have slept there, but I longed to find some warmth. So I talked myself, against all sense, into one town further along the road. In the darkness, at 75 miles an hour, I saw before me a wide-eyed bemused elk. Wondering at the lights I expect, so far out here in the Wyoming night. As tall as horses, these wild and rangy beasts, tottering on spindly legs, feet in point like ballerinas, barrel bodied, just the right height for smashing through windscreens. It was a brick wall suddenly erected across the road, nowhere for me to turn. I swerved for all I was worth and managed not to roll over… Wham! he hit the front wing and again the rear door in a sickening staccato. I was shocked, frozen, stuck in the moment, needing to stop. I pulled over but was too far along the road to find him, have no idea if he lived or died. I suspect the latter. The air was warmer out and the sky finally clear. High stars burned overhead and a deep peace was on the land. It put me in context—with my still shaking hands, and the nimbus storm of mixed emotion churning in me. Relief? I guess. But much more anger and regret. My death had been averted for now—at the cost of his—and was shelved for another time. The unnecessary injuries to the beast made me sick to my stomach with guilt. The unnecessary injuries to my car, which I was now returning to a workable state (cranking panels off tyres with a jack and tyre irons, bashing fenders back something like into place) made me angry with myself for not knowing better, for not stopping at Gillette.

I made it into Buffalo for the night, and slept strange dreams recovering from the shock. Incredible the way our deep biochemical and instinctual selves get on with things when the constructs of our character are temporarily compromised. I equipped myself for the mountains in this mountain town—camping gas and a percolator, string, all that stuff. I'd made more repairs to the car with clingfilm and scissors from the general store. In the mountains I saw a little along the road a brilliant blue warbler-like bird, landed on a post right by the road. A red tailed hawk stooped on something in the brush. A small group of elk were hesitating in the white-floored forest's skirts, so I stopped and looked at them, thinking of the one left broken somewhere on the Interstate. It's a strange thing, but somehow I felt real connection between me and the deer, in the strange tarantella of life and death in which I am caught. I am the killer, however unwilling, my life saved, even though I failed to save his. It feels like it links me into this place—no more a passer by, a stranger capturing the light trace of lives, without effect. Part of my heart that is so sad for that death, feels locked to this earth, now, until memory and thought desert me. Not a stranger, or a sight-seeing traveller—for better or worse on this land my mark is stained.

CAR ACCIDENT—U.S. 66, BETWEEN WINSLOW AND FLAGSTAFF, ARIZONA

After one of *The Americans*' most immediate images, Frank offers us one of his most intelligible juxtapositions. We all follow a road of sorts, from the door where it began. For these Americans, lying anonymous beneath a filthy tarpaulin in the sleety rain, the journey has come to an end. After picturing an automobile altar, Frank soberly acknowledges the sacrifices demanded by it. *Car accident—U.S. 66, Between Winslow and Flagstaff, Arizona* sees four people standing outside in the rain, cautiously staring at a cloth, covering corpses. The composition unmistakably echoes the preceding image, the palm trees replaced by onlookers, the silk-covered car by tarpaulin-covered bodies. A couple of humble buildings stand in the middle distance, behind them the expanse of America is cut only by telegraph posts and cables. The whole image is of the most melancholy, monotonous grey. Only some of the clothing and the inside of two buildings feature any darker tone. This is in stark contrast to the bright sunlight of *Covered Car—Long Beach, California,* its crisp shadows and saturated tones—sooty blacks and brilliant whites. The certainty of those beach lives, the order and satisfaction of everything in its place, everything protected, contrasts with these random deaths on a grey day, on an unremarkable stretch of highway, in nowhere in particular. American adults cherish their cars and are killed by them: as is so often suggested in the art and literature of the American Dream, they are the victims of that which they love. Frank uses again the style of his pictures to reinforce their theme. The image Frank chose for inclusion is sombre, respectful and reverential: his contact sheet reveals the full random horror and misery of the fatal collision.

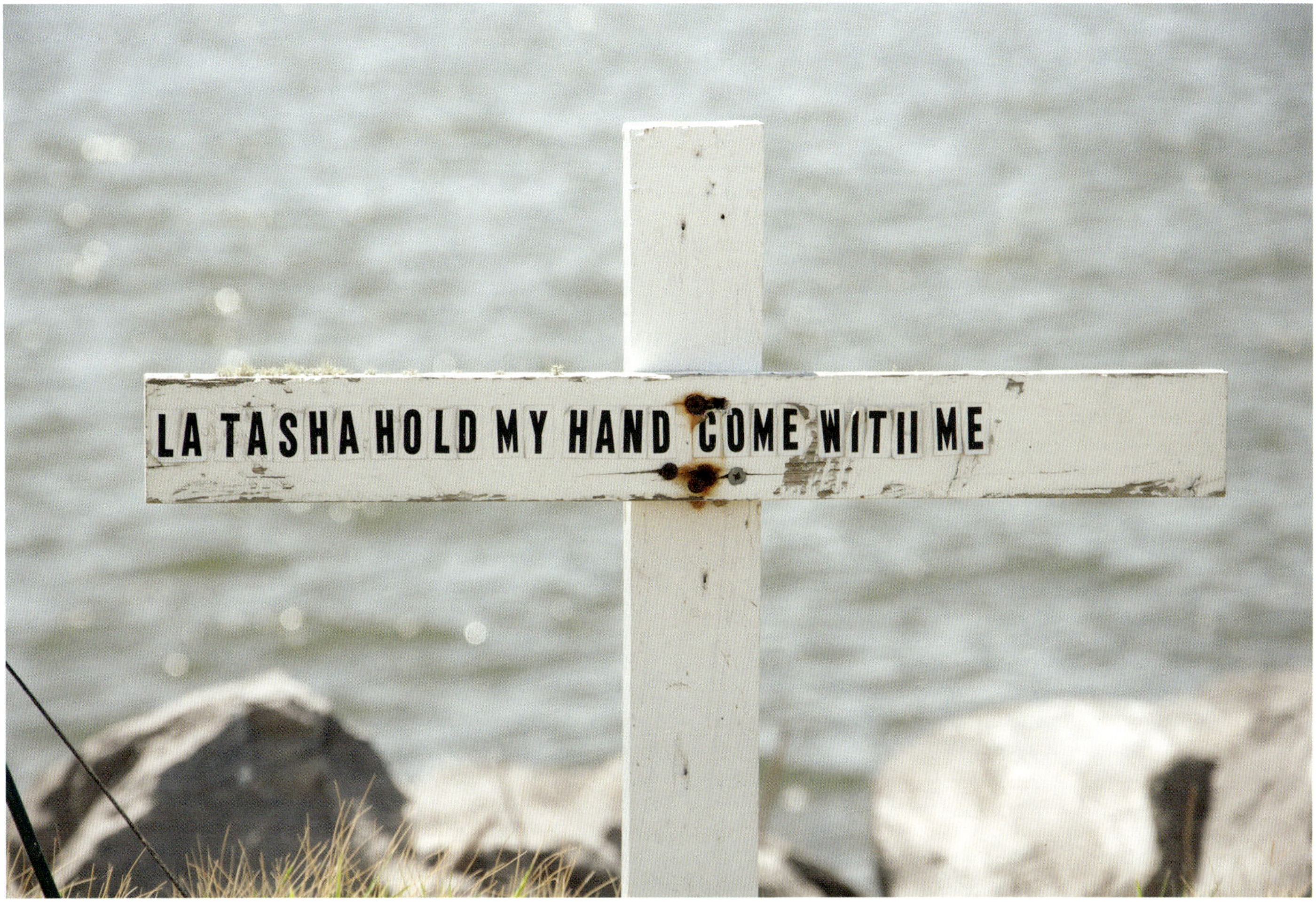
LA TASHA HOLD MY HAND COME WITII ME

I RODE THE LONG MILES OF *US 285, NEW MEXICO* BLISSFULLY, finding another answer to a Frank puzzle. How did he catch on film a silver shining desert road? It is heat haze, an aery mirror makes it shine, alchemically twisted by his black and white into silver on darkness. The time is wrong for me, the haze is fitful in the morning, a light that needs the afternoon. It's fine—I'm not trying to steal his pictures. As always the challenge is to re-vision the image, capture something contingent but in a different way. Sometimes you just can't... Off the road was a collapsing old white painted brick shack. For just a flash I thought I saw the ghost of Standard Oil, so turned the truck around on the hot road and headed back. It was an old filling station, advertising slogans barely visible any more, but for sure it was Standard Oil. The long decayed remains of a white wall tyre lay on the disused turnoff road in front, now buried under vegetation, detritus and dust. I wonder if this was a service road or maybe the original 285? It a lovely moment, a kiss through time into the world of then, the experimental archaeology of my journey. I could almost hear the tread of Robert's shoe in dust, or the cackling laughter of Marylou, wild and lost in the backseat of Kerouac's Cadillac. Are we ever as free as when we are lost?

U.S. 285, NEW MEXICO

Frank described his goal for this journey as "lying in wait, pursuing, sometimes catching, the essence of the black and white, the knowledge of where God is" (Frank 1991: after plate 63). The still-new American interstate network and the wide, wild vastness of America were an appropriate place to look. There is an association between travelling these roads and the spiritual: they are an analogue for the journey we all undertake. *U.S. 285, New Mexico* shows the highway at its most open. Ruler straight, it bisects the semi-desert and the photograph. A tiny car in the middle distance is the only other object in the photograph. This heightens the smallness and impermanence of the traveller next to the monumentality of the road. Light reflects off the tarmac as far as the distant horizon. It bifurcates in the foreground, following the ruts left by tyres. The illuminated road cuts across the dark desert like a highway under some enchantment. It rises in the distance, appearing to point up into the sky. The overtones of a charmed path leading to a bright place, perhaps paradise, appear to be denied by the lowering sky. But there is more—a thin band of light stands between the illusory apex of the road and the dark sky. The light appears almost to leak along the horizon, as if the shining road has punctured the darkness. Is this the promise of the end of the road—Kerouac's 'pearl' or Frank's "knowledge of where God is"? It is literally the suggestion of enlightenment, if only the end may be reached. However uncertain the destination, the road to it is undeniably luminous. Whatever the journey's end may be, the travelling will be along its brightness, riding between darkness to the left and right. This figuring of the road echoes Dorothy's journey along the Yellow Brick Road in the film *The Wizard of Oz* (Fleming, 1939) and F. Scott Fitzgerald, writing thirty years before Frank, who said:

> Out of the corner of his eye Gatsby saw that the blocks of the sidewalks really formed a ladder and mounted to a secret place above the trees. He could climb to it, if he climbed alone, and once there he could suck on the pap of life, gulp down the incomparable milk of wonder. (Fitzgerald 1994[1925]: 118)

Gatsby, like Frank, Kerouac and Dorothy, dreams of paradise at the end of the road. Frank's engagement with this particular road is obvious. It dominates its environment. The entire lower three-quarters of the image are filled with tarmac. The camera angle shows Frank is on this bright road, photographing as he drives. Only the tiny, distant car speaks of others: this photograph's lack of street furniture, with its implication of community, leaves the bare road as the most basic mark of civilization on the wilderness. This is a place of pilgrimage, an appropriate place for a journey of the spirit.

Clearly, the car and the road are powerful icons of American civilization, and they lead easily into the following ten depictions of other icons of American culture.

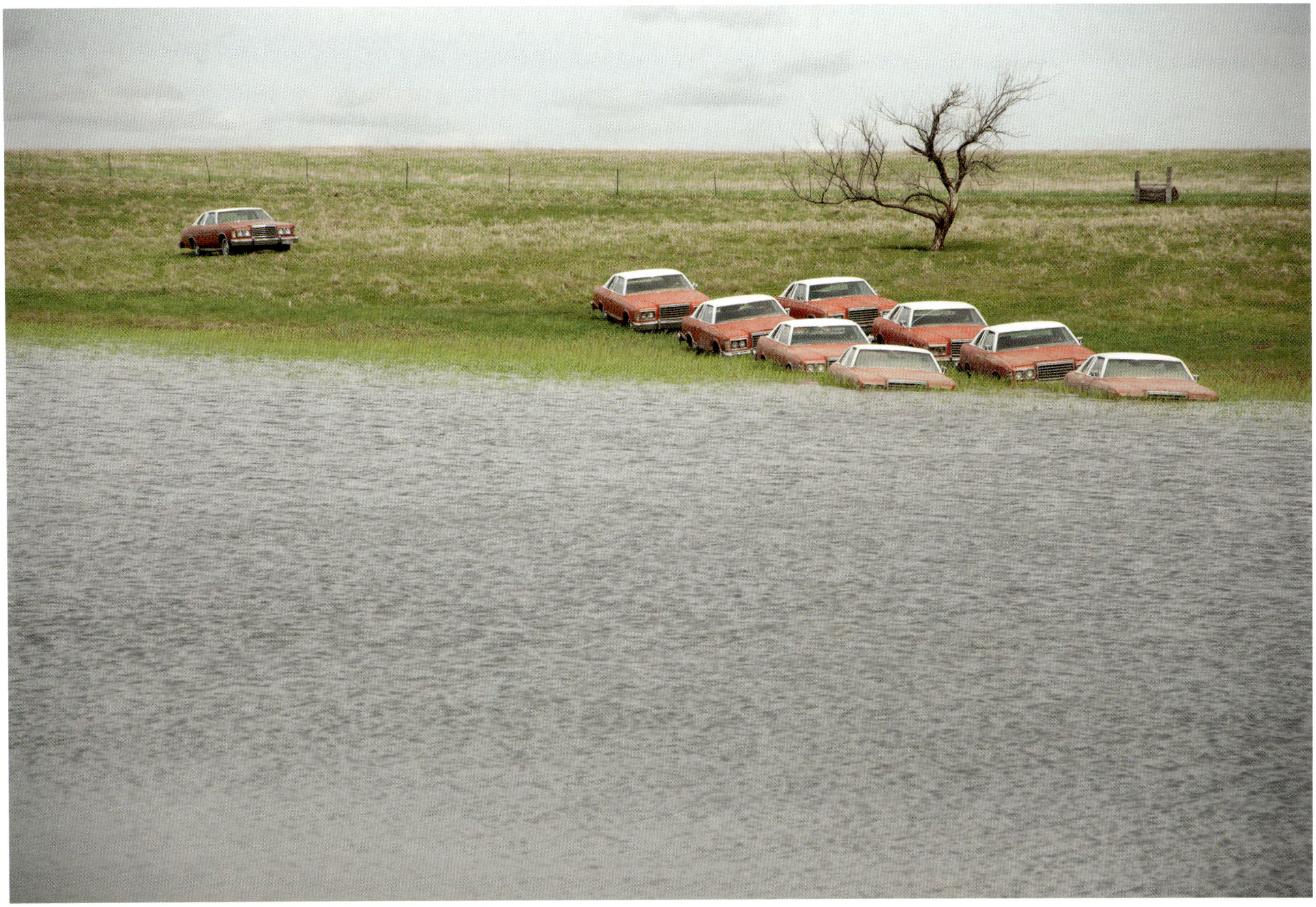

IN THE LATE GREY LIGHT I FOUND A PLACE CALLED WHISPERING PINES. In the cold rain I took a cabin, a tiny one roomed log built shack, with heat but no water. What a warm and happy night I spent there—only to be lectured over breakfast by a T-shirt, explaining why guns are better than women.

Through the craggy ancient granite I followed a sign for Mount Rushmore. I knew what to expect—I've seen *North by Northwest*. So consternation was mine when I turned a bend and the signs changed direction, pointing back where I had come from. How could it be? I hadn't passed a mighty mountain valley, over which the stalwart leaders of a conquering race declared their final and absolute rout of the previous incumbents, at the heart of the vanquisheds' most holy place. So I turned around and finally saw it. Tiny against the mountains (the faces about 18 metres high), nothing at all like I'd imagined. I'd bought the line Hollywood had fed me, with their mighty mock ups in some studio somewhere. Really an archetypal American spin, making so much out of so little.

Bemused, I moved on to the slowly emerging sculpture of Chief Crazy Horse. Conceived as a post-colonial riposte to the Presidents, it is a few miles away, heading south. The Head is clear now on the skyline with some definite work underway, but it doesn't look much different to the time I first saw it on TV, many years ago. Not sure I'm impressed—such a song-and-dance gargantuan effort for what will be quite a small thing, matching Rushmore scale for scale. In relation to the hills themselves? These carvings speak of humble powers and a species in love with an expanded (and unjustified) sense of its own grandeur. The size of the Black Hills puts these little ant works into context. Having said that, the infestation of roads, souvenir stores and cabins is much more impressive. Some geologists are calling our times the 'Anthropocene', when men are deemed the most significant force for change on the Earth. I am undecided, sincerely doubt this is true. If we really are so influential, then it is not carvings and monuments that make it so, but roads, mines, housing estates, aluminium distribution sheds and shopping malls.

BAR—DETROIT

From the wilderness of New Mexico, we plunge straight into *Bar—Detroit*. This is pure *On the Road*, which so frequently juxtaposes the boggling immensity of the American hinterland with just such intimate and human spaces. *Bar—Detroit* is another flag picture and initiates Frank's third notional 'section'. The photograph records the upper part of a bar's wall and some of its ceiling. Central to the image is an illuminated American flag, caught between darkly toned portraits of George Washington to the left and Abraham Lincoln to the right. It is captured in mid-flap, frozen in what appears to be vacuum-moulded plastic. It is illuminated, its warm reassuring heart spotlighted or powered, perhaps, by a bulb burning within. A plaster cornice delineates the ceiling, and faux half-timbering covers the wall beneath the trio of portraits and flag. These architectural details provide a rooting in the everyday world for these airy symbols. The framed portraits embody an older world, one of formality and even decorum. They speak of a serious world in which appropriate *gravitas* is reserved and required for these American founding fathers and inspirational leaders. This *gravitas* contrasts markedly with the illuminated flag—an industrially mass-produced rendition of the Star Spangled Banner. Furthermore, the moulded flag appears to be slowly collapsing, wilting under its own weight and peeling away from the wall. This juxtaposition of presentational modes is powerful and reveals the iconoclasm wrapped up in the industrial consumerist explosion. The old forms, with all their seriousness and immanent value, are ranged alongside the cheap, ephemeral and industrial; both expressions are seen as equally appropriate carriers of American identity. Beneath this trio, a sign saying 'You must be 21 and prove' hangs near to a cartoon-like carving of a fish. Frank is celebrating the facility of the vernacular decorators who created this assemblage. The grandly patriotic, the pragmatic and the utterly kitsch are combined without self-consciousness. The works of the painters' hands and the work of the plastic moulding machine sit together on the wall, both accepted as contributors and representatives of national identity—the icons are given equality by their proximity. These Americans happily hang long-dead presidents next to something more akin to Mickey Mouse. It is not seen as inappropriate: America exists within both these

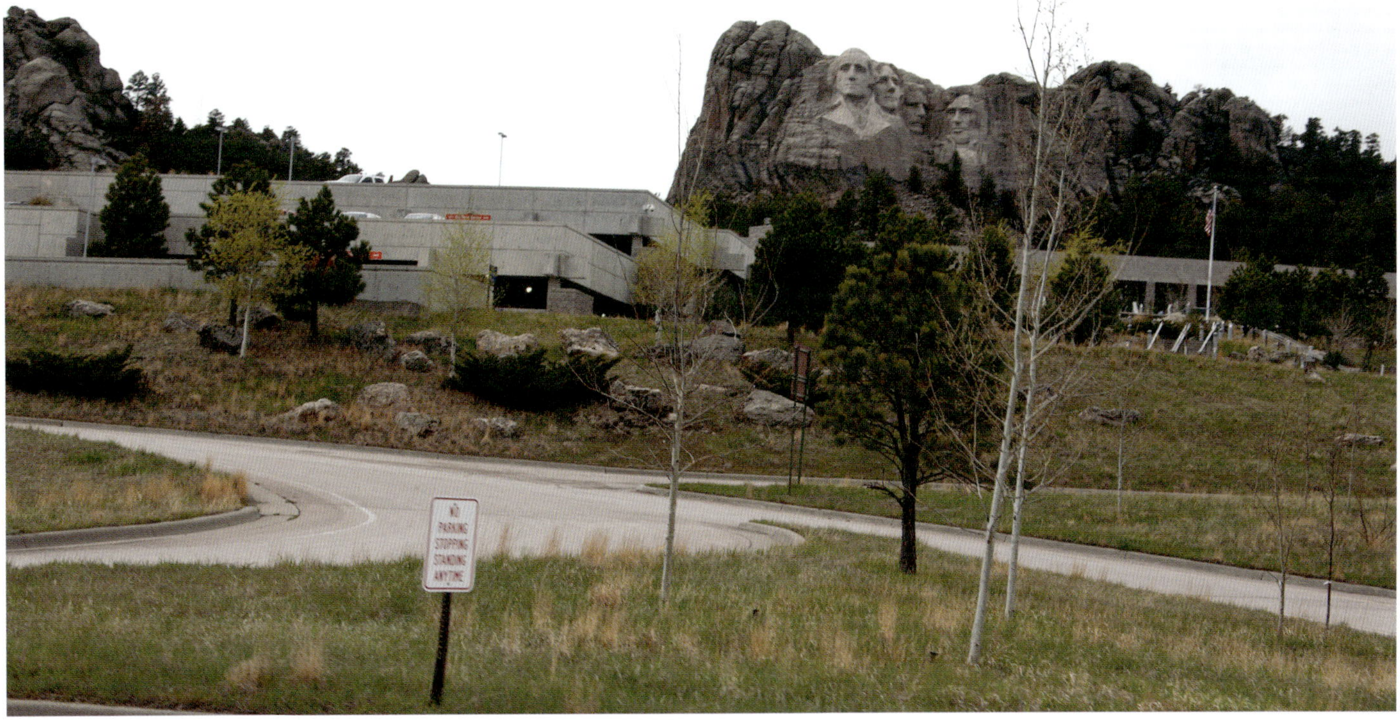
NO
PARKING
STOPPING
STANDING
ANYTIME

visual strophes, and within their relationship to each other. Both are essential to an understanding of this civilization.

Much of the joy of *The Americans* lies in its visual playfulness. I am very attracted to a final possibility within the image. The ceiling of the bar is spangled with spots of light. It is difficult to see how this has been achieved, whether there is reflective material included in the stuff from which it is made or whether some glittering light-source is responsible, but these glowing dots cover its expanse. They fall into the waffle-like pattern on the ceiling's plaster. All of this is reflected in the glass of Lincoln's portrait. The rectilinear pattern and the shiny dots conspire to produce an accidental stars and stripes, not preconceived or intentional, draped around the president like a stole or the aegis of a Greek god. Next to a plastic realisation of the real thing, an architectural accident drapes the president in a self-emanated celebration of nationhood. Manifest destiny in Detroit. I can almost see the ironic smile on Frank's face.

SURPRISED TO LEARN THAT THE FERRY IS CANCELLED—a severe shoaling of the Hatteras channel, apparently, following the storm. What should have been a leisurely hour's drive, with breakfast in the beautiful Chicamacomico—a place that has a somewhat mystical power for me—is now frustrated. Cheese and bacon biscuits, heart attack on a stick, delicious. I retrace, instead, the road back over Roanoke, to Alligator River and take a left into the depths of the river-estuary reserve. The southern East coast of America is an imagination: it barely ever exists. In the place of coast there is a debateable land, more mud than solid earth, melding slowly with the ocean, barely perceptibly becoming water. Navigating this indecisive country is challenging—you could lose a lifetime on the dead-end swamp roads. And that would be no bad thing. In the brilliant Carolinian light, I felt like a Hazardous Duke, hurtling along deserted roads through life so vital and intense it was consuming. The stench of trees and water beneath the brilliant sun, a long black snake sliding across my path. Turtles sunning on muddy banks—what a world of muddy water is theirs, creatures whose shells and skin just about differentiate them from their green and viscous homes. A giant Turkey Buzzard startled up as I turned a corner, its wings huge and bracing against the sunlight. Mile and mile and mile, so much space...

I passed a few fish huts, coming without intention to Engelhard. Perhaps because it's so hidden away, it remains a place in touch with its colonial past. Weathered wooden houses, small porticoed, some white-washed, aping memories of palaces in marble in the old lands. This is not McClellanville, where Frank found his Barber shop, but it is of a piece, a couple of streets in an immensity of forest, one foot in the delta water, one foot on the land.

I like the Engelhard houses, humble in actuality yet grandiose in intention, a statement back to the diasporic homelands, a finger flicked at the things these people were told they could not have, and here, by dint of muscle and will, have cut from this unforgiving place. I like that it has become humble and ironic work, whatever its original intention.

Everything is flooded four or five times each year by hurricanes. These few fields cut out of the swamp oak are, even in this brilliant light, only a little less than waterlogged. The forest cut back beside the road is crouched like an almost sentient thing, waiting to spring forward at the slightest moment's inattention and take back its lost places. The forest misses its children and resents these two-legged upstarts, and their certain to be frustrated, so-temporary civilizations.

Around one bend is a deserted and collapsing barber shop. The Barber Shanty Pop Inn. Rank and rotting chairs inside, creeper covered and bee buzzing, giant bees, bees not to be messed with, long black bodies like treacle toffees, or translucent like liquorice blackcurrant drops. I sense the jaunty Boaters here, bright ribboned once like those on the mourners' heads in Frank's *Funeral—St. Helena.* A busy yet comfortable place for men, full of hair oil tonic, hair nets and bonhomie. I hear so faintly the voices of the ghosts, foul-mouthed and laughing. Driving around the corner, though, they are quickly quietened, becoming suddenly contrite and earnest around the tiny colonial church.

I am in the heart of a delta, here, a place more of water than land—and boats, as Blackbeard knew, are the appropriate way to travel. Soon I will sit and drink coffee beneath Carolina Jasmine and Mimosa at the Ocracoke Coffee shop, which is the Barber Shop renewed, for our co-educational world.

BARBER SHOP THROUGH SCREEN DOOR—MCCLELLANVILLE, SOUTH CAROLINA

Frank claimed many things for *The Americans*. He was trying to "see freshly" and to "speak of the things that are there—easily found, not easily interpreted". He said "This project is essentially the visual study of a civilization [...] carrying its own visual impact without much word explanation." (Frank 1954, in Greenough 2009: 362). These words help us to see his purpose; they tell us his intentions. They are not, of course, to be found anywhere in *The Americans*. Instead, Frank chose to visually communicate his purpose and wordlessly reach his conclusions.

Barber Shop Through Screen Door—McClellanville, South Carolina is, on one level, a clear depiction of a celebrated

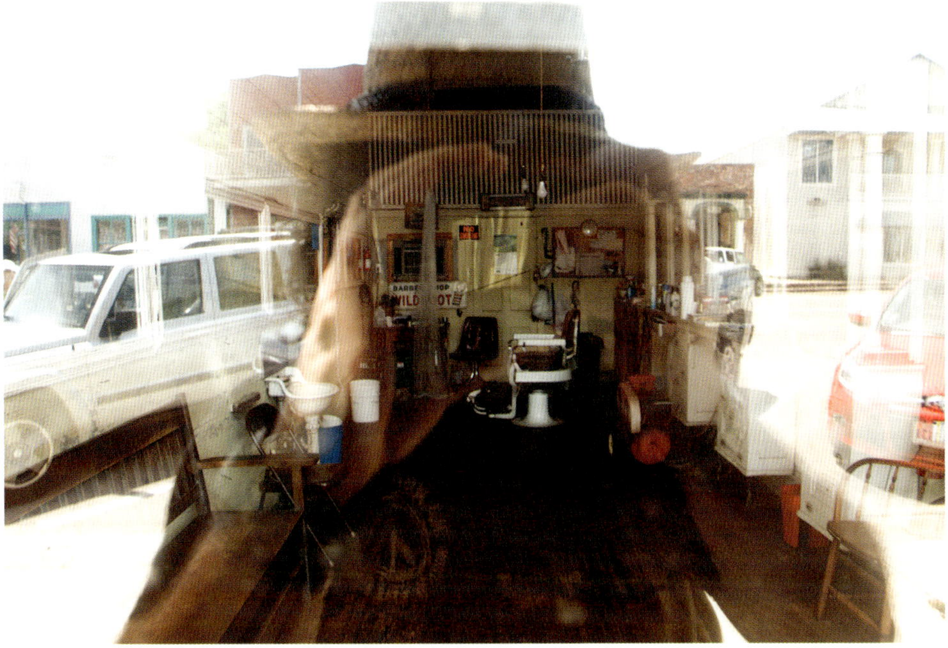

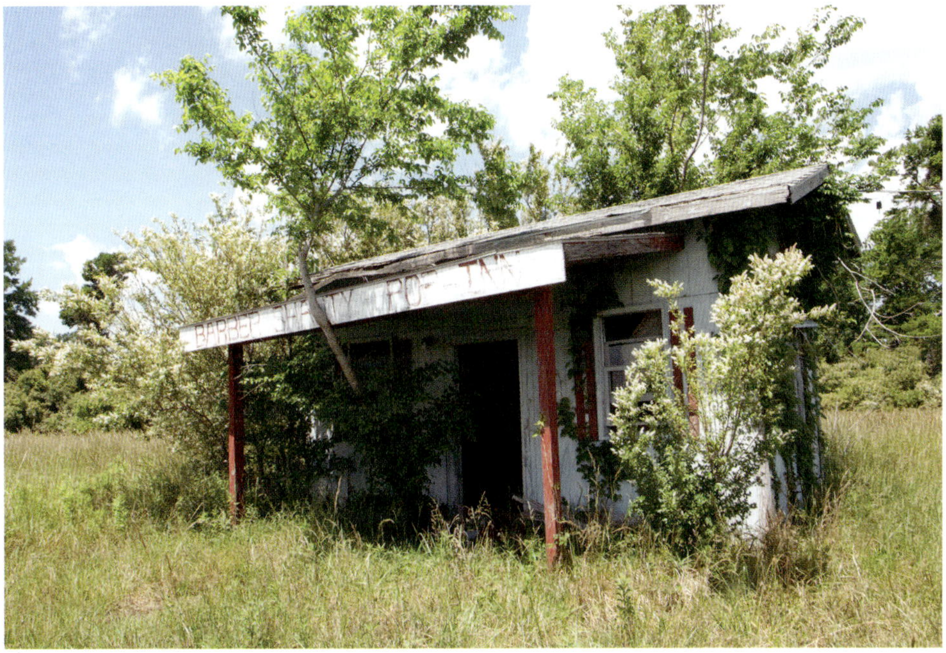

American icon. Frank is referencing his mentor Walker Evans' work here, whose *Barbershop, Havana* (1933, estate of Walker Evans) similarly depicted just such an interior. This image is unremarkable in many ways, typically Frank in its referencing, typical in its identification and presentation of an American symbol and typically Frank in the photograph's contribution to the wider structuring and intentionality of *The Americans*. There is, though, something that sets this image apart. It is Frank's pictorial signature, his 'thesis statement' for the book. He communicates this by the manner in which we are shown the interior of the barber shop. We don't just see through the window, as in Evans' picture, we see into the shop through the shadow cast by Frank's head and shoulders as he holds his camera. This falls on to a screen door which is reflecting the street scene opposite—a number of unremarkable houses and hedges across a road. We only see the barber's chair and ranged bottles because of Frank's shadow. He is showing us that this is the America he sees, a shifting and mercurial place only captured according to his vision and, literally in this case, seen through his head and his Leica. Not just here but throughout *The Americans*, we are seeing the world that Frank saw, the roads he walked, the cars he drove, the people and the things that filled his days. He is contained by, but here also containing, America.

If we accept *Barber Shop* as a kind of 'thesis statement' from Frank, if Frank is indeed communicating his intentions pictorially, then we should also, later, be able to find a pictorial conclusion. Surprisingly, given his immense efforts to avoid the predictable or expected, this exists, as we will see, in the book's final photograph.

Despite its significance, this photograph fits perfectly into the sequence: the barber shop is an American symbol, an icon, and it continues the study.

I'M COMING TOWARD THE END OF MY JOURNEY NOW. Mountains and solitude have made time seem flexible, less fixed. I slept last night at 9000 feet in the company of the oldest living creatures on earth. Trees no taller than I am, rooted to this same mountain for 7000 years. At 5.00am I struggled across snow slopes in the thin air to sit for a while and try to listen to their story. I let a tree encircle me and slowly relaxed deeply into its embrace. I felt incredible patience, astonishingly careful, contained lives. They face the freezing nights and baking desert days by refusing the rash, never taking risks or over extending, growing only the tiniest amount each year in their high severe home. Thus they have endured, the antithesis of the ever prowling, active and short lived wolf.

Now LA seems a frantic nest of rush, people rocketing here and there, absorbed in their everyday. It's as if all the activity throws a wall of white noise against the wild; invisible, adamantine, absorbing every whispered wilderness sound. The quiet voices of the wind blown stars, the winter surviving creatures and the mildest of trees are lost here, all that they can teach us neglected, crowded out by the mass of existence and the drowning sounds of the manifold creations of our hands.

I meet an old friend and drive to Venice Beach—the Pacific reached at last. It's raucous and strange, after weeks in the wilderness. All the panoply of urban society is here. Rich people in enormous cars, and homeless, pushing their stuff around in supermarket trucks. Almost too much for me, these moments of incredibly affecting ugliness. My eyes are too open still, not yet focused down from the desert horizon, still set for seeing from its frozen heights.

We are a people who love signs—all these pictures here are signs of a kind. There are signs aplenty on Venice boardwalk: an old man's 'smoking accessories' are plain for all to see, like another old man's flag-like stripy canopy, pictured here 50 years ago, in a back yard. It's a questionable place to end my drive across this continent, almost a third of the way around the earth. But I think on *It's a Mad, Mad, Mad, Mad World*—this place is an American icon, at the least. A plane flies over dragging another sign behind it. Written there on the Pacific sky, above an ocean that stretches for half a world, "The Market at Santa Monica Place Now Open". Listen to the wisdom there, in these our early attempts to colonise the air. It tells us about our deepest desires and most pressing needs, crowded here on this noisy beach. For we are creatures that first must eat, drink and shelter from the storm. A wall of noise built against the silence. I remember Shelley's 'Ozymandias', crumbling into sand: "Look on my works, ye Mighty, and despair!"

BACKYARD—VENICE WEST, CALIFORNIA

In *Backyard—Venice West, California*, an ancient old man sits beneath a cobbled-together striped canopy, resembling the American flag. Surrounded by huge vegetables and scrub trees, this garden wrested from the wilderness sits behind a single-storey, white-painted board house. Between bungalow and old man is a derelict car. Its paint is peeling, boxes sit on its roof and a garden hoe leans against it. The 'steed' of this retired knight errant is likewise retired. The conduit of his great and glorious deeds, whatever they may have been, is incorporated into his retirement garden with him. As he hangs up his spurs, so his car, the essential partner to his exploits, is decommissioned. Frank's composition captures the brilliant Californian light leaping from every surface in this image. It describes the vitality of the world. The old man hides from it under his canopy and the corrupted paintwork of the fading car refuses to shine. They are passing beyond this light.

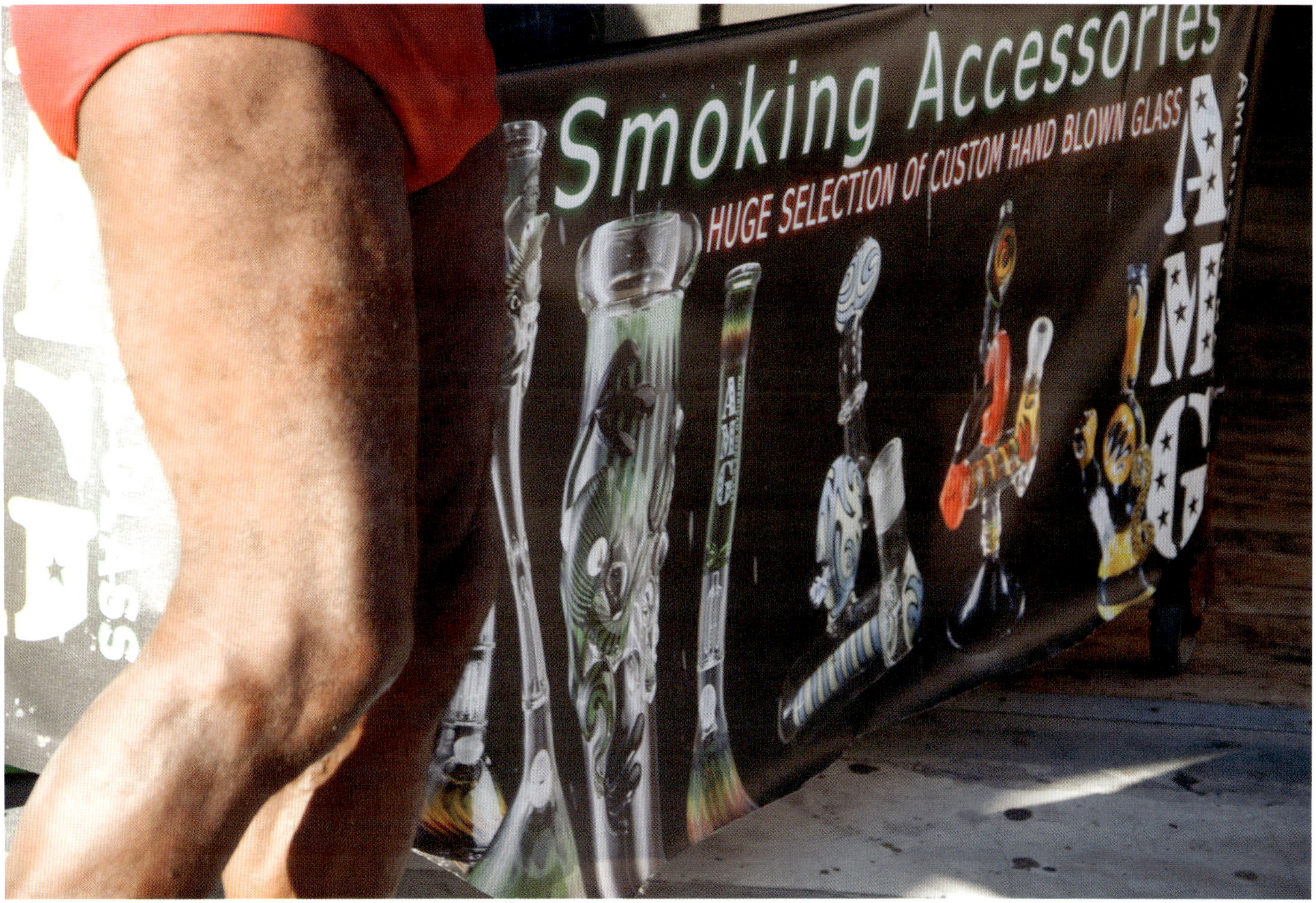
Smoking Accessories
HUGE SELECTION OF CUSTOM HAND BLOWN GLASS

A TALL SKINNY MAN IN A LIVERIED LEATHER WAISTCOAT, dripping chains, was Preacher Ray. Smiling and kindly, surrounded by children, wrapped in the soft fire comfort of kith and kin. Around us on rough pine tables, or in knuckly clusters, sat deep country men of impressive girth. Their country wives wore ratty singlets and tiny cut off shorts, dressed down for the outdoors day. They had not, though, sacrificed their hair, piled soufflé-high salon style—some things must endure, whatever the weather, only 15 miles from Pigeon Forge and it's Backwoods Barbie's *Dollywood*. Here at the Dragonfire Mountain Music Festival, there are resonances of my own early industrial life. Not in this landscape of rolling broadleaved groves, but the intense sense of community, the unquestioned acceptance of both the shining and the shipwrecked. I quickly and deeply felt the commitment to each other of the Hardcore Biker Church—outcasts from a wider society and, as 'The Peaceful Few', rebels even from that world.

I wonder what they thought of me, these friendly disciples? Wandering in off the road in sandals and denim, the wild of Balsam Mountain still in my eyes and hair. What did they hear as I strummed my songs? Did they recognize a pilgrim, road dirty and full of grace?

NEWBURGH, NEW YORK

Newburgh, New York pictures a biker on his motorcycle. There appears to be an expression of hostility and suspicion in its subject's face, an expression much beloved by Frank. Two similarly garbed associates flank the rider, suggesting perhaps a biker's club. One of these wears a badged hat, reminiscent of the one worn by Marlon Brando as he played the leader of just such a biker gang in *The Wild One* (Benedek 1954). The film carried messages of freedom from convention and examined personal revolution in a trammelled and conformist society. These were expressions of the same motivations that fuelled the Beats, notwithstanding the clear visual and philosophical differences. The look is archetypal '50s chic, and the motorcyclist bears a striking and amusing resemblance to the singer George Michael, who would later adopt this same image for a while. His aping of this style reflects the contemporary importation into Europe of American motorcycle culture, mixing Harley Davidsons and Hell's Angels with, in England, the indigenous 'ton-up' boys, with their Vincents, Nortons and Enfields. My father was such a biker.

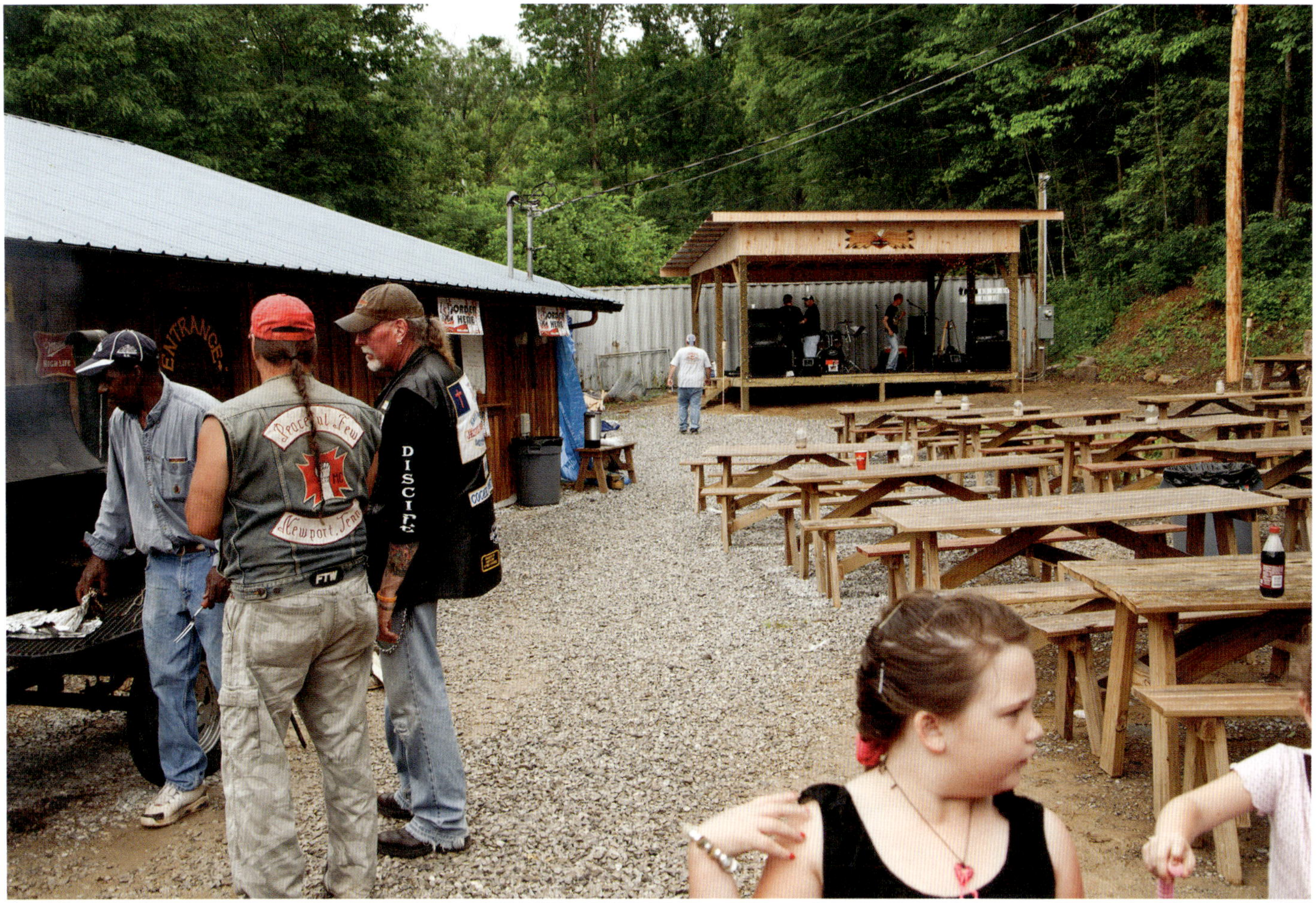
ENTRANCE
ORDER HERE
FTW

DRIVING HELL-FOR-LEATHER DOWN FROM THE 5 O'CLOCK DESERT MOUNTAINS, I hit the heat of Death Valley—like driving into an upholstered wall. It sucks at all movement, as if you're caught suddenly in gelatine, in slo mo. Trapped in a bowl of mountains, cut way down beneath the level of the sea, the air turns turgid with superheat and evaporates everything—water, vegetation, life. Somehow in the centre, though, a few creatures survive. Two ravens, as crackly as pinecones, ruffled their parched feathers for me, appealing for food scraps with the harshest razor blade rasp. A rattler-sidewinder slid across the road on tiny shifting points, a reptilian primadonna as fluid as water. Now there's an irony. And people, too, in their techno caves, glittering pipework in the impossible light, carrying away the heat, cleverness keeping them alive.

Too hot and impossible to stay for long, I headed back over the mountain wall and on towards LA. Somewhere out there in the desert, on the side of a two lane, I hit Trona. A few scrappy buildings, a gas station and a rail yard. Lots of deserted buildings—was clearly a community once, some time ago. Out across a cracked salt lake, a wind devil lifted the baked soda into the air—quicklime on the wind, like snow blowing across the town. Silver pipes, maybe a metre wide, enormously long, fire arrow-straight into the lake, carrying who knows what for who knows whom. A ramshackle, falling sign listed the churches of Trona and their opening times, a litany for the lost. Stuck on the side of a soda lake in the burning desert—isn't that a thing? Doesn't it say something about who we are? I doubt they are still open, barely enough people left now to fill one. You never know. It's all too much and I turn around, back to the filling station to interrogate the town. Like finding a motherlode, this desolation, both natural and manmade, destruction in harmony. A mother serves me and her daughter cooks me lunch. The water they drink is poisonous, she says, so everyone has left save those who can't. Shocking she thinks it is, something should be done. Whether the chemicals are made by nature in this lake-size solar still, or are sucked out by the company—who can say whose fault it is? The mother is handsome but losing her teeth, another with no dental plan, I guess. Her daughter is solid and pretty but carries skin grafts, uglily done. Like Hubba Bubba stuck to her skin, only toffee brown and veiny. Of course I don't ask, try not to look. She is pretty and friendly, can't help wondering what will become of her, born here, a child of borax.

LUNCHEONETTE—BUTTE, MONTANA

Continuing his examination of essential US icons, Frank next presents *Luncheonette—Butte, Montana,* an image featuring an American diner. This relatively minimal photograph pictures at centre a gaming table. It looks similar to a pool table, save that it has only two pockets, each flanked by mushroom-shaped wooden pieces, with a further eight such pieces in the table's centre, forming a cross. This table is typical of the kind of diner furniture featured so liberally in *The Wild One* (Benedek 1954) and *Rebel Without a Cause* (Ray 1955), arguably the first significant 'teen' movies. Behind the table is a series of equally powerful American objects: campaign bills advertising candidates for state and county office. This level of democracy, the election of particular administrative officials was, and still is, uncommon in Europe. In England, for example, the electorate does not vote directly for the prime minister, for financial officers (like the state treasurer pasted to this wall) or for members of the legislature, like the attorneys, both general and county, pictured in this photograph. Democracy is always faux, but in England it is a semblance, a simulacrum and a sham. Democracy is also, of course, one of the mostly widely traded and most seriously compromised ideas with which America seeks to be associated.

Perhaps the most intriguing aspects of this and the next two photographs are their intimated religious analogies. We have already noted Frank's deep interest in new symbols of belief in America: jukeboxes, automobiles, the road. Here he evidences new kinds of self-emanation. Just as some believers find the Madonna in a rock outcrop next to a river, or see the face of Jesus appearing in snow melt against the ground, others in India can point to deities incarnated in ice crystals or the Buddha 'appearing' perfectly in a tree. These 'emanations' confirm—for some—the reality of the transcendent world. So Frank pictures a cross, salvation and the voice of God appearing apparently unbidden in the American landscape, across the next three images. The cross of wooden 'mushrooms' on the table, and the oblique angle of the tabletop, will be visually echoed in the next image, *Santa Fe, New Mexico.*

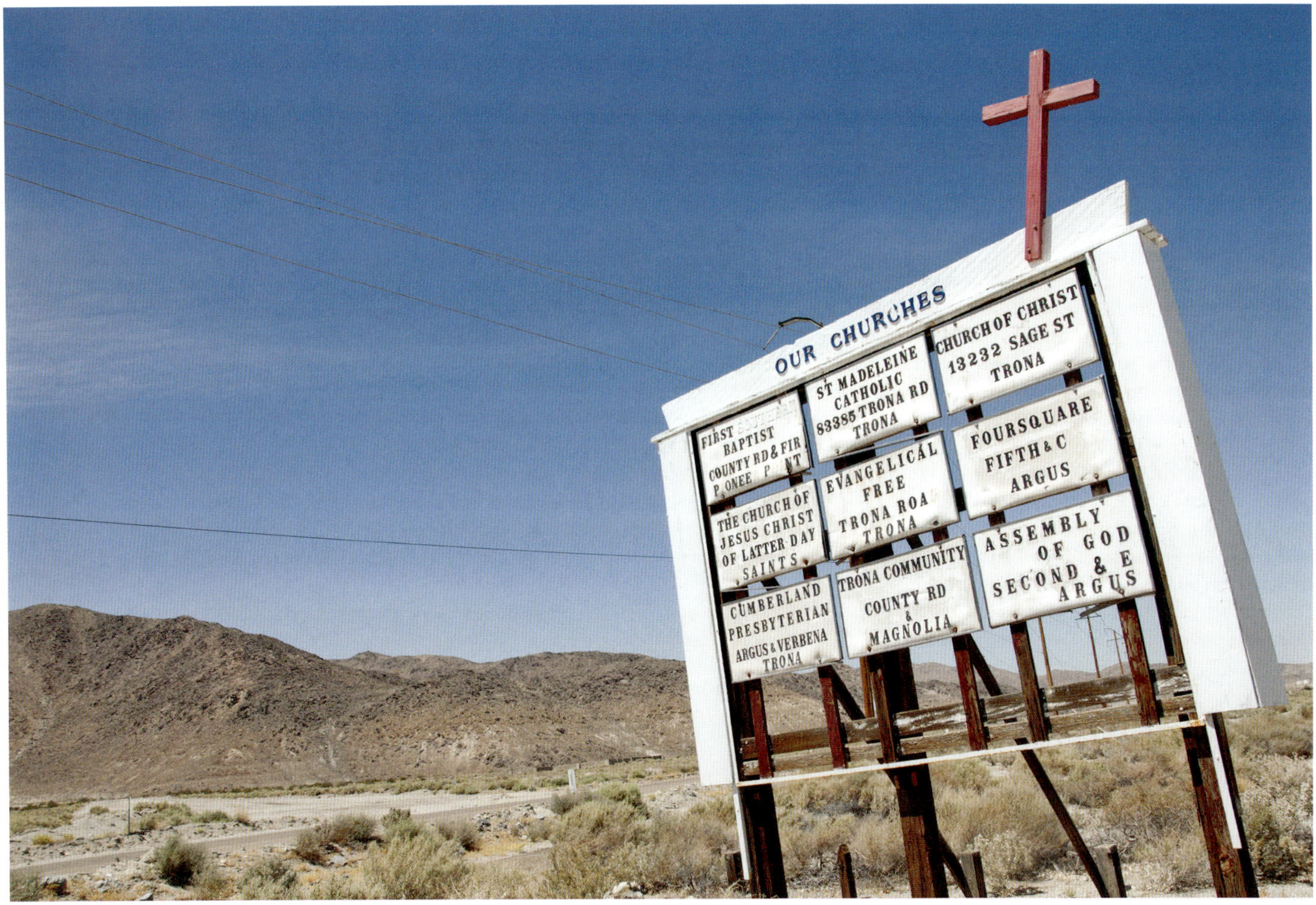
OUR CHURCHES
FIRST BAPTIST COUNTY RD & FIR P ONEE P NT
ST MADELEINE CATHOLIC 83385 TRONA RD TRONA
CHURCH OF CHRIST 13232 SAGE ST TRONA
FOURSQUARE FIFTH & C ARGUS
EVANGELICAL FREE TRONA ROA TRONA
THE CHURCH OF JESUS CHRIST OF LATTER DAY SAINTS
ASSEMBLY OF GOD SECOND & E ARGUS
TRONA COMMUNITY COUNTY RD & MAGNOLIA
CUMBERLAND PRESBYTERIAN ARGUS & VERBENA TRONA

THE END IS COMING OF THE AMERICAN ROAD—or at least the road as we have known it. We're gas-fracking now, pumping toxic sludge into the ground, and open casting hundreds of miles of oil shales, so pressing is our need. Petroleum like a mantra, lifeblood of a world. Nothing new, though, these techno changes, always novel processes ringing down our years—promising a bright forever, only to fail and wear out always sooner than we'd thought. I guess it will be no great tragedy, the passing of the car and road. Maybe replaced with something better—but certainly representing an end. It's happening already all over the States: most notably for me in back-country Texas, where towns built to serve the roads are a heartbeat away from death, deprived of the passing trade, which now overflys.

There's an irony, then, in Frank's *Santa Fe, New Mexico*. Taken when the roads were full of promise, vital, controversial, with an uncertain and contested enchantment hovering just behind the horizon. A photograph taken in the light of a thousand happy filling station pictures, many from the Standard Oil Picture File. Like Ed Rosskam's *Lee's Grizzly Station, Cut Bank, Montana; August 1944* (Standard Oil Archive, University of Louisville), picturing a small-town station and a young woman happily checking a customer's tyres. Pictures in bright sunlight and in an ordered smiling world. Pictures that seem to say, 'We have made it now, this is how it will always be'. I remember journeying once, by white-sailed felucca against a cerulean sky, and then finally by camel with my young son steering, across the desert to the Monastery of St Simeon in Aswan. Here the desert fathers eked a living from the sand, their cells surrounded by fortress walls—wrapped up against wind and its abrasive hand. Cut into the walls was a giant cross, behind which they attended an all night fire. For the lost and hopeless out in the wild, this fiery cross burned a desperate hope. No less a one, I guess, for the New Mexican voyager, travelling the wilderness on white walled tyres, seeing this sign against the darkness, promising fuel, food and water: a refuge for a while. The sign in Frank's photograph is turned off. He sees the patina of time, foreshadowing the station's return to rust, musing on the giant 'Save', held up against the evening sky (the word 'Gas' is all but invisible without its inner light). This is thus another sigil of salvation—not in a temple or a church, but held out here in electrical tubes, a talisman against desert waste and the night.

The pumps are slightly anthropomorphic—robotic perhaps—with illuminated head-like discs, sitting on human-sized shoulders, hoses hanging like arms. They are monolithic, immovable, standing in an almost circle, henge-like. An American Avebury, or Callanish. The deserted station looks ancient, abandoned, the pumps like broken teeth in the skull of a civilization—as strange as Stonehenge, as mute as Teotihuacan. These are the enigmatic signs which America has created, perhaps the way it will be best remembered.

How telling is this future that Frank sent us, the seeds of corruption in a culture at its height. It's a postcard from the wilderness—petrol Salvation with its lights turned off, the last of the gasoline dripping from these pumps into the sand.

SANTA FE, NEW MEXICO

Frank's fascination with sigils hidden in the everyday continues in *Santa Fe, New Mexico.*

Following a cross made of wooden mushrooms on a gaming table is a sign, this time literally, of salvation. It belongs to a petrol station. Jukeboxes and automobiles have been seen to define this civilization, strange objects, for sure, but a petrol pump is stranger.

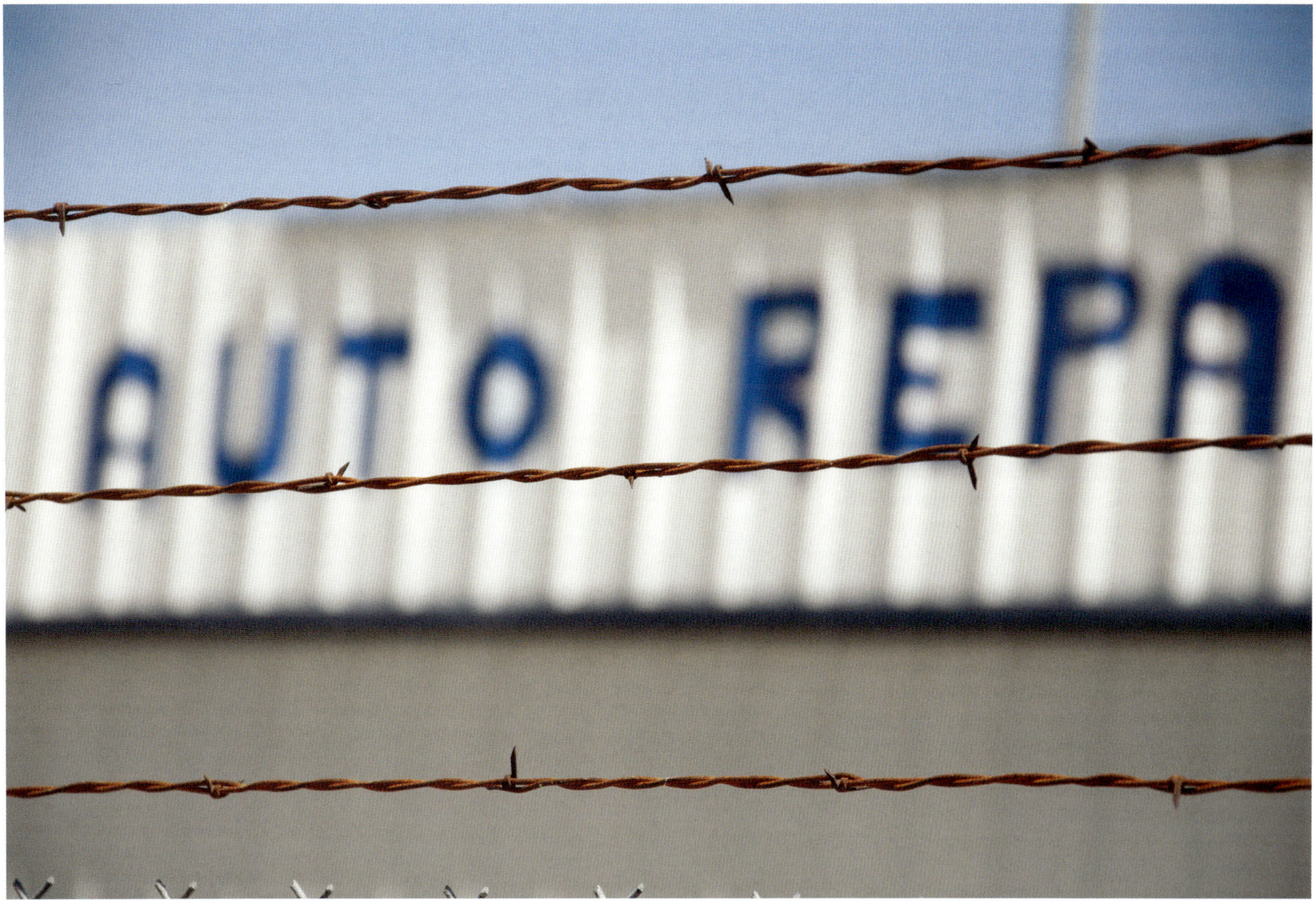
AUTO REPA

WE HAVE SEEN THE WORDS OF ETERNAL LIFE SCRAWLED IN NEON across a desert sky, and will see, later, the Christians' holy sign, trotted out in manifold plastic form, and held up blessing a car lot and a road. Not so strange then to see an angelic visitor—as Frank's juke-box seems to me, lit by its own inscrutable glow, in a dark and tawdry Bar—New York City. It proclaims the words of new prophets, the voice of Metatron disguised as Patsy Cline. Perhaps it is light that draws us to hidden mystery, like the lotus reaching up from the muddy water's bed. Or perhaps it's the jukebox's sparkling interface, a semi-permeable veil behind which magic is held. Like the walls of caves to Neolithic Hunters, which were a stony membrane between them and spirits within, or the temple curtain that Christ tore in two, or the silver cinema, or TV—places we look for wisdom, enacted stories that tell us how to be. Now above all we have the monitor and phone to aid our thinking, hold our memories, give us direction and sing us to sleep. Behind these veils of stone, celluloid and pixel, we hide our secrets and dream our dreams. The angel-possessed jukebox in New York I like—a glowing intervention, a musical life-support. Of the million screens I am not so sure, mysterious, functioning largely without our consent or instruction, hidden, arcane. We invest so much of ourselves in them—they will take everything with them, when eventually they go.

BAR—NEW YORK CITY

Bar—New York City is the notably vague caption for this image. The icon featured here has been seen several times already: it is the jukebox. In this photograph, though, Frank's communication of his understanding of this object is as clear as it ever gets. The robot-like jukebox sits in an unremarkable bar, in front of a partition, across from customers sitting at a table. A further customer is just caught, motion blurred, as he leaves the frame. The jukebox at the heart of this photograph glows with a white light, the traditional pictorial attribute of angels, saints and the Holy Spirit. The brilliance of the light has burned the photograph out: it spills beyond the jukebox into the surrounding air. Frank has given the jukebox a halo. This inner light is also reminiscent of the engines of spaceships in contemporary science fiction films, or images of nuclear fission carried by myriad popular magazines. It lights up the place like an angelic visitor, a modern-day Gabriel trumpeting in song the arrival of a new age—to an almost entirely indifferent audience.

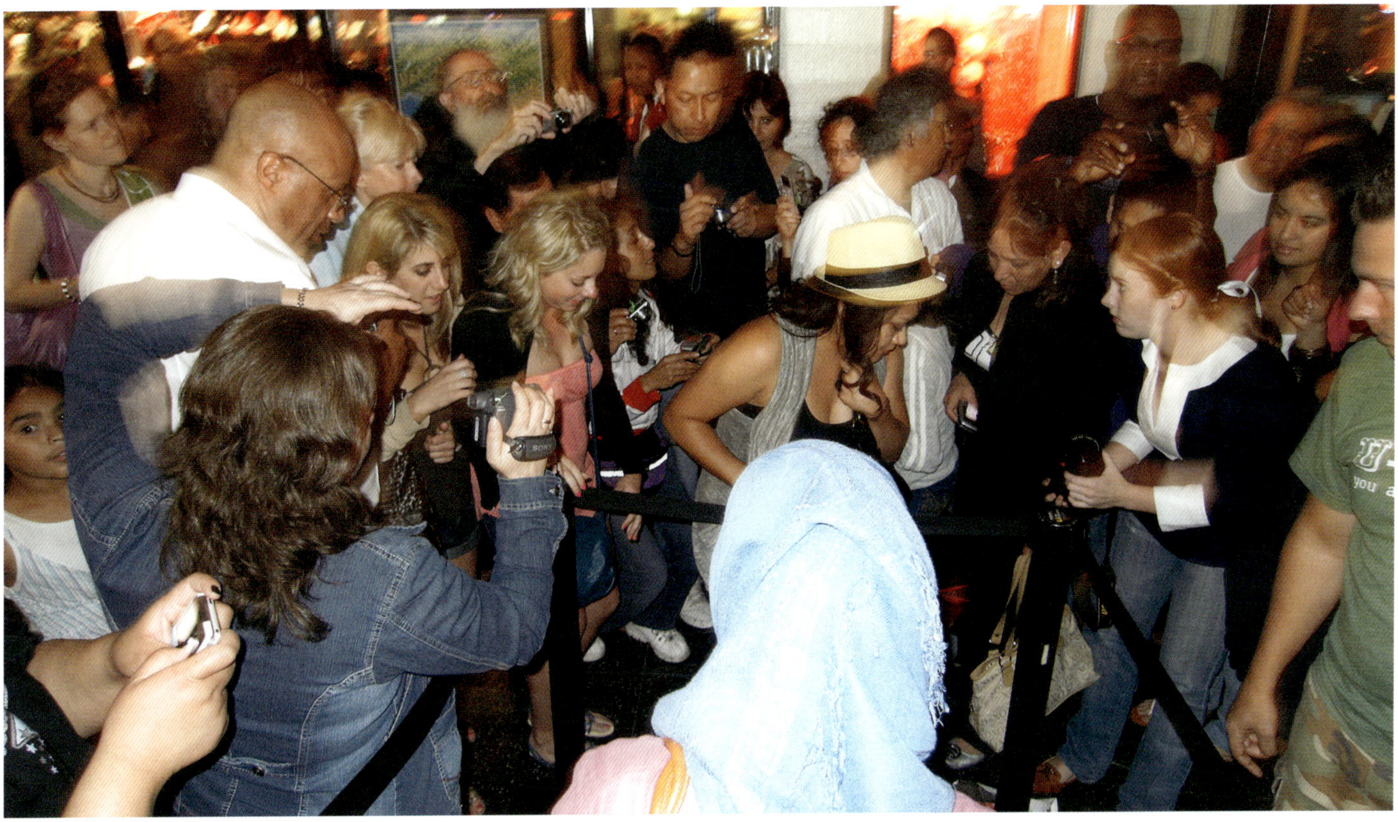

FRANK'S 'ELEVATOR GIRL' IS A PHOTOGRAPH ABOUT THE RIGOURS OF WORK, that's for sure. But there's more I reckon, through the eyes of a traveller. It's her beauty and attitude and the thoughts that flesh is heir to. Kerouac saw it, and wrote in his introduction:

> That little ole lonely elevator girl looking up sighing in an elevator full of blurred demons, what's her name & address?' (Kerouac, in Frank 1959: 6)

Many times a face, a smile, the flash of a leg, the tone of a voice or the curve of a hip has caught my eye. Kind of instinctive I guess? Sometimes, though, it is more than casual—some deeply felt thing that happens rarely. Like an explosion of colours, it feels, or an overwhelming scent of summer flowers. Ah that sounds like corny Hallmark greetings spiel, but how else to describe something so definite and important and a justification for my days? These meetings feel so powerful and invoke some kind of 'meant to be'—psychological feedback maybe, making life seem pre-ordained (move away from the spun string of my life, you Fates, and put away your scissors).

Walking once through the streets of a town, unexpectedly through a window I saw the waist, back and neck of a woman—a secretary I would guess. She was wrapped up tight in a pencil skirt, fitted blouse and extensive underwear, like a coiled and taught spring or a bent bow, or a shot about to fire. In my mind I saw her slowly unwinding, free of work's strictures, spreading loose and relaxed.

Another time I'd been out in the wilderness for several nights, barely speaking to anyone. I'd almost met my death on the road. I'd just driven the Chief Joseph Highway out of Cody, the only way into Yellowstone before the thaw. Between ramparts of snow, I saw otters and marmots in the high wild melt, was overflown by cranes and hawks, and watched a wolf and a grizzly just up above my car. At the Park entrance, completely unexpected, was the most beautiful Ranger. She took my breath away. It wasn't just her face under a crazy wonky straw Ranger hat, and I had no idea of her figure, dressed in four layers of National Parks' issue insulated clothes. It was her self, her so-warm charm, the field of content she radiated that made me feel five times as alive as before.

The next morning I saw her again and she remembered me, and wondered if I had any more questions. I wanted to ask "What are your dinner plans?" and then maybe in time marry her and have her children out in the wild forest. Instead I listened attentively to the condition of the South Exit, which was my entirely unsatisfactory response. Time and mission seem to dominate me—inevitable, regrettable, I drove on with a sigh. Ah but what a moment, there in those high mountains, in the twinkling of her eyes, half a world away. She took a smidgeon of my soul and I left it willingly.

Like Frank, standing in front of an elevator—the choices we make construct us. If only her elevator bell didn't 'ding'. Going up…

ELEVATOR—MIAMI BEACH

We've already discussed Edward Steichen's *Family of Man* exhibition and Frank's responses to it in a number of the photographs in *The Americans.* One of Steichen's themes was men and women working. Included in his show were images of sweat and toil in dusty, dirty conditions—like the Bolivian woman breastfeeding her baby in a quarry with a shovel at her feet (G. Thorlichen, Museum of Modern Art, New York), or a black man standing between resignation and despair inside a stone-crushing plant (D. Kessel, Museum of Modern Art, New York). A Welsh child with a bandaged finger holding up his miner's lamp, dirty in the pit (F. Scherschel, collection of *Life*) is another example. These photographs are accompanied by the text "If I didn't work these worlds would perish", a caption taken from the *Bhagavad Gita*, an Indian religious text credited as the dictation of the incarnated Krishna. What relevance do the words of an Indian deity speaking of his divine activities have to this context? The exhibition's implication is clear. All of this work, however squalid or painful, is necessary and desir-

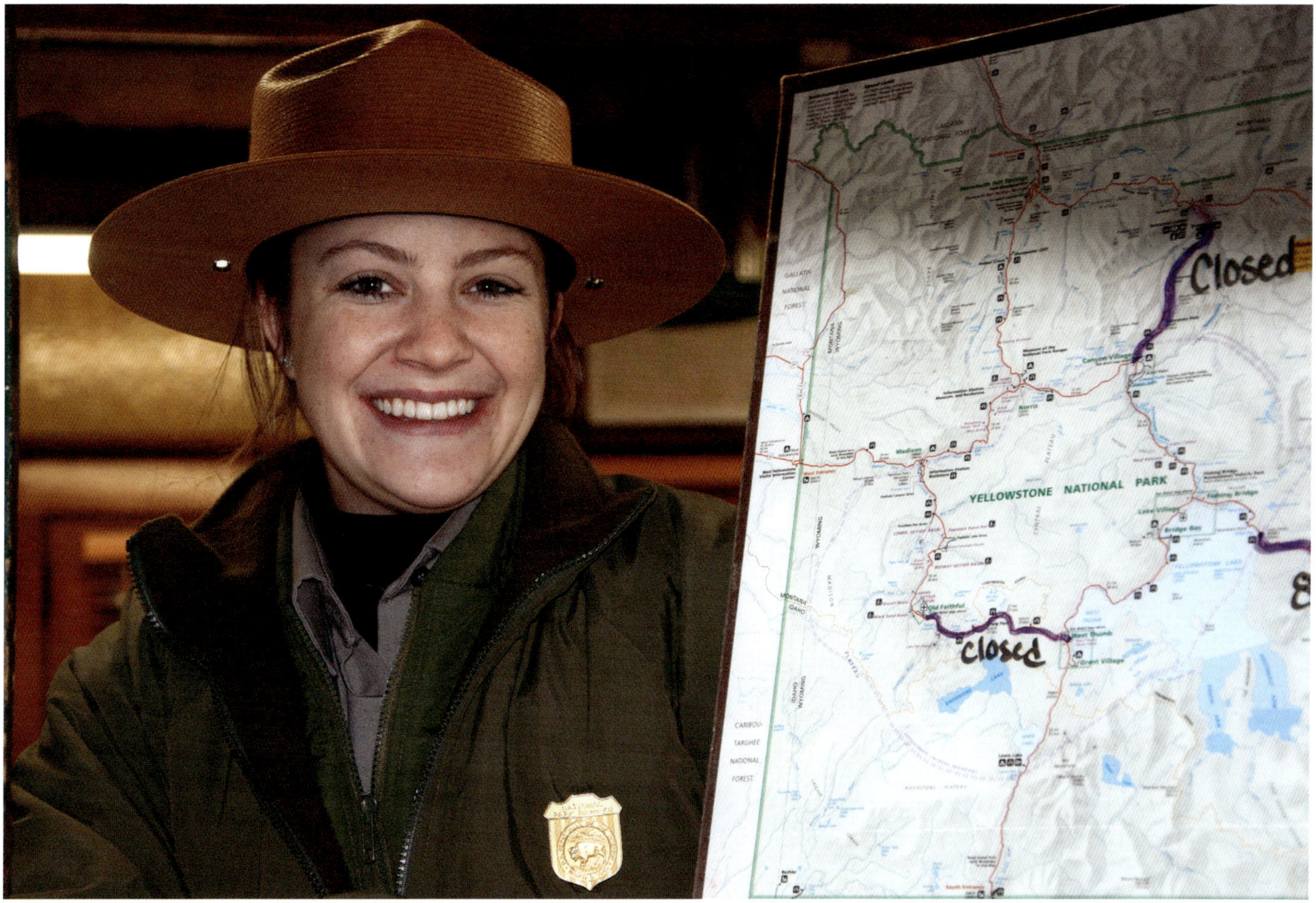

Closed
GALLATIN
NATIONAL
FOREST
YELLOWSTONE NATIONAL PARK
Old Faithful
Closed
CARIBOU-
TARGHEE
NATIONAL
FOREST

able. Steichen hammers his point home further. A Russell Lee photograph, originally taken for the Farm Security Administration, shows the crippled arthritic hands of a woman (collection of the Library of Congress). This sits above the caption "Bless thee in all the work of thy hand which thou doest", taken from Deuteronomy 14:29 in the Bible. Karl Marx's description of religion as the opiate of the masses (Marx 1977 [1843]: 127) could not be better illustrated than here. The implication is that a life of crippling work is God's will, and these useless hands that are its fruit should be worn like a trophy.

One of Steichen's worker images is a Bill Brandt picture of a young dark-haired woman, called *East End Morning*, taken from *A Camera in London* (1948, estate of Bill Brandt). She is scrubbing the tiled floor of a hallway, with the door open, allowing the viewer to see her. Her body describes a beautiful arabesque as she wets her brush or cloth in a bucket. She looks down and to the right, in a traditional Madonna-like pose. She seems perhaps wistful, perhaps a little sad, a delicate female at her work.

Frank's *Elevator—Miami Beach* features another brown-haired girl. She is uniformed and at the controls of the cited elevator. The dark form of a bald man blurs across the photograph's right. To the left, a woman in a white fur stole is similarly blurred. The operator herself is static within this movement and looks at neither of them. Her expression almost defies description. It contains the longing for something more, hatred of the tyranny of the time spent endlessly riding this elevator, delivering faceless people whom she doesn't see, doesn't especially care about and who similarly neither see nor care for her. Her uplifted eyes appear to see nothing; she has retreated into herself, waiting for her life to recommence. Yet she is not cowed. She is defiant. Her impatience is burned across her face. She wants to live, though she has to endure this work. There is nothing of the Madonna here, no wistful long-suffering. Here is a flesh and blood woman, working because she has to. No amount of captioning or religious quotations will change her essential nature, revealed in this "look of sadness" (Frank, in Maloney 1958: 115). Frank does not depict an archetype or a cipher, or attempt to generalise or universalise working. His woman at work is real enough to arouse Kerouac.

MARYLAND WAS A BLISS OF GREEN FIELDS, BRIGHT IN THE SUN, watched over by the tidiest of farmhouses. Germantown and Berlin were tiara-ed with 'Historic Quarter' signs. Down into Virginia's long green miles with the sea slowly encroaching on both sides—thrift shops, churches and cabins on the quiet road. I stopped for lunch at the Meriopac Seafood Shack, its tiny rough-timber room stuffed full of people. They were picking up baked clams, strangely-shaped fillets and dark, bready crab cakes. Most everyone friendly, most of them black, chatting the gossip, chewing the cud—letting the blissfully warm day slip along, as this ocean freshness, straight out of the Atlantic, sizzled in the fryer on the café hob. Deep freeze chests around the walls, decoy ducks for twenty species, fishing lures sparking rainbows from their ribbons, moved by a breeze in the brilliant light. A fat, aggressive white man barked his order across the counter, never a 'please' or 'thankyou', as if everyone here had earned his personal hatred. He waited outside in his truck while his food cooked, glowering through his windshield at the afternoon. Good to see the eyes of a hard-line hater alongside the pleasant, mild café crowd. On the table sat cell phones, ketchup and a bible—no sense here of the incongruous. Unopened, the black book sat with authority, like a cipher book to decode the day. Alongside food, light and company, the things we need for survival, another need we have it seems—to explain it all some way.

RESTAURANT—U.S. 1 LEAVING COLUMBIA, SOUTH CAROLINA

Restaurant—U.S. 1 Leaving Columbia, South Carolina is a subtle and powerful comment on the decline of America's traditional faith. On the most immediate level, this image is one among several pictures examining the nature and character of the American diner. This interpretation is valid: Frank chose to exclude any information as to the identity of the man on the TV in his caption. It is difficult on visual evidence alone to attribute anything to him. He is serious, perhaps even sour-faced or aggressive. Contemporary Americans may have recognized him, but the Europeans who saw *Les Americaines* (1958) probably would not have. This photograph is one of those chosen by Frank for his retrospective book *The Lines of My Hand* (Frank 1989). Here the picture carries the caption 'South Carolina, Oral Roberts on TV'. The identity of the broadcaster is significant. Roberts was one of America's most famous television evangelists, notable also as the cousin and denouncer of rock and roll singer and pianist Jerry Lee Lewis. Despite being well known for his Christian faith, Lewis stormed out of his cousin's church after being continually harangued for performing the 'devil's music' (McBride 1989).

As a TV preacher, Roberts is presumably declaiming about something that he might call 'light' (his face has an expression of dour sincerity, symptomatic of media evangelism). He is speaking, though, on a tube illuminated by the bombardment of florescent spots by billions of streaming electrons. Frank is contrasting the simulacrum with the reality—the small TV cannot compete in a room filled with brilliant sunlight. Kerouac, in his introduction to Frank's book, called it a "holy halo I never thought could be captured on film much less described in its beautiful visual entirety in words" (Kerouac, in Frank 1959: 1). Frank compares the artificiality of the TV screen and the constructed understanding of the world explained by Roberts with the commanding reality of a glorious morning. So then, not surprisingly, no one is listening to Roberts preach. They are all gone outside—all of them, that is, except the man behind the camera, quietly fulfilling his secret and personal purposes.

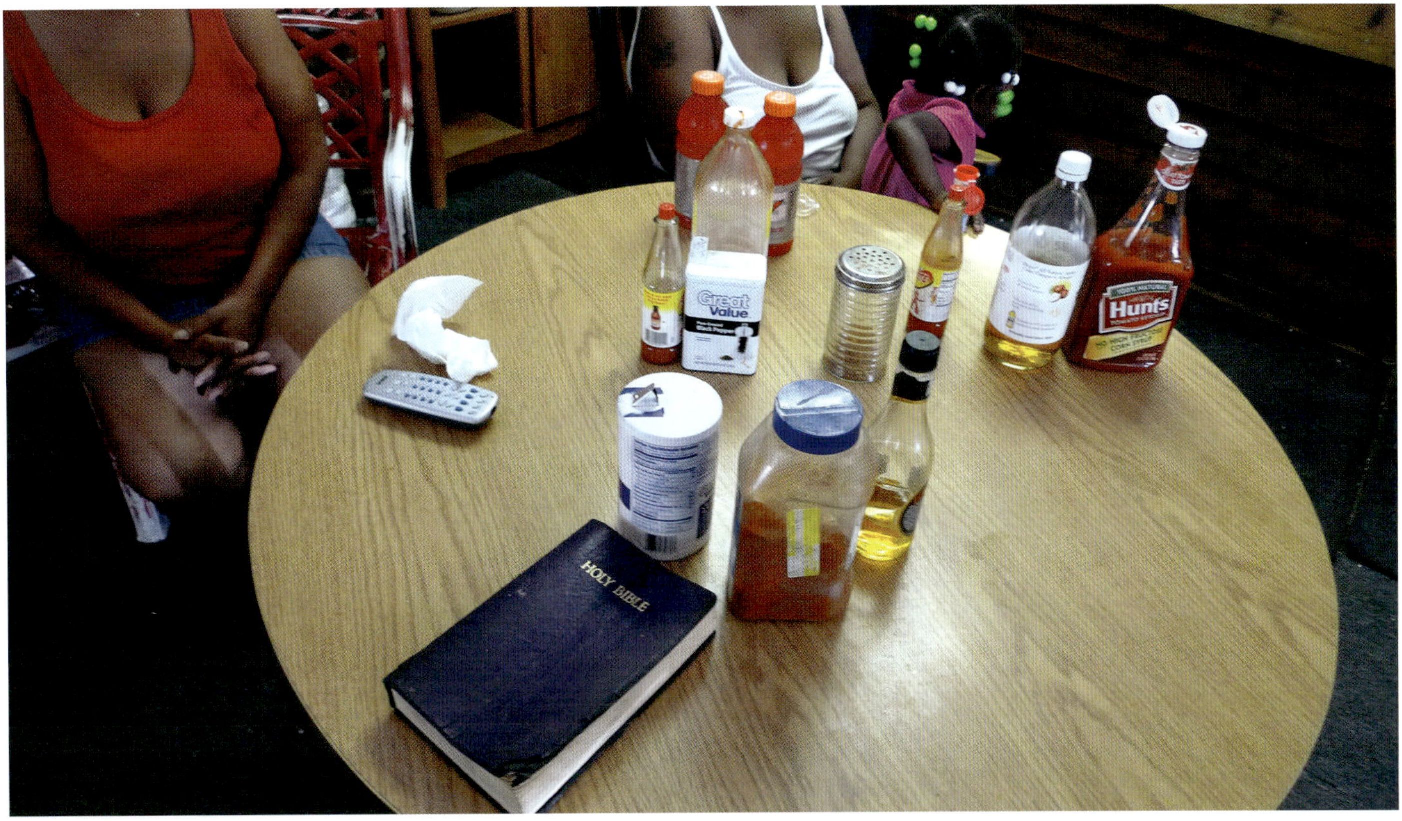
Great Value
Hunts
HOLY BIBLE

I GUESS I TOOK THIS TRIP TO SEE IF IT WAS TRUE. If the America that had wet-nursed me ever really existed, or if it was a glamour I had cast, conjured from the flowers and sulphate-blue chemical plants of my own mind. The many mid-wives at the birth of my imaginings, like Kings in a stable, attested to its truth—Carlos Castaneda, Gram Parsons, Crosby, Stills, Nash and Young, Todd Rundgren, Emmylou. But I wanted to see it for myself, catch the last echoes of its fading away. It strands us all, the turning tide: we are not designed to last. We are stardust, as Joni Mitchell celebrates, and stardust-to-dust is our destiny. The world which we arrive in carves its accidental nature onto our skin and bone, its music, art, religion, political systems and social relationships cutting grooves across our being like the geometry of keys. So there is a lock we fit, a time and place that will always indelibly feel like home. It's a place that recedes and is lost, ever more quickly now, as we breed out of control and technology tries to match our frightening replication. This time of Frank and Kerouac, Ginsberg, Coltrane, all of the Beats, is foundational for me, the words of life itself, the glass that I look through to see myself. Not so, though, for the so-many others whose natal stars shone with newer light: an exercise in history this is for them, illuminating perhaps, interesting maybe, but lacking any of that elemental power.

We can, even so, empathise—step outside the scars of our creation and see in imperfect flashes how it would be to look through another's eyes. And some things endure across the generations: our creations, styles and fashions are not equally ephemeral and evanescent. Occasional things persist, helping others on their way to survival.

And so it is with *Drive-in Movie—Detroit*. They're mostly gone now, these giant light shows, dancing beams of Technicolor projected at the night. Occasionally, still, there's a remnant—some festival or celebration projecting images onto buildings or trees. They are, in any case, no more a part of the everyday. I was lucky enough to go to one as a child, in Joubert Park. There's something really powerful about images we've made interacting with the endless sky. The antithesis of the cineplex, where we dive through homogenised darkness into the worlds inside our minds. Anchorless, there, and sensually deprived by the banality of surroundings, we drift in an entirely inward place, robbed of context, of the conditions of our being.

So there are little messages for now in these remnants of the past, quiet and unassuming, for ears that want to hear.

DRIVE-IN MOVIE—DETROIT

As well as continuing the 'icons' theme and further examining their religious nature, *Drive-in Movie—Detroit*, like the last image, contrasts man-made light on a screen with the power and immensity of natural light. As it connects back, so it also looks forward: the next three images are linked by lighting, all of them being taken in the 'golden hour' of sunrise/sunset. *Drive-in Movie* captures flickering characters on a large screen, watched by a couple in a cabriolet and innumerable others whose presence we must assume, hidden as they are inside their sedans. The film's plaid-shirted protagonist, occupying perhaps a twelfth of the image, is intent on something in his screen-bounded reality. He seems insignificant against the vastness of the evening sky—human life and all its insularity and self-obsession put into context by the immensity of this, and every, evening.

The crowd's serried attention in the drive-in is contrasted sharply with a lone man in the next photograph, who is also looking away into the sunset.

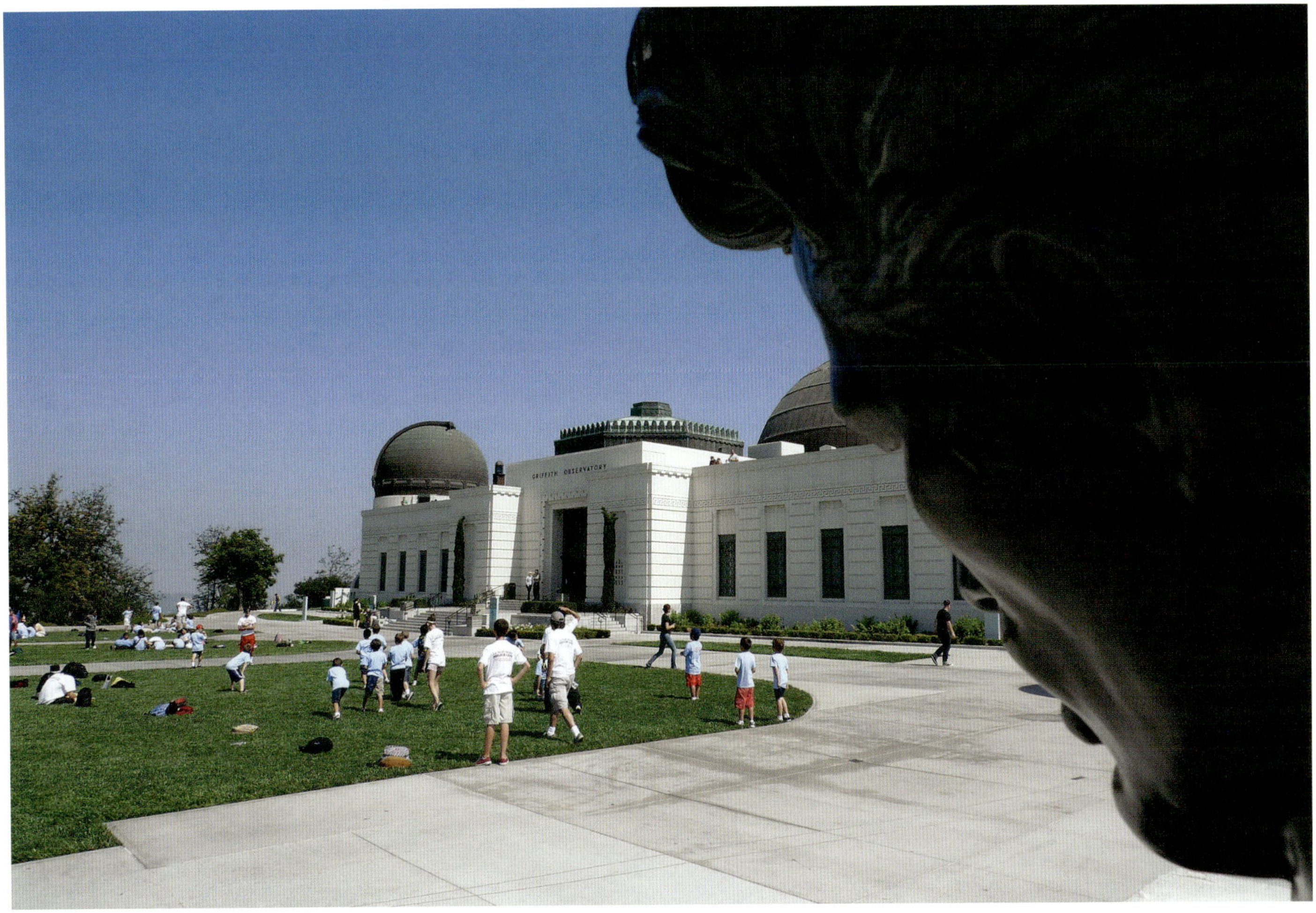
GRIFFITH OBSERVATORY

SUNSET WAS A FIRE ACROSS THREE MILES OF MISSISSIPPI WATER. So strong the stain and the spirit of this flood, I was sure I could smell the snowmelt still, starting down from faraway Minnesota, telling me softly its secret name. Long miles then into Arkansas. Flat, flat river lands, orange Western sky, a full moon brightening the set. So tired when I saw a motel in Marked Tree—really old and not owning a chain name I'd seen anywhere on the Interstate. I swung by and it looked shabby—worn, cracked, like something from the old song—"Trailer for sale or rent, rooms to let fifty cents". Well twenty-five dollars, but hey. Asked a guy who called by the office for some soap; he says, "It's good for twenty five dollars". My lock was smashed off the door, the room smelled strongly of something not quite rancid. Heavy flock wallpaper, worm brown around the edges, set off with a kitschy painting of a forest cabin in a gilt frame. I think once this place was more than it is now—left on the roadside, an unreconstructed relic of another age. Most of the clients are itinerant—transient agricultural workers, eyeing me suspiciously, living out of battered trucks, up early, home tired, not earning much. I barricaded myself in and slept... surprisingly comfortably.

MISSISSIPPI RIVER, BATON ROUGE, LOUISIANA

The crowd's serried attention in the last photograph's drive-in is contrasted sharply with a lone man in this picture, looking away into the sunset. Instead of a screen at the heart of the image, he holds a cross (the next three images all feature a cross). He is wearing white robes, which distance him from the workaday and contemporary, clearly in a deliberate act of demarcation. His simple white cross, and the book from which he reads, denote a Christian element to his devotions. He appears to be praying, as the *Mississippi River, Baton Rouge, Louisiana* flows ponderously by, mirroring the light from the evening sky. His supplication is across the huge river facing into the sun. What mystery is he enacting, what soul poetry does he read to the evening, unheard, unregarded? While 'St. Francis' in the next image is frozen in stone, expostulating silently to the myriad cars and to Sunset Boulevard, here at the heart of America, apparently oblivious to the regard of others, be they individual or corporate, a priest from an unknown order reads his quiet liturgy to the wide land and inevitable sky. Kerouac said of it:

> mysteries like the Negro priest squatting underneath the bright liquid belly mer of the Mississippi at Baton Rouge for some reason at dusk or early dawn with a white snowy cross and secret incantations never known outside the bayou... (Kerouac, in Frank 1959: 5)

The man we see praying was known for his practice of walking up and down the river as a pilgrimage, praying as he went. Frank encountered him at a ferry crossing, moving around the cars as they waited for and then boarded the boat. Frank has pictured him away from even that restrained action, thereby heightening the sense of solitude. This is one of the few photographs of traditional religious observance in *The Americans* that does not raise an eyebrow or wag a finger in consternation. I wonder, though, how aware the pilgrim was of himself as Frank's subject: a photographer and he together on the riverbank. Was he complicit in the creation of the picture? Although Frank has shown repeatedly that he embraces, and offers no apology for, his presence and his shaping vision, there would be irony in one of *The Americans*' most sincere photographs being essentially staged.

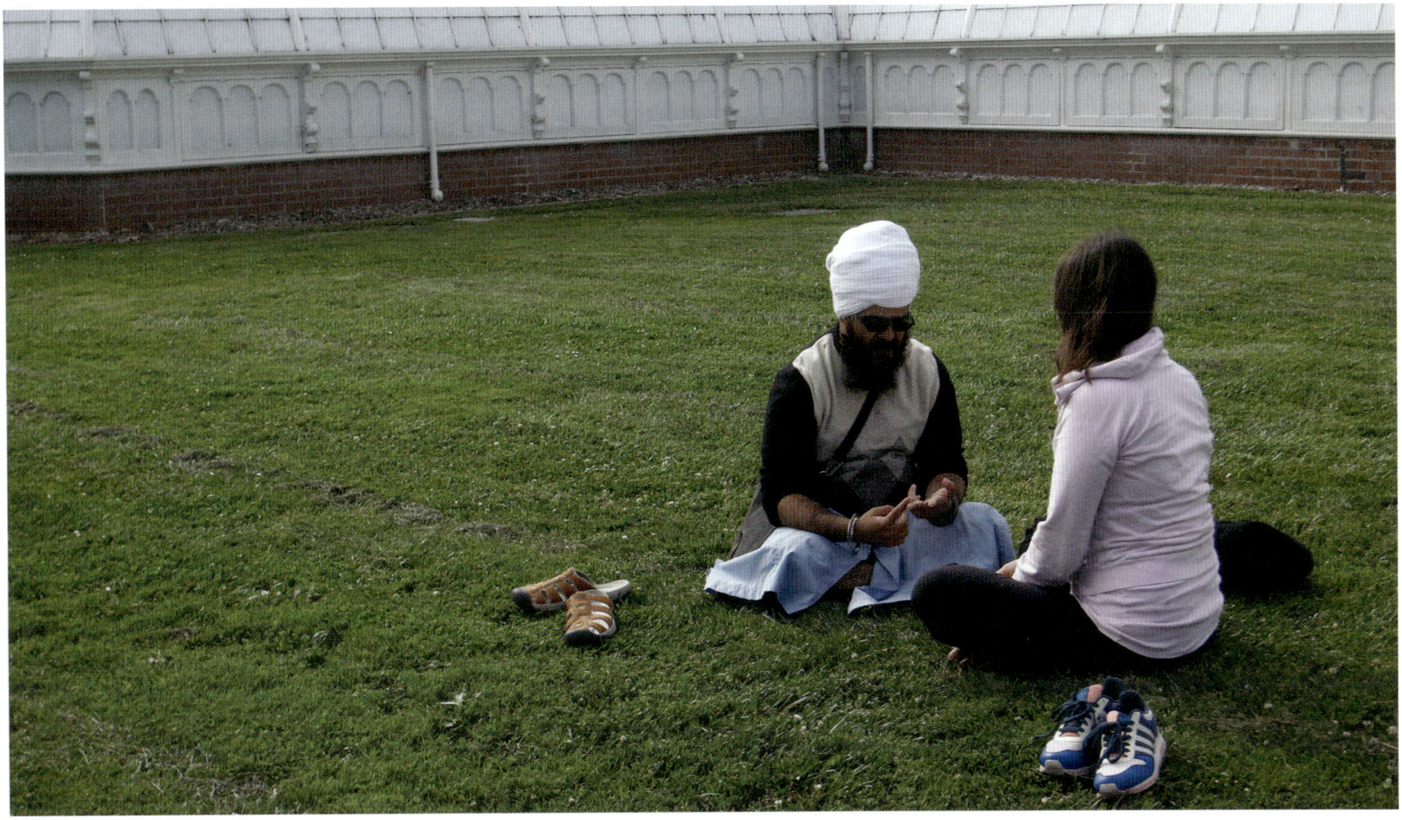

I'M WRITING AT A BENCH WHERE I CAMPED LAST NIGHT IN THE HIGH ROCKIES. My fingers are so cold I can barely type—the seat so cold I have to take off my quilted waistcoat and sit on it to write at all. I've been much interested this trip in the Kerouac and Beat idea of the 'experiential transcendent'—moments of such joy and intensity that time and death are effectively negated. On this high mountain, heading now slowly home with a joyful certainty and, short of disaster, inevitability, I think I see why this was not enough—why, dissolute and whisky-damaged, so many of the Beats died young. However intense the experience, however mind-altering that kind of high, it always and inevitably ebbs, the hangover or come down manifests, the damage done demands a reckoning. Watching the early sun on the snows, I hear the twittering of strange yet somehow familiar birds. Although I've never seen them before, they seem somehow right, here, with a start of recognition that says, "Oh yes, of course, that is beautiful and that makes sense". In this happy place I think again of one of the heart sources of Beat philosophy, the Buddhist Dharma. I only really know this at all, and that in part, from Zen. The idea of enlightenment is contained there, achieving a state of being that can endure and be less transitory.

I guess the 'experiential transcendent' is the inevitable consequence of Dharma pulled through sensibilities born in a '50s materialist-consumerist world. Looking for the hit, for the wildness of the strange and unexpected, packaged up and for sale in myriad shifting material forms—searching for the 'transcendence aisle' in some kind of American metaphysical supermarket. The City Lights guide to a kool-ade life.

In any case, looking at the sun in this high place I think again that this is all there is, and all there needs to be. My life as it is: I have enough, I am enough, I do enough. In a warmish bubble of mountain jacket and boots, here in this high brilliant moment I see again that this stillness is the heart. I think perhaps in my life before this journey—writing and music, records, press and gigs—I had forgotten that, falling again for the lie that achievement or status can ever be sufficient. They cannot. Thrills certainly, but nothing of the quiet heart and assuredness. I am very happy to find this again, near the end of this trip, in this high place.

As I drive down into woodlands, I realise the mountain and the storm have given me their benediction, worth more than any gold: a peaceful mind and a quiet heart.

ST. FRANCIS, GAS STATION AND CITY HALL—LOS ANGELES

Like the last two images, *St. Francis, Gas Station and City Hall—Los Angeles* is bathed in a quiet sun. This hazy light is, I suspect, in the early morning, given the geography of the image. The sun at Baton Rouge is setting on a passing world—here in Los Angeles the morning sun of another day is rising on a petrified saint, caught out by pell-mell progress, like a troll at sunrise. The hulking building at left is not City Hall, as the statue is not St Francis—I don't know if Frank was mistaken or disingenuous—but the rise in ground level to the right is familiar and suggests that the image is looking from west to east, across what was then Sunset Boulevard (this section of road was later renamed Victor Chavez Highway in honour of the public figure). The duplicity within the image raises questions certainly, but it does not destroy the power of the depiction. This robed man (St Junipero Serra, in fact, now relocated a few blocks away on a quiet street), cross held high, church clutched under his arm, is preaching passionately to the rising sun, to a highway and a car lot. Temporal power, represented by City Hall (had it been City Hall), has moved away from the gospel of this preacher—cut off by the road, separated by the technology of travel. St Francis famously preached to the captivated birds. In this image, even the cars look somnolent, distant and disinterested. The tiny church beneath his arm also seems anachronistic in this world of pistons, rubber and asphalt.

The black priest in *Mississippi River, Baton Rouge, Louisiana* also holds a cross and a book. 'Francis' echoes his posture, save for the kneeling, but his location could not be more different. The wide river and wild sky and the still enraptured, still living priest contrast sharply with car-ridden Los Angeles and its petrified saint, silent as stone. Serene, car-free clarity stand against a grey, smog-bound city morning.

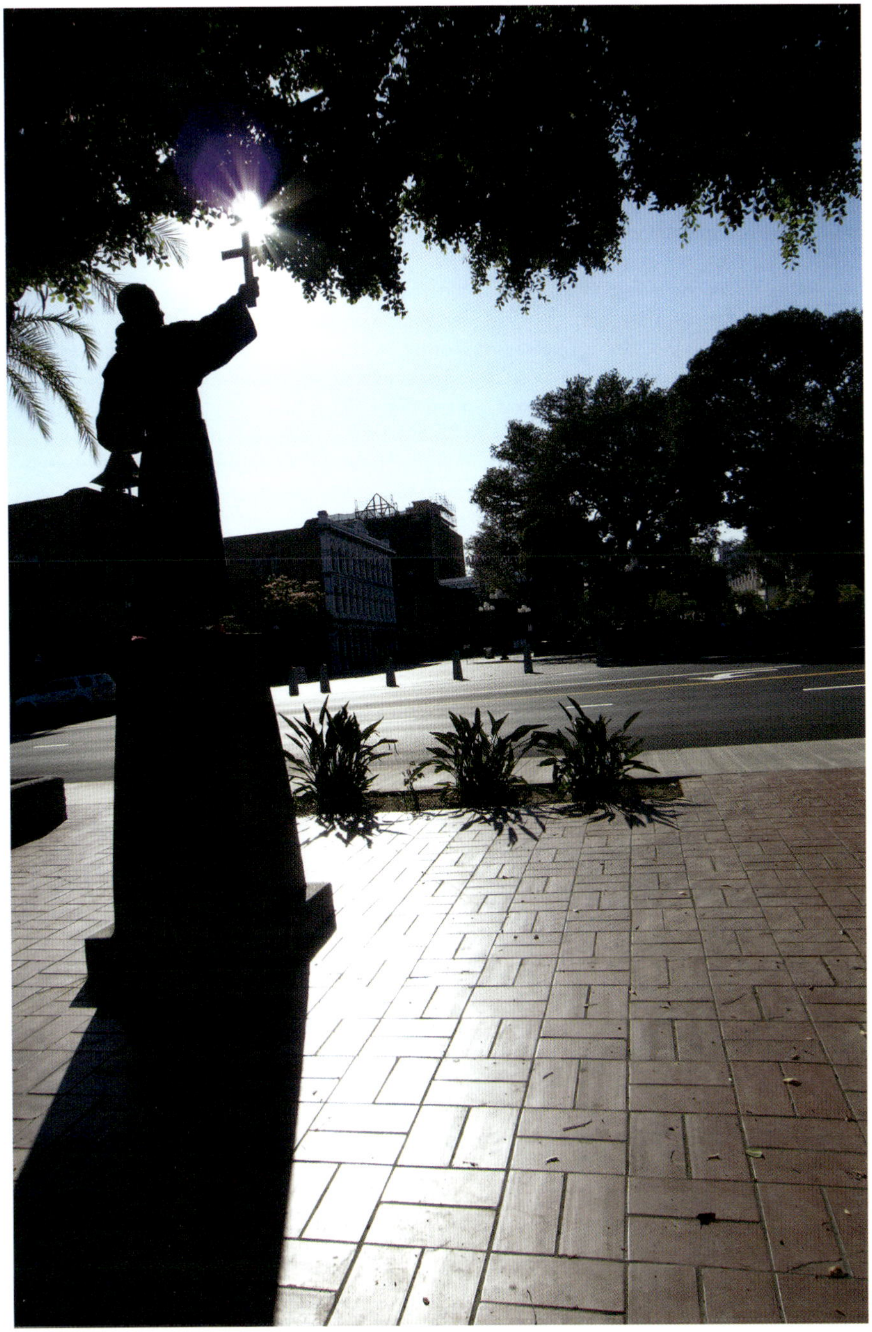

OUT TOWARD THE PRAIRIE, AFTER SLEEPING IN THE BLACK HILLS. Stopped at Hot Springs, in the morning sun, next to a clear river running boisterously, like boys playing with puppy dogs. I stopped for a music shop. Not much business out here, I guess. An old lady showed me round, friendly and enthusiastic—obsessed with Ovation guitars, made of plastic. Coffee from a bar next door, the server another of those long brown-haired American girls. Save me. An old prison in the parking lot, stalls off the road selling trinkets. On into Wind Cave—rolling hills and grazing bison—of course it's a national park: old America is only available in aspic. Slowly, slowly the hills subside, like ripples washing the Black Hills' feet—until all sense of tide is gone and the hillocks are windchop, chaotic, without orientation, washing this way and that with the constant fitful wind. Endless ice-sheet moraine, covered in the thinnest skin of grass. Where the grass is cut the land erodes, in brilliant green and brown striations, like mouldy dripping chocolate cake. Not for the first time it feels like sailing out under this endless sky, speed turned down to the sense-of-snails-crawling: impossible to judge distance, nothing here but bumpy green. Over one such bump three crosses are off to the side. State funded, perfunctory, a warning for the living, all sense of tribute denied. "X marks the spot—THINK—Drive safely!" But here three real and blood rushing people came to an end, their lives eked out on this green ocean. All traces gone now of car wreck, horror and tragedy. Someone loved them, clearly, and could not leave these signals naked, just a statistical State-marker on the road. So with infinite care they wrapped them in red tinsel, and shaped one heart for each, remembering a life. Rustling in the endless prairie wind, glistening in the sunlight, dripping in the rain. The colour of blood fresh spilled, fighting forgetfulness, staining the snow.

CROSSES ON SCENE OF HIGHWAY ACCIDENT—U.S. 91, IDAHO

Frank often sought nothing so resolutely as to photograph the indescribable, "the essence of the black and white, of where God is" (Frank 1991: after plate 63). A beautiful example is *Crosses on Scene of Highway Accident—U.S. 91, Idaho*. Frank photographed a road flanked by three simple crosses, an image that could be read as simply a memorial to three road accident victims. It is followed by *Assembly Line—Detroit*, a car factory staffed by oily, busy line workers. This later can be seen as a comment on the means of the victims' destruction. People make cars, which then destroy them.

Streaming from the top of *Crosses on Scene of Highway Accident* is a flare of light. The light is unnatural looking, most probably the result of a fault or crack in the lens (Day 2011: 144; Livingston 1992: 307). The intense centre beam, flanked by two fainter subsidiaries, recalls many Renaissance depictions of the opening of heaven and the descent of the Holy Spirit. Titian's *Assumption of the Virgin* (1516–1518, Basilica di Santa Maria Gloriosa dei Frari, Venice) is an example. For me, though, the most poignant resonance is with Rembrandt's powerful etching, *Three Crosses* (1653, Rijksmuseum, Amsterdam). In both Frank's and Rembrandt's work, this light from above falls onto three crosses. The ones in Frank's photograph are small, probably metal, cruciforms, stuck into the verge of the highway mentioned. Most likely it is a roadside memorial for people fallen in just such a road accident as was figured earlier between *Winslow and Flagstaff, Arizona*. Here, in a place which a moment's inattention would miss, Frank has discovered the contemporary world's refiguring of the image underlying the iconography of the crucifixion. Rembrandt's suffering Christ and broken beggars are gone now, and these tin memorials are left, along with those they remember, silent and alone in the vastness of the American heartland.

The shaft of white light above the markers contrasts sharply with the dirty greys of the factory that follows, giving the latter an almost infernal suggestion. Frank conjures heaven and hell in the almost invisible space between his pictures.

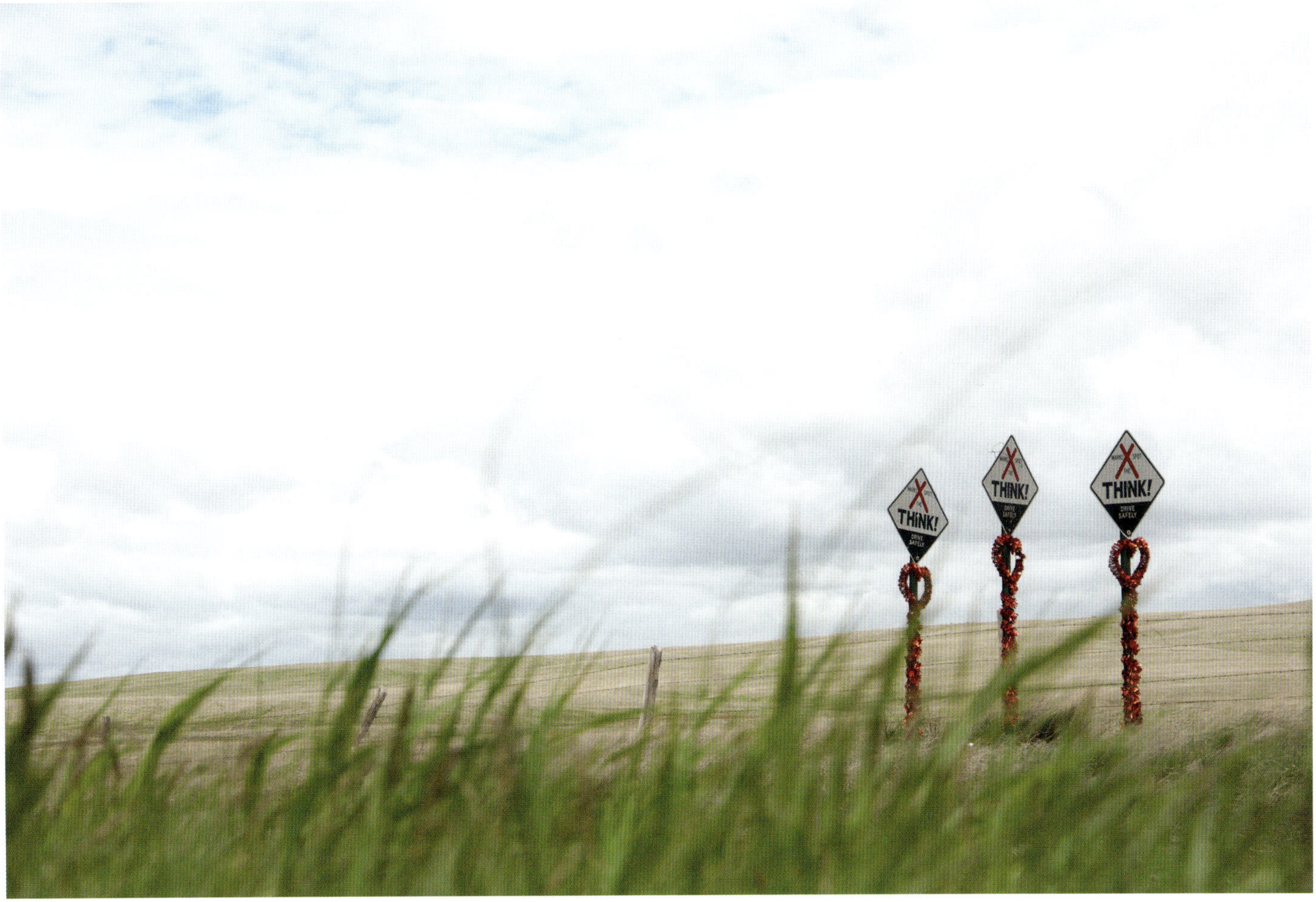
THINK!
DRIVE SAFELY
THINK!
DRIVE SAFELY
THINK!
DRIVE SAFELY

SOME COMMUNITIES IN DETROIT HAVE TURNED TO SUBSISTENCE FARMING, in gardens and parks, since there is no work to be found, nor benefits to be had. People are still making cars for sure, just mostly in Asia now, where workers are cheap and health and safety and unions mostly unknown. Our faux democratic governments turn a blind eye, since they—our so-called 'representatives'—own the companies that run the Asian factories.

There is nothing wrong with machines. I like them—cogs and pistons, realised imaginations and bits of cleverness, easing our passage, often keeping us alive. This trip of mine, this holy and less holy escapade, has a single machine at its heart.

Frank's *Assembly Line—Detroit*, taken in the midst of machines, is, though, demonic and dingy, despite its overhead light. I know the life lived sitting by these machines, covered in slurry, hands tattooed by oil-filled swarf gashes, blinding flare from arc welders, missing fingers from the grinders. This was one of the worlds in which I grew. My grandfather had only half of one hand, after a mishap on a machine one day. My father is deaf from the forge hammers. Their factories are gone now—the gates have closed, and the plant all gone away East.

It is not the machines that are to blame. Mass production is the devil in the oily detail, instigated originally by the US Army, which wanted interchangeable parts in their weapons to ease repairs. Pioneered by Smith's Armoury, Colt, Singer and Ford, interchangeable parts need machine tolerances, and it's more efficient for each machine to do a single, repetitive task. Men become servants of the machines, not their masters—and its better to have workers who can stand to be bored. So this grey assembly line and the harrowed ennui of the workers sitting alongside it. Profit and capitalism, the anti-humane mantras of our world, rivet these humans onto greasy seats, for every day of their lives, until they die. Doesn't have to be this way—machines and work can be cut to a human scale. By accepting less and espousing equality. The only possible future.

Parts of Detroit have returned to subsistence farming, in gardens and parks, since there is no work nor benefits to be had.

ASSEMBLY LINE—DETROIT

A feature of *The Americans* is its lack of text. Frank clearly felt he did not need words to explain his photographs; they are themselves eloquent. As his mentor Walker Evans argued, "Pictures speak for themselves or they fail" (in Maloney 1958: 90). This was a radical position at the time Frank was working, with many believing words were essential for the understanding of images. Art theorist Jean Clay agrees, feeling that until the 19th century artists mostly saw and depicted that which could be described in words:

> This subordination (of image) to language goes so far that the artist in his observation of the outer world sees only what he can delineate, outline, quantify. Nature is a nomenclature. The rest participates in the 'unmentionable'—and therefore in the unfigurable. (Clay 1978: 14)

Frank lived with a community of painters before beginning *The Americans*, and watched them working. He, like them, wanted to access this 'unfigurable'. From the mid-nineteenth century, avant garde painters, principally working in France, had begun to abandon the traditional differentiation between highly worked, significant foreground objects, and the background which simply served to contain them. Paul Cezanne, for example, questioned the notion of visual hierarchy and gave equal attention to foreground and background. He began to integrate these in works such as *Fruit Bowl with Glass and Apples* (1879–1882, location unknown) or *Mont Sainte Victoire Seen from Les Lauves* (1902, Philadelphia Museum of Art). The Cubists took this further in their destruction of the separated integrity of objects. Painter George Braque's *The Portuguese* (1911, Kunstmuseum, Basle) or Delaunay's *The Eiffel Tower with Trees* (1909, Guggenheim Museum, New York) exemplify the interpenetration of what were previously distinct objects and ground. This breakdown of boundaries facilitated a discussion in these works of things not easily depicted, which exist behind or between objects—'time' and 'energy' are examples. These are mercurial forces which cannot be directly seen, and whose presence must be intimated through their effects, visible all around. Figuring them is almost as difficult as seeing them, and must be accomplished in an analogous manner.

Frank sought to picture both the material and the immaterial in his photographs. His was the modern world, the machine

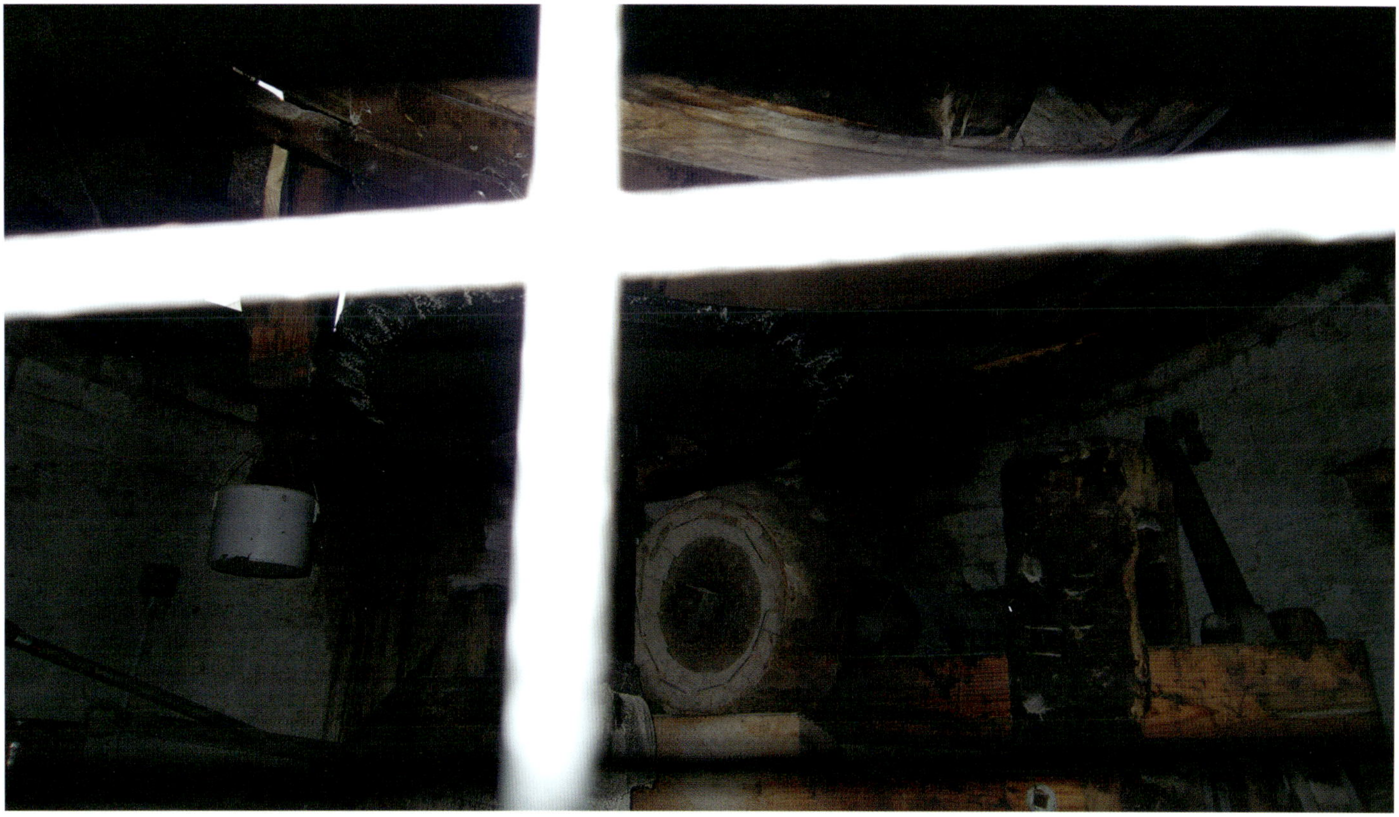

age of materials and consumerism. So he pictures the everyday, the (possibly) mundane. In these people and objects, he sees through the matrix of happenstance to the intimations of the ineffable beyond.

So here, following an evocation of heaven on the dusty roadside of the I 91, he conjures this infernal counterpart. The images are linked visually by the placement at the top centre of a block of light: this time it is artificial, falling from overhead incandescents, illuminating the factory production line. Black and white workers are busy alongside each other, labouring to construct the vehicles that ultimately claim the lives of people like those remembered overleaf. The car, rather than the cross, is the wheel on which they are broken.

Pablo Picasso said, "It's useless to paint what it's possible to describe" (to J. Metzinger 1910, in Clay 1978: 15). This painter, so hugely influential in the art scene in New York in the 1950s, is effectively describing Frank's faith in the power of the image. Paul Valery said, "poetry is the space between word and meaning" (Valery, in Clay 1978: 15). Between the physical materiality of its compositions, and that of which they speak lies the poetry of *The Americans*.

The social articulation explored in *Crosses* and *Assembly Line* instigates a short section of images that explore "the faces of the leaders and the faces of followers", as Frank described it (in Greenough 2009: 362).

THE OVERALLED WORKERS OF *ASSEMBLY LINE—DETROIT'S* heavy industry are followed by a crowd of smartly dressed men in *Convention Hall—Chicago*. Their earnest activity, name tags and indecipherable button badges give the event the look of a political convention, but this is not anywhere stated. What is clear is that the huddle of men in the right foreground are engaged in apparently sensitive negotiations. The central figure, who has his back to the camera, is surrounded by three others. Of the two we can see, one is looking downwards with concern and the other, cigar in hand, is conciliatory and placating, while retaining an air of invulnerable confidence. Behind these figures, another older man is pointing in a confrontational and accusatory manner. Behind this foreground group is a hall brimful with faces, all front-facing. These are mostly, though not exclusively, male. We can't know the details of the American policy, perhaps, or personnel movement, or financial shenanigans at the heart of this moment, but the universality of the political instinct in human beings is presented for us here with all its partiality, dissemblance and compromise.

CONVENTION HALL—CHICAGO

The contrast with the previous page is marked. These clean-shaven, suited and self-satisfied men are the balance to the busy labourers of the previous image. Each is tied to the other with bindings invisible to the eye, but as certain as steel. Even though they are never likely to meet, they are symbiotic, mutually dependent. In the American capitalist industrial system, the financiers and powerbrokers rely on the labourers, just as the labourers, more or less willingly, sought their lesser gains in the enterprises of the entrepreneurs. Perhaps 'symbiosis' is too good a word, since each cooperating organism should benefit equally from the relationship. This is clearly not so here. We cannot call the convention attendees entirely parasitic either, since the factory in Detroit could not have run without them.

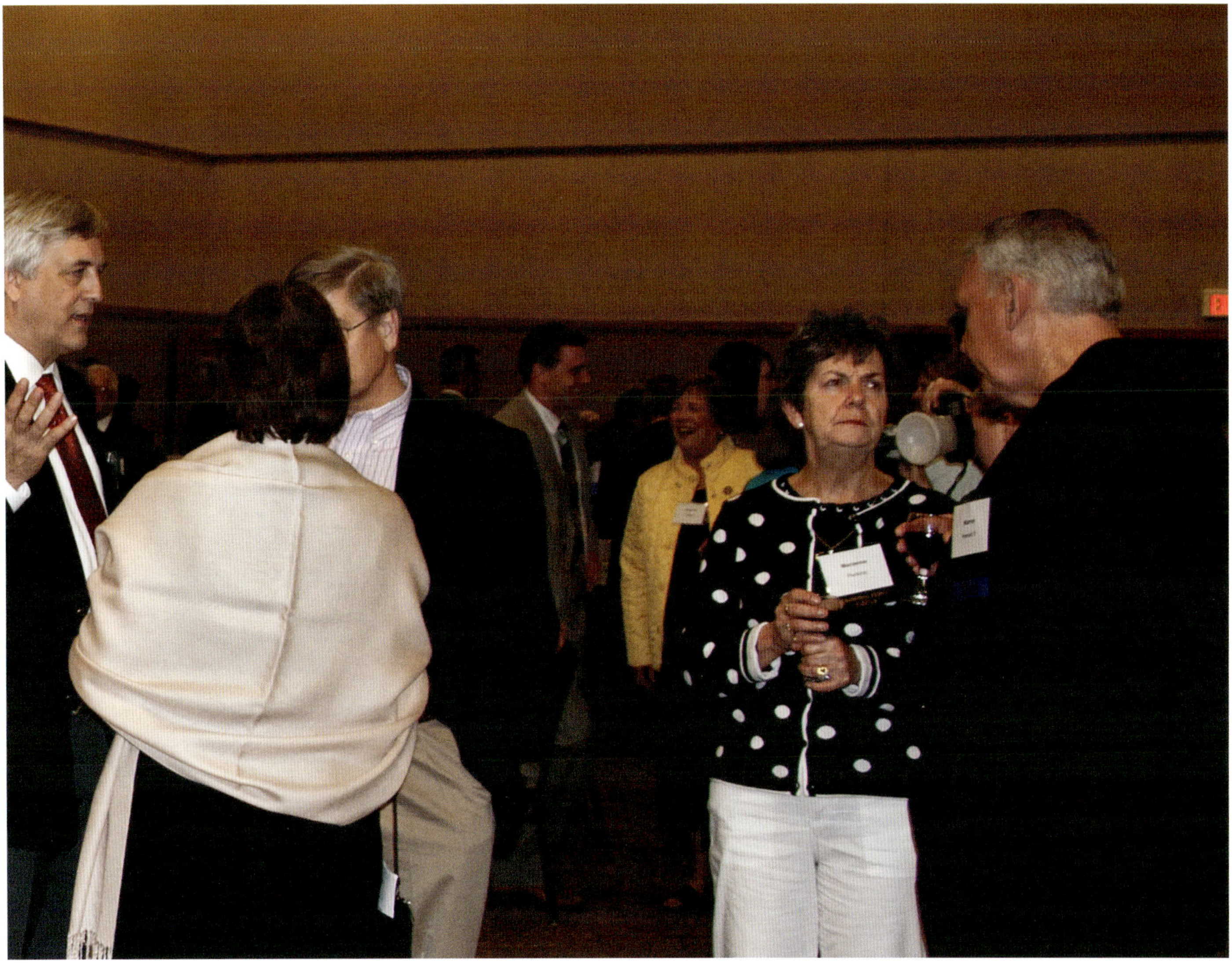

DEEP IN THE BELLY OF A RAILWAY STATION, the enormous kind that only cities spawn, I needed a toilet. Signs led me around corner after corner, up and down entirely purposeless seeming steps. Eventually, as if hidden away like a treasure, there was a men's room, wrapped in a concrete and strip light womb. Stuck with little mosaic tiles, of a dirty terracotta tone—burnt umber perhaps, or something other—designed to complement the colour of piss. The tungsten light stained it yellow on yellow, a place to forget about, to ignore. In the corner an old man was impish faced in a white overall jacket—standing by a table arranged with toilet paper and a mug for tips. I asked if I could photograph him, here in this netherworld—a kind of purgatory it seemed to me, not hellish, quite, neither rattling heaven's door.

My camera decided to mix him up with the street outside on this snowy night, bringing some kind of air and light to the eternal buzz of filaments and the distant rumble of tunnelled diesel trains. Somehow this image has become a thing for me of beauty, capturing better than anything that frozen winter town. The biting air, the bitter sky and the incalculable masses, marooned there with little option—land of the free, home of the brave.

MEN'S ROOM, RAILWAY STATION—MEMPHIS, TENNESSEE

Men's Room, Railway Station—Memphis, Tennessee swoops down from the acquisitive and moneyed world of the last image into what Kerouac called "the loneliest picture ever made, the urinals that women never see, the shoeshine going on in sad eternity" (Kerouac, in Frank 1959: 5). A blue-collar worker certainly, stooping and overalled, is cleaning the shoes of a suited man enthroned on a high seat. The chair was clearly constructed to save the back of the cleaner, but emphasizes thereby the difference in their stations. The suited man hides his face with his hand as if he, like Kerouac, is aware that this is a scene not meant for universal consumption, a secret place of sorts. Perhaps he is aware, too, of the lowliness of the moment. The cleaner's implements lie around the men's room, reminding us of his other duties: he tends the feet and the urinals of others. The loneliness of which Kerouac speaks is palpable, but it is not all that is here. The toilets are clean and well maintained, and the attendant seems engaged in his work. We tend to pity those we feel are less fortunate than ourselves and, if we are sympathetic, to look down from our self-assumed positions of superiority and castigate ourselves for our complicity in their situations and circumstances. Kerouac stops short of this, but the scent of it is in his commentary. This is not necessarily true in Frank's image, however: no one asked the attendant how he felt.

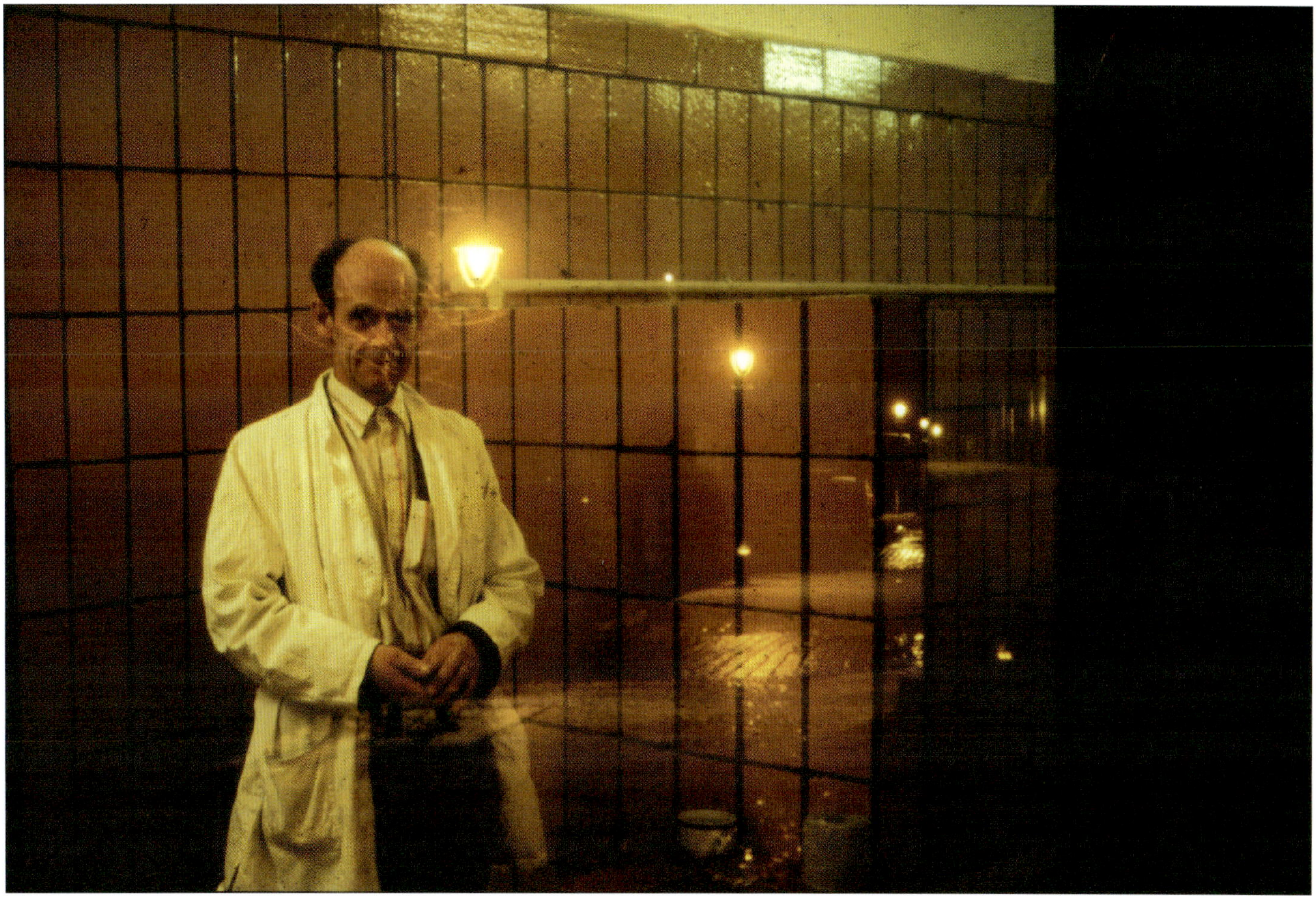

TOO TIRED FOR DOWNTOWN, I HEADED TO DANNY'S BAR, ADVERTISING LIVE MUSIC. It was in sight of my Days Inn motel and advertised live music: I hoped the bar, unlike the hotel, would taste of more than curdled tofu. This is Music City after all.

The stench of stale cigarette smoke was life-threatening—been a while since I smoked and I could hardly breathe. I took a table by the stage and was brought a Miller. The first guy up was barely in tune, and his story of regular appearances on radio stretched the audience's patience. After a couple of songs a swarthy young man walked with absolute confidence to the stage and forcefully offered him a beer to stop playing. The singer was devastated, visibly struggling to assimilate this latest humiliation and still believe in a future. I did not see how he could easily find that way.

On the table next to me a group of middle aged were drinking heavily and giving off the signs of having something like a good time. One of them seemed strangely childish, despite his white mullet and goatee. He didn't seem to like me, I don't know why. The house band finally got up and waded, competently, through some country classics. They had some skill and were not awful, but I could see why they were not playing Downtown. I don't want to say, here, that it seemed tawdry or desperate, this Saturday night. I don't want to believe the exuberance of my neighbours was a frenzied grasping for the best that they could get—which, in the end, wasn't actually much. I was tired. Perhaps saying that is enough? I walked to the beer pulls and paid the barmaid, who smiled beautifully and said, "Hello stranger…" A beer, 40 cigarettes smoked passively and a smile. Thankyou, Nashville, and goodnight.

COCKTAIL PARTY—NEW YORK CITY

The subterranean, hidden world of the men's room leads into a *Cocktail Party—New York City.* The people pictured are not overtly workers, although social networking is, of course, an essential aspect of business. The men at extreme left and right are smart and taut, framing the women at the centre of the photograph. They are smiling and polite, their body language suggesting mannered and superficial engagement with each other, with only the woman second from left implying any kind of real intimacy. These wealthy and leisured individuals present yet another face of the complex social interrelationships that characterise, and weave between, the Americans Frank is observing.

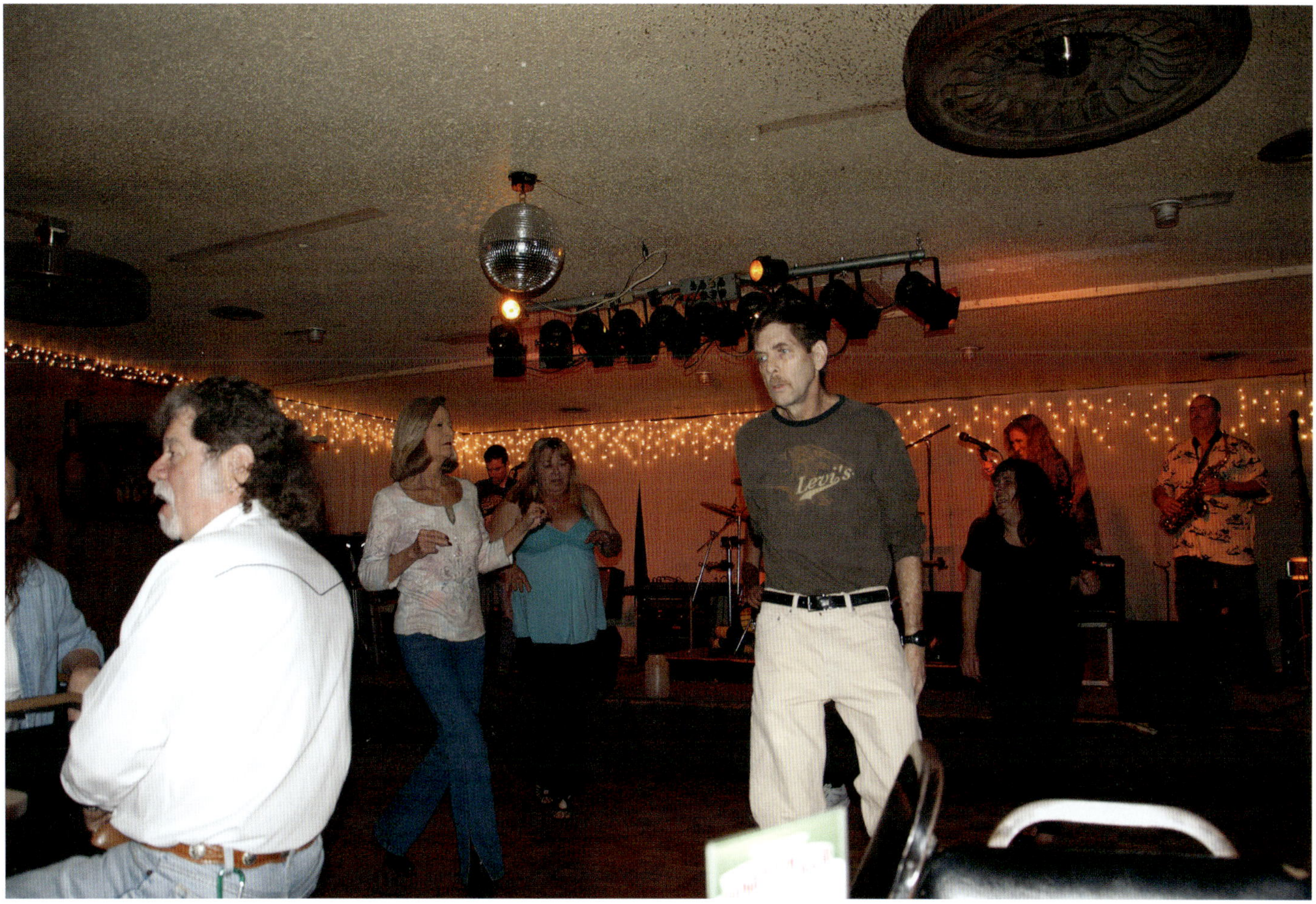
Levi's

NOW A CHILL POTATO PATCH FOG GRIPS THE MORNING: chill and damp, the Golden Gate a hollow maw, deepest grey. Last night a jazz trumpeter played as the homeless howled a night long litany outside my boutique hotel. It's on a street filled with commercial galleries, Picassos for sale by the score, Dali, Rembrandt, Lautrec. Not even any security. And just across the daytime thresholds, beyond the open arty doors, people in dirty rags push trolleys, full of bags and bottles. They just don't enter. 'Bums' and galleries, each with an overwhelming sense of place—they exist in the same city on the same street without ever interacting, an invisible interface as hard as iron between the inspiration and the expression. I walk between those worlds, an unconvincing art buyer (though I was not ejected), a more convincing bum.

Later, in the darkness, I came across a beautiful man catatonic on the floor. He had pissed himself, a river flowing from his loins, like the Hindu story of us all, conjured in the vulva of Shakti and sent out into the world on the wings of her dance. He looked like Jesus, lying there under an art school sign. A black guy shouted at me "That's something I've never seen, taking a picture of a man when he's like that!..." I guess that's my limit, as far as I'm able to go? Taking his picture, showing it to you. I'm no doctor of medicine or Samaritan, doubt I could have lifted him if I'd tried. But there is another reticence, maybe more powerful, that holds me back. This is his life, his decision, as it was Kerouac's. I think maybe I respect him that? He is beautiful lying on the floor—and I am simply sober.

SALT LAKE CITY, UTAH

Salt Lake City, Utah is another of those wonderfully anomalous images that serve to disrupt Frank's work and dam the sequential flow of his images. It is a real maverick, having little relationship to any of the other photographs in the work. It is an architectural photograph, so relates vaguely to other photographs dominated by buildings, such as *Rooming House—Bunker Hill, Los Angeles*. *Salt Lake City* pictures a darkly sinister building. We can easily see from its signboard that it is an art school, however much it may resemble the Bates Motel from Alfred Hitchcock's celebrated film *Psycho* (1960). The low light renders the entrance gate, the steps and the roofline an almost-silhouette against the pale sky. Amusingly, the image is a study in shapes, with the rectangular noticeboard, spherical gate ornament and the conical roof of the tower all describing the geometry that Cezanne believed was at the heart of all of nature and that, through him, powerfully influenced the development of Euro-American art in the twentieth century. Is that all this is, a quick smile between Frank's other considerations? A momentary nod, perhaps, in his inimitable way to Moholy-Nagy and others, for whom geometry and form were of the most pressing significance? A formalist moment discovered by Frank in the nether lands of America? How ever we understand it, it is a moment in his progression around the country, and is an intriguing and unsettling pause in our progress through the book.

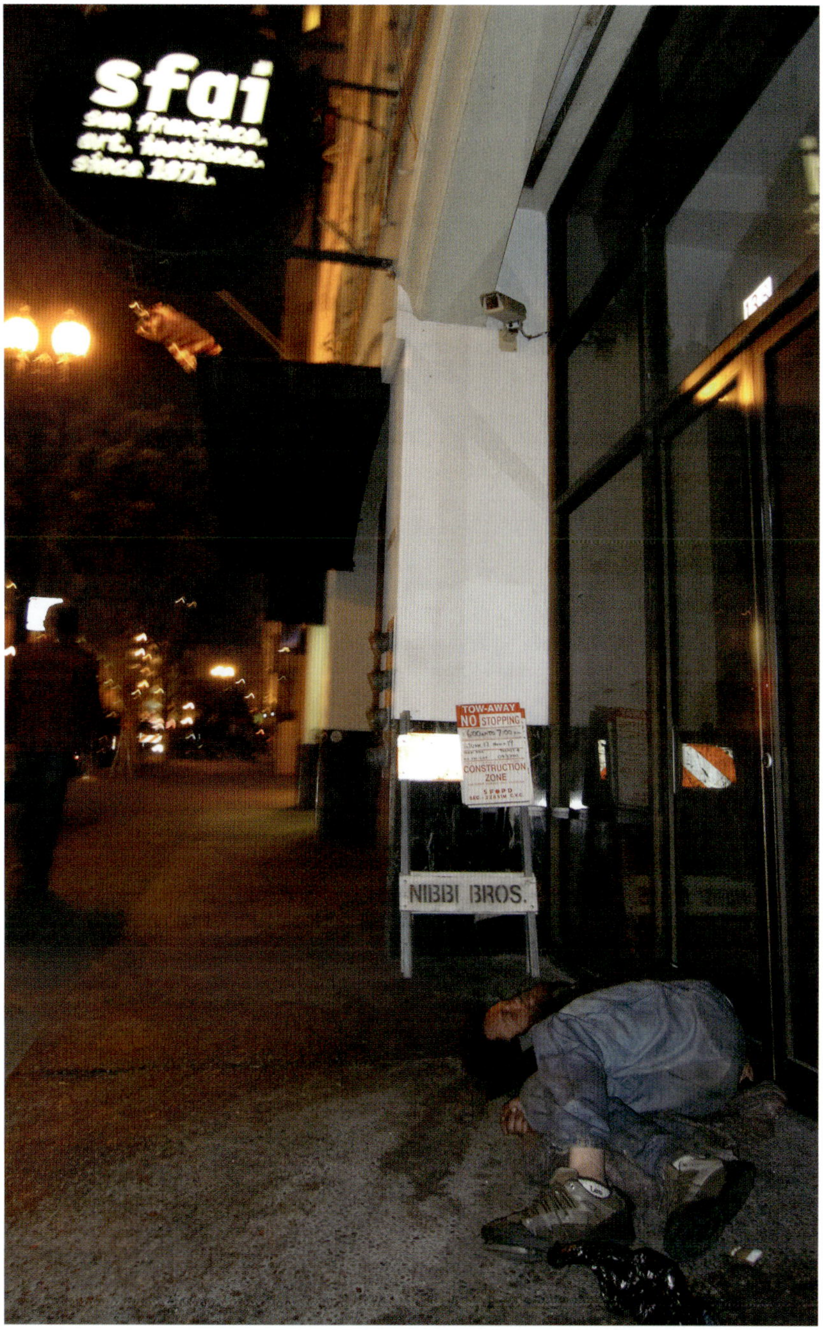
sfai
san francisco.
art. institute.
since 1871.
TOW-AWAY
NO STOPPING
CONSTRUCTION
ZONE
NIBBI BROS.

A WHITE PAINTED VIADUCT SPANS THE INLET, across the waters from Beaufort, South Carolina. This is the ocean, salt water in these creeks as they braid themselves indecipherably amongst islands and islets. Arriving hot and sticky from the journey, a soft wind blew across the waters to me, like a zephyr from the islands, carrying the faintest trace of an unfamiliar but beautiful song. I had to go there.

I drove across the steamy water onto St Helena, which set off an avalanche of thoughts… This was the place Frank had found his funeral, and a baby rocking the jukebox in a cafe and an evening laughing woman, smoking serenely in the last of the brilliant light. These are Gullah islands, I realised, a place made for themselves by the Black People of the South—this is where Martin Luther had A Dream, and James Jamerson learned the rhythms which Motown Records would sell to the world.

I walked into a little park. There was a gaggle of black people there, sitting amongst the trees. One toothless old man spoke at a ferocious speed, and I could not understand a word. Nor, even more confoundingly, could I sense any real communication between us when I looked into his eyes. What did he see when he looked back at me? An affluent white man, bizarrely walking into his local and familiar place? One of his companions smiled for a photograph and showed me a poem. I couldn't read it without my glasses and he demurred to read it aloud, instead giving me a web address. He was interesting, interested and there was connection between us. Too brief though, and I knew I could not stay to see the sights he recommended.

Across from them a little way a man called to me:

"What you doing?"
"Taking pictures."

He mentions five dollars. A slightly older woman next to him shifted uncomfortably, unhappy at the proposed exchange of money. He backed down and shuffled away. An astonishingly beautiful young woman next to her laughed and said, "I'll do it for five dollars." She leapt from her chair and struck a pose. Her skin was as black as night and her eyes sparkled like stars. For a moment she filled with light, a coruscation in the park pavilion, the viewfinder and the frame. No effort needed, I just recorded straightforwardly what she gave; vitality, the perfect contours of her face, an engaging edge of crazy. For the first time I understood Frank's photograph: it is joy he was trying to capture, joy in the face of all the woes and against the odds, irrepressible, needing no justification or premise, joy for its own sake, joy a nose thumbed at ill fortune, a nose thumbed at the Fates. Kerouac said: "The only ones for me are the crazy ones, the wild ones." So often, for me too, I guess. I do not know if she knew Albert Camus' (2005[1942]) writing about Sisyphus, who rolls his rock eternally up the mountain, only to see it fall again to the bottom every evening, as a punishment for denying the Gods. His heroism lies in his continued defiance—do what they will to him, he smiles in the teeth of fate, undefeated, indomitable. I so much wanted to know more about the world of Elizabeth Smith and something tangibly tugged at me to stay. I could have, could still be there today, living somewhere in a clapboard shack, finishing this book in a different way, used now to the humidity and deeply tanned by the sun. But the press of journey was on me, so I smiled, gave her five dollars and walked away. So many times I've moved on when maybe I should have stayed. St Helena is a potent and important place, where a race declared themselves independent, in no one's thrall, raised their flag, raised their heads and cried to all the world their freedom. Maybe one day…

BEAUFORT, SOUTH CAROLINA

Beaufort, South Carolina, is another tricky image. There is little direct relationship between it and its predecessor, revealing a black woman sitting outside in another sunset. She, her chair and a high distant cross are the only marks of humanity on this landscape. She is looking off to the right, smiling. The cross, as we noted, was a major linking element in several earlier pho-

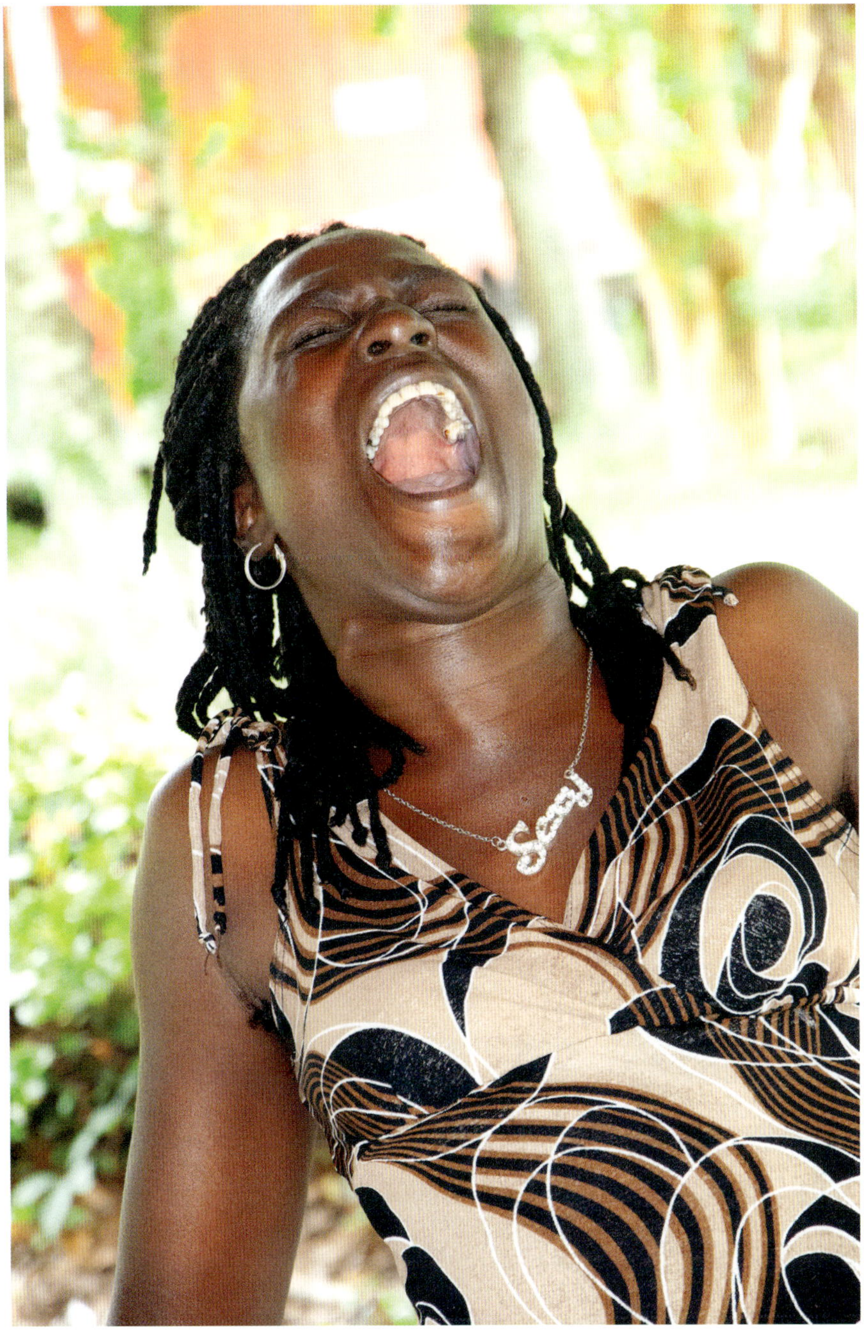
Sexy

tographs and is reprised here. It prefigures the next image in a way, since the following photograph is the first of three images concerned with death. The cross theme also surfaces in another image nine on from this one, where it is even more overtly linked with death. The palpable peace of the sitting woman smiling into the evening, at rest in her chair, contrasts powerfully with the following images of life's extinction. How rare are these moments of satisfied stasis, in the dynamic, uncertain and never-resting experience we all share, plunging headlong, if so often indiscernibly, towards the grave? How is it possible in the flood, carried on the tide of our experience, to rest and be at peace? In this image, Frank records someone who has found a moment of it. Kerouac described her as "One incredible I think Seminole woman pulling on her cigarette with thoughts of her own, as pure a picture as the nicest tenor solo in jazz" (Kerouac, in Frank 1959: 3). All that notwithstanding, she is sitting just along from the *Funeral—St. Helena, South Carolina.*

DEATH AND THE MEMORIALS OF DEATH. Like a sting or wound, burning and insistent, is the actuality of another's dying. It grabs you like an assassin, threatening for a moment all you know, all you are. Our equilibrium shivers and threatens to fail. Takes a while, but we process it—consign quickly the once alive to that other category, the departed, the lost. We close ranks around the living to block out that howling, knowing all that they were is forever gone. So unbearable is that loss, viciously dragging its red claws across our lives, that we make memorials to seal it away. A place and a thing to hold the anguish, so we can half open it when we need to remember and then safely put it away again. I've seen a deal of death on this journey: the Ludlow massacred miners' wives and children, killed long ago by the National Guard, and the tiny child whose nativity was marked by a star—his living became dying so quick and unexpectedly, leaving a tiny memory smudged across the high plains, a tear shaped tear in the Rio Grande. My own death stared out of the enormous glazed brown eyes of an Elk, whose innocent accidental threat I'd fought with beneath Wyoming stars. And Elvis' tomb, which I watched between a woman's proudly exhibited thighs. Surrounded haphazardly by teddy bears and candles, the gifts of the faithful. I think he would have liked the shortness of her skirt.

Life through a lens, somehow, is trammelled, its rawness taken away, immediacy subdued. Like a friend who was commissioned to record an abattoir and could only look at it through his camera. If he lowered it and let himself be there, he threw up. Fine though, through a viewfinder. So, in the presence of death unexpected, everyone approaches looking through a lens. The immensity of the spectacle captured first, to make sure it is safe. Then, perhaps, for a moment we look with our eyes, engage with our minds, experience the vision unmediated, feel the sting of sharp reality on our face. Before the warm fuzziness of a life safely secondhand tempts us back, drawing us into the glow on the other side of the glass.

FUNERAL—ST. HELENA, SOUTH CAROLINA

Such an image of balance, we saw back a page; contentment in her sitting, an equilibrium in the wild storms that come her way, a time out for a cigarette at the ending of the day. Across the Beaufort sound then, over the white viaduct, Frank too had made his way, where he found her cheek by jowl with *Funeral—St. Helena, South Carolina.* Frank has made images of death before in his book: this is the second one taken at this event and bearing this title. In the first *St. Helena* image, the faces of the mourners reflect death as they lean on their cars. It was found, also, lying beneath a tarpaulin on the *U.S. 66 between Winslow and Flagstaff.* In this second *St. Helena*, the faces of the black men are looking down, two of them at the floor, one of them contemplating the corpse. The manicured dead man is smartly dressed and appears as though he is sleeping. The expression of the living man in the foreground mixes curiosity and empathy with fear. This contemplation creates a connection between the young man, standing tall along the left hand side of the image, and the dead man lying to the right. Together they constitute the foreground plane of the picture, from which the other mourners stand back. The obvious tension between a young, living black man and an older one, now dead, eloquently examines life and death. Their similar suits extend the juxtaposition. The mourners celebrate all that this man has been and all that he has meant to the world. Frank communicates the profundity of this moment, among all of this ephemera, through his use of light. A good part of the image is burned out. The sky outside the building in which the dead man is lying is brilliant, this same light eating into the adjacent vegetation and haloing the men on the sunward side of the group. The floor of the building is similarly brilliant, biting at the edges of the coffin and the trousers of the men next to it. This invocation of light and darkness occurs very often in the rites of passage from life to death. From the burning of burial ships by Northern Europeans to the Ghats of the Ganges, humanity associates light with life and celebrates that light in the rituals of life's ending. This is not surprising: we are the only creatures to control fire. Light and fire are, then, sigils for our species—invoking them for a human passing is entirely appropriate.

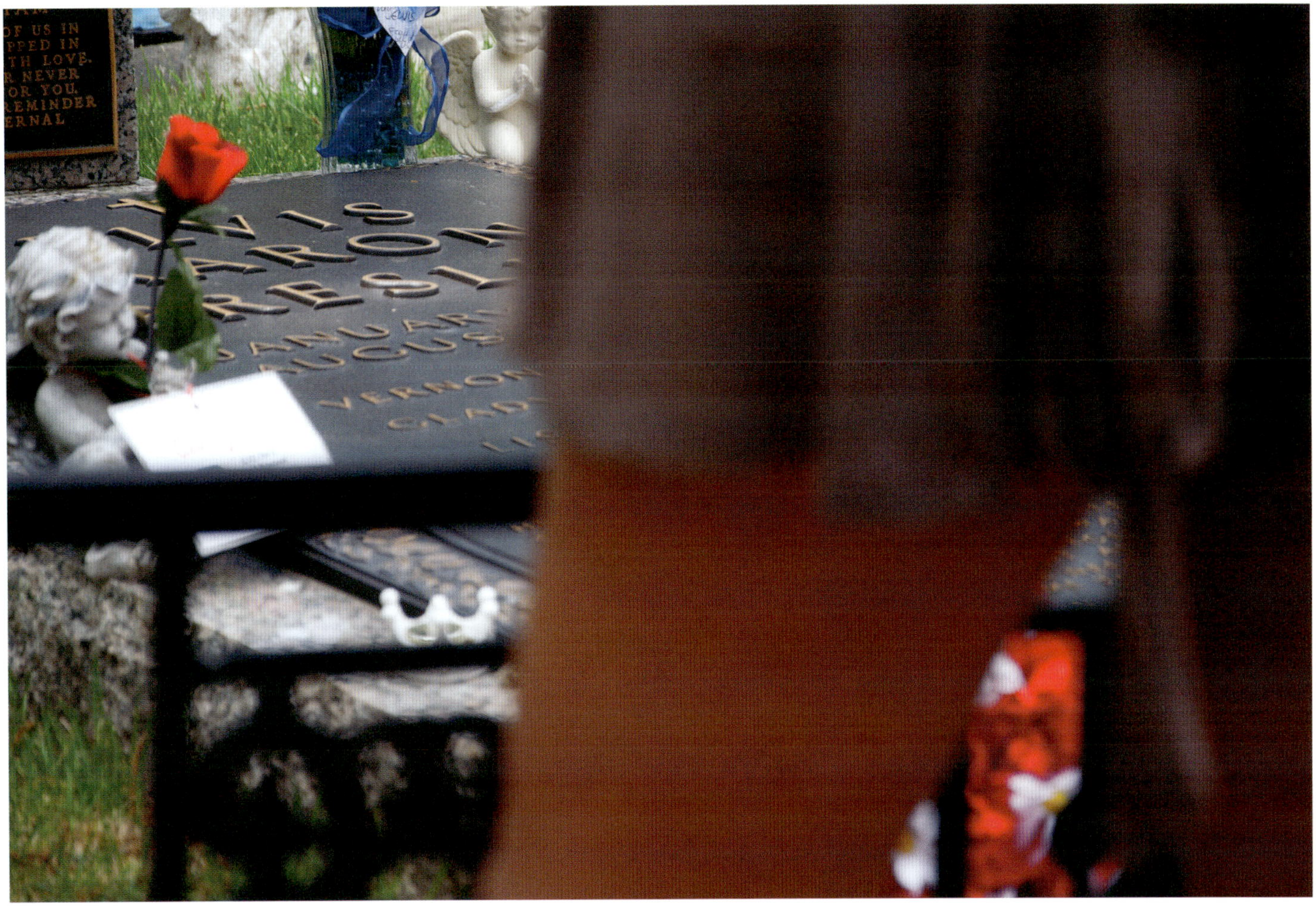
OF US IN
PPED IN
TH LOVE.
R NEVER
OR YOU,
REMINDER
ERNAL

THIS IS THE MODERN WORLD, FOR SURE. As someone said, "Modern Life is rubbish". There's a truth to that. When I first saw Frank's *Lincoln, Nebraska*, in which a department store is flogging cheap plastic memorial crosses, I felt a sense of how Frank was appalled by this readiness to reduce even the most sacred symbols to mass produced consumer goods at bargain prices. We are on the other side of that Rubicon, hard to see how we can make it back. We're stuffing all our world's hollows with landfill, obsessive little craftsmen we, bulimic humanity consuming acres of stuff, only to vomit it into holes to make room for some more. The profit optimising formulas of planned obsolescence and engineered failure—it's hard to stay positive with our idiocy sometimes. At the moment of death, too, and in its memorial, we know our offerings won't last for long.

I don't think, though, that this in any way lessens the sincerity or the heartfelt emotion that sits behind these tributes. People are existing in and responding to the nature of their age. Thomas Hardy so wonderfully described the passing of all things when he wrote in *During Wind and Rain*, "'Down their carved names the rain-drop ploughs" (Hardy 1917). Memorials, for him, were cut from stone; for us they are of made of sticks and sticky paper. This doesn't render the feeling, or the profundity of what is recalled, any less genuine.

CHINESE CEMETERY—SAN FRANCISCO

Somehow we want light to accompany death. Maybe we see it as the antithesis of dark, silent nothingness—and that is why we have Christmas, Up Helly Aa and a hundred other fire festivals to keep the winter night at bay. The last picture, *Funeral—St. Helena*, is so much about light. Frank's image is, interestingly, foreshadowed by the wonderful portrait of *Victor Hugo on His Deathbed* by Frederick Nadar (1885, J. Paul Getty Museum). The celebrated nineteenth century French portraitist uses light streaming from above to stunning effect, communicating an engagement with the 'transcendent unknown' that we all contemplate, at some point or other, and most often in the presence or environs of death. Frank figures this mystical signifier in *St. Helena*, just as he figured it earlier, shining down on *Crosses on scene of highway accident—U.S. 91, Idaho.*

More sombre, then, and melancholy is *Chinese Cemetery—San Francisco* for its lack of light. During one of the city's famous dense fogs, Frank has photographed a jumble of wreaths and white-painted sticks: one assumes that this was a standing tribute of some sort, now collapsed. Indistinct in the foreground are white shapes, which look like Chinese character-bearing prayer papers, but might equally be fallen flowers or leaves. A line of windswept conifers tapers away across the sky of the upper part of the image. The broken earth of the burial is contained within a wooden former of some sort, describing an 'L' shape on the ground within the photograph. These hard geometrical shapes are the marks of man, drawn beneath the enormity of this ocean-born, foggy sky. In this palpably damp and lonely space, they are ineffectual, peremptory and perfunctory. This is the end of all life—dust to dust, ashes to ashes—and the end, also, of all memorials.

Kerouac, in his introduction, senses the loneliness:

> blown over Chinese cemetery flowers in a San Francisco hill being hammered by potatopatch fog on a March night I'd say nobody there but the rubber cat. (Kerouac, in Frank 1959: 6)

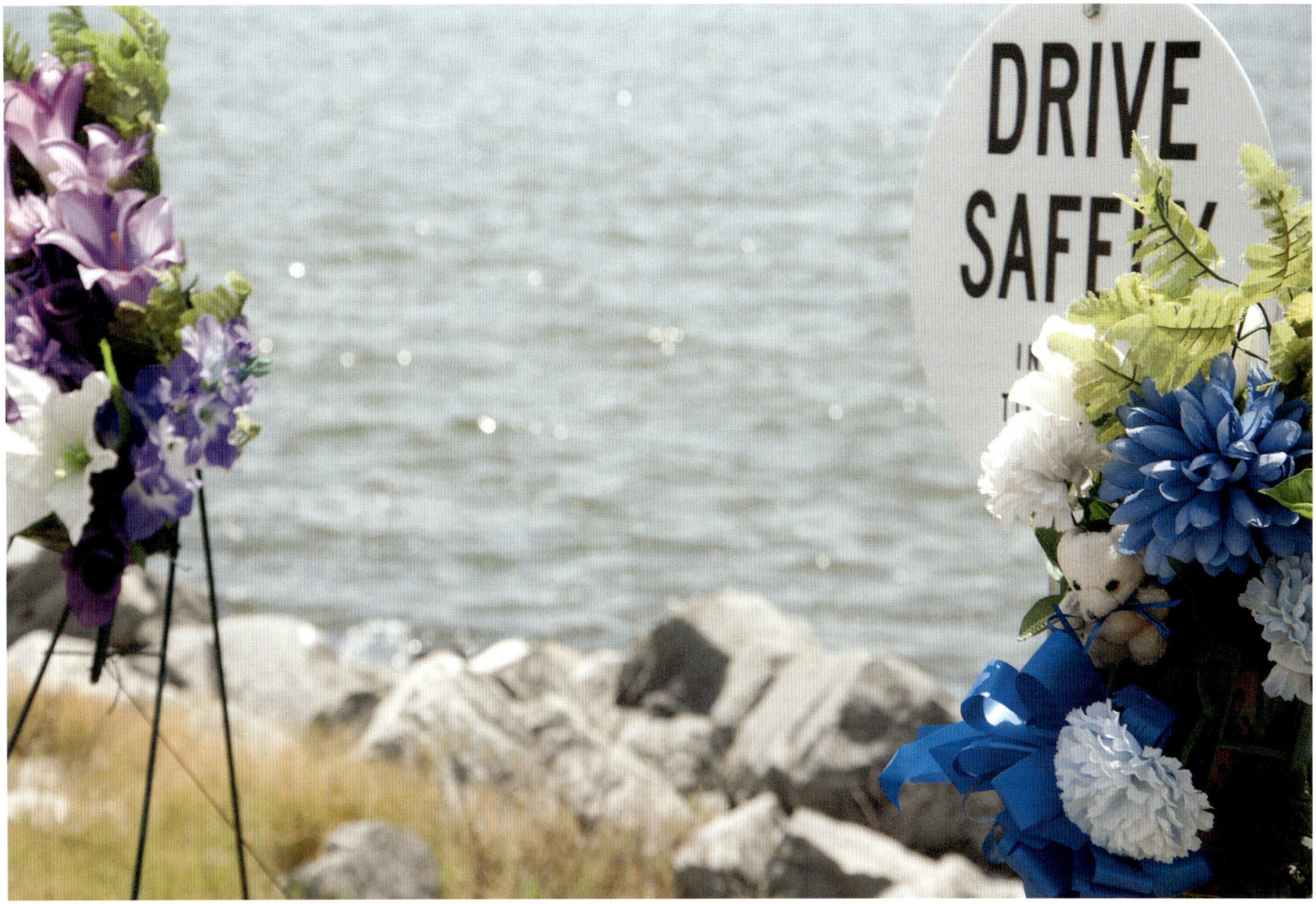
DRIVE

FOR WHOM did the bandsman give up his head?

POLITICAL RALLY—CHICAGO

Political Rally—Chicago, the final section-initiating image, is witty and in many ways a joke. Its depiction of a sousaphone-playing bandsman is playful, echoing something of Cartier-Bresson's bonhomie. This is Frank, though, so of course the image functions in other ways too. As with the woman at the beginning of the book, in the window in *Parade—Hoboken*, the bandsman is rendered headless, this time by his instrument. His body is a compound of flesh, uniform and metal tubing, creating an image of a composite being whose clear purpose is to act as a mouthpiece. We are shown what this mouthpiece is for by the flags which appear to stream out of the horn, festooning the building with stars and stripes. The instrument itself speaks so powerfully of America, invented as it was by an *emigré* musician who combined an aspect of his name 'So', with 'USA' in order to create himself anew in this new world. The performer here sports a badge, 'Adlai'.

There are two images in *The Americans* entitled *Political Rally—Chicago.* This repetition is inviting us to consider this image alongside the much earlier portrait of an effusive, suited man, declaiming his faith in something or other from a ledge. The building stone in both images is similar, and it may well be that the members of this band are the suited man's heralds, sonorously supporting his rhetoric from below. The implication, of course, is the loss of self. The bandsman's individuality and self-determination are sacrificed, along with his head and face—such powerful signifiers of selfhood—to his vocation. What price the work of a mouthpiece?

We've noted that this final flag image replicates and comments on the book's first, *Parade—Hoboken.* Both are decapitations, and they bracket the book's consideration of this most powerful symbol of nationhood. Although the circumstances and complicity of the participants in these images are very different, both photographs evidence the stripes of red, white and blue that America indelibly paints across its inhabitants. While one is uncertain and tentative, perhaps even a victim, nervously holding her hand to her mouth, as if to quiet her doubts and fears as the celebratory parade passes, the other is a feet-first adherent, gladly taking his role as uniform and herald. The first seems ambivalent and uncertain; the latter is fully committed to his immolation.

In his exploitation of the flag as introduction and punctuation, Frank states his intention for *The Americans.* He wrote to his parents, "I am working hard not just to photograph, but to give an opinion in my photos of America" (Frank, in Tucker and Brookman 1986: 28). His opinion is expressed in his celebration and deconstruction of the flag. Frank's photographs catch the flag with its guard down—they depict it outside of its conventional settings, in situations without beauty or heroism. By this shifting of context, Frank questions and reveals the processes by which the Star Spangled Banner's meaning is constructed. He tears it away from the White House and Iwo Jima, and shows its reality in Hoboken or Jay. Frank tests the symbol in order to understand the civilization for which it stands.

His conclusion is ambivalent. The sousaphone player is subsumed by the Stars and Stripes, his identity destroyed, while the flag in Hoboken, for all the uncertainty of its flyers, may be all they have of colour and joy. Is it the nearest thing to hope in that desolation? The people of Jay trot out their much-repaired ensign and ignore it—it doesn't dominate them. In Detroit, the flag is merely one symbol among many, pressed into service by the owners and drinkers in a bar. It satisfies their needs. If the red, white and blue consumes some of its people, other Americans take it and mould it into their own likeness.

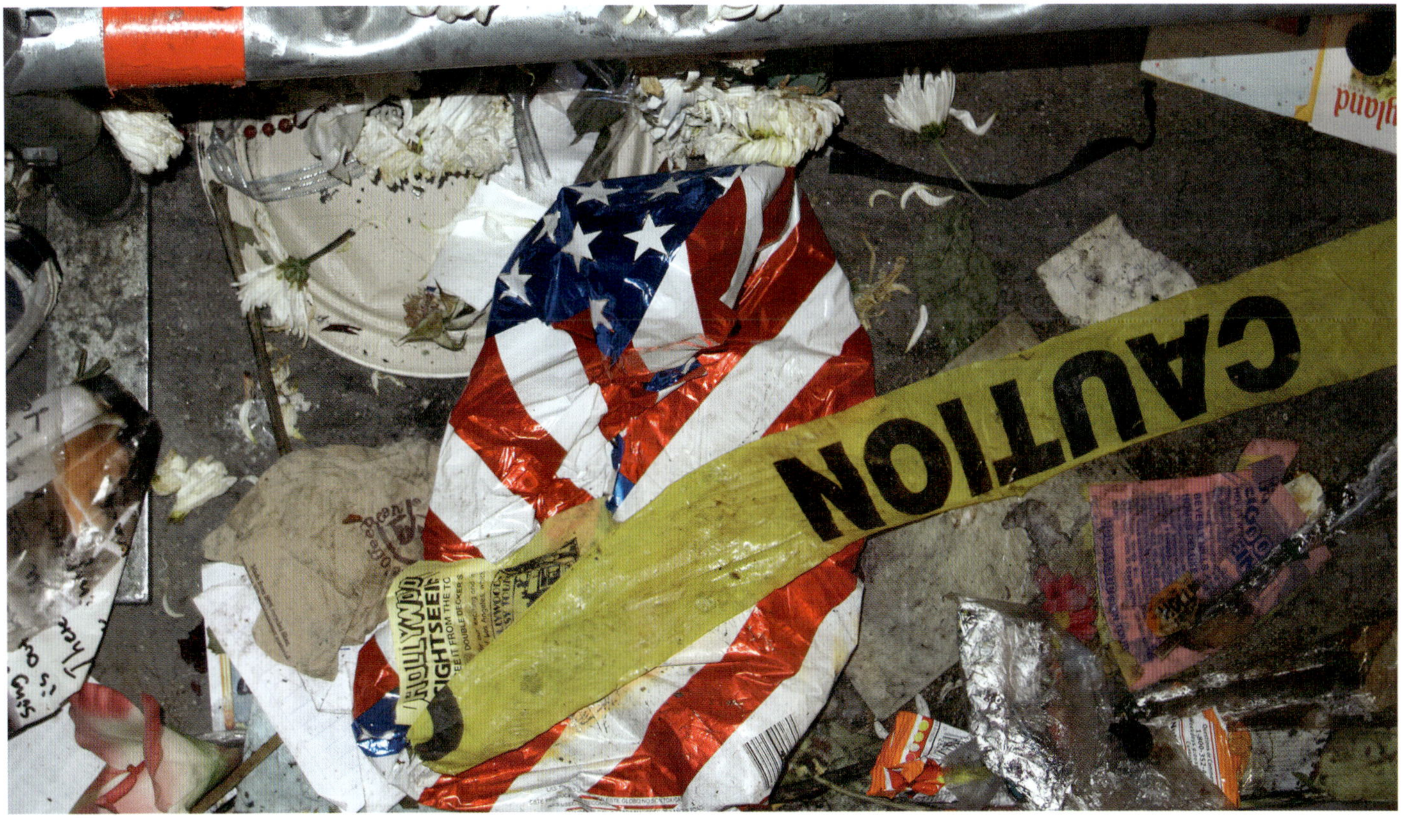
CAUTION

STORE WINDOW—WASHINGTON, D.C.

Store Window—Washington, D.C. continues the political theme from the last image, although subtly. A mannequin sporting a formal suit provides the link— like the sousaphone player, it is headless. The dummy advertises the shop's business; its 'Formal Wear' sign is visible at the top of the image. For some reason, the shop front's window is missing, replaced by what appears to be plastic sheeting. A refit is, perhaps, being undertaken. This creates an intriguing and beguiling uncertainty in the image's depiction of depth. After consideration, it becomes clear that the political portrait, which looks like Dwight Eisenhower, is stuck to this plastic, causing it to curtain. This disembodied head, floating in the confusing space adjacent to the headless mannequin, is a bizarre echo of a gallery-hung painting, or a display box filled with curiosities.

Frank's hopscotch connections are coming ever more to the fore in these later images, with a visual and/or conceptual linkage picking up on the previous image and another extending forwards into the next. The headless bandsman of the last image led us to the headless mannequin in this, as the pasted photograph of a disembodied head vignetted on a shop front leads us into the disembodied head of a TV presenter, vignetted on a TV screen in *Television studio—Burbank, California.*

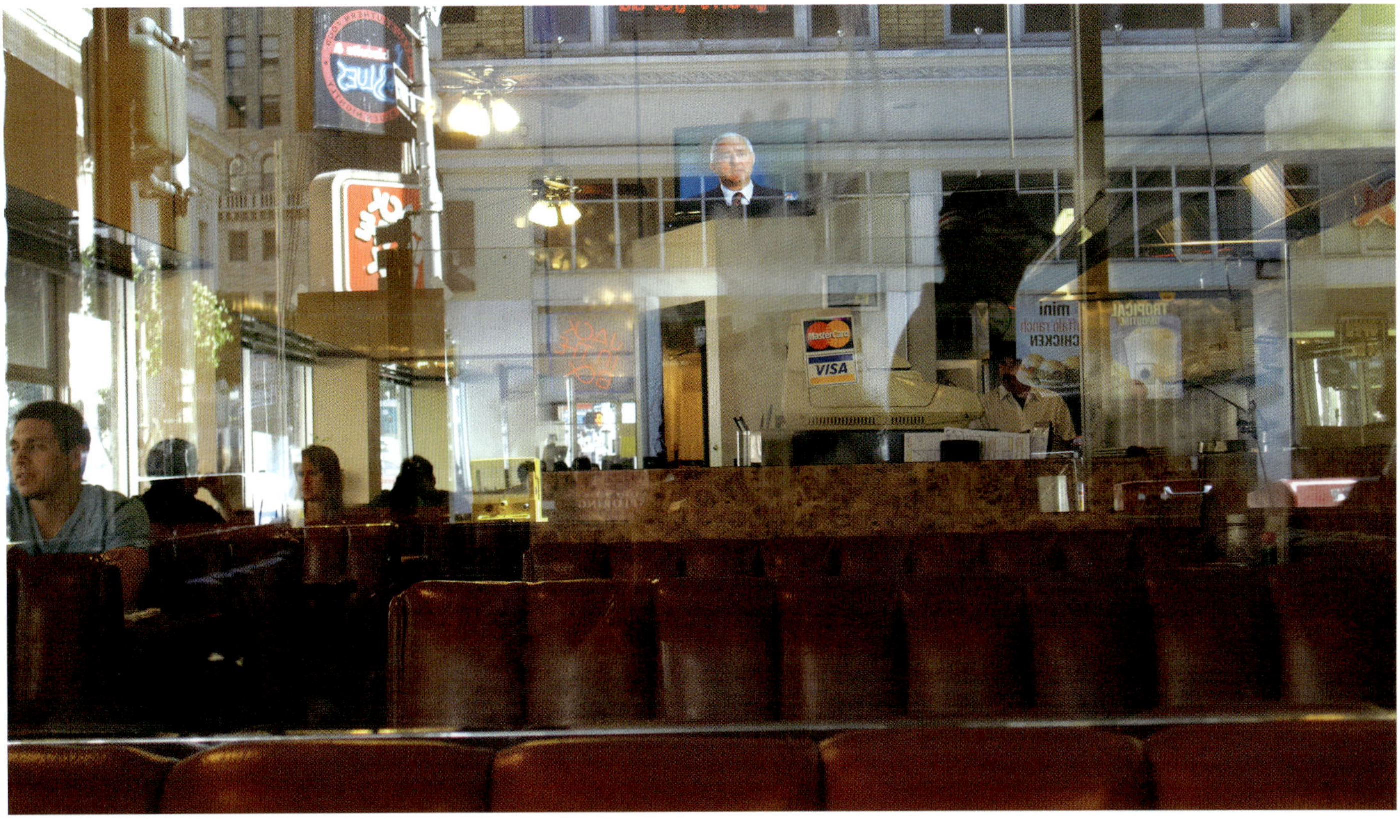
MasterCard
VISA
mini
CHICKEN
TROPICAL

DRIVING ALONG THE MUSIC HIGHWAY OUT OF NASHVILLE, I stopped at the Patsy Cline Rest Stop and Toilets. Nothing wrong, I guess, in being remembered with something useful. Plaques around were proclaiming this the hot-bed-road on which American music was invented, going on to capture the ears of the world. I see it, I think. The huge hinterland behind Nashville, spreading like ink into Smoky Mountains and Blue Ridge, country picking songs in the evening, full of humming birds, high balsam and mountain blasted men. It turned in my mind and flooded like a deluge, music flowing out of the mountains, narrowing, funnelling, getting ever more concentrated until finally it drip, drips—potent moonshine and acidic, into the bars and studios of Music City.

At the other end of this road is Memphis, the jewel in the crown of the Mississippi delta. Sitting at the apex, listening to the field-hands holler and the chain gangs howl, an old crone rocking on a porch, ears full of the traces of gumbo and the Monde Creole, carried up with the smell of mud and harvest on the wind.

Like enormous electrical conductors, these two Tennessee towns—building up an irresistible charge until finally they earth each other along Music Highway, in a sound like the howl of a coyote and the howl of a train, the buzz of a bandsaw and the buzz of a hummingbird.

TELEVISION STUDIO—BURBANK, CALIFORNIA

Just as the headless mannequin in *Store window—Washington, D.C.* followed the headless bandsman at the *Political Rally—Chicago,* so the bodyless head pasted to the same *Store Window* leads us into *Television Studio—Burbank, California.* Here, a very real presenter at left looks across Frank's image at a monitor showing her head, decapitated by television. Frank is playing with levels of reality and artifice in this picture. Neither of the presenters is real, obviously, one is recorded directly onto 35mm silver halide film, while the other arrived via cathode ray tubes and radio waves. The image includes another visual joke. The television studio set uses a series of linked diamond shapes, suspended at either side of the presenter, to frame her space. The angle Frank has chosen for his photograph renders these diamonds arrow-like. Her gaze seems to follow these arrows from her studio seat to the screen on which she appears, as if she is watching and musing on her projected self. The arrows also serve to illustrate, in a way redolent of 1950s graphics, the process by which she is captured by the camera and 'delivered' to the TV set. The arrow also links this picture into the next one.

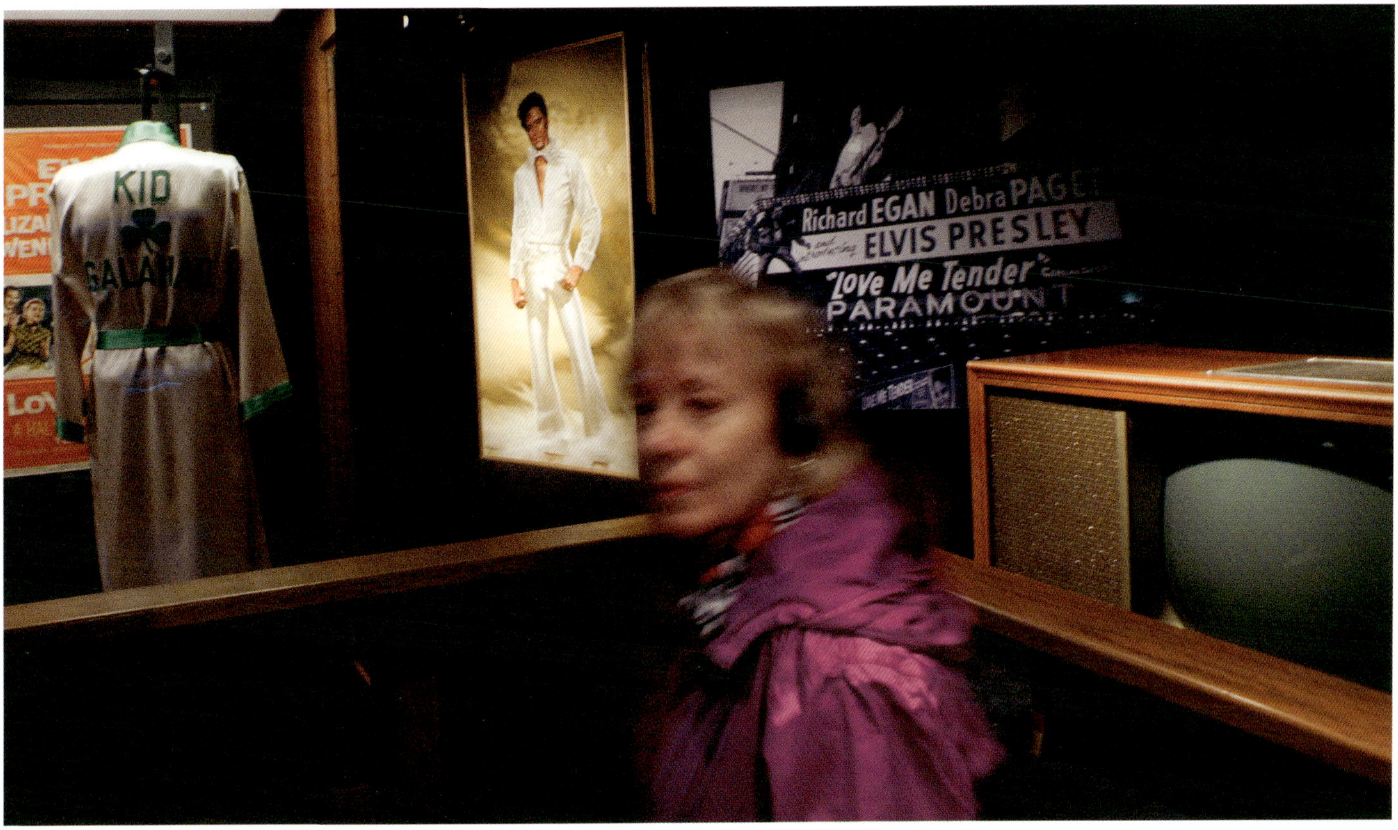
KID
Richard EGAN Debra PAGET
ELVIS PRESLEY
"Love Me Tender"
PARAMOUNT

I SLEPT LAST NIGHT ON THE SUMMIT OF MOUNT MITCHELL, highest place east of the Mississippi, miles high in a storm. The wind scraped at the summit like talons, scraps of cloud catching in branches, desperate for relief from the hurdy gurdy hurl, for something to hold on to. All night the wind rocked me, wrapped in three sleeping bags and a down coat. But I was truly happy—this is where I was made to be. Jet lagged still, and with clocks akimbo, I woke when I thought it was time to get up. Pitch black and blundering, I went outside for nature's call and to clean my teeth. I dinged my bear bell repeatedly as I was the only non-native creature this high up. The chill factor was astonishing—I needed three jackets. To my consternation there was no light at all. I thought in my confusion that my watch might be wrong, so lay down again to sleep: time turned out to be 3am.

Eventually the early light seeped sullenly into the day: I was irritated to be awake, longing for another hour in bed. Without ceremony, the cloud lifted a little and there before me was the whole of the Blue Mountain Ridge, stretching in a great 'S' up into the north-east and Virginia. I went outside wrapped in hats and gloves and in the freezing wind one thought came to mind: "When I get off of this mountain I know where I'm gonna go, straight down the Mississippi river to the gulf of Mexico..."

So I drove down to Asheville and into the Great Smoky Mountains. I was unprepared after the wilds for such a concentration of leather and tattoos, bright orange and green melons on dusty, broken-glass stuck lots and smiling brown toothed mid-day lounging boys, sat outside barbers and bars and motel shacks. Climbing slowly on roads where flotillas of Harleys drifted by on growling winds, everything was biker-black, except t-shirt prints and bandannas. Half way up came a mighty wind, a wind of biblical proportions, vanguarded by a rolling tumble of leaves. Too strong to look into or stand outside, it was followed by a huge downpour and lightning—the stuff of life. Daytripping bikers, who had ridden cocky and t-shirted into the morning sun, scurried now back for their shelters, enormous bellies shrink wrapped by sodden cotton. For one rider it was too much for even his Harley to handle, and an ambulance sirened past.

I was standing beneath a giant sign. It was neither Springsteen's "Exxon sign, that brings a fair city light" ('Jungleland', 1975) nor the eyes of Fitzgerald's Dr T.J. Eckleburg, looking from his enormous yellow spectacles, brooding over the solemn dumping ground. It was a sign that seemed especially for me, carried here and dumped by the Dorothy–Kansas wind. Or maybe it was me that was lifted and carried to this car park by the storm. Miraculously before me in pale letters metres high, a giant arrow pointed at the mountains and sky and said: "The Most Photographed View in the Smokies"—lest I in my ignorance might have passed it by.

LOS ANGELES

The arrow fired from the last photograph, *Television Studio—Burbank, California*, is caught in *Los Angeles* on the side of an otherwise dismal, featureless building. This is one of my favourite images in *The Americans*, speaking so concisely and so eloquently of our species' hunger for meaning and direction within a mass of indifferent dark shapes and dead ends. The neon arrow glows in the shadows of the claustrophobic street, pointing apparently at nothing, leading perhaps nowhere, but demonstrating such certainty and confidence, such brilliant poise and self-belief as it burns amid the dirty and beaten bricks and stones. It is a theme we've seen before in *Jay, New York* and in the fatuous faces of politicians in *Hoboken.* A torn, tattered and compromised reality is whitewashed over and adorned with bright distractions. This is the heart of the America Frank has come to know. As he wrote:

> I was aware that I was living in a different world—that the world wasn't as good as that—that it was a myth that the sky was blue and that all photographs were beautiful. (Frank, in Johnson 1989: 37)

There is no blue sky in *Los Angeles*, and the nature and quality of the American myth is revealed and celebrated wonderfully in this image. The arrow is a profound and recurring symbol in human culture. I can't help but think on the iconic quality of the mark-making in Jackson Pollock, Willem de Kooning or

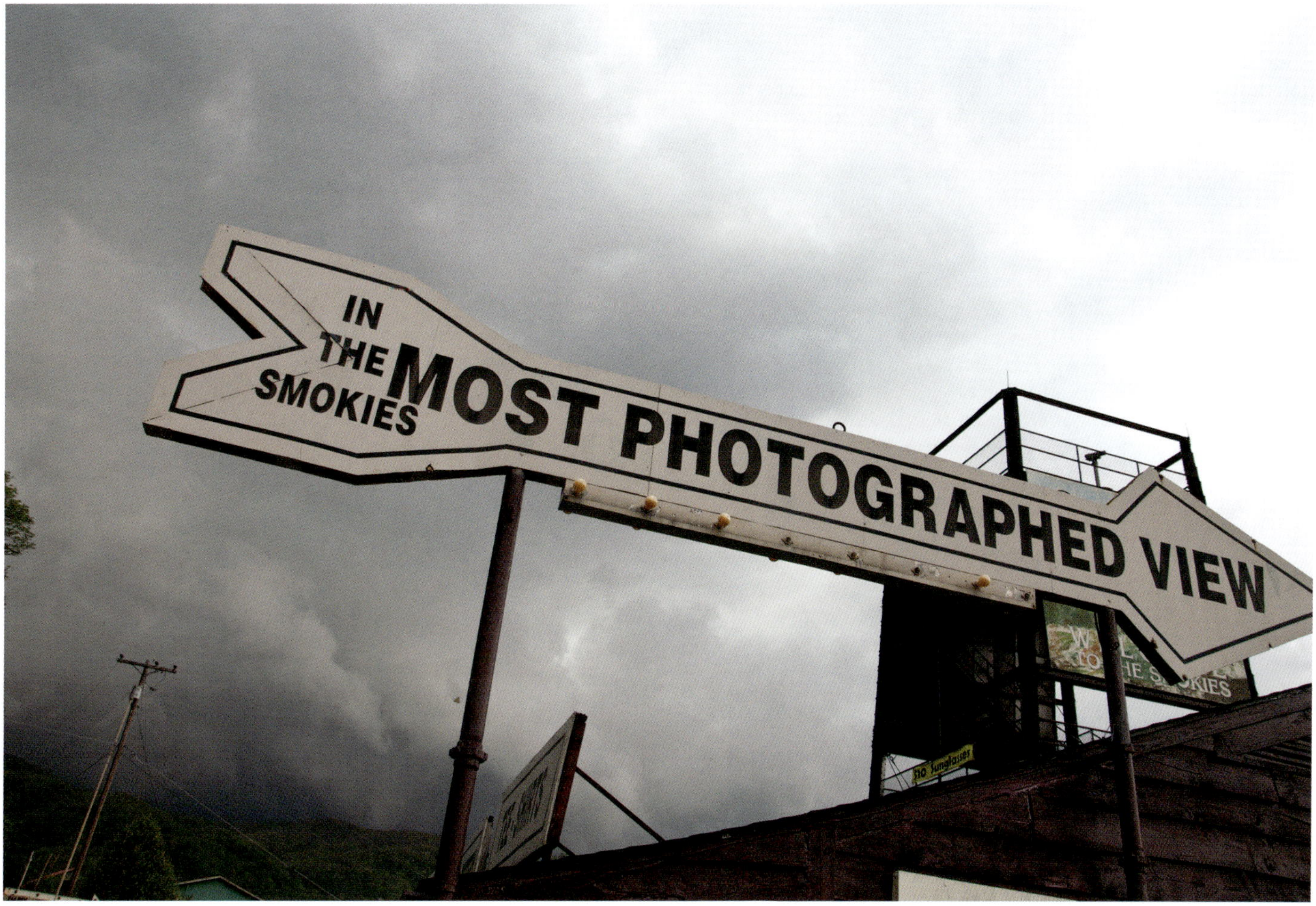
IN THE SMOKIES
MOST PHOTOGRAPHED VIEW

Alfred Leslie's painting, each of them seeking to identify and exploit just such significant symbols. I generally avoid the notion of the 'universal', limited as our intelligence necessarily is to the viewpoint of men, but if we accept that limitation, this somewhat spurious notion may be invoked here. The arrow takes us back to the days of stone and has been inscribed by us for millennia on walls of rock, wherever we have passed. Frank's photograph continues and comments on that tradition. It lacks the dignity of time that petroglyphs claim, and doesn't even have the elevated context of a gallery-displayed painting. This, of course, is its strength. Frank has caught this unself-consciously human moment, in which a sign is at once openly deceitful in its masking of the sooty reality beneath, and almost noble in its relationship to the walking man following its direction. Let's think again of Camus' (2005[1942]) model of nobility described through Sisyphus, who is doomed to roll his stone always up the hill, only to see it fall each evening back to the starting point. Sisyphus, nonetheless, smiles his defiance into the teeth of the indifferent Fates and rolls once more. This solitary man on a sidewalk in Los Angeles is, in his own striding way, engaged in exactly as noble a pursuit. As a footnote, it is worth remembering that Los Angeles is naturally a place of blue skies. This image must be either a twilight shot, which is consistent with the glowing neon, or might be taken beneath the city's smog, or during the famous 'June gloom'.

THE NEW MEXICAN SUNRISE WAS A BALL OF FIERY RED, hauling itself up over the horizon. I had rested here, at last—something more than the necessity of sleeping. I'd found in the high desert a comfortable place for my heart.

Two days I'd been driving up from the Bayou and the *Monde Creole*. Long, long miles of greening, through sundown and the dying light. Baton Rouge was half a silver shiny-scaled fish, half mud-brown squatting toad, sucking on the juices of the Mississippi. A fecund land, vegetable laden and bowed down with fruit—oranges and melons, round, firm and ripe. The brilliant sun was caught in the leaves, escaping only here and there to break across the road, like the last few kids in a game of British Bulldog. The roadside fruit-sellers waited indifferently in brown-boarded sheds, the colour of their rich earth, born of the same soil. I made Shreveport in the dark—hot, humid and buggy—another of those American towns that seem startled by a traveller, or at least one who is not American. A peroxide kid behind a checkout was delighted to meet an Englishman, claiming a bundle of online friends from there. He was mischievous, like a small-time not-so-villainous Disney character. The truck stop was the size of a small town—brash, filled with the noise of busyness, truck brakes snorting their derision, roaring cruisers decibelling the night.

After Louisiana, Texas was restive. Maybe it's the heat—up to the high 90s, not even summer yet. The metroplex of Dallas-Fort Worth was enormous—easy to see how this could seem all there is, all that matters, to someone born and raised here (how could anything, anywhere be bigger than this sprawl?). It's a dangerously unremarkable terrain, no mountains, or ocean, no wide and endless seeming plains. I wonder for those who call this muted landscape 'home', whether a more decisive topography might be disturbing, even malignant seeming, perhaps? A waitress in Wendy's Diner says she "tried leaving once and didn't like it". To be so sealed in a place, centred, only ever looking out at the wild and other elsewhere—it's conducive to ideas of 'us' and 'them'. The Metroplex—an entire civilization, isolated, self absorbed, stranded and sprawling in the Texas heat.

Wonderful then to drive north west and watch the trees slowly shrink and thin. The semi-arid maquis scrub appeared seamlessly out of wide arable and rangelands—river beds became starved of water, bare hills looked a little wind scoured, buttes in embryo. What a place, what a continent, this tarmac filigree lets me career around, high on travel, across climate zones in a day.

Well rested in high New Mexico, I headed out along the desert road. In the early morning I drove just long enough to find a diner, in Tucumcari, for breakfast. One of the uncompromised delights of the American road, these oases of comfort so liberally dispersed across the land. There's such an enormous variety of culture in these barely United States, but in every one the diner is there, reassuringly familiar. The one I'm in now is old, attested to by time-worn timber; comfortable though in the quiet dawn. Coffee, bacon, cheese and eggs, maybe grits and pancakes, orange juice. Breakfast in America will kill me, eventually. But I might just die smiling.

BANK—HOUSTON, TEXAS

Bank—Houston, Texas pictures a suited, bald man sitting behind a solid desk, at the rear of a room full of vacant, opulently upholstered chairs arranged around other solid desks. On one of the desks in the middle distance sits, incongruously, a hat. The direction and appearance of determination and dynamism in the previous image are juxtaposed with clutter and stasis here. A grimy backstreet, which might be the setting for a certain kind of heroism, is contrasted here with the trappings of opulence, and a man contained motionless, like a caged pet, in his moneyed world.

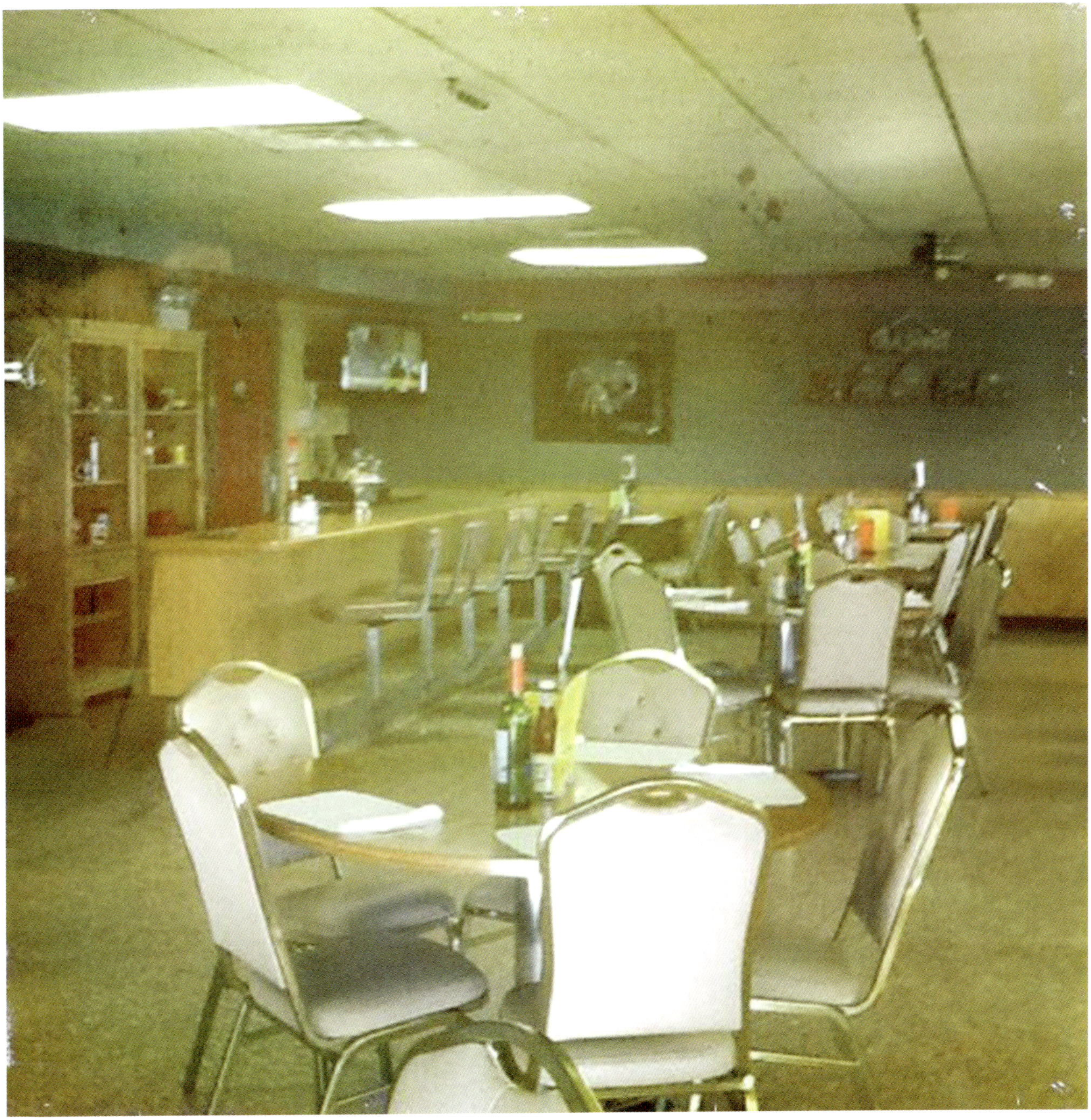

ALONG AWAY FROM GRAND ISLE, in among the dendritic turns of water and silt, I found a man called Ray. Raymond, in the *Monde Creole* Arcadian French, like my kids' favourite firefly in *The Princess and the Frog*. What a man he was, sitting immoveable, as if the strength of ages held him by rights to this place. Fastened to this soil with the roots of trees, chained to the Bayou by birth, need and predilection. He sat outside a shack selling live bait—Minnows at 20 cents, live shrimps at 15. Knocked together out of bits of plank, impermanent as the shifting land. Behind him was his 'house' of sorts. It's a trailer home, not too unusual that, but hanging 5 metres above the ground, held by a rickety looking rank of hand built timber hangers. Ray has hoisted his world above the worst of the Hurricanes' force. I'm guessing he is one of those who stays…

I'm fine to take his photograph, he says, but endures it like a kid getting a haircut or having his face cleaned with an aunty's spit-moistened handkerchief. "Caught me 12 redfish last night, right here in the creek" he exclaims, sure that will leave me amazed. If I could properly describe how I saw those imagined monsters, as red as tandoori powder, lit from within, electrical down there in the murk and the muddiness, woven into swamp grass, eating monstrous many-legged things. It's a little awkward between he and I—he's a man of few words I can see, more used to boats and bait than conversation. But I linger, nonetheless, next to his cigarettes and root beer, just to wonder how it would be to live here and be him, in this mermaid land of water. I can feel the treacle-dense darkness, covering everything in its quiet flood, hear the water plop of giant redfish taunting me with every swallowed fly, taste the half-salt half-silt fillets which, after an excess of eating, leave him almost as much fish as they. I pull on another cheap Pall Mall cigarette, take a slug of Barg's root beer and wake up from my afternoon drowsiness, bid Ray farewell and get out of there.

FACTORY—DETROIT

We've noted that Frank wished to contrast white-collar and blue-collar workers, and he continues to do that in *Factory—Detroit*, following a man who appears to be a bank clerk with an image of an overalled man outside a factory. The photograph is mostly filled with a wall, stretching away towards a gas-containing tower in the distance. Frank is standing in what appears to be an entrance, with a workbench, complete with engineer's vice, almost obscured in the shadows. Three steel bollards, sunk into the concrete pavement, protect the wall and are scored with marks left by passing vehicles. The lone man is sitting against the wall, looking quizzically, perhaps suspiciously, at Frank. He wears a hat, again linking this image into the last one. This time it is an engineer's cap, favoured by such iconic TV characters as Casey Jones, the heroic railwayman, solving problems and saving America from chaos in every town through which his engine passed. The contrast between this cap and the trilby of the last image is an eloquent description of America's financially predicated social system.

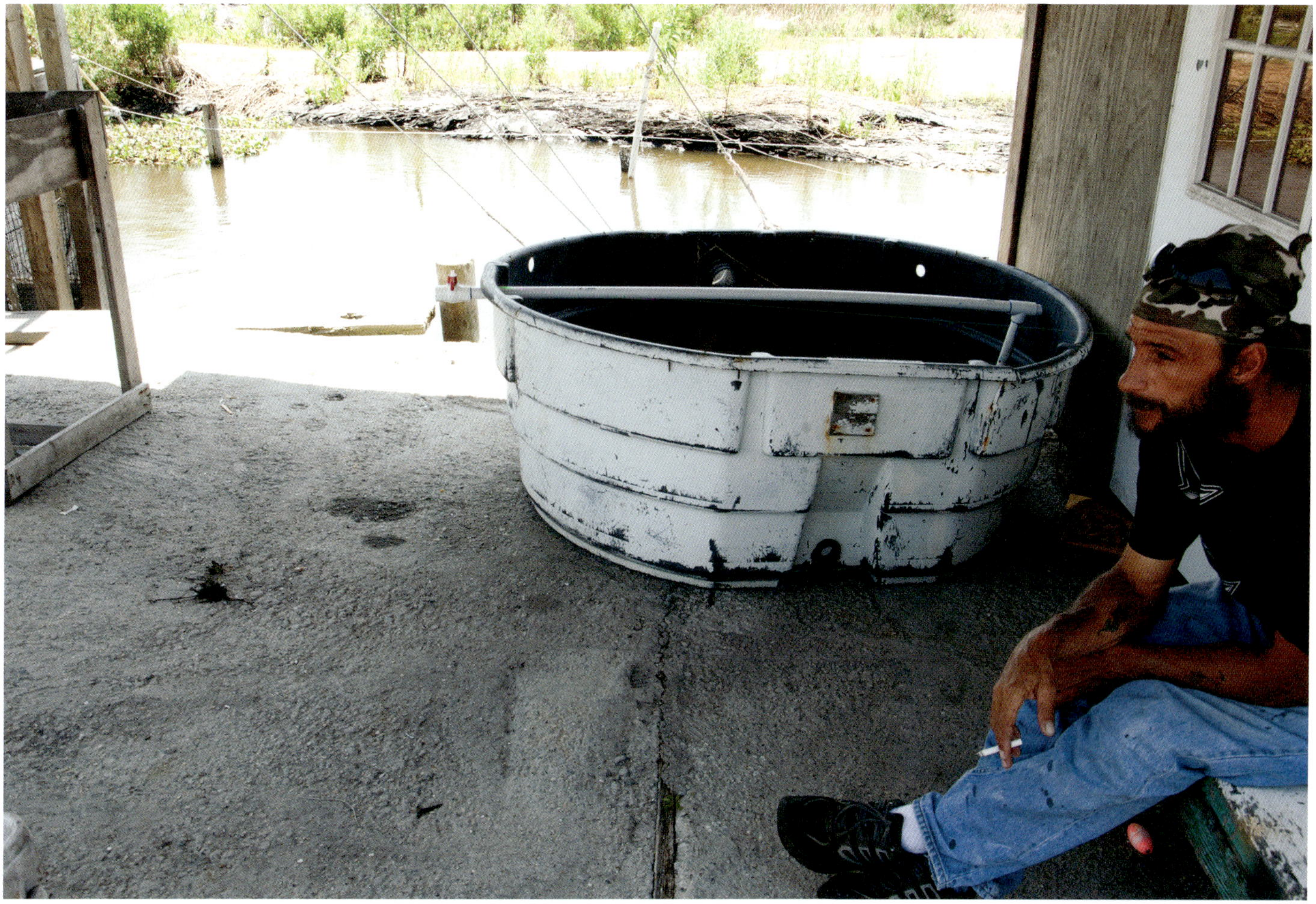

I VISITED THE TOMB OF ELEVEN MURDERED MINERS THIS MORNING. Because of a song I'd heard years ago by Woody Guthrie (and sung often myself) about the rapaciousness of power companies and their utter lack of concern for any lives but their own. Here on the skirts of the Rocky Mountains, striking miners were attacked by the 'National Guard'—bandits and ne'er-do-wells employed by overweight and out of work ex-Army Officers. The miners were resolute, so they were evicted out of Rockefeller company homes into tents, in the winter. The Guard killed the miner's leader. Caved in his head with a rifle butt and shot him three times. Then they started shooting randomly into the camp. The miners dug cellars for the children and women to sleep safely in. The Guard torched the camp site—in one cellar eleven women and children asphyxiated. So the miners armed themselves and fought back, necessitating the despatch of Federal Troops. They won a victory for wages and rights, which is remembered in this granite tomb, sharp in the sunshine of a fresh May morning. A hollow victory though—their descendants are mostly unemployed now; the work has gone to Asia. Fertile new fields for the corporations, without Unions or health and safety.

As I thought about the dead, and some men's inhumanity, looking at the child in her mother's arms carved on this aesthetically unremarkable tomb—around the monument skipped a tiny girl, dressed in turquoise and pink, as bright as a button, sunnier than the sunshine. She jumped on the memorial's lowest step and smiled the most beatific smile for me and my camera. She was oblivious of context. Like a ghost or spirit unsummoned, seeing her there, a flesh and blood refraction of the children who had died.

Old men milled around outside the tomb, Mineworkers Union of America custodians. They tell me again the story, and say it must never happen again. They wince at the mention of Abu Ghraib, and the Foxconn workers in Shen Zhen, making Apple products (designed in America) leaping off their factory roofs—sacrificing themselves so their families get insurance—still dying in search of a better life.

DEPARTMENT STORE—LINCOLN, NEBRASKA

Jazz was an enormous influence on Kerouac's writing, and is evident too in *The Americans*. Many of Frank's early images established the major themes for his book, just as in jazz the musical theme on which a piece is based—called the 'head'—is stated at the beginning. In jazz these themes are then explored, expanded on and exploded in successive solos. *The Americans* works in the same way: as we have moved through we have seen Frank comment on, deepen and sophisticate his examinations by presenting images which counter, augment and question each other. Now, as we near the end, these themes are brought to a conclusion. *Department Store—Lincoln, Nebraska* and the two images that follow are a staccato section, a 'rat-tat-tat' of pictures referring back to earlier photographs, commenting on, refining and concluding Frank's consideration. *Department Store* recapitulates the earlier section examining crosses and death in the same way that so many musical compositions refer back to earlier motifs and movements from within 'development' and 'resolution' sections.

Department Store examines the erosion of human values by consumerism and the mass-produced. 'Hested's', as the sign in the photograph says, helps us remember our loved ones for 69 cents. These identical white plastic cruciforms echo and reflect the cross that was held so reverently by the white-surpliced wanderer beside the *Mississippi River, Baton Rouge, Louisiana.* They recall the cross held aloft with passion, remembered in stone in *St. Francis* (actually St Junipero Serra, as we noted) and echo the quiet commemoration of the dead beneath a brilliant flare of light on the side of *U.S. 91, leaving Blackfoot, Idaho.* They further bring to mind the sad displacement in the face of the young mourner in *Funeral—St. Helena, South Carolina*, and the weather-blasted grave in *Chinese Cemetery—San Francisco*. Frank is bringing his considerations to a conclusion as we approach the end of the book. The unselfconscious manner in which these store operators degrade and commercialise this symbol is a powerful closing statement on the iconography of the cross in Frank's America.

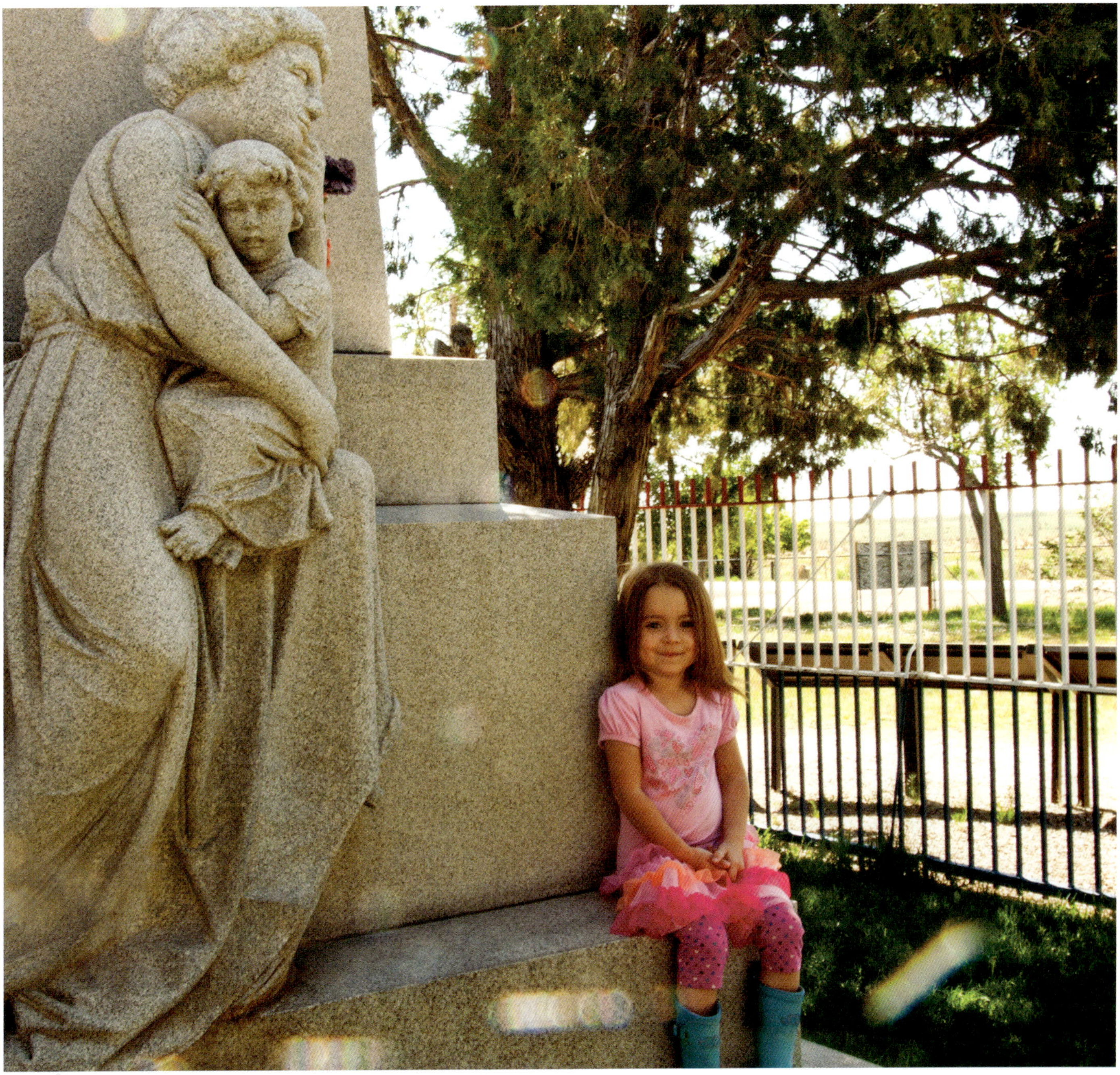

I'M SITTING DRINKING COFFEE IN A DINER, across from an old man in a black Stetson and a crisp pink Western shirt. He is tall, fit for his age and tucked into Levis and boots. He's sitting with a younger lady—she is solicitous, some kind of carer or samaritan neighbour of the old man. Her affection is genuine and contagious. He is still a rancher-of-the-old-ways, she says, maybe one of the last. She shimmers with wonder telling of his fields of mares and colts—wishes she could take me out there. I wish it too, but this journey-life all of us share doesn't have room for everything. He is mostly silent, only semi-involved in this discussion about him, like a scrubbed up child at a school parents' evening or bashful in the doctor's office. He is hard of hearing that is clear, and I'm guessing hasn't learned the knack of reading lips. He proudly tells me he is the subject of a book, and shows me a copy: "Don't get a god-damn cent out of it though", he says with a smile.

RODEO—NEW YORK CITY

Just as Hested's completed Frank's consideration of the cross, *Rodeo—New York City* concludes his examination of the cowboy. It recalls other images: *Bar—Gallup, New Mexico* captured a moment of apparent tension with a solid and stalwart Native American or Mexican looking man, four-square across the drunken composition. *Rodeo, Detroit* recorded a cigar-smoker looking rather like the Hollywood actor Paul Newman. The current New York cowboy leans against a wire waste basket, lighting a cigarette. He is cross-legged on a kerbstone, flanked by a puddle. He is the only obvious trace of the captioned rodeo, bizarrely transplanted into this city block. Frank has caught the heart of the dichotomy and surreality of this displaced 'cattleman', who no longer has a home on the range. The final joy of this image is the truck just along the street, behind the cowboy. In easily visible letters it advertises its manufacturer, 'Dodge'. This was the city at the heart of so many stories of the Old West, sometime home of Wyatt Earp and location of the infamous Long Branch Saloon and China Doll brothel—lending it the epithet of 'wickedest city in the West'. On a gritty and unremarkable street Frank images a man playing out his own movie, behind his eyes.

In case we miss the point, Frank restates it for us in the next image—of a corsaged *ingénue* at a *Movie premiere—Hollywood.*

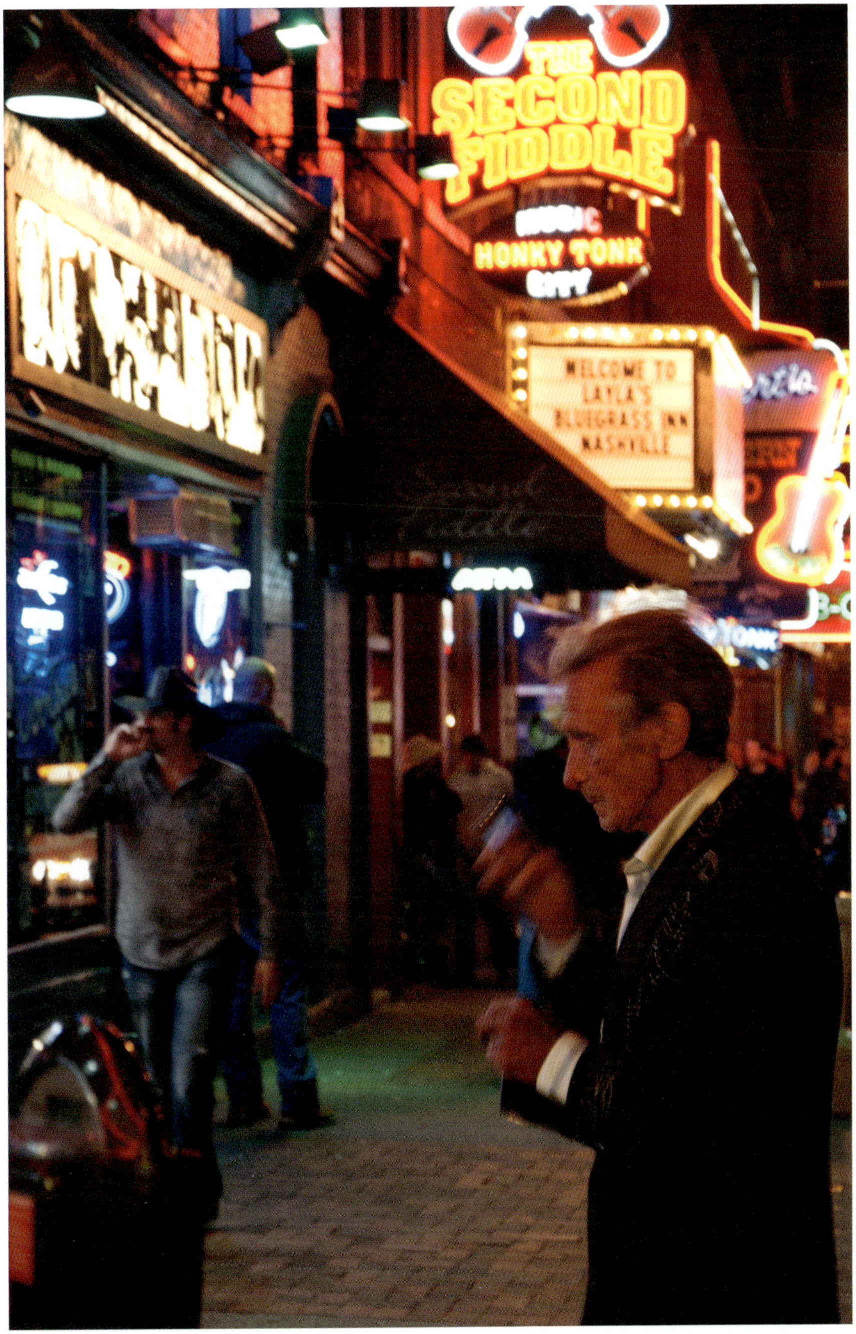
THE
SECOND
FIDDLE
MUSIC
HONKY TONK
CITY
WELCOME TO
LAYLA'S
BLUEGRASS INN
NASHVILLE

PLAYING THE ROLES OF STARDOM, the front of a stage is like a membrane with a magical behind. The corner of a bar will do—needs must—or a space bounded on the street by a bit of rope. Step through this veil and suddenly, temporarily, we participate in some kind of mass and historic suspension of disbelief. Pick up a guitar, put on a suit that turns you on, and for the duration, if you don't mess up too bad, you're truly a star. Then step back out, take the adulation: it won't last, so no need to worry. Pick up your bag, out to your truck, back on the road as if nothing ever happened, and no one out there knows. Nothing did happen, save on the inside of your listeners and yourself, a heavily human interchange, of not much interest to the circle sky and the silent stones.

I saw Nashville all around me as a huge halftone map, immense and stretching in shades of grey to the horizon. Scattered around in brilliant colours were all the bands playing the thousand bars of this hopeful's town, hung hierarchically like a champagne fountain, or ornaments on a Christmas tree. Looking always to move on up to the next rung of song, until finally making it all the way—and being allowed to play for tips on Broadway.

Maybe you could sell a billion, live in a mansion, marry someone pretty. Like Keith Urban on the same day I was there, whose name on a slab was laid into wet cement, beneath a sky of indifferent grey. I did not attend: through the window of my bar I saw it was lightly raining. I listened instead to a so-sweet voiced Virginian, singing *You'll Never Leave Harlan Alive* at my request. Between my coffee pot and her unflattering corner space, we conjured up a vision of mines and forests that carried us away. All for a dollar in a jar.

She had seen a look in my eye and knew she was really communicating. All the pragmatic and necessary barriers we put up to protect ourselves came down, for only as long as the music lasted. Real communion, being to being, deep, important, amazing. We passed the songs through the fire to renew them: in that sacred space we renewed ourselves, our connection, our humanity.

Make music into an industry about money and celebrity if you like, but these things are incidental, and neither help nor hinder our approach toward the sacred fire.

MOVIE PREMIERE—HOLLYWOOD

In *Movie Premiere—Hollywood*, a carefully coiffured and expensively dressed *ingénue*, corsage at her bosom, fills much of the photograph despite being out of focus. This lack of clarity directs us past her to the onlookers behind. It would appear that the young woman is a guest at the premiere and the people behind, overwhelmingly women, are spectators. Their expressions vary from smilingly engaged to the slightly perplexed look of those who adore the thing which is before them and are struggling to cope. Significantly, the lookers are not looking at our blurred subject. They look instead behind and beyond her. Like the cowboy in the last image, she too is living her own fantasy—a starlet perhaps, but not yet a star.

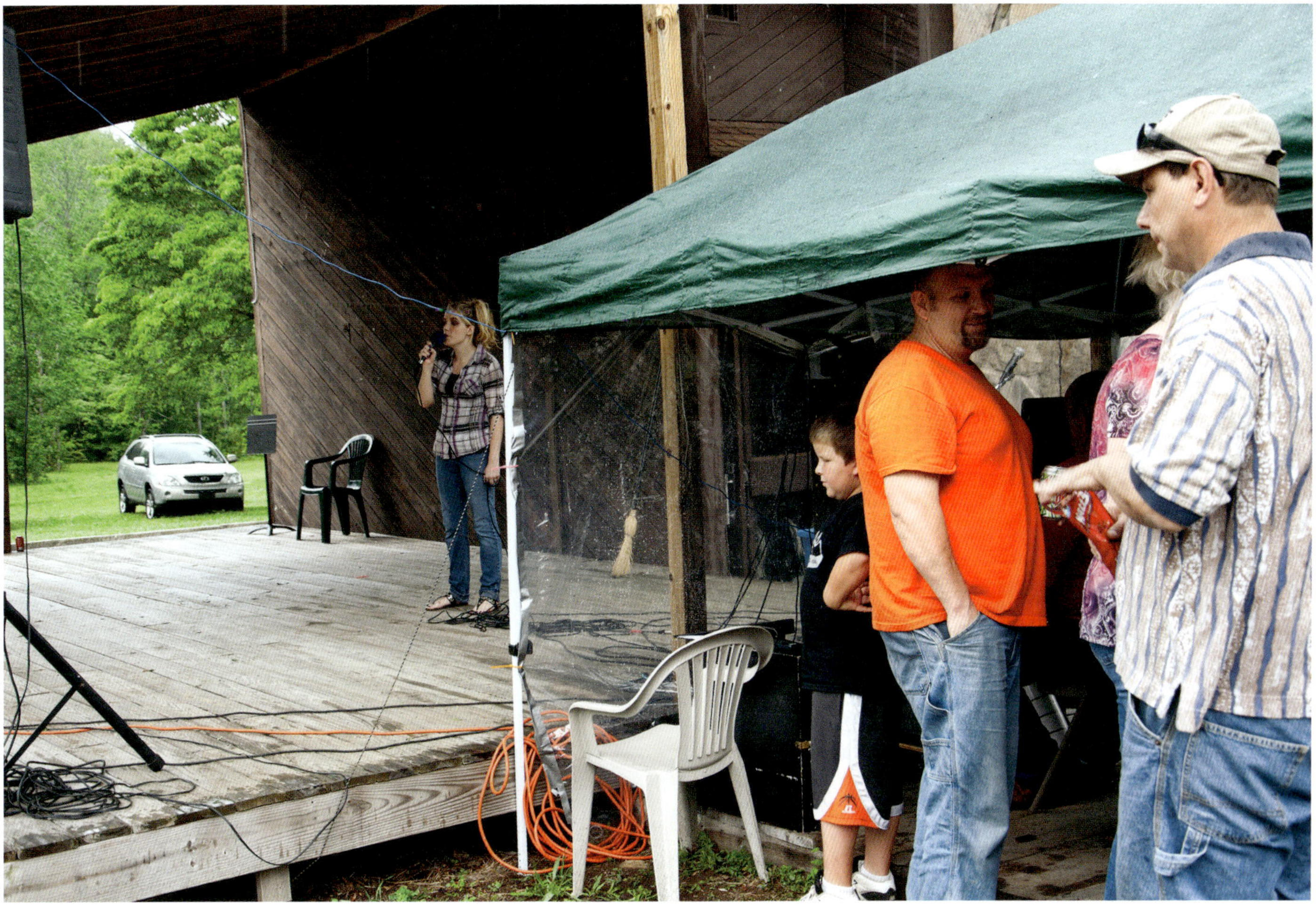

DEEP IN THE SMOKY MOUNTAINS, completely lost, driving aspirationally along a byway, hoping for a sign. Suddenly Jesus is there on the verge, frozen in concrete, pastel bright. Mary is nearby in her pale celestial garment, arms raised in endless benediction. Between them are two giraffes—not to scale, but attractive nonetheless—and a wizard, full of mysteries, star spangled and ominous. As an attempt to balance it all, I suppose, a small urinating cupid completes the assemblage, holding his useless (disconnected) member, waiting with infinite patience for the water to come. They are the angels of the epiphany for a small place of pastures, meadows, and streams. Some of the houses are combed and cosseted, some as ratty as a William Egglestone dream. Lovely. I can see why Billy Ray needs to be making his way back to Tennessee—or maybe these country roads really have taken me home.

Crosby Volunteer Fire Service summer party, still in the sun-after-rain, pulled off the road in a beautiful land, I feel a little over the rainbow. Way up high in ancient forests, watching a bluebird fly. Is it dirt road Shangri-La, at last? The washed mountain air is as fresh as line-dried cotton. A strangely faced karaoke singer, eyes wide as a guppy, make up applied with a potato spade, is singing Taylor Swift with a passionate fire palpable in her eyes. In that grassy Appalachian field, under a plastic awning by a wooden shed, she sees stadiums and screaming fans—is on a world tour in her head.

In the dappled sunlight, I look with interest at bear droppings, varnished and caressed by a Rescue Ranger at his stall. A disabled Viet Nam veteran is selling all things Native American, next to two old ladies charmingly running an animal shelter stand. A friendly lady sells me cakes for later, wondering I suspect "Who is this stranger?" but too polite to ask. Most remarkable, though, is the wonder, the deeply satisfied wonder of it all…

CHARITY BALL—NEW YORK CITY

In *Charity Ball—New York City* a bejewelled lady sitting at a table accepts the embrace and kiss of the dark-haired and suited man behind. Like the cowboy and the *ingénue* she is playing out a role, performing herself into being through her lavishness, clearly enjoying this version of herself. How curious that in this guise and this guise alone—one of the very many she will have played out in her life, mother perhaps, lover, teacher, counter clerk—and for only the length of this tiny moment, will she ever be known to the wider world.

Again, we are in part following Frank's interest in 'leaders and followers', this confident and powerful woman preceding a rather less powerful man—mirroring other places in the book where Frank has imaged powerful men following disenfranchised women.

The rich accoutrements and conspicuous consumption of this couple begin a series of four images which examine eating.

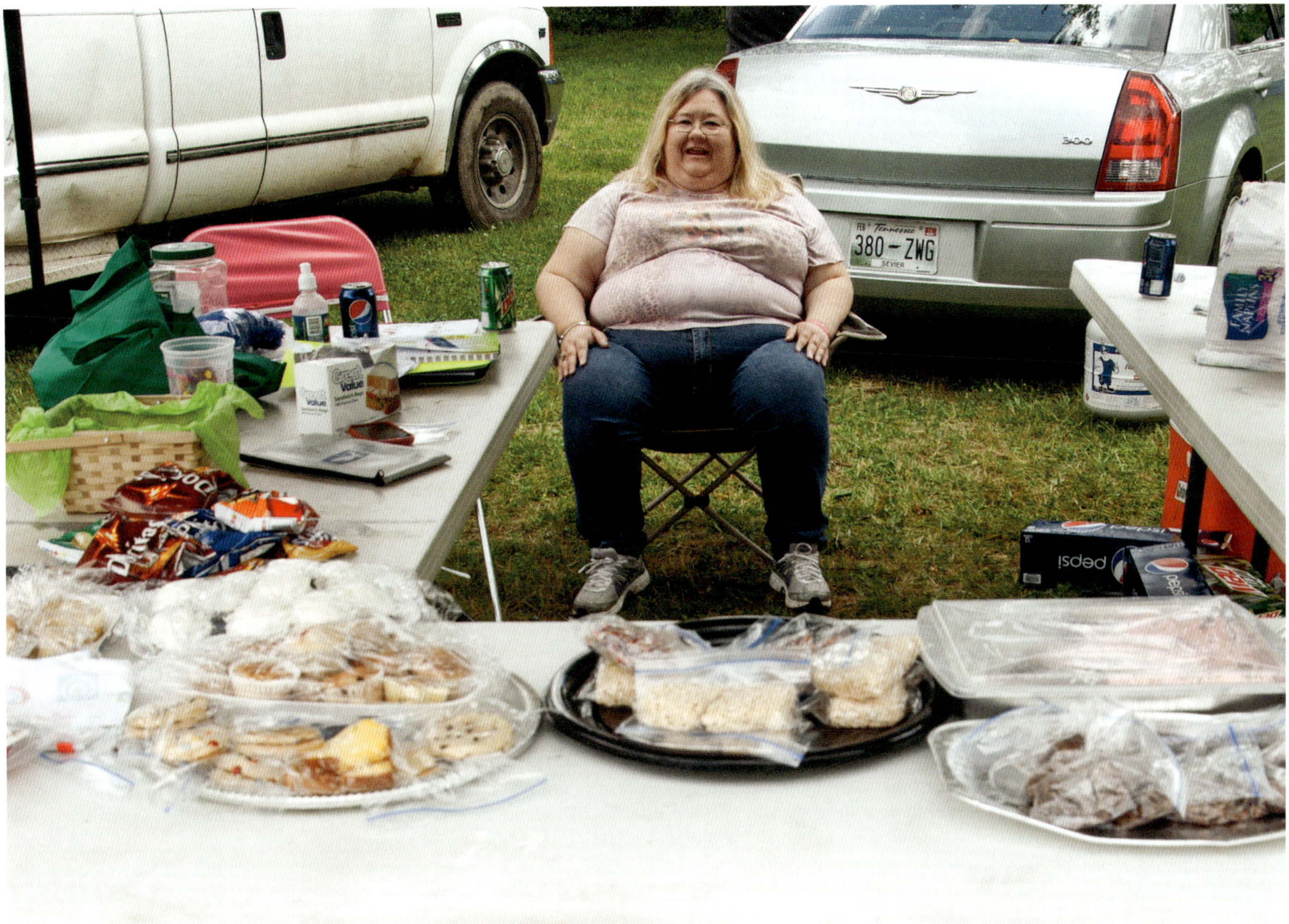
380-ZWG
SEVIER
Great Value
pepsi

DRIVING THE I 95 ON A HECTIC HEADING SOUTH OUT OF JERSEY. I like this road for its arrival associations—the slightly nervous first miles on the wrong side of the road, adjusting again to the freedom of lane discipline, huge girders in the waste land, nondescript bits of rusting ironwork lying in fetid tide pools. I like it for its associations. This road goes on and on, down to the Garden State Parkway perhaps, through Asbury Park, or straight on for Baltimore and the sweet winds of the South. Best of all the I 95 is the home of the Walt Whitman service station. Nothing remarkable about the place, outstandingly unremarkable actually. Staffed almost exclusively by second language Thai women, with the usual Roy Rogers burgers and Nathan's hot dogs, adorned with 'no soliciting' signs—it is the name which makes it special. I would love to read Whitman describing this honouring of him, see where his sparkling, alliterative, over-weight mind might wander, how it would attempt to alchemise the essence of this place. Drip its tarmac, washrooms and mustard and ketchup stained detritus through his subtle and arcane distillery and capture it in a few drops. I quietly wonder if he would keep an eye on the strutting boys in their finery.

Oh such memorials we in our modern wisdom make, for Roy Rogers and Walt Whitman and a hundred others so 'honoured' on the Interstates. We weave them thus into the weft of our everyday—tawdry, regrettable, tolerated only for their base usefulness. Do these poets and screen heroes bring inspiration to these places smelling of cooking fat and piss? I can't speak for any others, but there is irony here that raises my smile every time I pull in, happily, once again.

CAFETERIA—SAN FRANCISCO

Frank continues his examination of Americans eating in *Cafeteria—San Francisco.* This echoes another widely distributed image from Standard Oil's Picture File, taken to promote the oil company and its work (Day 2011: 113). It is part of *Trucking Story* by Sol Libsohn (1945), a series of photographs taken in support of the war effort, recording drivers delivering aircraft parts. *Charles Henry eating steak at Martin's restaurant, Darlington, Pa.; March 1945* (Standard Oil Archive, University of Louisville) sees driver Charles squeezed into a suit, shirt and tie. His clothes look as though they will burst at any moment, as he resolutely cuts into a plate-sized steak, lips parted in anticipation. His hands are corpulent, wearing a large, square ring. The dark tones of the photograph suggest warmth and safety. The child at top left who looks with apparent longing at Charles's dinner strikes a slightly jarring note: an unintentional one, I suspect.

Frank's photograph follows Libsohn's composition quite closely. The man pictured in *San Francisco* is sitting in about the same position as Charles, also eating steak. His table is squalid, though, covered in the remains of other people's meals. The man's clothes are not as smart as Charles's, yet neither are they threadbare. The room does not have the protective darkness of 'Martin's Diner'; it is well lit. The back of a hat and coated man suggests a busy and impersonal place. Perhaps the most defining characteristic of Frank's picture is the expression on its subject's face: it is exactly that "look of sadness" (Frank, in Maloney 1958: 115) which Frank was seeking. He may be eating steak, his clothes may be reasonable, but this is a despondent image of a man for whom no amount of cafeteria food will bring joy or inclusion. He takes little delight in the meal; his mind is on other things. He is an individual who sits in this American institution untouched by its mythology; its disorder and sense of alienation emphasise his absorption in his own experiences. The image which preceded this one, *Charity Ball—New York City*, reinforces its loneliness. The photographs contrast conditions of wealth, certainly, but more than that they contrast a deep sense of contentment and satisfaction with despondency. One of these photographs pictures people in relationship, the other a man who is signally alone. The diner does nothing to alleviate his evident suffering.

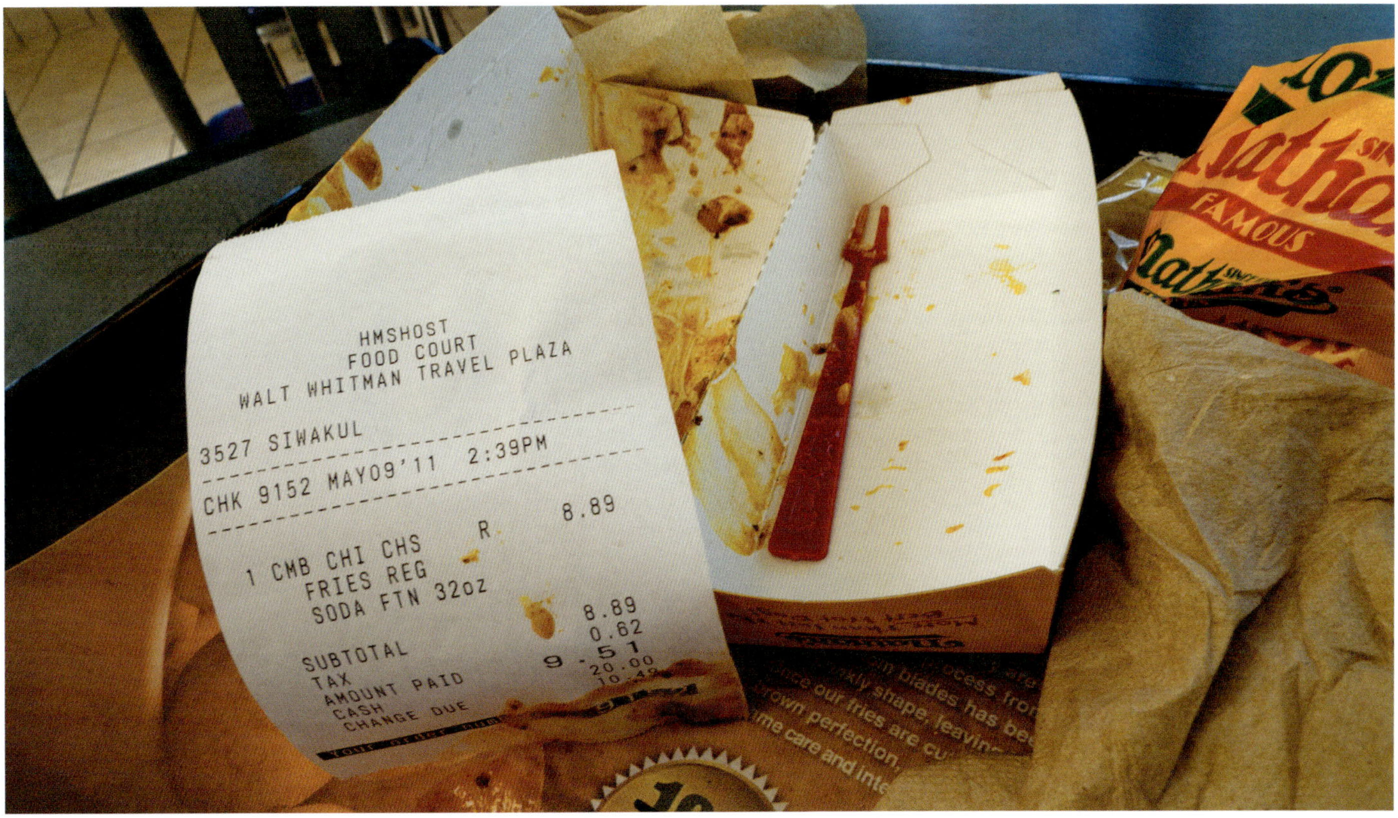
HMSHOST
FOOD COURT
WALT WHITMAN TRAVEL PLAZA
3527 SIWAKUL
CHK 9152 MAY09'11 2:39PM
1 CMB CHI CHS R 8.89
FRIES REG
SODA FTN 32oz
SUBTOTAL 8.89
TAX 0.62
AMOUNT PAID 9.51
CASH 20.00
CHANGE DUE
FAMOUS

DRUG STORE—DETROIT IS ANOTHER OF FRANK'S PHOTOGRAPHS that relate closely to earlier images from Sol Libsohn, taken for the Standard Oil Picture File (Day 2011: 113). It reinforces the reflexivity of Frank's work, so often seeking to reframe images and thereby comment on their content. *Drug Store* strikingly echoes Libsohn's *Lunch counter in the Trylon Diner, Clinton, New Jersey, May 1945* (Standard Oil Archive, University of Louisville). The angle of the shot is identical, firing along a counter from around its curved end. The line of male diners, too, is the same. Behind Libsohn's counter is a single waitress who, unlike the ladies in Frank's photograph, is white. *Trylon Diner* is an image of order, overalled men are animated, looking chatty and clearly having fun. The waitress is much younger—she smiles at their conversation. Everything seems proper, yet fun. No one is tired, no one is sweating. This is diner utopia again.

DRUG STORE—DETROIT

Frank leads us quietly to the side of this staged idealisation and shows us other, mostly unself-conscious diners in his *Drug Store—Detroit*. Nothing is really amiss with the diner, it isn't dirty or squalid. The harsh contrast with Libsohn's *Trylon* lies in the faces of its customers. None of them are smiling: they look bored, dissolute and uncomfortable. Two of them look with suspicion at Frank as he photographs them; it is the kind of suspicion that might erupt into disapproval, even threat. One baseball-capped customer covers his mouth protectively with his hand. He stares into space, oblivious of his companions. The sloping diner counter leads the eye across and down to a black-haired man at far right. This leading of the eye echoes *Parade—Hoboken*, which similarly focuses on a face at the right. The man here hunches over his milkshake in a primal gesture of protection, like a predator over its kill. He has an aggressive look, the kind that demands space, demands that it is not disturbed. None of the customers is engaged in any interaction with the others. There is no community here, only a group of disparate and dissociated individuals, who nonetheless sit closely together in a temporary truce, regimented before the counter. Frank's composition shoots obliquely along the counter from its corner, foreshortening its sweep and compressing the space occupied by each of the diners, revealing and heightening their mutual isolation. This claustrophobia is heightened further as their personal and pictorial space is invaded by huge cardboard glasses of Orange Whip (at '10 c. each, King Size 15 c.').

It is impossible for us, now, to know with any certainty whether Frank knowingly re-created these Standard Oil images: he has said that his memory of those times is not good (Greenough 2009). The visual duplication is remarkable, and the thematic counterpoint makes exactly the points that Frank mentioned over and over in his writing about *The Americans* project. Take a look at the image and see if you are not convinced.

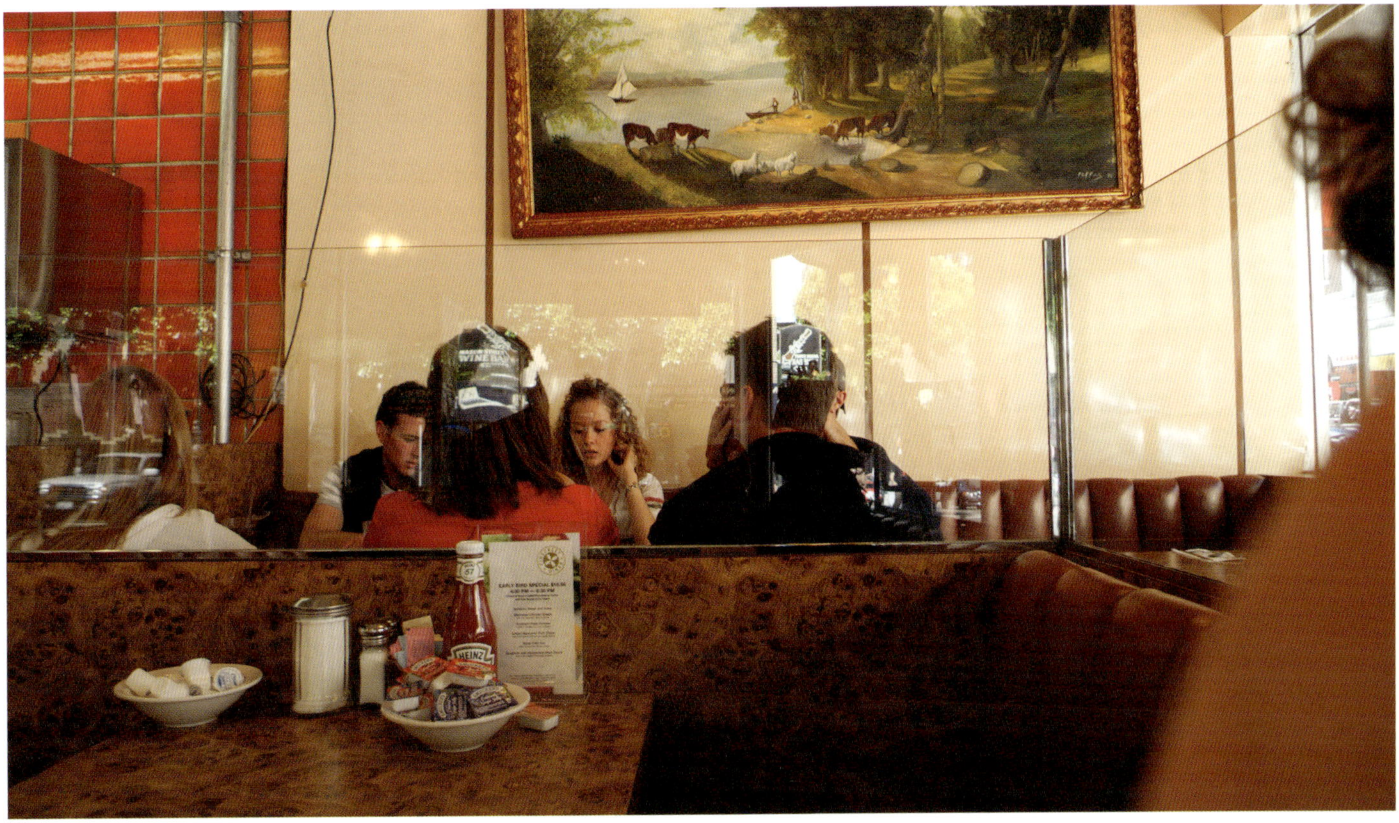
HEINZ

LAUREL CANYON SNAKING UP INTO THE HILLS. Here 40 years ago is where I, for so long, wanted to be. Typically tardy of me, arriving at the party after it has moved on. The tall trees sheltered by the walls of this arroyo welcome me nonetheless, and I think I sense the faintest traces of the past, the quietest, quietest echoes of Crosby, Stills and Nash, Neil Young and—best and most compelling of all—a young Joni Mitchell. Trying to project, I drag my muso friend into the convenience store and coffee shop, mirrored and psych-muralled, at the crossroads near the sacred sign. I buy American Spirit cigarettes (I quit! Really, I don't smoke anymore…) and am wrong footed by the ageing clerk. He doesn't need the usual ID, he says, he can see I am good by my eyes. The server, barely higher than the counter, is a Native American woman. I've no idea where she has come from, maybe one of the so-called 'Mexicans', indigenous people re-populating this stolen land from South of the border. She is as perfect as an Olmec greenstone, olive skinned, divinely proportioned—and kind, so gentle in her conversation and expression. I loved being with her, love that I have known her. Although the rigours of our timetabled lives and the million expectations of our manifold social intercourses made the meeting brief—and probably rightly so and for the best—when I look at her face caught on celluloid, I can dwell again in that moment, luxuriate again in the warm place of her smile.

Railway Station—Indianapolis was one such moment for Robert, I guess—beauty looking quizzically across the counter, amused, without censure or hatred. So often travelling alone, these moments of passing kindness have such power, last a lifetime.

COFFEE SHOP, RAILWAY STATION—INDIANAPOLIS

Coffee Shop, Railway Station—Indianapolis finishes off the series of diner pictures. As with many of the images in this final section, this piece represents a conclusion. Frank has examined the diner and Americans eating in depth and at length, concluding, significantly, here. It's significant as Frank argued that his critique was from a perspective of love. A young woman stands behind a coffee shop's counter, and has turned and caught Frank taking her photograph. She has the so-often recorded expression of surprise, but she does not repeat the aggression we have observed so frequently elsewhere in the book. There is a gentleness and a kindness in her demeanour. Amid the stainless steel, donuts and hamburgers, she has the look of a Vermeer. Her over-the-shoulder glance is powerfully reminiscent of a mirrored *Girl with a Pearl Earring* (Vermeer, c.1665, Mauritshuis, The Hague). This is the apotheosis of the disinterested and impatient assistant in *Ranch Market—Hollywood.* Unlooked for, in a corner of a mid-west town, there is gentleness and beauty to match anything, anywhere.

The love that inspired Vermeer, and that looks questioningly at us in this photograph, is the subject of the rest of the book. Typically, there are counter-images and images that punctuate: two photographs show single men and one records an unoccupied car, but the remaining ten all record some aspect of romantic or familial love. Equally typical for Frank, there are other themes invoked simultaneously. Public parks create a sub-series of six images, while the car plays a major part in the final series, with only one of the last seven images lacking a vehicular presence.

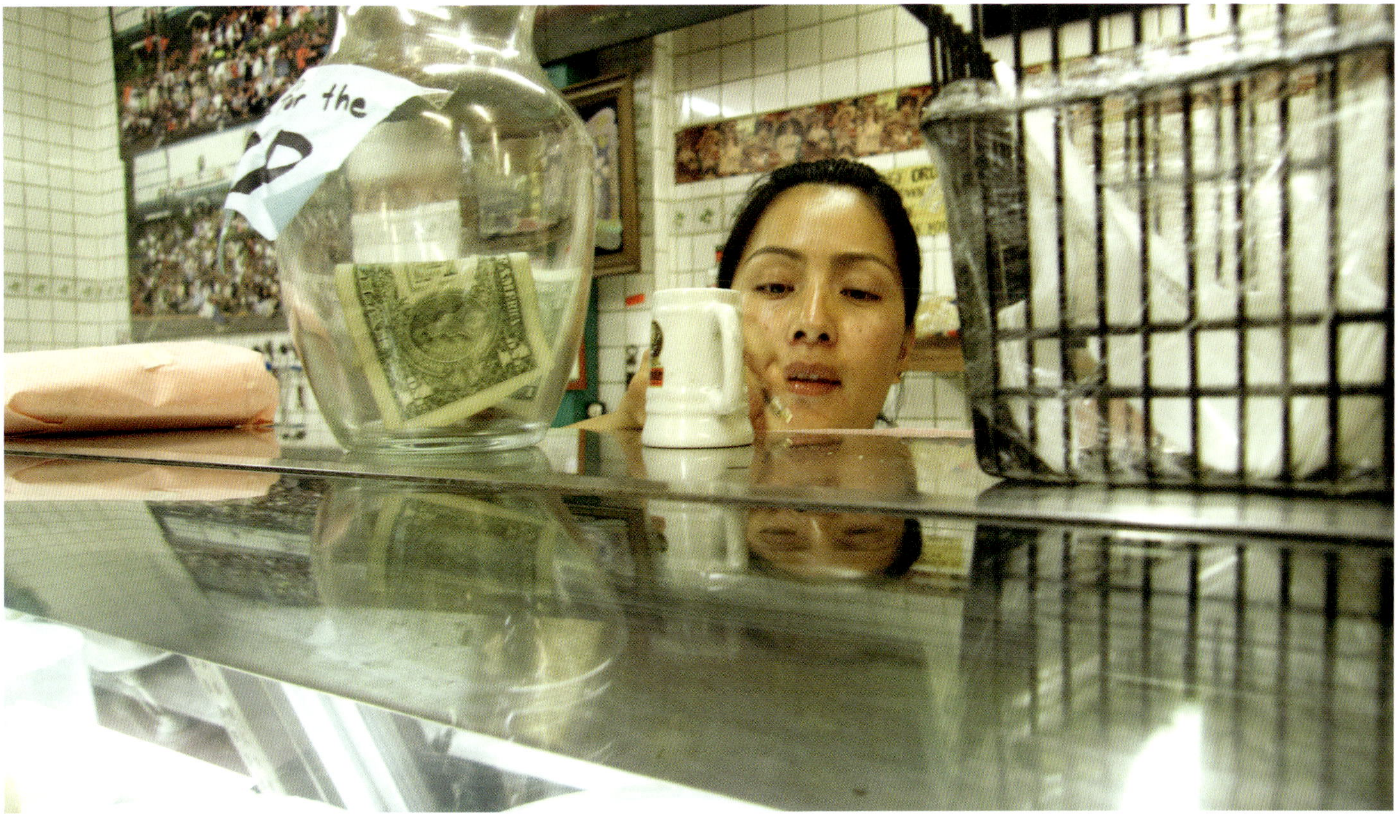
for the

FASHION AND MUSIC ARE BOTH THE VICTIMS OF AGE, since they are overwhelmingly about sex. That's not meant derogatively or quizzically or with mal intent. Sex is who we are, what constructs us, the warp and weft of existence. Good to engage in it often and, through our children, shape the world to come. Good to abstain from it often, for the sake of clarity and to appreciate the quiet universal voices, inaudible against the primal blood beat in our ears. Fashion lets us tell the world something about how we dream ourselves into being. Music has something of the primal rite, the overture to ecstasy, a signpost saying 'This way to the transcendent'. Great music, even when it is avowedly not at all about sex, is still incredibly sexy.

So, then, Frank's beautiful couple in Chattanooga. Hep cats, present in the morning light, young, energised, relishing their moment. Slicked, eyebrows plucked, an hour in front of the mirror underwriting every swagger, yet disguised beneath an unmistakable "As if I care…". I kind of love them, these two, takes me back to my own days of preening—happy times, young and as lovely as I was ever going to be. They being in the '50s, in Tennessee—the days of Elvis and Chuck Berry—how could they fail?

Where to look now, though, for couples *à la mode*? Impossible it seems to me—too many modes to choose from, and the fashion rules far too arcane for an outsider such as I. Cosplay in downtown, hip-hop city kids in South LA, Preppies in the Hamptons? Postmodernism and multi-style have left us adrift in a sea of particularity. Maybe that is the attraction, part of the essence of this black and white—a time when culture was homogenised and everyone knew what was what? Or is that, too, a dream, only possible looking back, nostalgia for something that never really was, that we only think we remember? Ironic, anyway, that *The Americans* has become a book about collective memory, when almost everyone at the time felt its messages and pictures were wrong-headed.

CHATTANOOGA, TENNESSEE

We have noted that love is at the centre of this concluding group of photographs. It is young love that occupies Frank's *Chattanooga, Tennessee.* A swarthy young man is smartly dressed, with impressively padded shoulders. His diminutive, very fair-skinned partner is equally large of shoulder. The very white girl and the possibly Latino young man look with bemusement out of frame to the left. Their location, in Tennessee in the American South, begs many a question as to the possible source of their disapproval. In a wonderful echo within the composition, an older couple walks away from us to the image's right. The old man is fair-haired and in a light jacket, while his out-of-focus companion is dark of hair and outfit. This attractive visual symmetry is echoed by the conceptual one: youth approaches us as age walks away. New love, preparing for a life of family, house purchase and work, is in clear focus, as those who have completed these challenges become ever more distant and remote.

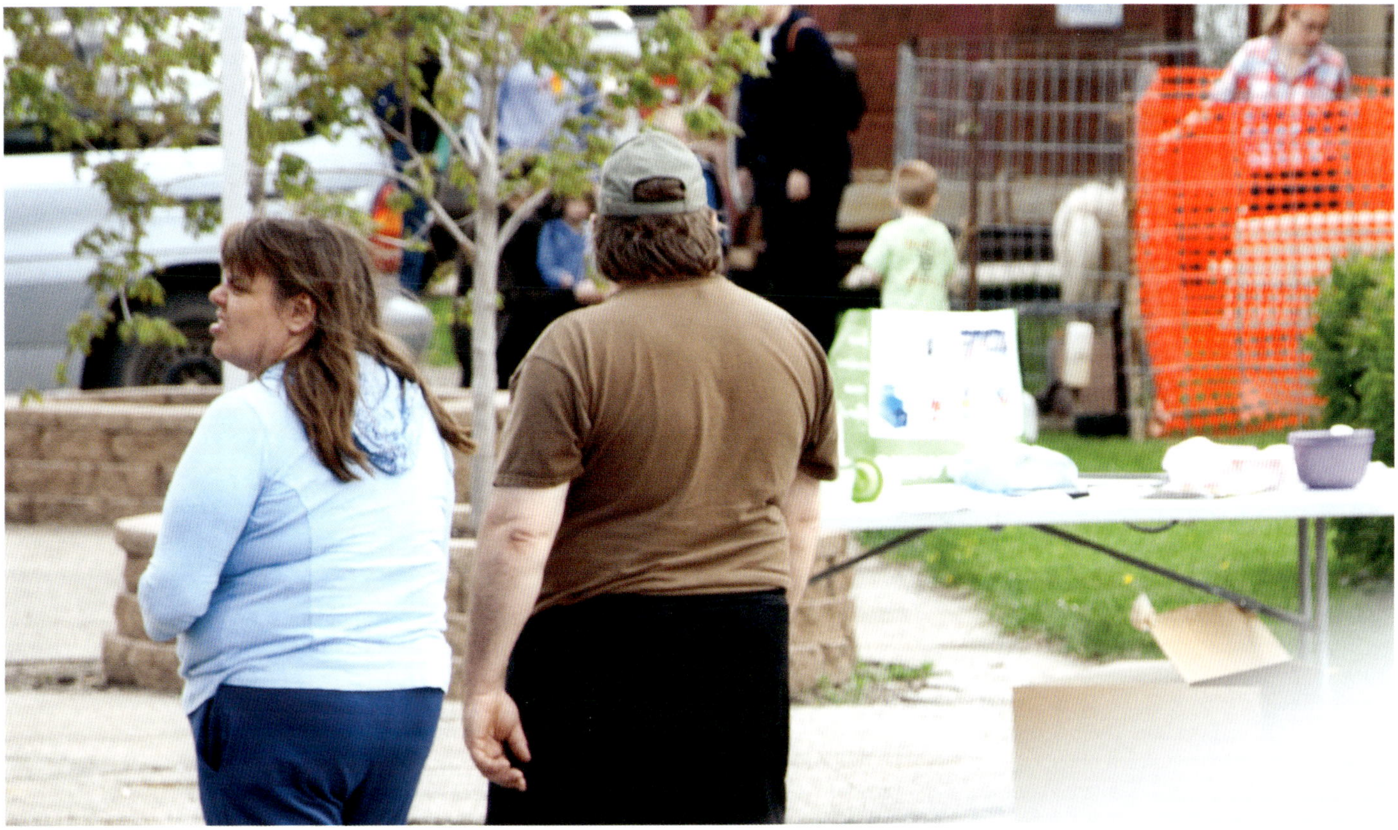

OUT IN THE MORNING FROM THE KING GEORGE HOTEL, hot under my collar for coffee and buns, burning to get on with the day. The homeless ones who howl all night and whimper seem to scurry away with the morning, getting out from under the city workers' feet, perhaps—not invisible but withdrawn into alleyways and corners. I walk down to a bus stop for Haight and Ashbury, so excited to finally see this cauldron of the culture of my young life. It's 10,000 miles from Johannesburg, and it's taken a good number of years to get here, on this chill potatopatch fog morning—'nobody here but the rubber cat'.

The initial excitement was lovely, photographing the street signs, hippy this and that, up and down the lines. Board houses in every direction, a gentle hum of morning town wrapping around sidewalks and squares. Did not persist for long though—not that anything was really wrong. Hippy shops sold cliché tie-dye, Grateful Dead guitar picks and the paraphernalia of hashish. There were a couple of salvation hostels for the institution-tolerant people of the street. I guess it was a sense of 'the party's over' that poked me, the inevitable morning come-down, dawn-light soaking like water into tissue paper, revealing the secrets, rendering the magic night humdrum. And humdrum it was, clean as a piece of new paper, everything fresh painted and gentry. Still Cheshire-cat smiling its fame and global stature, but for no reason that now remains, a pretty housing estate, nothing more.

I walked to Alamo Square looking for Frank's San Francisco houses—the Victorian 'Painted Ladies' I'd seen in a tourist guide and was sure were here. What delight then to walk around the place, through groves and trees and patches of grass, finally finding exactly the place where his lovers had been. I touched the earth and short circuited the years—to the days of my childhood's black and white dreams. I'd quickly realised on this journey that it was pointless trying to re-photograph Frank's scenes. His photographs are about the moments, and the way those traces of light reflected his dreams and vision. So I was not enslaved by geographical tracing. On this day, though, I made an exception, and was glad I did. A wonderful view in the eventual sunshine—so little has changed in 50 years. Lovers still in the mown grass and sunshine, strange lone photographers still stealing the scene.

SAN FRANCISCO

San Francisco is another in this final series of photographs engaged with images of love. Following on from the hip and aware young couple in Chattanooga, this picture records a black couple lying on the grass of a public space, high above the city. They have noticed Frank and his camera and are staring confrontationally at him. The love which is strongly evident in their body language to each other, coexists with the dislike and the very evident threat contained in the man's expression. Here, love is revealed as conditional, contextual and far from the cure-all of the so many songs soon to be penned a couple of blocks away on Haight and Ashbury.

We've noted already how often Frank's images relate to the photographs of the *Family of Man* exhibition. Curator Edward Steichen included a number of images of lovers. One of them, originally published in *Life* magazine, is by Ralph Morse (collection of *Life*), and another by Edward Weston (Museum of Modern Art, New York). In these pictures happy lovers embrace, apparently oblivious to the camera or the world beyond themselves. The challenging stare of the couple in Frank's picture, clearly discomfited by his presence, leaves no possibility of the *Family of Man's* suspension of disbelief. The photograph is revealed as the product of a particular process, with intrusive and voyeuristic overtones. Frank's lovers are disturbed by him and, through guilt by association, by us the viewers. The oblivious lovers of Morse's image and the consenting ones of Weston's serve the fiction of the photograph as impartial observation. They equally serve the fiction of loving as a universal panacea. Frank's subjects, who moments before were lying together on the grass, are in an instant ready for conflict.

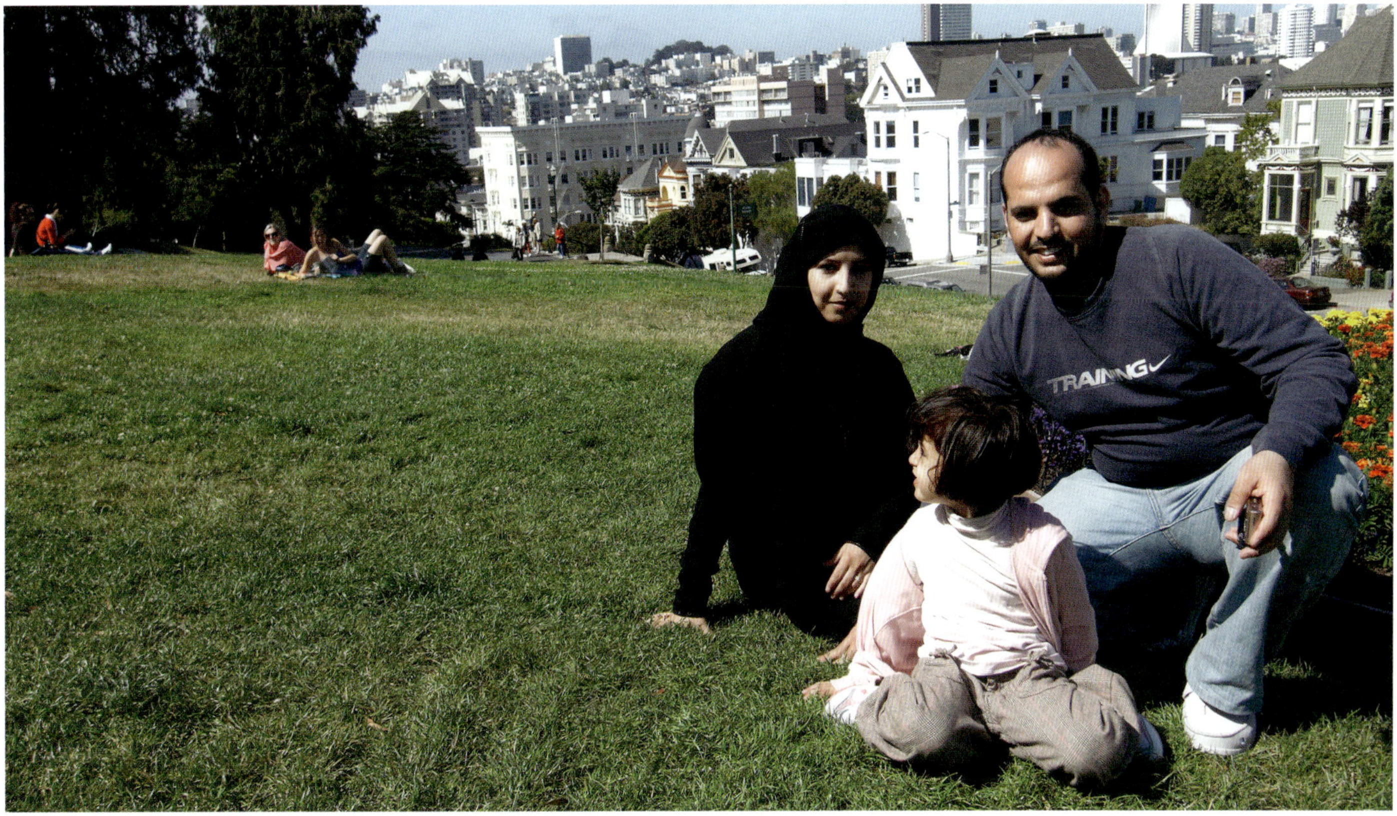

A BLEACHED HAIRED LADY, TIME WORN AND EXPANSIVE, gave me Dr Pepper ("cold from the car") in a park. I'd played some songs on a little festival stage and she thought she knew me from a Newport (Tennessee) bar—a town I've never been to and likely will never see. Just have 'that kind of face' I guess. Her daughter was flitting around, playful, wilful. A beguiling girl, intrigued by the stranger, full of life and hope, excitement which in her mother had ebbed, maybe died. Deeply tempered, in any case, by the heat and hammers of experience. Her mother said "don't worry, she's a little wild..." A child of the hills and trees, open to her wide-open homeland, empty enough to still hold secrets.

BELLE ISLE—DETROIT

Another park, *Belle Isle—Detroit*, is the scene for a family outing. This is a photograph that contrasts loving inclusion with separation. It may be fanciful, but its figures, water and darkly silhouetted tree recall for me something of George Seurat's painting *A Sunday Afternoon on the Island of La Grand Jatte* (1884–1886, Art Institute of Chicago). As with Seurat, Frank is interested in the ordinary people who occupy his space. Paris in the 1880s was in the throes of enormous development and industrial expansion, so Seurat was recording the new lives of the working class and the bourgeoisie. Frank is doing the same thing in the American 1950s. Seurat's rich man is replaced by a serviceman in Frank's photograph, and the Parisian 'lady of easy virtue' (check out the coded monkey she is holding in Seurat's painting, a symbol of base licentiousness) with a young woman holding a child on her hip, and an older woman who is pregnant. The latter looks, a little sadly, out of the frame, as does the couple in the Seurat.

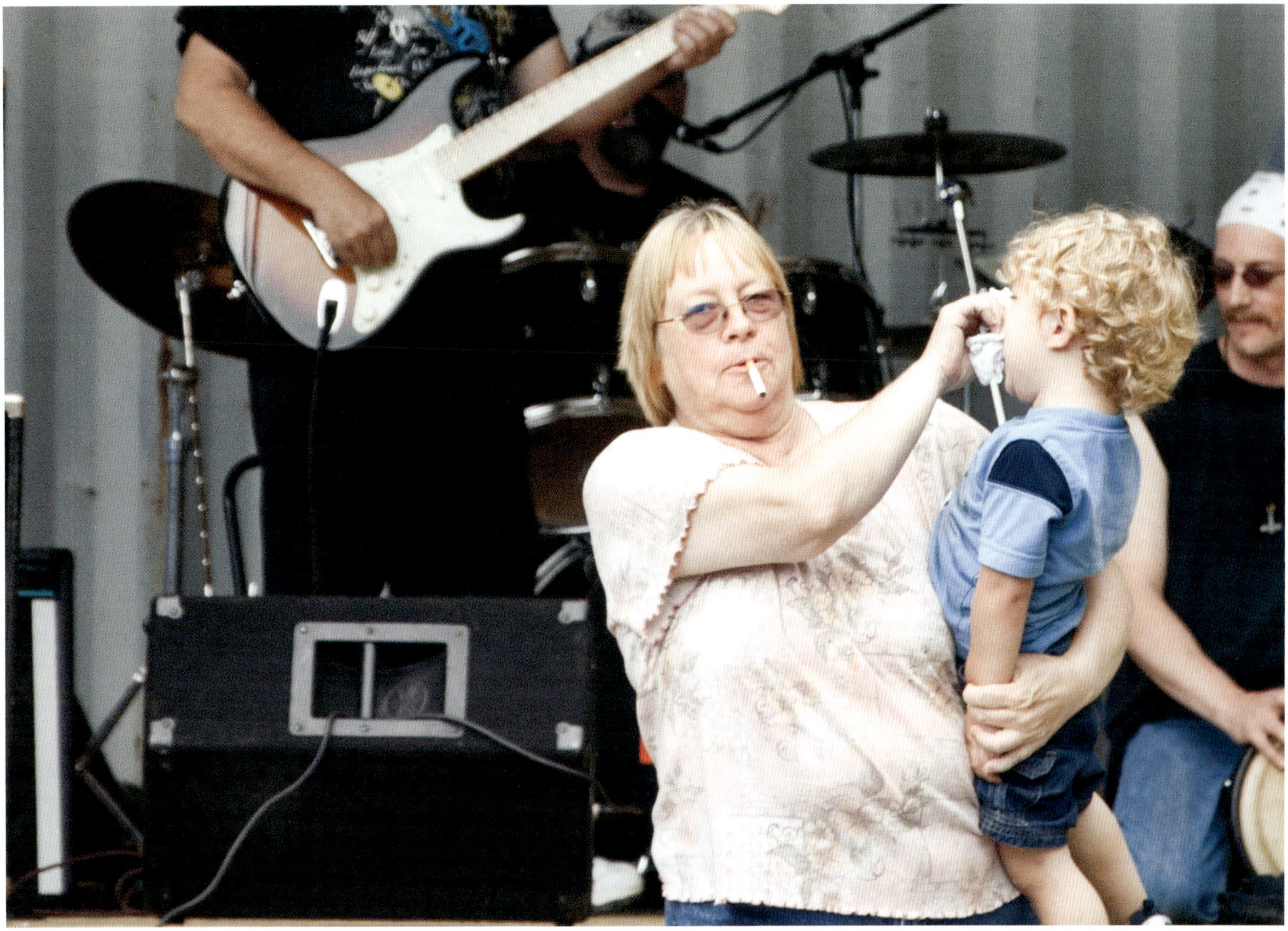

OVER THE SHOALING SEA TO CEDAR ISLAND. The ferryman told me there are lots of Days living here. Fascinating—though unlikely—that they may be somehow distantly and fortuitously sprung from my stock, their divergence both profound and irreversible. The small wooden houses stand at the sufferance of the ocean and storms—most are well kept, hale and hearty, others show the marks of the nights of hurricane winds and the highest of tides. One is 'to let', and the wide sound at the end of the garden, barely a yard lower than the lawn, makes me want to take it. So far from anywhere, the bright sun on the pines.

Forty miles of small settlements, wide flat salt marsh and soggy forests led me eventually into the developments and sprawl of Beaufort NC. A place of lovely houses hundreds of years old, marking the ancient founding of this town: every bar is 'Blackbeard' or the 'Queen Anne's Revenge'. I'm here for the music festival—local rock bands are competent and the Austin, Texas headliners banal in their reductionist, crowd-pleasing roots rock. Pretty girls and flop haired boys, this is an affluent place. I meet a travelling couple, the husband feral eyed and crudely tattooed—stigmata of his four years on the road, adverts for his chosen lifestyle. His wife is young and has the vaguely lost look of someone running from something, desperately hoping that her dreadlocks, edge-living partner and beach-sleeping will bring her lasting peace. Is her rejection of regular society and its expectations a sublimation? A transference, perhaps, leading to this table of hand-made jewellery on a rich town's boardwalk? Her spectacles are expensive and I wonder who bought those for her. She is friendly, he is distant and suspicious. I am apologetic, as if my car-borne journey is in some way a compromise, born of an older man's comfort needs. I think of my teenage self, also running—from unbearable ugliness, of both environment in my industrial town and of the desperate relationships I saw in my family. I can still feel those days so strongly. I remember another festival, quite like this one, in Tonder Park—it was raining. I spent the evening watching a Celtic band on blagged tickets with the most beautiful Danish painter. She was blonde and finely figured—we walked into the early hours talking, arm in arm. Finally she kissed me so gently in the night, her embrace was like the gentle rain. I want to reach out to these young American fellows and let our commonality cross the generations, let out a 'whoop' for the wonders we have seen. But my crooked smile was rejected: the young man remained suspicious, and his girl, sensing it, quickly withdrew into sales pitching. The moment was lost—reaching out is a two way thing, sometimes you just have to let it pass. I was saddened, nonetheless, by this failure of fellowship—I guess a little of me somewhere still wants to walk between the worlds.

I made my escape and drove back some miles into the quiet, swampy, seabreezed back country. I had a less than comfortable night on a ferry car park, myself now feral and vagrant. I guess the teenager, all those years ago, looking to be comfortable in the heart of the darkness got his wish, eventually. I, older now and organised in a hire car, give him a gentle smile. I miss the youth, his strength and ability to carry off clothes. The rest of him is here still, fulfilled now, contributing to these words. I have no tattoos as stigmata and it's nearly forty years I've been on the road. Maybe there is something in my eyes? If not, then I am content: I see no need to advertise. Maybe the sweetest winds really do blow across the South, and tonight I'll let them carry me home.

PUBLIC PARK—CLEVELAND, OHIO

The sense of community generated by the assemblage in *Belle Isle—Detroit* and the love clearly expressed by the woman and child at its centre lead into yet another park image, this time *Public Park—Cleveland, Ohio.* Again, a tree is central to the image and partially protects a single man from our gaze, as he sleeps on a tatty quilt. A sense of well-being emanates from his peaceful face and is supported by his neatly placed shoes. He is young, his hair modishly cut, and he sports a tattoo on his arm. He is alone but not lonely, contentedly lying in the sun. Given the exploration of love in which we are engaged, I wonder whether the voluptuous pin-up on his arm is important, representing his engagement with the pursuit of love, from which (perhaps because of which) he is temporarily resting? We have seen, though, that Frank repeatedly uses counter-images to interrupt a thematic flow, forcing his viewers to reconsider and re-engage with the photographs. I prefer to see this fashionable young man as taking time out of love, carnal or otherwise, rather than denying it.

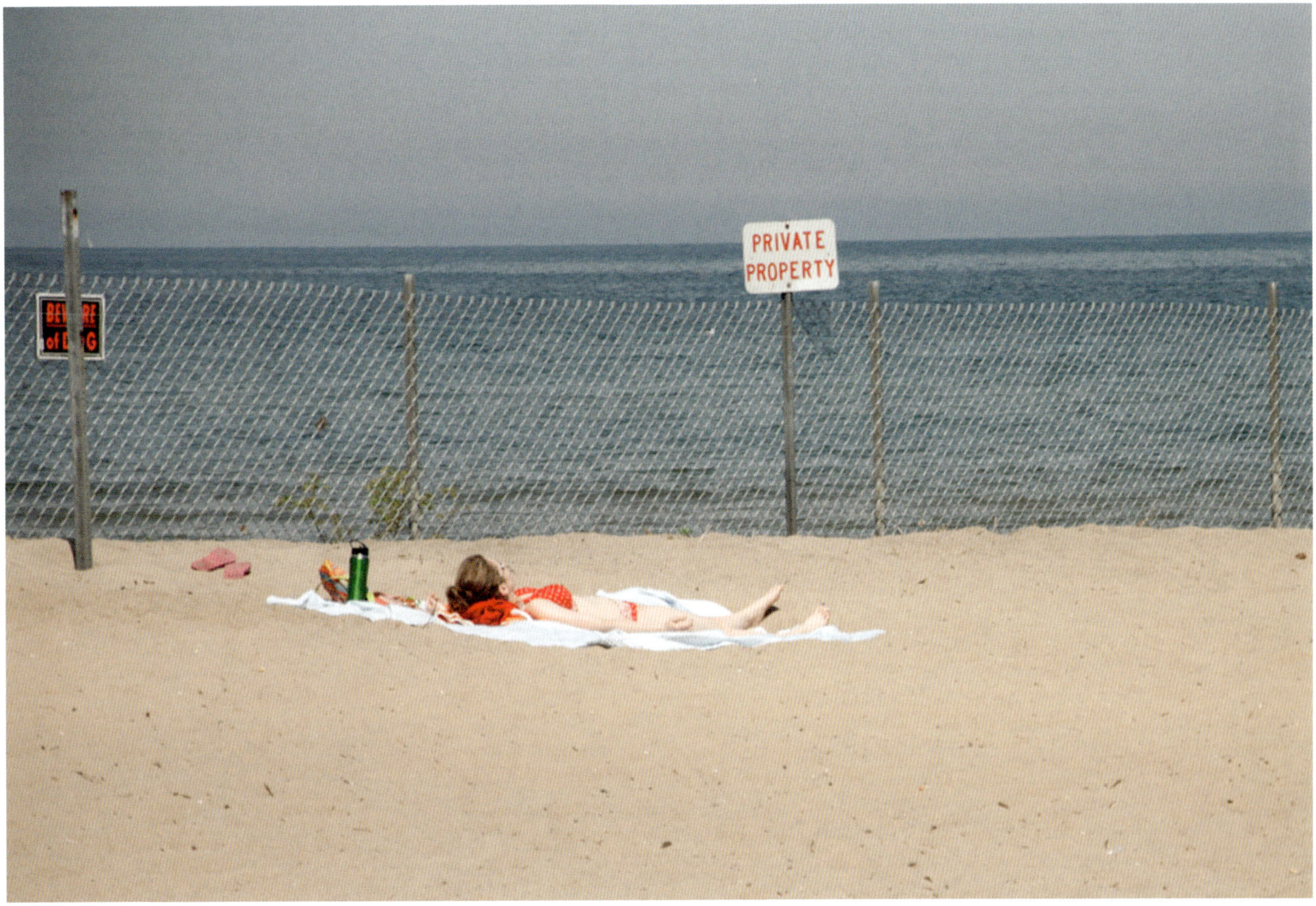
PRIVATE
PROPERTY

BUMPING ALONG THE WHITE GULF-SAND COAST, I had no place to go. I bought coffee from a Dunkin' Donuts, against my better judgement, to think about where I wanted to be. The lady server was very young and a little flirtatious, which was disconcerting given her state of advanced pregnancy. "I'm from Georgia," she smiled though her braces, "Oh my God, I love your accent" she said, smiling again, sheepishly. The coast down from Tallahassee had been kind of rural—forests all around with a wild enough back-country—but the entire coast was nailed down by strip developments, barely a bit of undeveloped beach anywhere to be seen. The houses spread like wildfire into the west as the sand turned from brown to white, backing up impatiently inshore, crowding the beach. Seafoam green water and white snow sand, with barely any space to breathe. I headed to a State Park campsite, looking for some air and space. The gates were dropped and locked, as usual, so I drove cross-country across the ornamental beds. Only one space in the whole place, between enormous RVs, rank on rank—not really sure how my notion of wild camping fitted in here. The heat was appalling, so I rolled on out again, to see where the sultry wind would blow me. Anywhere so long as it was out of here...

Coastal strip developments as far as the eye could dream, and every car park or pull over pretty much marked 'No overnight tramping'. Guess I was weary, longing for some wildness and less heat, so I drove through half the night 'til it got cooler and fell quiet. Pulled up and dived into my sleep roll, needing to close my eyes. Much further than I thought I'd get, so the sun found me with a smile.

Out early, and down to Mobile. It all was close to silent in the morning light, enormous deep-red dockyard cranes rusting quietly against a chrome and eggshell sky. Oh I still see the brilliant light. The Gulf was the colour of a Fender guitar—smirking foam green, showing mermaid teeth every now and then, as the gentlest of waves bit into the sand. A lady called Miss Beverley, in Apalachicola yesterday, had told me what I'd see. Feeding me oysters in her café (for free, though I paid for the beer) she said how these colours would be. I haven't lived many perfect dreams—things usually are so much better in my imagining than they turn out really to be. But not the cranes, the sky, the quiet sea—and the mystery of Alabama stretching far, far into the North. Strung on my chain of perfect pearls, those hours, for my fingers to worry as I get old. A talisman against decrepitude, something to grip in my closing days and say, "This, at least for a time, was me".

COURTHOUSE SQUARE—ELIZABETHVILLE, NORTH CAROLINA

This is the fourth of six photographs engaged with people in parks, and the stigmata of love and loneliness that accompany them. The protective love of *San Francisco*, and the love expressed by the women and children in *Belle Isle—Detroit* led to the satisfied and glowing contentment of the solitary sleeper in *Public Park—Cleveland, Ohio.* The last two images featured a central and powerful tree, standing strong behind the little family, and acting for the sleeper as an *in loco* companion, seeming to protect him as he sleeps feeling safe in its arms. Another tree, this time on the image's left, acts as a seat in *Courthouse Square—Elizabethville, North Carolina.* Two older men are sitting closely together on the roots, looking for all the world as if Atticus or Scout from *To Kill a Mockingbird* (Lee 1960) could appear at any moment. Their physical proximity and their clear engagement with each other speak of a quiet and enduring kind of love. The friends are balanced by a younger woman and a number of other men who occupy the upper third of the photograph.

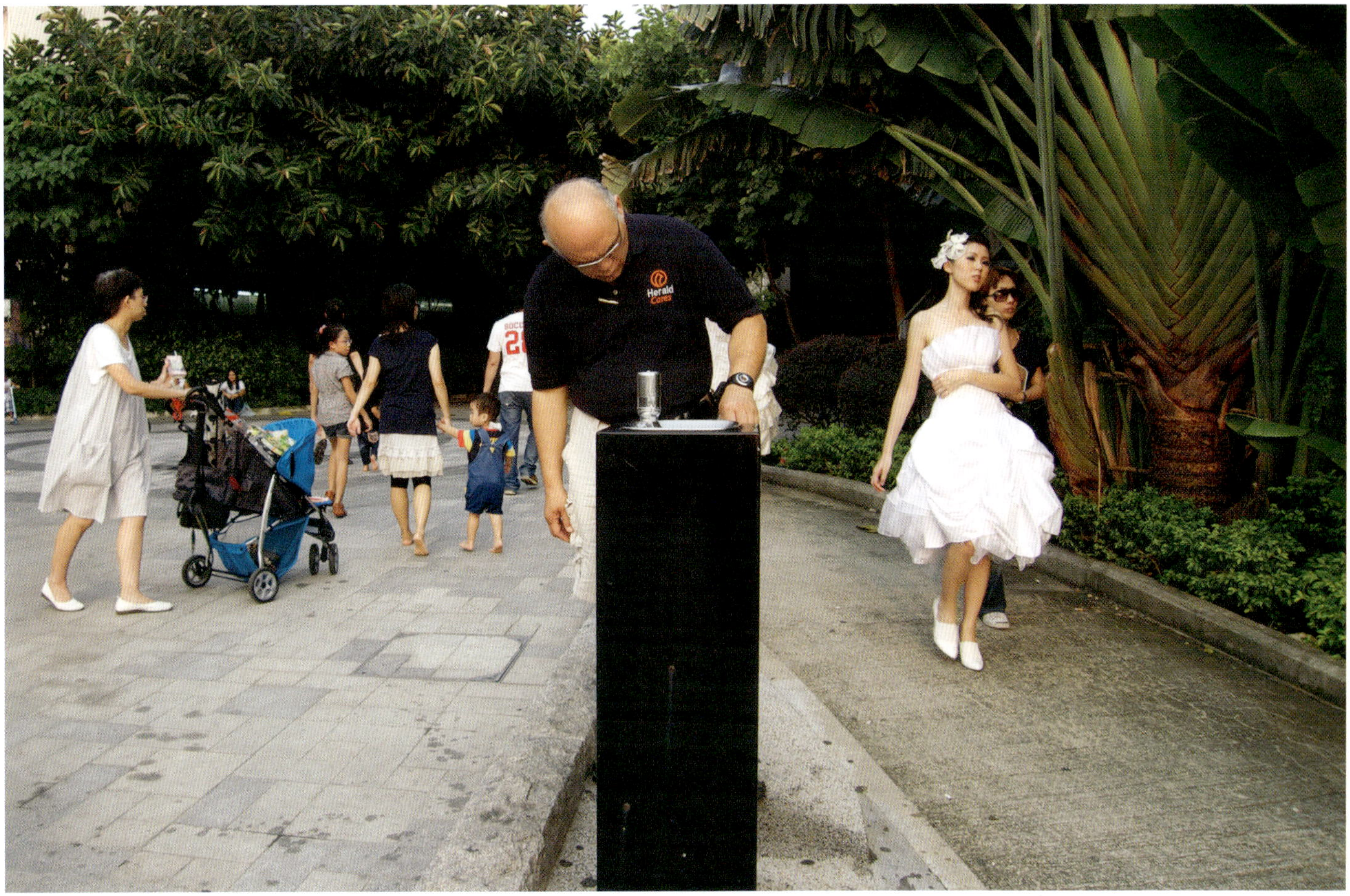
Herald
Cares

INCESSANT RAIN POUNDING ON THE ROOF OF THE CAR—a bear light on one of the RVs made a tree look like a stucco Madonna in its pale orange glow. Sleet is almost freezing in the air—I packed up camp shivering and turned up the heater on the way to Cooke City (all of fifty houses and a couple of stores) for fuel. Drizzly sky reached cloudy down to the steam rising all around from volcanic fumaroles. Around a corner I'm stopped short by a road filled with buffalo. Like a miracle, milling around my car, an ancient, surviving bloodline. They seem to me like trees crossbred with cattle, the deep calm of acceptance in their eyes. They walk slowly, their huge heads swaying rhythmically, their inscrutable eyes assessing me with an almost indifference. So engaged are they in their slow, grassy lives—the blood rush of their calves and companions is sufficient for them. They amble through a clearing, past a shallow pool popping with huge drips falling from branches. Along the way a little, I stopped again for a wolf, maybe four metres away, loping along the roadside ridge, supremely indifferent. Unexpected and wonderful, this wild spirit.

Cooke City is a vibrant little place—the gas clerk told me the Chief Joseph Highway, which I'd followed, is the only way in from the East and runs to 10,000 feet. Down to Silver Gate for breakfast in a 1930s café—octagonal, lodge pole pined, wonderful. Pancakes, eggs, bacon and peace. Journeying then through a little river valley, two enormous cranes buzzed my car, beating the air with a thrumming whistle—the music of feather and wing. They called continually to each other in a strange, rattley croak. Huge and dreamed of birds.

Along the roadside whole stands of trees are skeletal, black against the nondescript sky, poisoned by the shifts of sulphurous gas, as one earth pore closes and another opens. The looming eternal grey above and steaming flats of travertine beneath sandwich brightly coloured Chinese tourist groups. Pastel blue, yellow and tomato red scurry across the creamy steaming plain, like something Degas might have painted, from his window onto the Pont Neuf across the Seine. Sodden and cold I head back to my car heater and bitter coffee. Again the blasted leafless trees: their presence is one of infinite calm.

PICNIC GROUND—GLENDALE, CALIFORNIA

Frank moves from the group in the last photograph to a solitary man in a picture of yet another park with a tree at its heart. *Picnic Ground—Glendale, California* shows a random assortment of trees, benches and waste bins. The solitary man at its centre is sitting on one of these benches and views Frank, as so many others have, with suspicion. His unusually small size, in relation to the image as a whole, serves to emphasise further his isolation. Unlike the contentedly sleeping man in *Public Park—Cleveland, Ohio*, the single figure here, lost in the trees, speaks of loneliness—implicated it seems to me as the obverse of love.

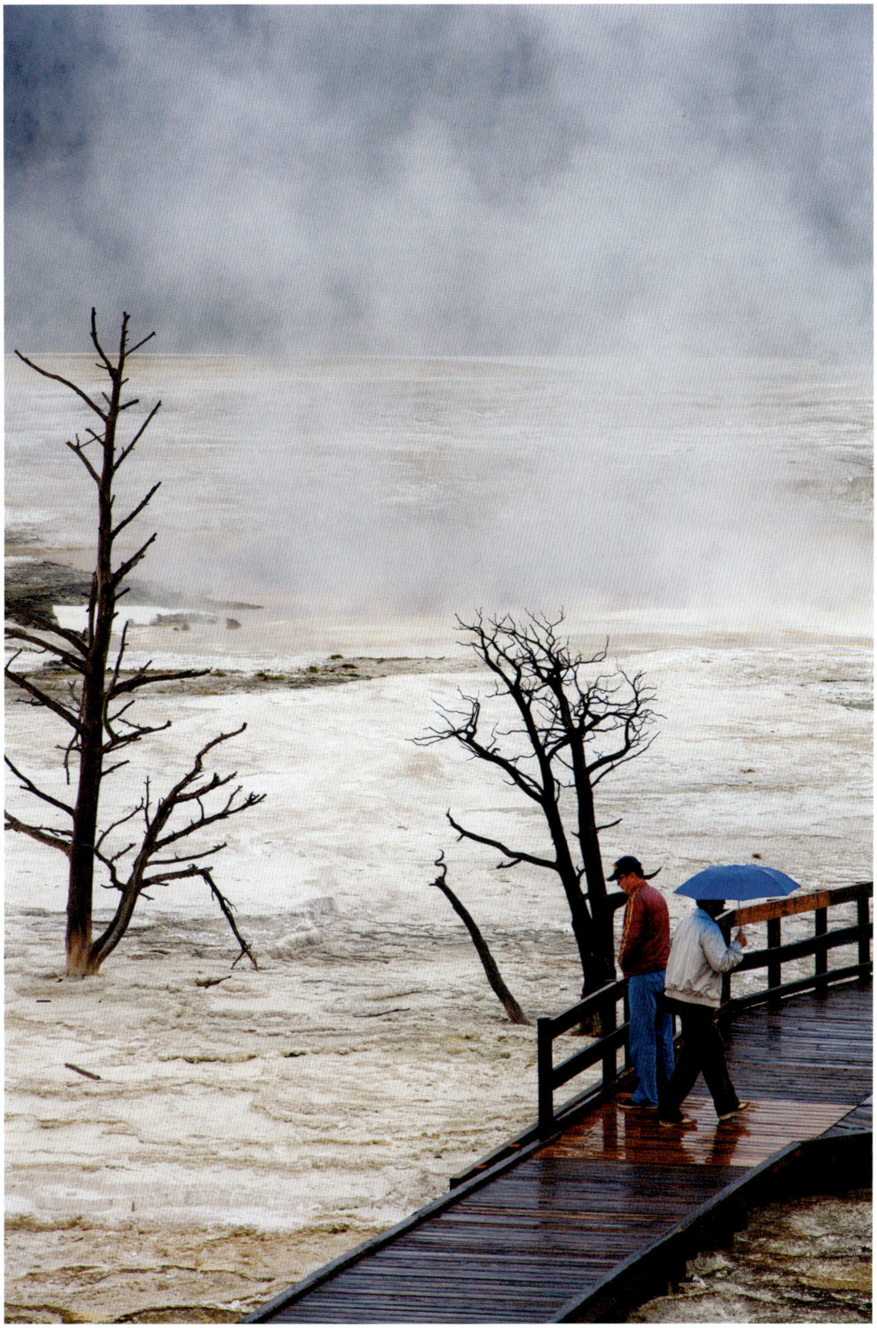

THIS SOFT AND GENTLE FOREST IS SO LIKE HOME, I see so easily how immigrants settled here. I walked this morning through self-heal, garlic-mustard and something like ragged robin, after a long, deep sleep. Yesterday evening as the light died into darkness, I heard over my engine-sound the strident and musical call of the Mockingbird. My daughter loves a book series called the *Hunger Games*. Rather like Takeshi Kitano's *Battle Royale*, but less nihilistic, more political and, for me right now, significantly set in America. The heroine's home ground is here, 'District 12' in the book, a recreation of the Appalachian coal fields. I first heard the call of a Mockingbird (in the book evolved through a complex series of events into a Mocking*Jay)* in our favourite dusty old English cinema, a 1950s' Odeon which has, remarkably and against all odds, survived intact and in business. I was watching the film of the book with my daughter.

I have been travelling the world since I was eight—at that age to Africa—and without too much of a break since. Sailing on the *Windsor Castle*, a lavender-sided mailship, from Southampton via Los Palmas to Cape Town, with my dad's job. We flew back over the Sahara at sunrise in a Boeing 707 filled with Irish stewardesses, landing just over the snow-capped Alps. Knowing so early how utterly amazing was the world behind the horizon—it set the agenda for my life.

Ah but children—what a thing to have children. Approaching 50, his body ravaged by alcohol and (I'm sure not knowingly) approaching death, Kerouac wrote that maybe a family was the only thing to get you through. He was a doting child, criticised by some as a mummy's boy, who yet denied the only child who claimed to be his—he was writing about what he did not know. Nonetheless, I think he was right. All of the fire-behind-the-eyes drive we have when we are young seems to mutate with age. We realise, I guess, that we are creatures of our gene-induced predilections—to mate, reproduce and compete for the materials with which to thrive. It's not all there is, of course, but these things drive us. I think of Elvis and Alexander McQueen, men who had everything that fame and fortune could supply, but both of whom died broken-hearted for loss of family. There are also, of course, many famous who thrive and live undaunted, deep into old age. I suspect family and kinship are crucial cogs in the machines of their life support. I do not think, in truth, that achievement is enough.

The Mockingbird/Jay took me straight into the smiling eyes of my little girl, into the heart of her wide-eyed delight at the world, her fascination with the smallest things, things that without her would seem to me tired and worn out. The Mocking Jay in the last of the ebbing, waning light was a call from home, a warm place for my heart to hang onto in my journey into the dark. This forest is powerful, and I lay, unable to sleep for a while, wrapped in its deep and humid intensity. The rear window of my newly acquired little van slopes enough for me to look up at the sky through the dense trees to the tiny puddles of deep blue eternity, speckled with starlight.

BELLE ISLE—DETROIT

Belle Isle—Detroit is a part of Frank's extended consideration of a life lived in cars, and it is also part of this final series concerned with love. The picture is one of exuberance and excitement. Four black children occupy the rear of a cabriolet, as two adults in front focus on whatever is ahead—perhaps looking for an exit after a day of fun, or maybe arriving and looking for somewhere to park. One boy is half-standing, with obvious pleasure and anticipation in his young face. His three fellows are sitting behind him. Their attention has been caught by something in the same direction as the camera—perhaps Frank himself, or something nearby. They are animated, all attention and entirely at ease with each other. This is family, whether blood relatives or good friends. Significantly, one of the adults has an arm around the trilby-hatted other.

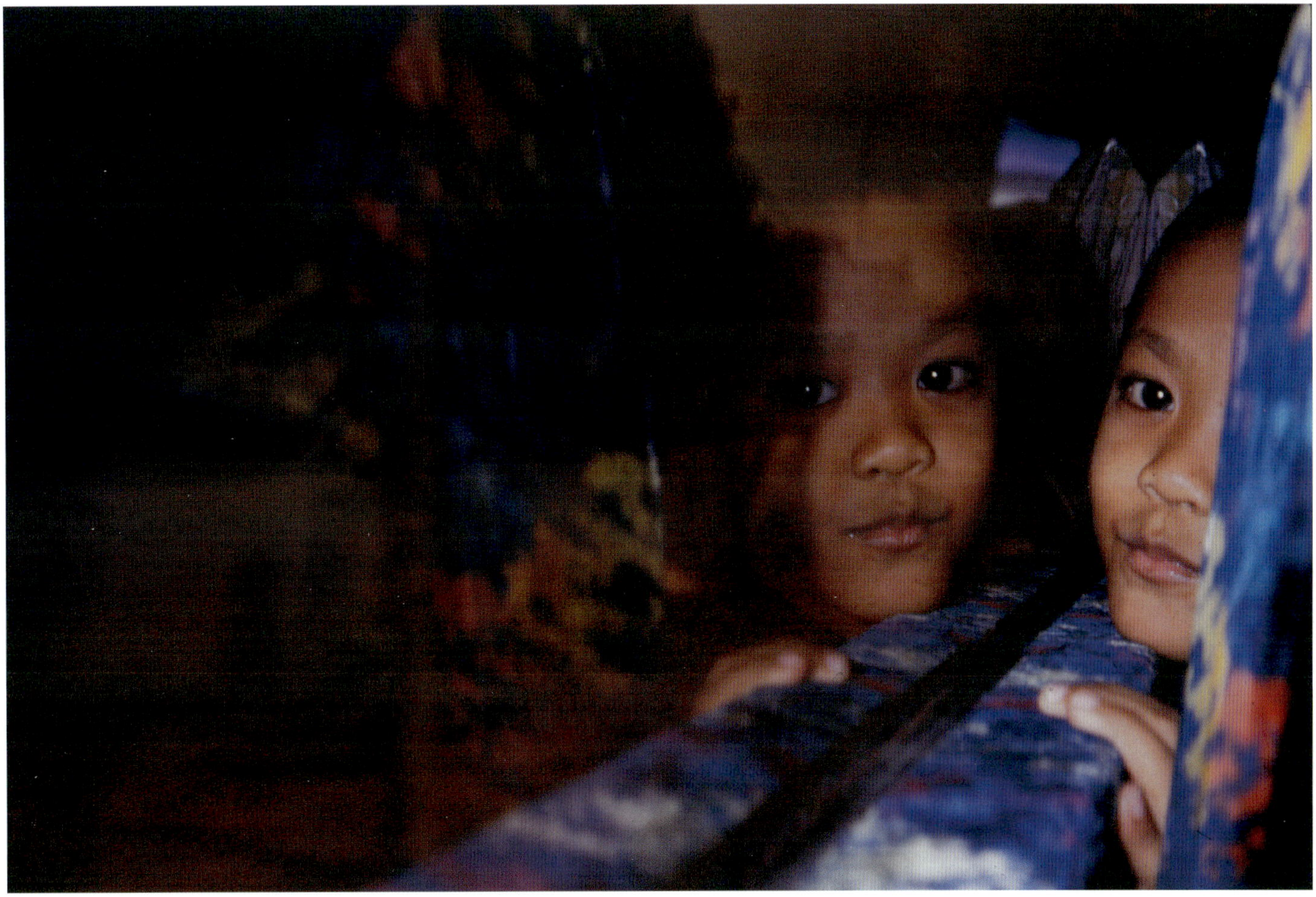

THERE'S SOMETHING DAUNTING ABOUT THE HOLLOW HEART of America. Dull green and dusty brown, the Great Plains stretch unconscionably far. They are a vacuum that sucks in air and spins it, sending it cavorting through Eastern farms, dancing a gavotte with hearth, crop and limb, garrotting lives. It sucks in courage, companionship, family, aspirations, hopes and dreams, all the details that constitute our small humanity—offers them up to the sky and forgets us. Completely. Extinguished. As if we'd never existed.

Down from a Rocky Mountain high, on a road running at 12,500 feet, into a gorge. Granite so fresh I could think it had just been baked, gnarly crystals at every serpentine twist of the Big Thomson River, brittle as toffee, the colour of caramel. Driving was like skiing, carving around the hairpins, trying to stay out of the water. I had a map book as a child, nothing fancy, my auntie's old *Philip's Modern School Atlas*. How I pored over it and dreamed of these mountain passes with their impossible railroads, cutting through this bright new world. I was sad, now, to have to speed through this staggering canyon, and sadder still at canyon's end to encounter Denver's extended sprawl. I hunkered down in my seat until I'd passed it all. It thinned eventually, and the prairie's steamy pall took over from the mountains. On this day I would cross Nebraska, or as far as I could get before the darkness caught me. The heat in my van was astonishing—my air con was fried. All windows down, firing at 70 across the Interstate, just about bearing it. Even so, waves of sleepiness washed me with danger, and I fought as manfully as I was able. Endless-seeming hours of brown grass shimmering in the heat, rolling country, frustrating vision, holding my eyes in the sandhills' claustrophobic bowl. Friendly people at an information stop gave me coffee; much less friendly was the town they served. No matter. Driving ever onwards into darkness, and the realisation that Nebraska was bigger than I could have imagined. I pulled into a truck stop, beyond North Platte near Cozad. After the pre-sleep rituals in the final minutes of consciousness, I read a typical rest-stop plaque, telling the story of the place. Battles everywhere around, apparently, in this solemn, hot and quiet land. Fights between Cheyenne and Lakota, US Cavalry and indigenes, and the slaughter of wagon trains, tattered canvas blowing cloud-white beneath the endless sky. A fellowship of some kind came between me and these unquiet dead. Irish and Scottish farmers and families looking for a life—only to find it horribly ended on the end of a knife in the half light of Nebraska. And with the red men on their warm beasts dressed in Buckskin, caught on a lance, or an arrow tip. How, I wondered, would it be to wander for ever lost in this featureless land. I felt for a long time after that some part of me was left there, that night, wandering forever those endless plains. Crying out to the Human Beings, searching for other spirits beneath the stars, eyes ghostly wide and appealing for comfort, never again able to hold the small hands of home. I feel a shiver now as I write, and the reality of dying there, never making it back, is real still for me, as my children sleep quietly upstairs and the English night rocks me softly in its arms. There is a strange sky too, outside, full of far-off fires I will never clearly see—but I am habituated to it, and this is as near as I will get to home.

DETROIT

After the love and exuberance of *Belle Isle* another Detroit photograph reveals an old couple sitting in a white, hard-topped sedan. They wear expressions of concern, perhaps uncertainty. The contrasts are clear: a young vibrant family, almost overflowing their open-top, against a roofed-over couple whose children, if they had any, have left and gone away. The balding, white-haired man and his companion are still together, though, and look out from their protected place at the bewildering and ever-changing world that has left them behind (as it now leaves behind Frank, and me also). They have not reached the status of the St Petersburg pensioners we saw earlier, migrating to Florida to be warm when they die: they are still motorised. Clearly though, they are in decline, losing their battle with the years, hanging on with fingernails. It doesn't look like it will be long until they and their car retire from the road into a back yard somewhere, like the one in *Venice Beach, California*. This final short series of photographs is more about love than cars, and love appears to have remained here, in their stalwart—if in this moment enervated—togetherness, sharing the solemnity of companionship.

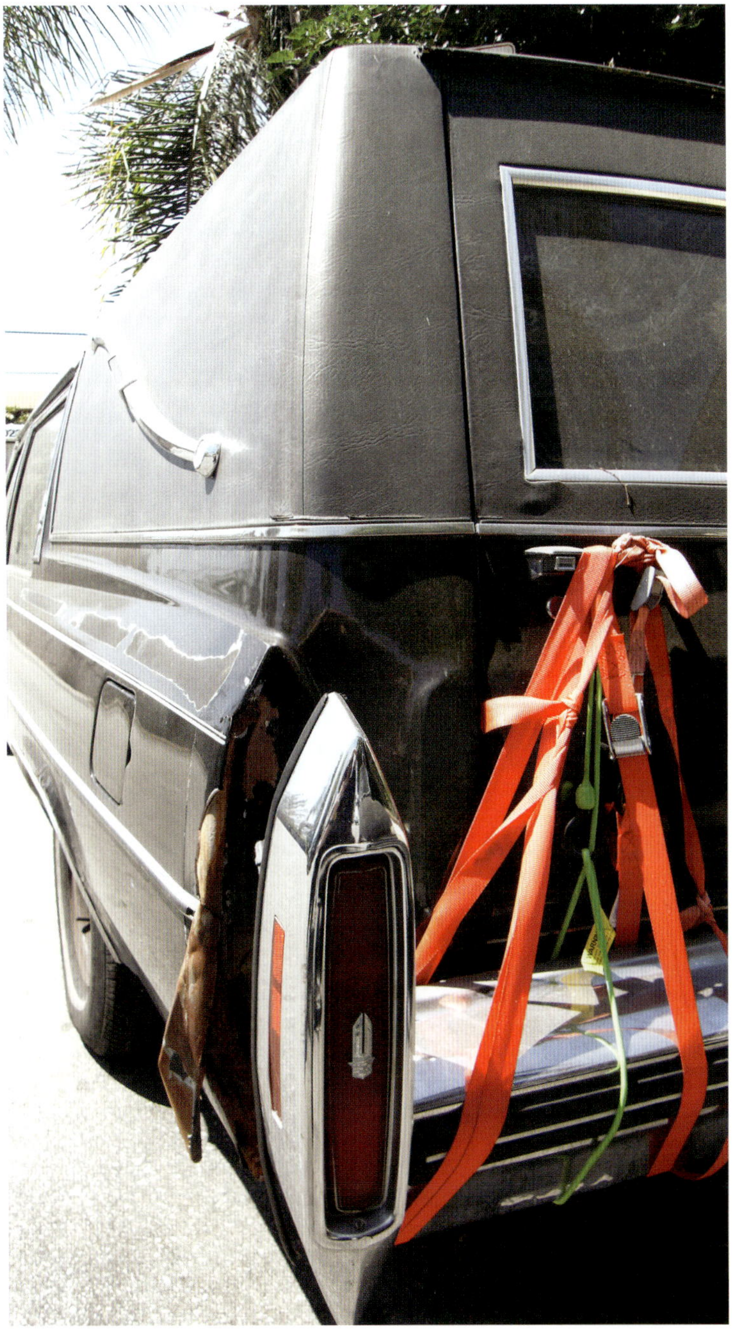

THE THIRD CAR-THEMED PHOTOGRAPH in this final sequence is a slightly aberrant image. There is no couple or family in this photograph. It features an empty black saloon, offsetting the occupied white car of the last picture. The parked car is in a just-discernible alley, dark walls rising to either side and a snippet of another vehicle just in frame at top right. Most of the high walls are visible as a sinuous reflection, drawing an arabesque of light and dark across the roof, rear window and trunk of the car. A spiderweb of girders, fire escapes and walkways is twistedly echoed at centre. Is this, then, another of Frank's finger flicks at structure, departing from his theme in these final pages filled with romantic and filial love? Perhaps it is, but there is another possibility. The car's licence plate supports a badge saying 'Christ came to save sinners'. Above this, in the rear window, another says 'Christ died for our sins'. Frank's capturing of these evangelical soundbites, which preach redemption through repentance and grace, appears to be ironic. The relocation of the 'words of eternal life' onto a dusty automobile parked in a back alley appears to speak of the debasing influence of materialism, consumerism and advertising. This is a theme Frank has certainly examined previously. I do wonder, though, whether there might not be a less ironic possibility. Above the licence plate is the Chrysler corporate badge. This stylized cross is caught by the falling light and starkly illuminated against the almost solid black shadow in which the rest of the trunk lies. Within this shadowy and shadowed place, the lightning-like trace of brilliant sky leads vertically down the image to the cross and the badge. Christ is called the 'Man of Sorrows', and was known for his preaching to the poor and destitute, his exhortation that 'blessed are the poor in spirit', his association with lepers and prostitutes and his eventual execution at the 'Place of the Skull'. We have seen already that Frank is prepared on occasions to depict religious practice with ambivalence, even with sympathy. Given the love theme in this last sequence, might we read his depiction of Christian words here in this 'city canyon', this back alley so associated in American popular culture with mugging, drug-taking and destitution, as positive? Is it, actually and against the odds, appropriate? Could the car be an angelic messenger, buried in the streets of the city? Frank has shown us a life lived in cars—childhood, adolescence, maturity, family, old age, dotage and death. So where to now in the cycle of the car? Perhaps we need to see heaven. Perhaps here is a car-carried evocation of afterlife. It is an intriguing possibility.

CHICAGO

What, then, is Frank's conclusion to his consideration of a life lived in cars? Many of his images are obviously critical. Hatred and criticism of the car were common among contemporary commentators. Charles Merz, writing before Frank set out, described the pointlessness of recreational driving:

> Impressions? Yes. Impressions of a never-ending road [...] Thrills? Yes. Thrills of scenery that would be worth stopping for if only there were time [...] Trophies? Yes. Trophies to bring back memories of this day of travel: postcards, toy balloons and paper bathing girls [...] Yet surely these are poor rewards for so much travel. Surely it is worth no man's while to drive three hundred miles from break of dawn on Sunday just to add another pennant to his string, or to hurry half the day for the apparent purpose of arriving at a point far enough away to make it necessary to turn at once and hurry home again. (Merz 1928: 19–20)

Frank is far more ambivalent than this. The car is protection in a *Motorama* as much as a killer in *Flagstaff*, liberation for the young men leaving Blackfoot as much as a fetish in *Covered Car*.

Frank sees what Merz figured without. Travel is a metaphor for change. It is the signifier of progress, of movement, the constant incremental approach towards the gates of paradise. Frank clearly echoed this in *U.S. 285, New Mexico*. For people tied to endless repetitive work and a daily struggle for survival, like the women in *Parade—Hoboken, New Jersey*, travel, even for one day a week, could represent an escape from the dreariness of everyday life. It is not a real escape, merely a symbol, a representation. It is no less significant for this. Many Americans in the 1950s spent their lives working in coal pits or steel mills, shipyards, shops or automobile plants. They sacrificed their youth and strength for poor wages and the slow growth of the US economy, finally to retire briefly and die. For them, this simulacrum was as essential as food or warmth. They needed

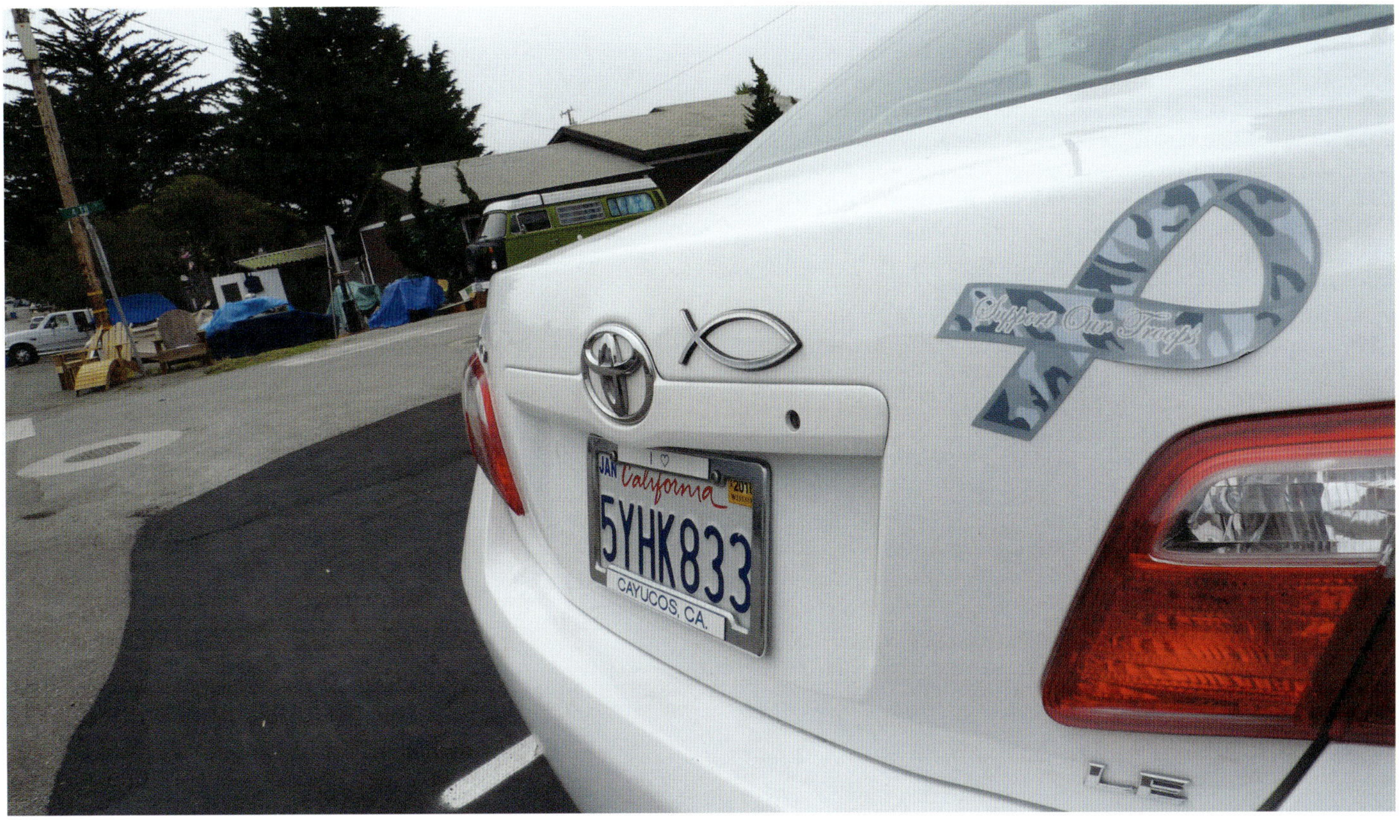
Support Our Troops
JAN
California
5YHK833
CAYUCOS, CA.
LE

this dream. The pennants at which Merz jeers contain, in their tawdry kitsch, the hopes of another, better, life. The memory of those few free-feeling Sunday hours sustained days of drudgery. We still, of course, live with this reality. Frank sees that for Americans the car and highway represent even more than this. In their living memory, theirs was the land of frontiers and pioneers, exploring an unknown world, with always the possibility of striking gold or claiming acres of fertile virgin land, bereft by the bullet of their Native stewards. By the middle years of the twentieth century, the country was consolidating its expansion. Journeys that had involved danger, adventure and promise had become safe, sanitized and, by comparison, fruitless. The everyday life of the Americans no longer necessitated travel. For a nation so peopled by refugees, prospectors, runaways and dreamers, both religious and philosophical, this change could only be deeply traumatic. The Pacific was reached, the interior surveyed, the 'Indians' pacified or, more accurately, annihilated. There was nowhere new to explore or to escape to. The loss of real adventure had to be replaced with an aesthetic simulacrum. It became symbolised in the thrill of a journey to some theme park or 'discovery cave', as the former were known in embryo. The pursuit of the Dream could no longer be invested in the mythical frontier and lived vicariously through pulp fiction, the newspapers or travelling Wild West shows. The frontier no longer existed. The echoes of the constitutional right of every American to engage in the pursuit of life, liberty and happiness, to bear arms and to be 'free' became, in the light of factory work, the imperative of poverty and the control of an ever more regimented society, a constant searching. They yearned for the time and place—on a Sunday afternoon, of course, and within easy reach of home—when truth and beauty would finally integrate in the harmonious music of the spheres, played as accompaniment to the ultimate orgasmic sensory overload. They searched for something that would change their lives for ever, the echo of what Frank describes as "where God is" (Frank 1991: after plate 63) or Kerouac saw as the moment when "the pearl would be handed to me" (Kerouac 1972[1957]: 11).

Frank counted the cost of the highway and the car while celebrating their metaphors. He travelled these prescribed asphalt paths in pursuit of their promise, aware that it may be spurious. He pressed these simulacrums into service as signifiers of the journey within, sharing the hope of so many whose writing was never read, whose photographs were never seen. Many of these anonymous Americans pursuing their Sunday afternoon dream were also aware of its chimerical nature, appearing to form for a moment from the heat haze or distant fog into the gates of paradise, only to dissolve again into nothing. One moment saw a flare of light over three crosses speaking of heaven, the next only a deserted desert road, fading sticks stuck in the dirt.

I MET A COUPLE OF TRAVELLERS IN A DUSKY NORTH CAROLINIAN SQUARE. I asked them about a place to sleep, and drove down the coast a little way to a beach they recommended. It was a concrete circle of car parks, a Civic and functional bathers' pavilion and a noisy bar or two. Beyond it was the beach—so far from anywhere I wanted to sleep.

In the heavy darkness I found a knot of black kids, drunk, angry, piled high on the hoods of old cars. Deep hard beats solidified the air, everywhere shouts at the DJs, screams, howls. Rage was palpable in the air. No white faces apart from mine, and across the street a watching group of cops—ready, unimpressed, unfazed, waiting, almost bored. In the deep darkness at the centre of this whirlwind of youth, girls strutted and bellowed at the congregation, emboldened by the heat and noise, in a world they'd spun out of rusty steel and blackness. I was painfully aware of my difference, shot pictures from the hip, not as an affectation, but a sense of self preservation. I skirted them, trying not to be seen, hoping to catch a stolen moment of their Saturday night. Reminds me of a line from a Springsteen song, "a barefoot girl sitting on the hood of a Dodge, drinking warm beer in the soft summer rain". No rain, this sultry Southern night, and I felt little romance in these angry kids. As with Kerouac's San Francisco, his beloved city of bums, which seemed to me a lonely place—lost humanity, howling at the night.

PUBLIC PARK—ANN ARBOR, MICHIGAN

Finally, as we rush towards the book's conclusion, Frank's last four images form a quadtych, following the development of a 1950s couple's love from inception to the point at which Robert and his wife Mary found themselves.

In *Public Park—Ann Arbor, Michigan*, semi-naked, bathing-suited young people are 'making out' between their cars. The car at centre shot, with its door wide open, is at most a yard from its mating occupants. Parked on grass, the cars reflect the brilliance of the light between and behind the trees that surround them. The couples prefer the proximity of their vehicles to the brilliant clearing behind. Is this a function of the irresistible pressure of time? Kerouac thought something along these lines in *On the Road*: 'Boys and girls in America have such a sad time together; sophistication demands that they submit to sex immediately without proper preliminary talk' (Kerouac 1972[1957]: 57). Or is it that these young lovers feel comforted by the presence of their automobiles? The cars, despite their toothy grins and chrome protrusions, seem to watch over the mating rituals like benign and protective beasts, providing escape routes from danger, and shelter from prying eyes. This is their modern world, and they appear as at peace with it as they could possibly be. Frank has caught one man's eye, and he looks quizzically from his front car seat out of the frame. He is questioning rather than aggressive, but eloquently reveals that the camera and the photographer are not as accepted or integrated into this world as the cars are. Frank is an outsider, the Buicks and Dodges are not. The products of mass production silently watch the process of human production. These technological creations are included in the ceremonies of procreation. This notwithstanding, the courtship moment in modern love sits at the centre of this photograph: the car is there at the moment of conception.

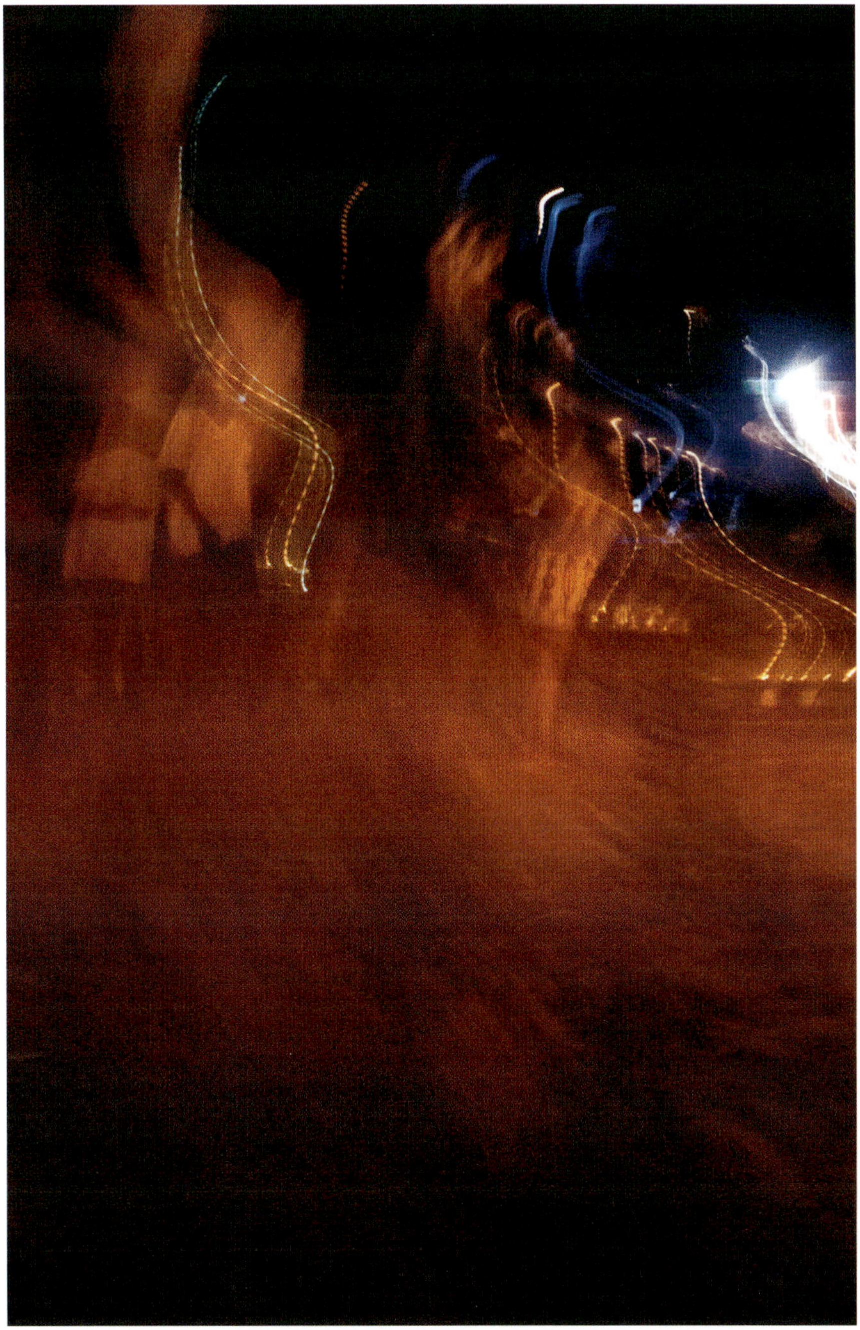

"AN IVORY TOWER BUILT ON A SEWER", THE TIBETAN BUDDHISTS SAY. It's imaginative language of course: we are not made of ivory. Save in our dreams of ourselves. Maybe a wedding is the time when people try their hardest to escape the blood and shit of our reality and dissemble successfully for a day. It's such a fantasy and requires so much effort—yet I have seen the look in the eyes of departing couples when their day has gone well—they are replete, knowing that for this one day in their lives, they represented themselves as they wished to be. They have the self-satisfied smugness of bankers. It is, though, a fantasy, and we tacitly acknowledge this at the celebration's end. Where I grew up, a wedding without a drunken brawl at its close was a disappointment to everyone.

So our semi-sewer nature can be a reason to turn away, acknowledge the things of the world of illusions and try to find ourselves in contemplation. Even this requires an uneasy compromise between the requirements of our flesh and the wishes of our hearts. I think Kerouac got as far as this turning away, scaling mountains in his gym shoes and living alone in fire towers for months on end.

There is, though, another aspect of Zen called the 'water buffalo pictures' and I would love to know if he knew it. There, too, is a turning away, in an allegorical search for the eponymous water buffalo—a metaphor for our errant and wilful nature, out of control. Through long travail and contemplation the buffalo is tamed, and starts to respond meekly and with gentleness. Finally—and this is the key part—all duality has vanished, and the enlightened and integrated self returns to the marketplace to celebrate the things of the world, without being bound anymore to, or by, them. Lao Tzu said in the Tao Te Ching "Always rid yourselves of desires in order to observe the Way's secrets; but always allow yourself to have desires in order to observe its manifestations." A thing of balance then, at the end, a return from the wilderness cabin of the mind. Kerouac achieved the turning away: I'm not sure that he ever successfully made it back.

There's no reason, then, to mock Frank's young 'just married' people or feel any condescending sympathy for the material challenges that face them in a life as yet unlived. They are simply full of potential on a bright Nevada day. The threats that crowd their future, reflected mutely by the city hall's frozen stones, may be ones that they will rise to. Their journey may be a successful one, as they grow wiser and less boisterous with time, like the couple coming soon in Indianapolis—weary and yet mutually reliant—or Frank himself and Mary, also out there somewhere on the road.

CITY HALL—RENO, NEVADA

City Hall—Reno, Nevada seems to me an entirely uncynical image. A young couple, barely older then the teenagers of the last image, are imaged against an opulent if rather cold interior, otherwise devoid of people. They have delight and excitement written large across their faces. The young woman is wearing a suit of Chinese silk, complete with pagodas, and the quiffed and Brylcreemed young man has on a suit. The implication is clearly that they are getting married. They are impoverished by the lack of significant others, family or friends, and they seem small and vulnerable among the marble and ironwork. Their vows, too, will be a legal formality in this functional building. Despite all of this modernity, Frank in his role as wedding photographer captures the genuine joy of the consummation of young love. This joy, full of promise and nervousness, is evidenced and underwritten by the couple's positive engagement with the camera, unusual in *The Americans.* The young woman looks shyly but happily down, while the young man smiles openly for the picture. The context, of course, is the point: people are more comfortable with a photographer at a wedding.

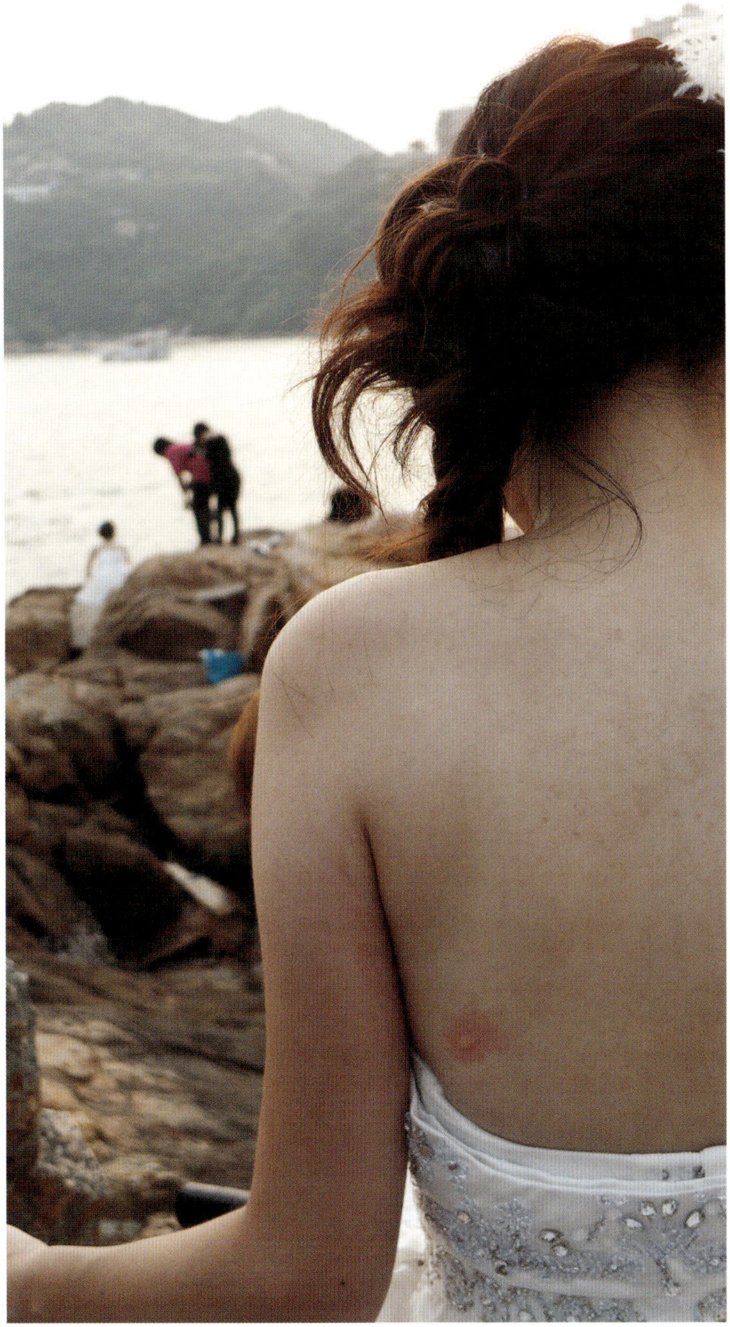

THE EARLY LIGHT CAME THROUGH THE HIGH MAPLES, dripping still from the rain storm, everything saturated—this is a rain forest. It was all so comfortable for me; I played a few songs for the trees and birds. My Triangulin sounded so sweet in the morning—in my head still the powerful and beautiful avian late evensong. There was a quiet intuited presence, too, of the Old Ones, also playing their tunes. This land was once teeming with mountain families, before they overfarmed the land and had to sell to the government in the '20s. Bob Dylan said his best performances are not on records, being left, instead, like offerings, somewhere out there on the road. Lost forever in air and time—for my sounds, too, this is the only epitaph. Clear, soft, fetched from wood and wire, in the forest, in the morning.

I turned back onto the Blue Ridge Parkway and drove a hundred miles of empty road. I want to just say that again, maybe the most spectacular and astonishing road in America, winding along the mountain crest, and it's empty. I drove from Otter Creek to the Peaks of Otter, where a strongly Virginian waitress served me bacon and eggs. I watched a red-headed woodpecker hammer, while brilliant yellow birds whizzed across my path. Dopey turkeys eyed me with something like disquiet, mixed with the deepest Republican disdain. Further along an iridescent bluebird flirted with the bushes and played kiss chase with the breeze. I kept trying, almost in exasperation, to describe this jump of a feeling brought on so often by this place. It was something that tasted of childhood and long ago wide-eyed pawing through picture books with my grandfather. I realised, abruptly, that it was joy. Oh the preserved little wood-pile pioneer shacks, hewn from the forest, sealed up with mud. Homes for our strange and inventive species, here so natural and sustainable, which yet we abandon for prefabrication.

Just into Carolina I was forced off the broken Parkway for a detour. I was at first astonished by the outside-the-park remnants of the mountain men. A burned out house with its burned out car still in front, as if the fire was yesterday and the owners are in a motel waiting for repairs. The caving in roof gives the lie to that thought: it's clearly been like this for a considerable time, just left there to rot.

And so into Laurel Springs, a Blue Ridge Mountain township. Here are the remnants of the pioneers who did not sell to the government and move to the factory towns. Some are clearly prosperous with neat iron-traceried porches. Picturesque and incredibly dilapidated trailer homes, too, and tiny, slowly toppling shacks. Blondie's Antiques has junk of the junkiest kind, mannequins dressed in bizarre assemblages, tattered film posters and Harley Davidson ephemera. Blondie of the enormous hair has one foot in the door of ancient. There is a sense of past glory about her, as if she is from another time. Stuck in the landfill of her merchandise, "every price negotiable" comes as no surprise. One door along the street is a deserted marriage shack, one more along is Freeborne's bar. I buy a coffee from Jen, a charming Carolinian, dressed in tiny denim shorts on this cool and misty day. Biker bar-maid gear *du jour*, she is lovely, and I take comfort in her easy smile.

INDIANAPOLIS

After the high emotion and gleaming faces at the wedding, *Indianapolis* evidences a more mature love. A couple sits on a Harley Davidson motorcycle. It is clearly a cherished object, adorned with studded leather panniers and punctuated with polished chrome. Their outfits similarly tie them to their vehicle: studded denim, a flying helmet for the woman and a Brando *Wild One*-style hat for the man. They are composed and elegant, their mirrored poses and easy physical intimacy communicating mutual reliance and sympathy. They are not, though, smiling or excited. They look a little sadly down, as if something has caught their eyes. Frank's contacts give us no clue as to what that might be: their expression is a thing of a moment as they move past him and his camera. This 'look of sadness' reveals a life that has moved on from adolescent high spirits into the more dogged and sustained challenges of adulthood. Their comfort and mutual support is, though, still very evident.

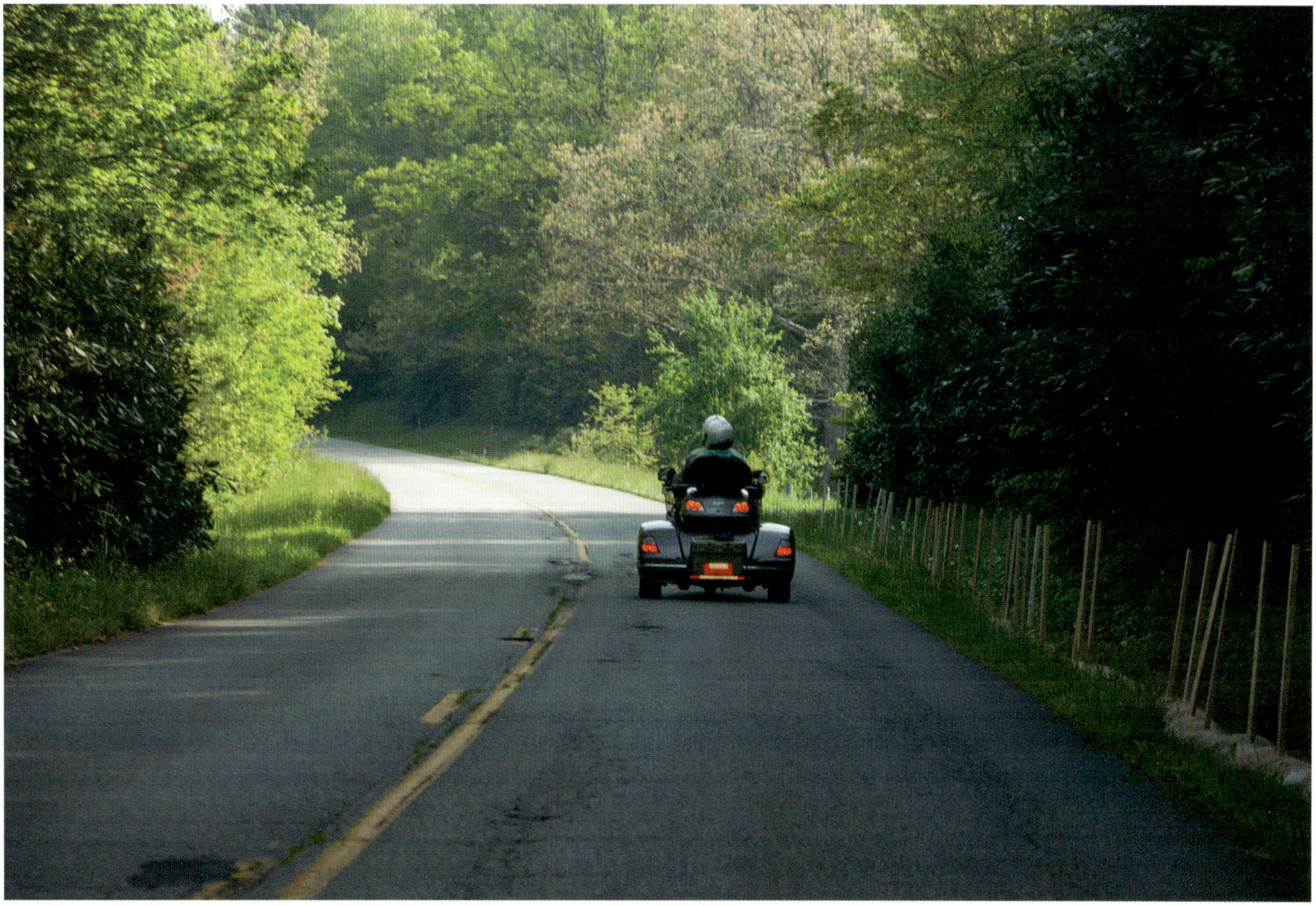

WHEN THE WHOOPING IS OVER AND THEY COME TO FETCH ME, what epitaph will I leave for the crows? Some wizened portrait of a pinched and painful passing, gripping everything tight, afraid of ever letting go? Or a glorious and ridiculous *pinyata*, of string and sticky paper, photographs and tacks? A happy celebration, I hope, with flashing lights and the most wonderful, heavenly sounds. Something funny for the children, but also so astonishing as to draw ravens and apsaras down. Or maybe something different still—whiter, more enduring. A photograph that has all but faded, the essence of the white and white. Something that just about acknowledges passing, speaks of departure, the barest trace remaining of something gone.

It isn't quite time for that yet, although it soon will be in this spinning life. The dark trees smile their knowing smiles and the high stars celebrate in fire, as I walk into light.

So here, as a farewell to you, is a picture of me missing—hat blown on the desert wind, red car waiting like the boat of Ra, desperate to get under way. I'd stopped for no good reason, here at a pull-in on a bend in the high Mojave Desert, near to Joshua Tree. I walked for no good reason along a little path, looking at the strange woody shaman shrubs, happy with them and they with me. I continued along the dusty path to the sun cracked granite for no particular reason and found there, unexpectedly, a cave, painted up and peculiar. A cross vibrated in lines of red and blue, sad memorials were hand-lettered on the stone, for someone clearly much loved and lost. I realised with amazement that this was for the dead Gram Parsons—his body had been committed here to the Universe. He was a singer, long dead now, whose story I had known since childhood. He had a pact with his tour manager that whomever of them should die first, the other would kidnap their corpse and bring it secretly to this ancient place, freeing it as ashes and smoke, trailing into the sky. For Graham, as much as anything, I had come here, but didn't know I'd arrived, until nothing in particular drew me to this place, to see what I could find. That was at the start of my journey. Peculiar. Twenty thousand miles and miles have left me, finally, back at the beginning.

U.S. 90, EN ROUTE TO DEL RIO, TEXAS

If we accept Frank's earlier photograph *Barber shop through screen door—McClellanville, South Carolina* as a kind of statement of intent, if Frank really was communicating his intentions pictorially, then we should also be able to find a pictorial conclusion. *U.S. 90, en route to Del Rio, Texas* is his revelation of himself to us, his signature and his benediction.

The photograph also, and importantly, comments on a classic Standard Oil advertising image. Sol Libsohn's *Charles Kitchen, Anchor Motor Freight Company trucker, driving at night on U.S. Highway 22; May, 1945* (Standard Oil Archive, University of Louisville) was part of a project called *Trucking Story*, on which he worked from March until May of 1945. Libsohn and Roy Stryker, Standard Oil's Picture File director, together produced a script detailing a routine two-day journey by two truckers collecting parts for war planes. The story was published in *The Lamp*, Standard Oil's expensively produced corporate magazine, with *Charles Kitchen* as its lead image.

Frank's *U.S. 90, en route to Del Rio, Texas* follows the composition of Libsohn's image closely. The line of both vehicles is approximately a fifth of the way in from the edge. The position of the windscreens, and the view through them of people inside, are very similar. Most significant of all are the lit headlamps, occupying about the same position in each picture. Notably, Frank has reversed the Standard Oil composition, literally mirroring it, as his photograph mirrors, distorts and comments on its meaning.

Libsohn's almost cinematic image presents the trucker as an archetypal worker-hero. Humphrey Bogart had played exactly such a trucker previously, in Henri-Georges Clouzot's *The Wages of Fear* (1953), heroically carrying nitroglycerine across rugged country in an effort to preserve life and limb. Kerouac acknowledged this archetype:

> ...what a driver a great big tough truck driver with popping eyes and a hoarse raspy voice who just slammed and kicked at everything and got his rig under way and paid hardly any attention to me. (Kerouac 1972[1957]: 16)

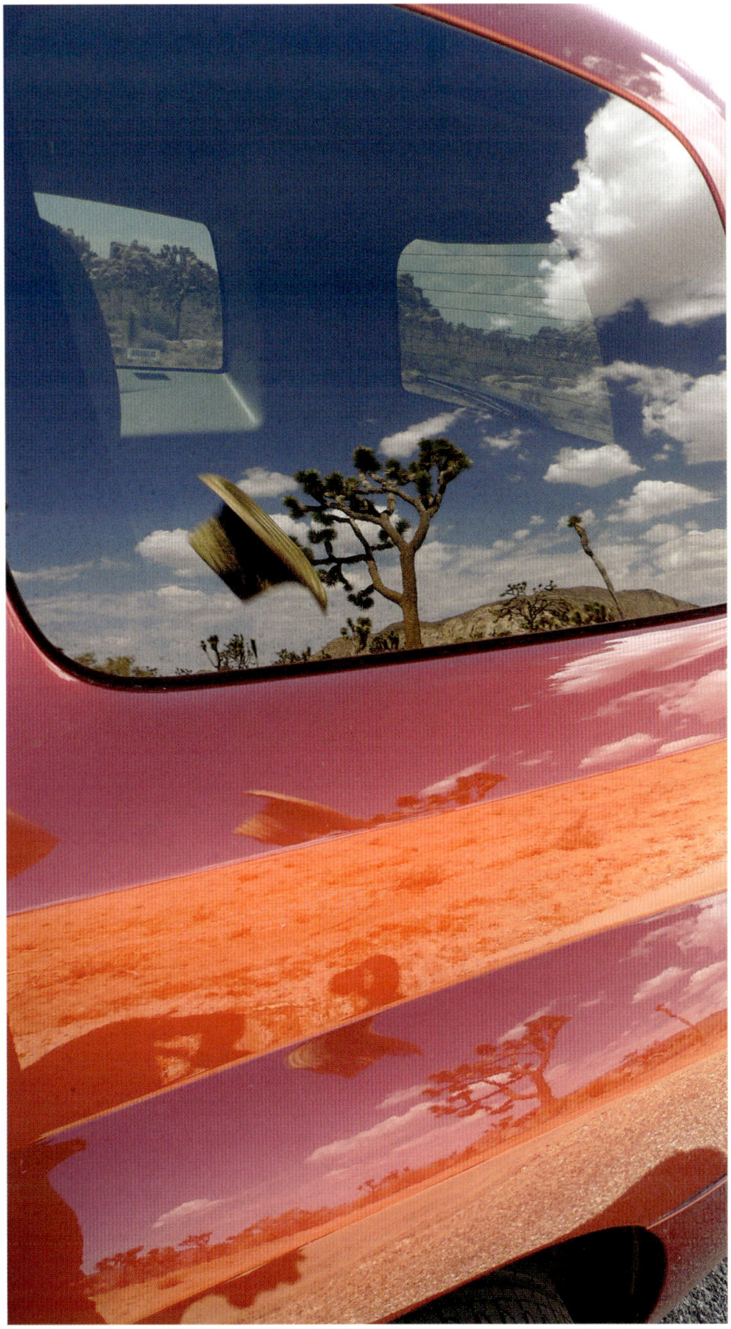

If the American Dream presses the road and the notion of journey into service as signifiers of a better life waiting just around the corner, then images such as *Charles Kitchen* identify the pursuers of this dream as heroes rather than victims. Advertising is mythologising the worker. It is the aesthetic humanisation of industry, the justification of hours of toil by the conferral of heroic status.

Charles Kitchen is a corporate image, full of machismo and power. The photograph's low viewpoint emphasises the truck's size; its lines are rectilinear and powerful. The glowing, eye-like headlamp sits above and to the side of the toothy radiator grill, grinning against the black bonnet. Charles's face is determined, lit dramatically from the side. His grip on the steering wheel is certain. Libsohn wrote, "His hands were big on the wheel. They seemed hardly to try when he turned the wheel" (Libsohn, in Keller 1986: 204). He is the master of this monster, controlling its huge power, driving through the night with his war-bound cargo, intent on his mission. The picture strives to embody not only the nobility of labour and of Standard Oil, but of America, intent on the defeat of the enemies of the 'free world'.

In contrast, Frank's image is taken from head height. This emphasises normality, facilitating an easy identification with the photograph's everydayness. The car is small and personal; its curves are feminine and humble. Frank's Madonna-like wife and child sleep easily. The car stands motionless at the side of a desert road in dim light. There is no urgency, no work to do, nowhere to go that can't wait. The only imperatives are personal, the only mission is the journey, the only cargo his family. Here, Frank has entirely subverted the notion of the highway as the conduit for affairs of state. Charles Kitchen is a cog in the wheel of the dream, aiding the American pursuit of 'manifest destiny', in this case by helping to win a war. He is a part of the industrial process; both he and the road are its servants. Frank's road is a private place, somewhere to watch his family sleep, somewhere that is as close as this wild-at-heart world comes to home. The road is the conduit of his personal journey, perhaps even of his dreams. He denies its role in the formulas of advertising men, and through it questions the orthodoxy of the American Dream. The road is revealed as an aspect of the wide world through which it runs, a world bigger than society's strictures, a strange, mysterious and wonderful place. Frank's photograph is an image of living, his existence and journey described by a family and a car, their travel through time and space described by the road and the desert.

Charles Kitchen is personally unimportant. He stands for faceless millions in his photograph. Another driver would have done just as well, without Libsohn even having to change the story. Charles is a representative member of society, his individuality serving the whole. Frank's photograph reveals an individual following his own obscure purposes.

Frank's earlier photograph *U.S. 285, New Mexico* was a picture of an empty, bright road running through darkness, an image of searching. In that image's distance was the elusive light—promising glory, its reality unknown, its nature obscure. The photograph suggests a driver's take through the windscreen of a car. In *U.S. 90*, the artist has stopped and is out of the car, turning back towards it. This is Frank's conclusion: there is no ephemeral bright destination. After two years on the road, he knows Del Rio will be another Main Street, another diner. The journey's end is this realisation. There is only now, only this moment, washed up on some dusty roadside. All that remains is those we love, who share our journey, at the dawning of a new day.

CONCLUSION

Sitting in the town of Speculator, in the Adirondack Mountains. Not really mountainous, more rolling and wooded—there is evidence everywhere, though, that they have a lot of snow. I think snow would make these hills seem more montane. Winding narrow roads, pristine and spruced holiday cabins next to dilapidated and collapsing mountain homes, yards filled with rusting 8 litre pickup trucks. One of these, still drawing breath, had 'Girls Love Muddy Rubber' stuck to its door. The fat driver bore testament to his bumper sticker: a svelte blonde was riding alongside. I'm sitting in a small park, hard by a lake. A little family with a couple of kids are quietly fishing a way off. A wonderful wind is coming from the west—more than a breeze, less than a hurricane, maybe the remnants of the rain storm that plink plinked all night on my truck in Wisconsin, or a balance perhaps to the she-Beryl that pounds the Carolina shores to the south and evacuates the islanders as I write. Fresh and cooling after a hot day, birthing lines of waves broken and uneven but, like all the Universe, there's a rightness to the jumble, a reassurance, a sense of home. This really is it, the last quiet moment before a botherment of business—packing, car returning, baggage handling, immigrating, sitting-up sleeping. The treasures that await outside the arrival gate are of such wonderment that I'm keen to undergo the whole shambolic irritation.

It's a wide country, drawing away from these quiet and civilised mountains—rising in the twirling blarney of the Blue Ridge, banjo picked and stilled in Great Smoky black forests, to the high white Rockies, South Parked and Arapaho. My journey is like a string, a thousand beads strung on it, burned in memory, assimilating even as I write. Maybe Wordsworth was wrong to lionise "emotion recollected in tranquility"—maybe all tranquility does is ameliorate the rawness. It's too wide to think of as a country, and most of its inhabitants don't really travel. More a federation, a place of easy borders and distinct but cooperative spatial differences.

The journey has been characterised by speed, often the need to move on detracting, it has seemed, from a deeper engagement. Inevitable of course, but what has been gained, as I see now, is a sense of the scope, range and size of the country, from the steamy South to this quiet Northern place.

The landscape needs no mediation, this wide, one-third of a hemisphere. The people, too, resonate deeply with me—the recent descendants of incomers from countries near my home, stirred like oil and water into the few more ancient American lines. This has been their peoples' home for much longer and they survive still, but in a so-much changed world. The Pueblos have adjusted and are using the fascination and ennui of the displaced white men to help their survival. They charge premium prices for their crafts, and hide away for celebrations. Even so, how must it feel to have been colonised so utterly?

Mostly I think I have a sense of quiet, of a huge land with room for people to breathe. And yet too, a sense of distance, alienation maybe, of a lost colony sometimes, of people who have moved away from home, made a new place that so resembles the old but are always aware that it is not it.

The evening is deepening, I am spruce from parasitising a busy campsite's afternoon showerblock, but have nowhere yet to sleep. I won't find rest here, the wish for home is too great for me to stay even these three or four hours away from the airport. Time to check in, time to leave.

The smell of pine, the call of the mockingbird in a black night, an orange spike of eclipsed sun setting over the Rio Grande, airless, open, wooded mountain valleys—the roof of the world. Wide, slow rivers, a brilliant smile in the brownest of faces, the glow of a European girl's eyes behind an American voice in a Wilmington, North Carolina café. The whirl and twirl of New Orleans busy and polychrome, hookered and harlot, horns in the evening, baritone rumble to the tune of tubas, out to its hinterland, through water and land, where people live in the air and park their fishing boats outside their houses, on a watery street. The strength, almost frightening, of the Rocky Mountain rocks, the scoured canyon of the Big Thompson, carved into the granite as if it was caramel, thrown and rowing its cascade. The churned and extruded high plains between Ten Sleep and Cody. A wonderful place—yellow, black and red songbirds into endless seeming farmlands of the Mid West, friends hunkered deep in their black lake soil—wonder if I'll see them again. Photographs given gladly to a smiling stranger, friendships in embryo, never to be fulfilled, but I the richer for their promise. Music beneath and around it all, swirling notes of potentiality, building from the softest, most unhearable beginnings until at some point I know they will break the surface of song and realise themselves in the white blur of a moment. I can feel them now, rising almost infinitely slowly from the depths, *de profundis*... Maybe an hour of light, enough for me to get lost again in the wildness of the American night.

BIBLIOGRAPHY

Agee, J. and Evans, W. (1941), *Let Us Now Praise Famous Men*, Boston: Houghton Mifflin.

Alexander, S. (1997), 'Robert Frank Discusses the Americans at George Eastman House, 17 and 18 August 1967', *Katalog: Journal of Photography and Video*, 9(4), p. 38.

Anonymous (1958), 'The Second Book of Samuel', *The Bible*, London: Collins.

Apollinaire, G. (1949), *The Cubist Painters: Aesthetic Meditations 1913*, New York: Wittenborn Schulz.

Aristotle (2003), *Poetics*, London: Penguin.

Aronowitz, S. (1990), *Crisis In Historical Materialism: Class, Politics, and Culture in Marxist Theory*, Minneapolis: University of Minnesota Press.

Avedon, R., Brodovitch, A. and Capote, T. (1959), *Observations*, New York: Simon & Schuster.

Benedek, L. (1954), *The Wild One*, Hollywood: UCA.

Brandt, B. (1936), *The English at Home*, London: Batsford.

— (1948), *A Camera in London*, London: Focal Press.

Brodovitch, A. (1945), *Ballet*, New York: Augustin.

Brookman, A. and Brookman, P. (1986), *Fire in the East: A Portrait of Robert Frank* (video documentary), Houston: Houston Museum of Fine Arts/Houston Public Television (KUHT).

Butler, D. (1953), *Calamity Jane*, Hollywood: Warner Brothers.

Caldwell, E. and Bourke-White, M. (1937), *You Have Seen Their Faces*, New York: Modern Age Books.

Camus, A. (2005[1942]), *The Myth of Sisyphus*, London: Penguin.

Capa, R. and Gerda, T. (1938), *Death in the Making*, New York: Covici-Friede.

Cartier-Bresson, H. (1952), *Images à la Sauvette* [*The Decisive Moment*], Paris: Editions Verve.

Cassady, C. (2007), *Off the Road: Twenty Years with Cassady, Kerouac and Ginsberg*, London: Black Spring Press.

Charters, A. (2007), 'Introduction', in J. Kerouac, *On the Road*, London: Penguin, p. 9

Clay, J. (1978), *Modern Art*, Secaucus, NJ: Chartwell Books.

Coke, V.D. and Du Pont, D. (1986), *Photography, A Facet of Modernism*, New York and San Francisco: Hudson Hills Press/Museum of Modern Art.

Corbett, J. (1995), 'Ephemera Underscored: Writing Around Free Improvisation', in Krin Gabbard (ed.), *Jazz Among the Discourses*, Durham, NC: Duke University Press, p. 224.

Cuirara, C. (2002), *Beat Poets*, London: Everyman.

Day, J. (2008), *The Politics of Navigation: Globalisation, Music and Composition*, Saarbrucken: Verlag Dr Muller.

— (2011), *Robert Frank's The Americans: the Art of Documentary Photography*, Bristol and Chicago: Intellect/University of Chicago Press.

— (2012), 'The Eviscerated Museum: bricolage, iterative hierarchy, *The Family of Man* exhibition and the Standard Oil Picture File in Robert Frank's *The Americans*', *2nd International Conference of Photography and Theory*, Cyprus: Thalassa Museum.

de Beauvoir, S. (1953), *America Day by Day*, New York: Grove Press.

de Saussure, F. (1995), *Course in General Linguistics*, London: Gerald Duckworth and Co. Ltd.

Dickinson, L. (1982), *Filming the Impossible*, London: Jonathan Cape.

Eliot, T.S. (1932), *Selected Essays 1917–1932*, London: Faber and Faber.

Evans, W. (1995[1938]), *American Photographs*, New York: Museum of Modern Art.

— (1957), 'Robert Frank', in *US Camera Annual 1958*, New York: US Camera Publishing Corp., p. 90.

Fitch, S. (1976), *Diesels and Dinosaurs, Photos from the US Highway*, Berkeley, CA: Long Run Press.

Fleming, V. (1939), *The Wizard of Oz*, Hollywood: Metro Goldwyn Mayer.

Ford, J. (1940), *The Grapes of Wrath*, Hollywood: 20th Century Fox.

Frank, R. (1957), 'A Statement', in *US Camera Annual 1958*, New York: US Camera Publishing Corp., p. 115.

— (1958), *Les Americaines*, Paris: Robert Delpire.

— (1959), *The Americans*, New York: Grove Press.

— (1961), 'Black and White are the Colors of Photography', *Aperture*, 9(1), p. 22.

— (1968), *The Americans*, New York: Aperture/Museum of Modern Art.

— (1989), *The Lines of My Hand*, New York: Pantheon.

— (1991), *Robert Frank*, London and Paris: Thames and Hudson/Centre National de la Photographie.

— (1993), *The Americans*, Zurich: Scalo.

— (1994), *Black, White and Things* (facsimile of 1952 edition), Zurich: Scalo.

— (2008), *The Americans*, Gottingen and Washington, DC: Steidl/National Gallery of Art.

Frank, R., Bischof, W. and Verger, P. (1956), *Indiens pas Morts*, Paris: Robert Delpire.

Ginsberg, A. (1956), *Howl*, San Francisco: City Lights Books.

Greenough, S. (2009), *Looking In,* Washington, DC: National Gallery of Art/Steidl.

Guthrie, W. (1997[1945]), 'This Land is Your Land', *Woody Guthrie: This Land is Your Land: The Asch Recordings Volume 1*, Washington, DC: Smithsonian Folkways.

Hardy, T. (1917), *Moments of Vision and Other Miscellaneous Verses*, London: Dodo Press.

Hicks, W. (1952), *Words and Pictures*, New York: Harper Brothers.

Hitchcock, A. (1960), *Psycho*, Hollywood: Shamley Productions/Paramount/Universal.

Hunter, J. (1987), *Image and Word*, Cambridge, MA: Harvard University Press.

Ilf, I. and Petrov, E. (1937), *Little Golden America: Two Famous Soviet Humorists Survey These United States,* New York: Farrar & Rinehart.

Ives, S. (2009[1996]), *Ken Burns Presents: The West*, Insignia Films: New York.

Janis, E.P. and MacNeil, W. (1977), *Photography within the Humanities*, Danbury, NH: Addison House.

Johnson, W. (ed.) (1989), *The Pictures are a Necessity: Robert Frank in Rochester, NY, November 1988,* New York: Rochester Film and Photo Consortium and International Museum of Photography.

Joyce, J. (1993), *Ulysses*, London: Penguin.

Kazan, E. (1951), *A Streetcar Named Desire*, Hollywood: Warner Brothers.

Keller, U. (1986), *The Highway as Habitat, A Roy Stryker Documentation, 1943–1955*, Santa Barbara, CA: University of California.

Kerouac, J. (1972[1957]), *On the Road*, London: Penguin.

— (1992), 'The Essentials of Spontaneous Prose', in A. Charters (ed.), *The Portable Beat Reader,* New York: Viking Penguin, pp. 484-485.

— (2000[1958]), *The Dharma Bums*, London: Penguin Classics.

Klein, W. (1996[1956]), *Life is Good and Good for You in New York,* New York: Dewi Lewis.

Koeppen, W. (1959), *American Journey*, Frankfurt: Suhrkamp.

Kramer, S. (1963), *It's a Mad, Mad, Mad, Mad World*, Santa Monica: United Artists.

Lacan, J. (1968), *The Language of the Self: The Function of Language in Psychoanalysis,* Baltimore, MD: Johns Hopkins University Press.

Lao Tzu (1963), *Tao Te Ching,* London: Penguin.

Lee, H. (2010[1960]), *To Kill a Mockingbird*, Arrow Books: London

Libsohn, S. (1945), 'Trucking Story', *The Lamp*, Standard Oil of New Jersey.

Lifton, R. (1970) 'Protean Man', in L. Hamalian and F. Karl (eds), *The Radical Vision: Essays for the Seventies*, New York: Crowell, p. 120.

Livingston, J. (1992), *The New York School Photographs 1936–1963*, New York: Stewart, Tabori and Chang.

McBride, J. (1989), *Great Balls of Fire*, Hollywood: Metro Goldwyn Mayer.

McCarthy, C. (2009). *The Road,* London: Picador.

Maloney, T. (1958), *U.S. Camera Annual,* New York, U.S. Camera Publishing Corp.

Manchester, W. (1989), *In Our Time*, London: South Bank Centre.

Marx, K. (1977[1843]), *Critique of Hegel's Philosophy of Right,* Cambridge: Cambridge University Press.

Mayr, O. and Post, R. (1981), *Yankee Enterprise: The Rise of The American System of Manufactures,* Washington, DC: Smithsonian Books.

Merz, C. (1928), *The Great American Bandwagon*, New York: The John Day Company.

Milestone, L. (1939), *Of Mice and Men*, Hollywood: Hal Roach Studios.

Mingus, S. (1997), 'Mingus', *Goblin Web Magazine*, 8, http://www.sonic.net/~goblin/8mingus.html, accessed 20 May.

Owen, W. (1994), *The Poems of Wilfred Owen,* Ware: Wordsworth.

Papageorge, T. (1981), *Walker Evans and Robert Frank: An Essay on Influence*, New Haven, CT: Yale University Art Gallery.

Plattner, S.W. (1983), *Roy Stryker: USA, 1943—1950. The Standard Oil (New Jersey) Photography Project*, Houston, TX: University of Texas Press.

Ray, N. (1955), *Rebel Without a Cause*, Hollywood: Warner Brothers.

Riis, J. (1998), *How the Other Half Live: Studies among the Tenements of New York,* London: Penguin.

Schuh, G. (1957), 'Robert Frank', *Camera 36,* (no. 8), pp. 339–356.

Scott Fitzgerald, F. (1994[1925]), *The Great Gatsby*, London: Penguin.
Shakespeare, W. (2007), *Othello*, London: Penguin.
Shelley, P. (2009), *The Major Works* (ed. Z. Leader and M. O'Neill), Oxford: Oxford University Press.
Springsteen, B. (1975), *Born to Run*, San Francisco: Columbia.
Steichen, E. (1955), 'The Family of Man' (exhibition), New York: Museum of Modern Art.
Stryker, R. (1947), 'Transcript of lectures at the Design Institute, Chicago, August', *Roy Stryker Papers*, Photographic Archives, Ekstrom Library, University of Louisville.
Tucker, A. and Brookman, P. (1986), *New York to Nova Scotia*, New York and Houston, TX: Graphic Society Books/Museum of Fine Arts.
Tudor-Hart, M. (1986), *Das Auge Des Gewissens*, Berlin: Foto-Taschenbuch.
Twain, M. (1992[1876 and 1884]), *Tom Sawyer and Huckleberry Finn*, Wordsworth Editions: Ware.
Various (1958), 'First Letter to the Corinthians', *The Bible*, London: Collins.
Various (1960), 'An Off-Beat View of the U.S.A.', *Popular Photography*, 46(5), n.p.
Various (2009), *Writings from the Zen Masters* (comp. P. Reps), London: Penguin.
Wall, A. (2009), *COOL*, London: BBC.
Webb, M. (2012), *The Amazing Spider Man*, Hollywood: Sony Pictures Entertainment.
Wheeler, D. (1977), 'Robert Frank Interviewed', *Criteria*, 3(2), n.p.
Wisemen, L. (2003), *Underworld*, Hollywood: Sony Pictures Entertainment.
Wordsworth, W. (1999[1798]), *Lyrical Ballads*, London: Penguin.
Wilcox, F. (1956), *Forbidden Planet*, Hollywood: MGM.

ABOUT THE AUTHOR

Black Country bred, I am the spawn of three hundred years of English Midlands' industrialism. I was conceived in a derelict church, on land left wild after its ruination by Roman iron mines. My mother was 18 and had no intention of making me. My grandmother, in turn, bore her at 17, fathered by a half-Irish sailor who died near Trinidad before my mother was three. My great grandmother was the daughter of a displaced Welsh coal-miner, who fled Abertyleri in a cattle truck after the pit-work dried up. She was loved by a factory owner's son, who she married. She saw him disowned by his family and left penniless. He died not too long afterwards, from pneumonia after a fall into the canal which ribboned the mill in which he worked. He left her destitute with two babies. Her second husband, my great grandfather, had been a horse trainer in a circus. She married him after he fed sandwiches to her starving children. She became an alcoholic, ate grass from the garden, converted to Adventism after seeing the devil and gave away all her money. There is little more left of them than this—I tell you it all to establish a credential.